Youth, Crime and Justice

Youth, Crime and Justice takes a critical issues approach to analyzing the current debates and issues in juvenile delinquency. It encourages readers to adopt an analytical understanding encompassing not only juvenile crime, but also the broader context within which the conditions of juvenile criminality occur. Students are invited to explore the connections between social, political, economic and cultural conditions and juvenile crime.

This book engages with the key topics in the debate about juvenile justice and delinquency:

- juvenile institutions
- delinquency theories
- gender and race
- youth and moral panic
- restorative justice
- youth culture and delinquency.

It clearly examines all the important comparative and transnational research studies for each topic. Throughout, appropriate qualitative studies are used to provide context and explain the theories in practice, conveying a powerful sense of the experience of juvenile justice. This accessible and innovative textbook will be an indispensable resource for senior undergraduates and postgraduates in criminology, criminal justice and sociology.

Cyndi Banks is Professor of Criminology and Criminal Justice at the Northern Arizona University. Her recent publications include *Criminal Justice Ethics: Theory and Practice* (Sage, 2012), *Alaska Native Juveniles in Detention* (Mellen Press, 2009), *Punishment in America: A Reference Handbook* (ABC-CLIO, 2005) and *Developing Cultural Criminology: Theory and Practice in Papua New Guinea* (University of Sydney, 2000).

Youth, Crime and Justice

Cyndi Banks

Routledge
Taylor & Francis Group

LONDON AND NEW YORK

First published 2013
by Routledge
2 Park Square, Milton Park, Abingdon, Oxon OX14 4RN

Simultaneously published in the USA and Canada
by Routledge
711 Third Avenue, New York, NY 10017

Routledge is an imprint of the Taylor & Francis Group, an informa business

British Library Cataloguing in Publication Data
A catalogue record for this book is available from the British Library

Library of Congress Cataloging in Publication Data
Banks, Cyndi.
    Youth, crime and justice / Cyndi Banks.
        p. cm.
    Includes bibliographical references and index.
    1. Juvenile delinquency. 2. Juvenile justice, Administration of. I. Title.
    HV9069.B294 2013
    364.36—dc23   2012035850

ISBN: 978–0–415–78123–7 (hbk)
ISBN: 978–0–415–78124–4 (pbk)
ISBN: 978–0–203–58396–8 (ebk)

Typeset in ScalaSans
by Keystroke, Station Road, Codsall, Wolverhampton

Printed and bound in Great Britain by MPG Printgroup

For James

Contents

1	**Introduction**	1
	Constructing juvenile delinquency	2
	Child savers	3
	Parens patriae	5
	Education	7
	Juvenile court	8
	Organization of the book	8
	Recap	11
	References	12
2	**Theories Associated with Juvenile Delinquency**	13
	Strain	15
	Loss of positive stimuli/presentation of negative stimuli	18
	Strain and class	19
	Criticisms of strain	20
	Social learning	21
	Control	23
	Labeling	27
	Criminology and gender	33
	Recap	38
	References	39
3	**Juvenile Institutions**	42
	History and development of juvenile corrections	42
	Contemporary juvenile corrections	48

"Waiting for the outs": experiencing juvenile corrections   55
Discipline and control   63
Recap   69
Notes   70
References   71

4   Gender and Juvenile Justice   **75**
Controlling girls: gender and history   77
Girls' violence: definitions and explanations   87
Programming inadequaces in the treatment of girl offenders   93
Recap   97
Note   98
References   98

5   Race and Juvenile Justice   **103**
African Americans: the urban underclass   106
Bias and the operation of the juvenile justice system   114
American Indians and Alaskan Natives   126
Comparative racial disparities   129
Recap   131
Notes   132
References   133

6   Youth Culture and Delinquency   **138**
Deviance and youth   140
Youth subcultures   141
The interaction between youth cultures and deviance   146
Cultural criminology   146
Acid house parties and the rave subculture   147
Writing graffiti   155
Skateboarding   172
Recap   183
Notes   184
References   185

7   Youth and Moral Panic   **190**
Moral panic theory   191
Adolescence   196
School shootings   197
James Bulger   202
Mods and Rockers   204
Mugging in Britain   206

Juvenile superpredators		208
Girl violence and girl gangs		211
Gang violence		216
Recap		220
Notes		221
References		223
8	**Restorative Justice for Young Offenders**	**227**
	Explaining restorative justice	228
	Restorative justice and community justice	232
	Authentic restorative justice?	233
	Restorative justice: theoretical foundations	235
	Restorative justice programs	237
	International norm formation	244
	Critiques of restorative justice	247
	Restorative justice and the public	250
	Recap	252
	Note	253
	References	253
9	**What Works?**	**257**
	Delinquency prevention: what works?	257
	Rehabilitation and treatment: what works?	259
	Effective interventions: examples	265
	Ineffective interventions: control-oriented programs	267
	Understanding culture: culturally specific programming	270
	Juvenile drug courts	272
	Restorative justice (RJ)	284
	Recap	285
	Notes	286
	References	286
10	**Transnational Youth Justice**	**290**
	Specificity of delinquency in Bangladesh	291
	Policy convergences and policy transfer of youth justice policies	296
	Sites of tension	299
	Child soldiers	302
	Girl soldiers	305
	Questioning childhood	307
	Why use child soldiers?	308
	Recruitment and training	309
	Agents or passive victims?	310

Child soldiers in combat   312
Restoring the child soldier   314
Recap   315
Notes   316
References   317

Index   320

chapter 1

Introduction

This is a book about current debates and issues in juvenile delinquency that takes a critical issues approach. It is aimed at senior undergraduates in criminology, criminal justice and sociology, and encourages readers to adopt an analytical understanding that encompasses not only juvenile crime but also the broader context within which the conditions of juvenile criminality occur. In articulating the connections between social, political, economic and cultural conditions and juvenile crime, this book goes beyond the conventional approaches to juvenile delinquency commonly found in such texts. Also, and rarely found in this field, the book makes significant use of appropriate qualitative studies to contextualize, provide explanations and meaning, and to convey a powerful sense of the experience of juvenile justice.

While this book surveys topics like juvenile institutions and delinquency theories that are ordinarily found in juvenile justice textbooks, it also broadens and deepens the debate about juvenile justice and delinquency by engaging with the topics of youth and moral panic, restorative justice and youth culture and delinquency. Augmenting the customary field of subject areas in this way enhances teaching approaches that combine issues in youth culture with more conventional subject matter such as the juvenile justice system and delinquency theories. The text offers a contemporary perspective on each topic that takes account of all important research studies, and engages with relevant comparative and transnational research studies.

This chapter provides a historical perspective of the development of the concept of juvenile delinquency and examines how the discourse of delinquency has changed over the historical record. It sets a foundation and context within which the subject matter of the book is located.

Fundamental transformative events and conditions in the development of delinquency have been: the social construction of delinquency over time; the *parens patriae* doctrine; the child-saving movement; and the creation of the Juvenile Court as a specialist court for adjudicating both juvenile criminality and cases of non-criminal dependency known as status offenses. These issues are reviewed in the following sections.

Constructing juvenile delinquency

Discourses concerning juvenile delinquency relate to specific sociohistorical periods. Understanding how those discourses originated and developed and the social forces and movements that prompted those discourses is central to comprehending juvenile justice development. For example, an understanding of the concept of juvenile delinquency is incomplete without first appreciating how the concept originated, who originated it and how modern definitions depend so much on outdated assumptions about youth. As Muncie (2009: 45) notes, the historical account of juvenile justice up until the 1970s was an idealist history that focused on individual acts of prominent persons which suggested that juvenile justice followed a trajectory from savagery to reformation. Delinquency was defined by reference to poverty and neglect rather than by reference to actual acts of delinquency which would ordinarily constitute crimes.

From the 1970s revisionist histories challenged these accounts, and focused on a wide range of social, economic and political factors that are now seen as critical elements in the development of juvenile justice policy. The humanitarian and reformist child savers are now seen less as saviors of children in trouble with the law and more as a distinct class of individuals pursuing a broad range of goals, including the transmission of middle-class values, racist thinking about immigrants and idealizations of the family and rural life.

According to Bernard (1992), the term "juvenile delinquency" was created more than 200 years ago. In 1816 the term appears in a report of a society in London which investigated "the Causes of the Alarming Increase of Juvenile Delinquency in the Metropolis" (p. 42). The Society found the main causes of delinquency to be the "improper conduct of parents," "want of education," "want of suitable employment" and "violation of the Sabbath" (Muncie 2009: 52–53). In 1819 the Society for the Reformation of Juvenile Delinquents was formed in New York City and the term "delinquency" began to gain wide currency (Bernard 1992: 42).

In America before 1760, crime was not a serious issue and parents were responsible for controlling their children. However, after about 1700, laws began to be passed regulating parents who failed to control their children

(Bernard 1992: 44). Initially, uncontrollable children were sent to other families considered to be better at parenting. While corporal and capital punishments were used for controlling juvenile offenders, by 1800 these punishments were falling out of favor and by the end of the 1700s juvenile offenders were being boarded out or detained in adult prisons (p. 45). After industrialization, crime increased, especially property crime. With industrialization came urbanization, and people moved from the land into the cities to work in factories (p. 47). In transitioning to life in the city, many families disintegrated and youth began to collect together in groups in public areas and to engage in petty theft. This constituted a new issue in crime control and the label "delinquency" was applied.

King (1998) argues that the perceived problem of juvenile delinquency was not related so much to increased criminal activity but rather to changing attitudes to childhood and the poor. While some suggest that the origins of delinquency can be located back to 16th-century England (Muncie 2009: 63), it seems clear that the creation of institutions for juveniles and legislation and social activity directed at juveniles in the early 19th century marked a significant turning point in defining and managing juvenile disorder.

Child savers

In the second half of the 19th century, a group of reformers became concerned about juvenile delinquency and founded societies to prevent children from leading depraved and criminal lives (Krisberg 2005: 31). According to Krisberg, the child savers "viewed the urban masses as a potentially dangerous class that could rise up if misery and impoverishment were *not* alleviated" (p. 31). In response, Charles Loring Brace and the Children's Aid Society of 1853 decided that vagrant and poverty-stricken children should be "placed out" with farm families on the Western frontier. This had the effect of idealizing the family as a kind of reformatory for wayward youth. It was believed that the city corrupted children and that country life would ensure children were kept away from criminality and safeguard their socialization as good citizens. Midway through the 19th century, state and municipal governments took over the administration of institutions for children, and by 1876, of the 51 houses of refuge or reform schools, nearly three-quarters were operated by state or local governments (Krisberg 2005: 33–34).

According to Platt (1977: xx), the child-saving movement was directed primarily by the middle and upper classes which devised new forms of social control to protect their powers and privileges. This movement should be seen within the context of the massive changes that took place in society including changes in forms of social control (p. xx).

Platt (1977: xxiv) argues that it was the professionals and special interest groups as well as the conservative elements of the feminist movement that carried out the mission of the child savers. Although made up of women coming from a range of class backgrounds, the conservative wives of the new industrialists and the daughters of landed gentry comprised the majority. For Platt, the child savers combined class attitudes of an earlier period with the social control imperatives of the industrial era (p. xxiv). Nevertheless, Platt concedes that many child savers were concerned about the living conditions of the poor even though they accepted the basic structure of the new industrial society.

The child savers believed that children who revealed their criminal tendencies through acts such as truancy needed to be regulated in the interests of society because they would otherwise become criminals (Platt 1977: 32). Platt (1977: 43) suggests that by the end of the 19th century conceptions of criminality focused on: marginalizing and dehumanizing "criminals" as a subclass of human beings; on the development of professionalism in the correctional response to deal with this subclass; and on the medical model and the approach of rehabilitation as the "right" approaches to employ in correcting delinquent children.

The motives of child savers have been questioned on the basis that their intent was fundamentally to control the children of the poor – the so-called dangerous classes (in other words, fear of the young), composed largely of immigrant groups. Green and Parton (1990: 24) suggest that large groups of Irish immigrants were viewed as corrupt and as unsuitable parents, and that in England the Irish were considered "wild and uncivilized." According to Schlossman (1998: 327), the label "juvenile delinquency" was applied to the activities of lower class, often immigrant children, living in the cities without adult supervision or with neglectful parents. Platt (1977: 36) suggests that the city environment was seen as turning unskilled and uneducated immigrants into criminals while immigrants of the 1880s and 1890s were considered less than human and incapable of adjusting to the American way of life.

The child savers' emphasis on the authority of parents in the home, the attractions of rural life and the independence of the nuclear family was intended to counteract the influence of urbanism and the new industrialization. Drawing on their middle-class values, child savers were not very interested in criminal acts as such, but rather in creating norms to regulate youthful behavior in terms of education, recreation, attitudes to family and personal morality (Platt 1977: 99). As Platt (1977: 99) notes, the child savers:

were most active and successful in extending governmental control over a wide range of youthful activities that had been previously ignored or dealt with informally. Their reforms were aimed at defining and regulating the dependent status of youth.

Their aim was to intervene in children's lives to prevent delinquency. These interventions therefore had the effect of blurring the distinction between delinquency and dependency (Platt 1977: 135) so that formal legal distinctions were not made between those who were delinquent and those who were either dependent or neglected (p. 138). As Sutton (1988: 65) notes, it was believed that parental neglect caused a child to become unruly, "and unruly children turn into adult paupers and criminals who in turn neglect their children." According to Bernard (1992: 26), since the time of the puritans, social movements and policy makers have attempted to control the behaviors of children perceived to be offensive even though not criminal. Status offenses apply only to juveniles by virtue of their status as juveniles. They include laws against truancy, disobedience to parents, running away from home, drinking alcohol and violating curfews (pp. 17–18). Some have argued that status offenses should be decriminalized and that social services should be responsible for such cases. Others accept that status offenses should be dealt with in the juvenile court but do not see them as necessitating incarceration. They therefore favor deinstitutionalization of status offenses (p. 26).

Parens patriae

This doctrine was adopted by the U.S. Courts and became the principal foundation for the development of juvenile courts. The doctrine of *parens patriae* originated in the English High Court of Chancery as a means of protecting children's welfare (Mennel 1972: 69). It can be traced back to medieval times where it was applied to cases concerning property and guardianship (Rendleman 1979: 60). Some have questioned the scope and legitimacy of employing the doctrine to adjudicate juvenile delinquency. For example, Roscoe Pound in 1923 noted that the foundation of the juvenile court was actually in criminal law rather than in Chancery Court proceedings because the latter were concerned principally with neglected and dependent children (Mennel 1972: 69).

In the U.S., *Ex parte Crouse* established the right of the courts to remove infants from their parents by applying the *parens patriae* doctrine. In 1838, Mary Ann Crouse's father tried to secure her release from the Philadelphia House of Refuge under a writ of habeas corpus. The Pennsylvania Supreme Court decided that "the right of parental control is a natural, but not an unalienable one" and asked whether "the natural parents, when unequal to the task of education, or unworthy of it, be superseded by the *parens patriae* or common guardian of the community?" (*Ex parte Crouse*, 4 WHART.9 [PA. 1838]). The Pennsylvania Supreme Court denied the claim for habeas corpus. As Rendleman notes (1979: 69), in *Crouse* the Court adopted the doctrine of *parens patriae* and, in effect, used it to justify schemes that parted poor or incompetent parents from their children. Rendleman argues that *parens patriae* served as a convenient mechanism under which the state, through the courts, was enabled to act against the poor rather than punish delinquency (p. 70). Under the doctrine the courts permitted delinquent children to be separated from their natural parents, most commonly by sending them to houses of refuge where the protection of the criminal law ceased to apply (Mennel 1972: 73).

The courts adopted the *parens patriae* doctrine as a way of legitimizing legislation that allowed children to be separated from their parents for reasons of poverty and neglect. As the Supreme Court noted in *Crouse*, the fact that children could be sent to a house of refuge for reformation rather than punishment and that a refuge was not a prison but a "school" formed the basis for this ruling (Pisciotta 1982: 411). Reformatories were intended to reform and not punish, and did not require rules of due process. In fact, as Pisciotta's research indicates, many institutions failed to provide the beneficial environment that the court accepted so easily in *Crouse* (1982: 413). An example of this divergence is that throughout most of the 19th century reformatory managers used a system of contract labor under which the institutions provided child labor to private businesses. The institution managers were paid for that labor with the children receiving only a minor payment or no compensation at all (p. 416).

Another example of how the systems used by the New York House of Refuge served as models for other institutions is that of apprenticeships (Pisciotta 1982: 420). In 1824 the New York House of Refuge was established, allowing the Society for the Reformation of Juvenile Delinquents to establish an institution where children convicted of crimes or "taken up or committed as vagrants" could be detained (Rendleman 1979: 66). The refuge managers had the power to contract the children as apprentices. Most of the detainees were vagrants and petty thieves (p. 67). Muncie (2009: 61) argues that in England the establishment of reformatories and industrial schools actually aided in the formation of juvenile delinquency as a distinct social problem.

Thus, children were committed to apprenticeships for indeterminate terms under which they received a nominal payment until they reached the age of majority. Boys generally worked for farmers and girls were always placed as domestics (Pisciotta 1982: 420). However, citing a sample of 210 case histories between 1857 and 1862 from the New York House of Refuge, Pisciotta shows that 72 percent of the apprentices ran away, returned voluntarily to the institution or were returned by their masters. Similar

youth, crime and justice

experiences occurred with other institutions where children complained of being whipped and abused (p. 421).

In the Illinois *O'Connell* case, Daniel O'Connell had not committed a felony but was institutionalized in a house of refuge until his 21st birthday because he was in danger of becoming a pauper when he grew up (Bernard 1992: 70). The Supreme Court ordered the release of Daniel O'Connell, applying reasoning directly contrary to *Crouse* (p. 70). First, the Court believed that O'Connell was being punished by being sent to reform school; second, the Court investigated the actual performance of the reform school; and third, the Court rejected the *parens patriae* doctrine and decided that due process ought to be applied where a child was detained in a house of refuge for between one and 15 years (p. 71).

As a result of the *O'Connell* case in 1899, the first juvenile court was established because *O'Connell* ruled that it was illegal to place children in reform schools unless they had committed a felony (Bernard 1992: 73). Establishing the juvenile court meant that Illinois was able to again commit poor children who had not committed a criminal offense to a juvenile institution (p. 73). Thus, the juvenile court developed not as a means of punishing delinquency but more as a mechanism to punish the poor for being poor.

In the *Gault* case, the U.S. Supreme Court ruled that where an adjudication hearing could result in a juvenile being sent to an institution, a juvenile had due process rights comprising: notice of the allegations, right to counsel, right to cross-examine witnesses and the privilege against self-incrimination (Bernard 1992: 115). The Court found, based on an assessment of the juvenile justice system, that Gault was being punished and not helped. It rejected the *parens patriae* doctrine and ruled that there was a need for due process protections (p. 116).

Up until 1899 when the first juvenile court was established, the juvenile justice system was represented by a varied collection of private and public institutions and programs including probation for minor delinquents and status offenders. Juvenile offenders whose actions necessitated a criminal court hearing were handled as adults. The fundamental effect of the doctrine of *parens patriae* was that the civil court acted to legitimize the entire system (Pisciotta 1982: 57).

Education

The introduction of compulsory education for children in the late 1700s created another forum where it was considered necessary to discipline and control children. Just as children who roamed the streets needed to be brought under control, children who broke school rules or played truant were also seen as requiring discipline (Pisciotta 1982: 56). As Pisciotta notes, "The juvenile was expected to be both obedient to both parents and teachers, and if he refused, he was held liable by the courts" (p. 56). Platt (1977: xxi) suggests that compulsory education with its forms of discipline and training was an extension of the corporate workplace and was intended to train children to become obedient workers.

Writing about the value of compulsory education, Charles Loring Brace noted the need for "a strict and careful law, which shall compel every minor to learn to read and write, under severe penalties in case of disobedience" (1880: 352, quoted in Platt 1977: xxi). Brace considered education as essential in the interests of public order and safety. Michael Katz (quoted in Platt 1977: xxviii) suggests that the reformatory represented the first mode of compulsory schooling in the U.S., indicating a link between the discipline of the reformatory and the discipline demanded by schools. According to Platt (p. 69), reformatories taught lower class skills and middle-class values. Life in a reformatory was tough and discipline in the form of military drill, hours of tedious labor and "character building" was part of the treatment (p. 73).

Juvenile court

According to Platt (1977: 3, 137), the child savers, and later the juvenile court system, called attention to and thus "invented" new categories of youthful misbehavior and reduced the civil liberties and privacy of youth. Platt relies largely on the insights of Howard Becker (1963) in making this statement and on Becker's contention that "deviance is not a quality of the act the person commits, but rather a consequence of the application by others of rules and sanctions to an 'offender'. The deviant is one to whom that label has successfully been applied" (Platt 1977: 8).

Why, therefore, have a juvenile court at all? The reason is that the juvenile court was established with criminal jurisdiction over children when it became clear that the civil courts could no longer process the number of juvenile cases entering the system (Ferdinand 1991: 207). In 1899, the first juvenile court was established in Chicago with jurisdiction covering all categories of juvenile "delinquency" including criminality, status offenders and neglected and dependent children (p. 209). By 1920, 30 states had established juvenile courts and by 1945 all states had juvenile courts.

Organization of the book

As mentioned earlier, this book reviews topics like juvenile institutions and delinquency theories normally found in juvenile justice textbooks, and also attempts to broaden and deepen the debate about juvenile justice and delinquency by exploring in the following chapters the topics of youth and moral panic, restorative justice and youth culture and delinquency.

Chapter 2, entitled "Theories Associated with Juvenile Delinquency," looks at the principal, mainstream theories associated with delinquency, namely: strain, social learning, control, and labeling. This chapter also explores criminology and gender, and, in light of the overrepresentation of men in criminal behavior, asks and examines the question of the extent to which gender constitutes a key explanatory variable.

Chapter 3, entitled "Juvenile Institutions," traces the history and development of juvenile corrections into their contemporary form and explores policy making on juvenile punishment. Drawing on insightful qualitative studies of the experience of juvenile detention the chapter reveals how juvenile detainees learn how to "play the game" and master the language of treatment to secure release from confinement. Molding the detainees for a life outside the institution means imprinting modes of behavior that are appropriate and fitting for the facility but lack relevance in the social world to which a resident will return. Treatment and detention approaches reviewed include the "tough love" applied to break down students in a "resocialization course."

Chapter 4, entitled "Gender and Juvenile Justice," examines how gendered laws punished girls who violated expectations of proper conduct by, for example, running away from home because of ill-treatment or sexual abuse, and how the juvenile justice system created a framework of status offenses that empowered the courts to control girls' sexuality. Understanding girls' delinquency means investigating gender stratification and mapping the social control exercised by the juvenile justice system, noting how that system continually reinforces female subordination by labeling girls as deviant. Explanations for the apparent increase in girls' violence are reviewed, including relabeling status offenses as criminal conduct and girls' involvement in domestic violence incidents during which police may make presumptive arrests of all or any family members. Qualitative studies again provide a rich source for understanding how girls experience violence, and the need for gender-specific treatment programs is addressed.

In *Chapter 5*, entitled "Race and Juvenile Justice," the social construct of race can be tracked through racial disparities in the juvenile justice system. This chapter examines how race effects may be direct or indirect, may be felt at various decision points within the system, and may accumulate as youth move through the system. A detailed review of studies examining decision points for racial disparities is provided. It is argued that gaining an understanding of the social, cultural, political and economic history and the contemporary circumstances relevant to minorities is crucial. A discussion of African Americans as an urban underclass explores the development of urban black ghettos, isolation, unemployment and the life-world of the ghetto and its association with black criminality. Qualitative studies illuminate social isolation and violence in the black ghetto and in the barrio of Spanish Harlem. The two indigenous minorities, American Indians and Alaskan Natives, are shown to be overrepresented in the juvenile justice system. Studies of comparative racial disparities reveal how in every country incarceration rates for members of some minority groups greatly exceed those for the majority population.

Chapter 6, entitled "Youth Culture and Delinquency," looks at aspects of youth culture and subculture that link to delinquency and deviance. Youth cultures are especially susceptible to labeling as deviant because they have become very significant, not only in relation to patterns of consumption, but also because young people have become a very distinctive group, one which is regularly labeled as linked to disorder and deviant activity. After a review of the theoretical developments in the study of youth cultures in the U.S. and Britain and associated critiques, the chapter engages with specific youth subcultures, namely: acid house parties and the rave culture; writing graffiti; and skateboarding. The insights of cultural criminology are drawn on to gain an understanding of delinquency that contains emotional or expressive elements, where individuals willingly accept risks in an interchange of emotion, risk, deviance and identity.

Chapter 7, entitled "Youth and Moral Panic," explores the notion of a moral panic and specific incidents that have generated moral panics, namely: school shootings; the James Bulger case; Mods and Rockers in the U.K.; mugging in the U.K.; "juvenile superpredators"; girl violence; and gang violence. These moral panics show how youth is associated with risk, how moral panics and "moral crusaders" engender a need to confront and control youth and how youth can be cast as "folk devils" so as to justify a punitive response in the form of greater social control. Moral panics have become associated with zealous policing, cultural conflict over moral values and often a media frenzy that spurs policy makers and legislators into imposing control measures that remain in place even after the panic has dissipated.

Chapter 8, entitled "Restorative Justice for Young Offenders," is a review of the development and contemporary application of restorative justice (RJ) in the field of juvenile justice. It is in the sphere of juvenile justice that RJ has had its greatest impact worldwide and advocates of RJ in juvenile justice see RJ becoming a viable alternative justice process through systematic reform and not as simply a "sideshow." This means that all functions within a juvenile justice system would be based on restorative principles. This chapter explores issues surrounding RJ and assesses its potential to radically reform juvenile justice.

Chapter 9, entitled "What Works?," examines what works in delinquency prevention and in treatment and rehabilitation. Treatment programs that have been judged a success in eradicating delinquency, and recidivism may still need to be scrutinized in terms of the way they are experienced by youthful offenders, as discussed in Chapter 3. This chapter links to the discussion of gender-specific treatment for girls in Chapter 4. Despite scientific assertions that certain psychologically oriented programs succeed, the public fascination with boot camps and other control-oriented programs continues undiminished. Effective and non-effective interventions are reviewed and the need for culturally specific programming is argued.

Chapter 10, entitled "Transnational Youth Justice," presents a set of analyses focusing strongly on the articulation between culture and youth justice in developing countries. Taking a thematic rather than a comparative approach, the chapter explores: policy convergences and the policy transfer of youth justice policies as well as heterogeneity in global juvenile justice policy making, with particular reference to parental punishment in Bangladesh; the creation and development of the child soldier in Africa and the failure of criminology to investigate human rights abuses and state crimes; and the process and elements involved in developing a cultural criminology in third world countries, using a case study about how childhood is culturally constructed in Bangladesh.

Recap

The selection of topics for this book takes into account time-honored approaches to juvenile justice that tend to focus on providing an overview of the U.S. juvenile justice system, giving some historical background, describing the operation and management of the juvenile justice system, theoretical frameworks, and an exploration of contemporary issues generally focusing on a limited range of topics such as juvenile justice law, juvenile corrections and treatment issues. The strategy employed in selecting issues for discussion in this text has been to present a series of critical studies of the principal issues in juvenile justice which includes an exploration of international aspects of the topic and to present a comparative perspective, where appropriate, and where available research exists.

Where appropriate, each study attempts to map the socio-historical background and also to identify the cultural, economic and political underpinnings of the topic under discussion in the belief that conditions such as social forces and climates of tolerance and intolerance about cultural practices, race and gender ought to be revealed and understood as part of any account of juvenile delinquency. In this sense, therefore, the book may be understood as offering a "thick" description of delinquency and as urging the criminological project of delinquency to disregard disciplinary boundaries.

In addition, the book pays attention to the worldwide contemporary conditions affecting juvenile justice or youth justice. It takes account of the internationalization of juvenile justice through the global policy flows and transfers in fields such as restorative justice, and of international treaties on child rights, as well as of the complexities associated with juvenile justice policy making in the developing world. The text therefore recognizes that progressively, in juvenile justice studies, it is not only disciplinary boundaries that need to be destabilized but also criminology's traditional parochialism and ethnocentrism.

References

Becker, Howard. 1963. *Outsiders: Studies in the Sociology of Deviance*. New York: The Free Press.

Bernard, Thomas. 1992. *The Cycle of Juvenile Justice*. New York: Oxford University Press.

Ferdinand, Theodore. 1991. "History Overtakes the Juvenile Justice System." *Crime & Delinquency* 37(2): 204–224.

Green, D.R. and A.G. Parton. 1990. "Slums and Slum Life in Victorian England." In S. Martin Gaskell (ed.) *Slums*. Leicester: Leicester University Press, pp. 17–91.

King, Peter. 1998. "The Rise of Juvenile Delinquency in England 1780–1840: Changing Patterns of Perception and Prosecution." *Past and Present* 60(1): 116–166.

Krisberg, Barry. 2005. *Juvenile Justice: Redeeming Our Children*. Thousand Oaks, CA, London and New Delhi: Sage.

Mennel, Robert. 1972. "Origins of the Juvenile Court: Changing Perspectives on the Legal Rights of Juvenile Delinquents." *Crime and Delinquency* 18(1): 68–78.

Muncie. John. 2009. *Youth & Crime*, 3rd Edition. Los Angeles, CA, London, New Delhi, Singapore and Washington D.C.: Sage.

Pisciotta, Alexander. 1982. "Saving the Children: The Promise and Practice of Parens Patriae, 1838–1998." *Crime & Delinquency* 28(3): 410–425.

Platt, Anthony. 1977. *The Child Savers: The Invention of Delinquency*, 2nd Edition. Chicago, IL, and London: University of Chicago Press.

Rendleman, Douglas. 1979. "Parens Patriae: From Chancery to the Juvenile Court." In Frederic Faust and Paul Brantingham (eds) *Juvenile Justice Philosophy: Readings, Cases and Comments*, 2nd Edition. St. Paul, MN, New York, Los Angeles and San Francisco, CA: West Publishing, pp. 58–96.

Schlossman, Steven. 1998. "Delinquent Children: The Juvenile Reform School." In Norval Morris and David Rothman (eds) *The Oxford History of the Prison: The Practice of Punishment in Western Society*. New York and Oxford: Oxford University Press, pp. 325–349.

Sutton, John R. 1998. *Stubborn Children: Counselling Delinquency in the United States, 1640–1981*. Berkeley: University of California Press.

chapter 2

Theories Associated with Juvenile Delinquency

Criminological theories attempt to explain youth crime. Theoretical paradigms are usually described by reference to biological, psychological and sociological categories. However, they can be regarded as advancing two general explanations for criminality: juveniles choose to commit crime, or juvenile conduct is shaped by internal or external factors. Positivist and scientific criminologies try to explain delinquency in biological or psychological terms by applying scientific methods to the study of youth conduct. Positivism is a search for data that represents "objective" knowledge, and positivists believe that the problem of delinquency may be understood once that knowledge has been acquired.

Following Agnew (2009: xx), this chapter will address the principal, mainstream theories associated with delinquency, namely: *strain*, *social learning*, *control* and *labeling*. Agnew describes an approach that does not attempt to explain all variants of the known theories; instead, the focus is on a synthesis of the four generic theories – strain, social learning, control and labeling. His perspective is consistent with the overall approach of this volume.

The gendering of criminology through feminist perspectives and feminist theory began in the 1970s. Before then, feminist perspectives were extremely marginal and gender was largely ignored in criminology. Contemporary feminist perspectives in criminology are now well established as part of the theoretical framework of criminology and delinquency, and are discussed below.

The notion that delinquency, or a propensity toward delinquency, is associated with a process of *social learning* as opposed to being a function of a biological or psychological pathology first appears in Sutherland's theory of differential association. The general approach is that youth become delinquent as a result of their associations with others. Social learning and strain theorists ask: Why do juveniles engage in delinquency? and focus on factors that push juveniles into delinquency.

Control theories operate on the premise that all youth would offend in the absence of some control that prevents this from happening. Social controls include modes of control that are external to the individual such as police, peers and family, and internal controls such as attachment, commitment, involvement and belief. According to Gottfredson and Hirschi (1990), youth will only refrain from law-breaking if special circumstances exist and this will only be so when a person has strong bonds with main-stream society. Four elements comprise the foundation for these bonds, namely attachment, commitment, involvement and belief. In the 1940s and 1950s interest in family influences on delinquency was displaced by a focus on social and economic conditions. Contemporary interest in the family and institutional factors such as schooling and religion is often expressed in terms of control theory (Shoemaker 2005: 167). Control theorists argue that motivation for delinquency is not important because they contend that we are all equally motivated since we all have unmet wants and desires that could more easily be satisfied by delinquency.

Strain, *labeling* and *control* theories are sociological in nature. Some control theories are associated with the idea of poor self-concepts contrasting with the labeling approach which argues that negative self-concepts are the outcome of having been labeled delinquent (Shoemaker 2005: 170). Strain and social control theories put the importance of structural variables, external to the person, at the center of explanations of the nature of delinquency (Walklate 2007: 26). Strain, social learning and control theories look at the characteristics of juveniles and the environments in which they live, and describe how those characteristics lead to delinquent acts. Labeling theory focuses on the reaction to delinquency – the official justice system reaction and the informal reactions of families, peers, teachers and the community.

Labeling, like social learning, is a symbolic interactionist theory of delinquency. Labeling theory examines the process through which a person becomes labeled as delinquent. Labeling theorists argue that society labels some persons as deviants and that those selected accept the label and therefore become deviant. Labeling youth as delinquent stigmatizes them, leads others to reject them and to treat them harshly, and this in turn results

youth, crime and justice

in the development of a negative self-image, increasing the likelihood of delinquency. Thus, labeling theory attempts to explain why some juveniles are more likely than others to persist in delinquency and perhaps subsequently engage in more serious delinquency (Agnew 2009: 146). The restorative justice model draws on labeling theory as a source and explicitly addresses the question of how we should or should not respond to delinquency.

Strain

Strain theories contend that delinquent conduct is the outcome of excess, stress or strain. Strain originates in the work of Robert Merton, who argued that there are institutionalized routes to success within society and that crime results from the constraints faced by the poor in achieving socially valued goals using legitimate means. Legitimate means are displaced by criminal conduct in pursuit of those goals. For strain theorists the key question is to ask what pressures cause a juvenile to commit delinquent behavior. Failure to achieve goals is regarded by all theorists as a major form of strain. The goals in question include money, status and respect, thrills and excitement, and autonomy from adults.

Acquiring wealth is considered by some theorists to be a central goal within U.S. society (Cloward and Ohlin 1960; Merton 1968). For Merton, the American Dream which postulated that anyone could succeed and become wealthy if they worked hard, ignored the reality that opportunities within society were not unlimited. Thus, as individuals discover that they cannot achieve their goals, they face pressures that can result in deviance. As Chapter 6 explains, contemporary youth subcultures are consumer oriented and adolescents are a highly valued market for consumer products. Studies provide some support for the argument that poor youth as well as middle-class youth experience strain through lack of money and therefore attempt to secure resources using illegal means. In the inner cities, where many forms of strain persist, especially lack of employment, money is a scarce commodity and, as noted in Chapter 5, activities like selling drugs have displaced legitimate methods of earning income to such an extent that they are now seen as almost normative. Thus strain is an outcome of the social structure of society that encourages persons to set unrealistic expectations and goals.

Status and respect

These are qualities closely associated with money because many judge others according to their wealth (Cohen 1955). Thus, anger is often the outcome of disrespecting another or giving unjust treatment. It is argued that the desire for "masculine status" is related to delinquency. Masculinity theory sees masculinity being accomplished through delinquency to demonstrate traits such as toughness, dominance and independence.

Thrill seeking

Thrills and excitement are often associated with juveniles who are termed "thrill seekers" and who seek to satisfy these desires through delinquent or deviant activities. An example is tagging or writing graffiti, as discussed in Chapter 4. Katz (1988) writes about the seductions of crime in relation to shoplifting, describing how students admitted to engaging in shoplifting not so much for reward as for the thrill of the act.

Seeking autonomy

Autonomy from adults relates to the desire of juveniles to be free of parental controls. The argument is that youth become involved in struggles with parents over autonomy in relation to issues such as appearance, school work and curfew hours, and this can make youth angry and frustrated, and more likely to engage in delinquent acts.

Subcultural theories

Merton provided a foundation for subcultural theories of delinquency such as Albert Cohen's work (1955) on the subculture of gangs in Chicago. Cohen suggested that lower class youth experience problems trying to satisfy middle-class standards, such as in education. This can result in status frustration and in seeking out youth in similar circumstances, thus giving rise to delinquent subcultures. Being streetwise and tough and engaging in risk-taking earns status rather than satisfying materialistic goals. Cohen saw social class as conferring a discrete set of values so that lower class youth were socialized differently than middle-class youth. Within the context of schooling, middle-class values predominate, and lower class youth are assessed according to those values. Thus, when lower class youth fail academically in school, they reject middle-class values and become "malicious," "negativistic" and "non-utilitarian."

Cloward and Ohlin (1960) argued that criminal subcultures develop in lower class neighborhoods where youth can observe and associate with successful criminals who become role models for juvenile gangs. However, not all youth are accepted into gangs and when they are rejected they may become alienated from society and abuse drugs or alcohol. Cloward and Ohlin make the important point that not all youth have access to illegitimate means of success, and contend that in neighborhoods without criminal opportunities, conflict gangs will organize around violence. Greenberg (1977) argues that a high rate of property crime among youth reveals the tension between wanting to be included in the consumer society and being prevented from doing so due to lack of resources.

A common method to assess strain is to present youth with lists of events that might prompt strain and associated conditions, and to ask them which of the events and conditions they have experienced. Some surveys contain over 200 items including factors such as divorced parents, parents who fight or argue, problems with friends, and money problems.

There are a number of versions of strain, including Merton (1938, 1968), Cohen (1955), Cloward and Ohlin (1960), Greenberg (1977), Elliott et al. (1979), Berkowitz (1993), Colvin (2000) and Agnew (2009). Each version is concerned with explaining the types of strain that may result in delinquency and the associated conditions. All theorists accept that strain does not generally produce delinquency, and so they focus on the variables or conditions that influence the probability of delinquency.

Merton suggests four possible adaptations to strain: *innovation*, *ritualism*, *retreatism* and *rebellion*. In *innovation*, while the innovator fully accepts societal goals, he or she pursues them through inappropriate means and this type of response is most likely to lead to delinquency. An example is selling drugs to pursue legitimate goals. In *ritualism*, a person over time surrenders the goal of financial success but continues to follow the accepted means of achieving it, knowing that the symbols of success are out of reach. Thus, a person pursues a dead-end job for low wages and does nothing more than survive each day. In *retreatism*, a person drops out and withdraws from society but, like the ritualist, does not opt for illegal means to achieve goals. In *rebellion*, a person desires a new social order and rejects both the dominant cultural goals and the means of achieving them. Street gangs and those following an alternative lifestyle best exemplify the rebel.

Agnew's review of strain theory, called general strain theory (GST), opts for a wider view of the sources of strain as being linked to delinquency, namely *failure to achieve goals* and *loss of positive stimuli/presentation of negative stimuli* (Agnew 2009: 105). Both the rich and the poor can suffer these forms of strain. Agnew's version of strain theory expands strain into a focus on negative relationships, thus providing explanations for a wide range of delinquencies. It is important to note that Agnew emphasizes individual adaptations rather than structural societal factors.

Agnew argues that the impact of strain on a juvenile results in negative feelings such as anger, frustration, depression and anxiety, and that these feelings create a desire for action to alleviate them. Anger and frustration are considered especially likely to result in a delinquent response because they lower inhibitions, energize an individual and prompt a desire to settle scores. Nevertheless, youth formulate coping skills and strategies to deal with strain and so only some strains involve delinquency. Examples of these coping mechanisms include: reinterpreting the strain so that to the individual it becomes less important or less bad, or it is conceptualized as having been deserved; employing relaxation techniques such as listening to music; where the strain is financial, relieving the strain by securing employment; and where the strain results from peer interactions, avoiding those peers. Delinquent strategies such as using drugs may also be the outcome of strain.

In the nature of things, some youth cope with strain better than others and strain theorists have identified several factors that influence whether or not strain will be met with delinquency. Thus, delinquency is more likely when:

- the strain involves key aspects of one's life such as challenges to masculinity or autonomy in the case of persons to whom autonomy is a key attribute;
- the person possesses only poor coping skills, for example, minimal communication or problem-solving skills;
- there is an absence of support systems such as friends and family;
- the costs of coping are low and the benefits are high, for example, where the likelihood of being caught for committing a delinquent act is low;
- the individual is more disposed toward delinquency, for example, because of having been exposed to it in the past, or where a person interacts with others who have so responded, or where a person believes an act of delinquency is justifiable.

Loss of positive stimuli/presentation of negative stimuli

When youth lose something they value – loss of positive stimuli – or when they have to tolerate negative stimuli, this can cause upset or anger and the outcome may be delinquency. The kinds of acts envisaged here include, for example, breaking up a close relationship, or being insulted or ill-treated in some way. When youth have been asked about events that anger or upset them, they typically identify interpersonal issues with parents, peers and teachers. According to Agnew (2009: 109), delinquency is associated with the following forms of negative treatment: parental rejection; arbitrary or erratic parental discipline or discipline that is perceived as excessively harsh;

child abuse and neglect; negative experiences in school such as poor relations with teachers; abusive peer relations; criminal victimization; homelessness; and experiencing discrimination on the basis of gender or race or ethnicity.

Strain and class

Generally, strain theories focus on the lower classes within the stratified American society. An upper class youth is likely to have access to high-quality education and business contacts as compared to a lower class youth. Strain theories can be regarded as class biased because they fail to take account of middle-class delinquency. However, it is also true that strain theories were not meant to explain middle-class delinquency (Shoemaker 2005: 135). As Hirschi (2009: 6) notes, one difficulty for strain theorists is to account for the fact that most youth who commit acts of delinquency later become law-abiding. Strain envisages that the conditions that precipitated youth delinquency do not change during the life cycle and that the position of lower class youth remains relatively fixed. As Shoemaker (2005: 137) notes, the strength of strain theories is that they suggest that societal frameworks are associated with significant levels of delinquency.

Criticisms of strain

As noted above, strain cannot explain middle-class delinquency but it is also unable to explain non-monetary crimes such as murder and rape because it is focused on crimes concerned with acquiring wealth through illegitimate means like robbery and burglary. Thus, strain accounts for some but not all forms of deviance.

Furthermore, strain fails to explain why reactions to strain differ. Why do persons in almost identical social situations react differently? For example, why does the ritualist continue in a dead-end job or the innovator become a drug dealer or the rebel join a street gang?

Empirical support for strain theory has also been lacking. For example, self-report surveys of delinquency suggest that income levels are not strongly associated with offending. Thus, strain was not concentrated among lower class persons and middle-class delinquency was also quite common.

Strain theory was most commonly tested by examining the disconnect between aspirations (goals sought to be achieved) and expectations (the goals a person may realistically achieve). If strain explained delinquency correctly it would be expected that those with high aspirations and low expectations would be the most delinquent category. However, studies have failed to support this hypothesis. Crime is found to be highest among those with both low aspirations and low expectations (Cullen and Agnew 1999: 119).

Social learning

Sutherland's theory of *differential association* was the first formal statement of learning theory, presented in its final form in 1947 (Cullen and Agnew 1999: 77). Before Sutherland developed his theory, crime was usually explained by factors such as social class, broken homes, age, race and urban or rural location. Sutherland contended that delinquency is learned behavior; that the learning of delinquent behavior occurs primarily in small informal groups; and that this learning is an outcome of collective experiences as well as specific events (Shoemaker 2005: 146). According to Sutherland, a youth commits an act of delinquency as a response to an excess of "definitions" (attitudes to the law) that favor violation of the law, and he or she principally adopts this attitude in association with others. This stresses the transient nature of delinquency which is always situational. The theory comprises nine propositions, one of which stresses that the learning of delinquent behavior occurs in intimate personal groups. While this also allows for learning by way of mass media influences, for example, the emphasis is on the importance of personal relationships.

Burgess and Akers (1966) further developed this approach in a restatement of differential association in terms of operant behavior theory, using notions of reinforcement and punishment with the aim of rendering the theory more testable. They joined Sutherland's differential association and concept of "definitions" with reinforcement and imitation theories drawn from psychology. Thus, for example, rather than referring to behavior being learned in primary groups Akers relates behavior to groups that constitute a person's major source of reinforcement (Shoemaker 2005: 149). He therefore proposed that delinquency is learned through associations with other delinquent persons, thus resulting in the reinforcement of delinquent acts. Akers (1998) argues that family, peers, schools, churches and other groups can promote or discourage deviance.

Akers' social learning theory attempts to more fully explain the process by which delinquency is learned. Therefore, he proposes that juveniles learn to engage in delinquency when others:

■ *Differentially reinforce their delinquent behavior* – whether persons will refrain from or continue to commit deviant acts depends on the relative frequency, amount and probability of rewards and punishments associated with the behavior (Akers 1998: 66).

- *Teach them beliefs favoring delinquency* – primary groups comprising family and friends are the most significant for the individual, but secondary and reference groups such as friendship groups and work groups become important later in life, as do churches, neighbors and law and authority figures (Akers 1998: 60).
- *Provide models of delinquency they can imitate* – Akers observes that for some, the most salient models are found in television, movies and video games (1998: 76), but overall, the most significant behavior models are persons with whom one is in contact in primary groups.

If juveniles learn to engage in delinquency from others, it is not surprising that families and peer groups are the most significant influences in social learning, although juveniles may also learn indirectly from the observation of others or from interacting with them, for example, through social networks on the Internet. Associating with persons who engage in crime is more likely to encourage a juvenile to also engage in deviance – having delinquent friends is the strongest predictor of subsequent delinquency, second only to prior delinquency (Agnew 2009: 117). However, while associating with delinquent persons may increase the probability of delinquency, it does not demonstrate the correctness of social learning theory because delinquency may, for example, be related to strain. Social learning theory will only be proved correct if it can be shown that juveniles actually learn to engage in delinquency from delinquent others.

Reinforcement

Reinforcement may be positive or negative; for example, money may be a positive outcome, or the pleasure derived from using drugs or enhanced respect from peers. In negative reinforcement, behavior results in the removal of some bad thing. Similarly, punishment may be positive or negative. Thus, positive punishment produces a bad outcome such as a reprimand from parents for a delinquent act, and a negative punishment involves removing a good thing; for example, where delinquency is punished by a ban on watching a certain television show.

There are three significant aspects of reinforcement for social learning theory: the *frequency* of reinforcement, the *amount* of reinforcement and the *relative probability* of reinforcement. Where these factors are all present there is a high probability of delinquency. Frequency relates to the likelihood that conduct is frequently reinforced and seldom punished (e.g. fighting where those who win and receive praise from their peers are more likely to continue to fight than those who lose and are mocked). The amount of reinforcement relates simply to the probability that those who receive a lot of reinforcement and little punishment are more likely to become delinquent than those who receive little reinforcement and a lot of punishment. The relative probability of reinforcement relates to the probability that delinquent conduct will be reinforced as compared to other behaviors, for example, that conflicts with others will be resolved through fighting, rather than negotiation where fighting supplies reinforcement and negotiation does not. Behavior is generally reinforced or punished by family members, peers, teachers and neighbors. As well, persons may self-reinforce and punish by internalizing standards of behavior from others and then evaluating themselves according to these standards with praise or self-criticism.

Social learning also views some delinquent acts as reinforcing or punishing in themselves; for example, getting a high feeling from drug use is itself reinforcing, and thrill seekers may receive a rush or thrill from delinquent acts, such as writing graffiti. Social learning theory argues that individual responses to reinforcement vary and so some are more likely to experience reinforcement than others. The parents of aggressive children may, for example, deliberately encourage that aggression because they regard it as an appropriate response to provocation. Research into reinforcement and punishment on delinquency indicates that delinquency is less likely when parents and teachers monitor behaviors and punish violations. Similarly, associating with delinquent peers increases the likelihood of delinquency because reinforcement is probable and punishment less likely.

A further development of social learning theory is the work of Sykes and Matza who, in 1957, advanced the idea of *techniques of neutralization* to explain more fully the "motives, drives, rationalizations and attitudes favorable to violation of law" in social learning. They argue that delinquents are able to engage in delinquency by relying on "techniques of neutralization" that, in effect, justify, in their minds, their delinquent acts. These justifications are employed before the act occurs and operate to neutralize the belief that it is bad (the authors argue that delinquents do not generally approve of delinquency; hence the need to neutralize it). The neutralizations are rationalizations and, according to Sykes and Matza, it is by learning these techniques that juveniles become delinquent (1999: 85–91). There are five techniques as follows:

1   *Denial of responsibility* – deflecting the blame away from oneself enables responsibility to be assigned, for example, to unloving parents, living in a depressed neighborhood or the influence of delinquent peers.
2   *Denial of injury* – it is suggested that delinquency can be neutralized by, for example, describing theft as "borrowing" and vandalism as "mischief," and by asserting that no one was really hurt because the injured party can easily absorb the delinquency (e.g. stealing from an already wealthy person).

3 *Denial of victim* – the delinquent insists that the injury is not wrong in light of the circumstances because it is not so much an injury as rightful retaliation – the victim is seen to be the wrongdoer and the delinquent is in the right.

4 *Condemnation of the condemners* – here the delinquent shifts the focus away from the delinquent acts to the motives and conduct of those condemning him or her, thus rationalizing that he or she is not deserving of punishment.

5 *Appeal to higher loyalties* – the delinquent rationalizes by appealing, for example, to the virtues of friendship over legal norms when faced with a dilemma.

It is commonly argued that attitudes of neutralization are not causes of criminal conduct because rationalizations are employed after the event and only when the delinquent acts have been discovered. However, this does not lessen the significance of the rationalizations because where they operate to neutralize guilt they also reinforce delinquent acts.

Differential association theory has been criticized for being simplistic in suggesting that criminality comprises only learned behavior given the complexity of motivations, or because it adds nothing new, or for ignoring individualistic factors. Others have argued that it fails to fully explain the process by which delinquency is learned (Cullen and Agnew 1999: 78). In fact, some argue that the theory better explains why some juveniles do not commit offenses (Shoemaker 2005: 150).

Measuring a person's "definitions" of the law is also problematic because it necessitates reconstructing his or her thoughts and moods at the time the crime was committed. When the situational circumstances also have to be reconstructed to show how attitudes at the time were influenced by events, the empirical difficulty becomes almost insurmountable (Shoemaker 2005: 151). The nexus between peer group association has, however, been studied empirically and the studies have generally supported the basic propositions. In fact, social learning and associating with delinquent peers are now commonly seen as one and the same (Vito et al. 2007: 183). Nevertheless, differential association remains only one of several factors that can be associated with an act of delinquency (Shoemaker 2005: 152).

Control

Sociological explanations of crime based on control theories were being articulated before the appearance of Hirschi's *social bond theory* in 1969, but Hirschi's work has emerged as the predominant statement of control theory (Cullen and Agnew 1999: 161). Before Hirschi, the "containment" approach developed by Walter Reckless attracted the most attention as a social-psychological explanation of delinquency. It is based on the notion that delinquency is the outcome of poor self-concepts. Containment conceptualizes delinquency as the outcome of drives and pulls that must in some manner be contained – checked or controlled – if delinquency is to be avoided (Shoemaker 2005: 170). According to Reckless, the most important outer containments were the family and the community, and inner restraint was associated with self-concept. Thus, it is argued that a low or negative self-concept contributes to delinquency (p. 171). Many aspects of containment found their way into later control theories.

Control theorists have a particular view of human nature. They argue that breaking the law provides a means of gratification and that people will therefore "naturally" break the law. Thus the question to be asked about breaking the law is not "Why do they do it?" but rather, "Why don't they do it?" (Hirschi 1969: 34). The response is that persons do not commit crime because of the control that society exercises over them. Thus, according to Hirschi (1969: 16), "control theories assume that delinquent acts result when an individual's bond to society is weak or broken." Explanations about why some persons violate the law more than others are therefore based on variations in control and not in motivations. The question is then: How does social control operate to prevent persons from following their natural tendency to commit crimes?

In *Causes of Delinquency* (1969), Hirschi describes the most influential variant of control theory which he termed "social bond" theory. It explains how an individual's social bond to society influences decisions to violate the law. Four major elements of the social bond are identified: attachment, commitment, involvement and belief. Attachment relates to the emotional connection to others and the extent to which one cares about their opinions; commitment refers to the investment in conforming to norms of conduct as against the costs of nonconformity; involvement relates to participation in legitimate activities; and belief involves accepting the conventional system of values – any weakening of that belief system, it is argued, increases the likelihood of delinquency (Shoemaker 2005: 176).

Hirschi contends that delinquency would be low among those who are attached to and care about others' opinions – especially parents – and higher among those who have no commitment to conventional morality, are not close to their parents and have low prospects for a successful future. Attachment involves an emotional connection to another, and when it is strong, such as with a parent, Hirschi (1969: 88) observes that "the parent is psychologically present when temptation to commit a crime appears. If, in the situation of temptation, no thought is given to parental reaction, the child is to this extent free to commit the act." According to Hirschi, simply being involved in conventional day-to-day activities constitutes a form of control and idleness presents opportunities for crime.

Social bond theory is principally an explanation of juvenile delinquency and focuses on the link between parent and child and child and school. However, studies have revealed that many delinquent youth do not become delinquent in their teen years; instead they demonstrate problem behaviors in childhood that evolve into delinquency, suggesting that the sources of delinquency lie in the early years and not in adolescence (Cullen and Agnew 1999: 163). Social bond theory has been tested empirically many times and overall there is fairly consistent support for the argument that weak social bonds increase the risk of delinquency (Hirschi 1999: 167). However, it is clear that the Hirschi thesis is ahistorical and astructural, and does not explore how social changes might affect social bonds as between classes. In addition, it cannot explain why a lack of social bonds might lead one person to take drugs and another to become a shoplifter (Walklate 2007: 26).

In 1990 Gottfredson and Hirschi wrote *A General Theory of Crime* which argues, in marked contrast to *Causes of Delinquency*, that a lack of "self-control" is the principal source of criminal conduct. In place of the association between social bonding and society, *self-control theory* sees the site of control as internal to the individual. Thus, crime is sourced to individual differences that develop early in life and affect the entire life course, and the impulse to commit crime for gratification is constrained by self-control and not by social bonds. Self-control theorists claim that a person's level of self-control is set before the age of 10 and remains stable throughout the life course.

In relation to juvenile offenders, the family and what parents do are key elements in shaping a child, and a child who exercises "self-control" will refrain from delinquency. While Hirschi stressed the significance of indirect control and the psychological presence of parents, Gottfredson and Hirschi argue that direct control is the key element in effective parenting (Gottfredson and Hirschi 1999: 175). Thus, unless parents monitor their children and teach them that rule-breaking has consequences, self-control will not be engendered and a child will be "impulsive, insensitive, physical (as opposed to mental), risk-taking, short-sighted and non-verbal" (Gottfredson and Hirschi 1990: 90).

Self-control is not seen as a biological agent but as an outcome of how a child is raised by his or her parents, and parents who monitor for deviance and correct it will instill self-control. It follows then that the chief cause of low self-control is ineffective child-rearing practices (Gottfredson and Hirschi 1999: 183).

Hirschi and Gottfredson argue that once established in childhood, the level of self-control persists and generally affects a person's life. This, according to them, explains why those who lack self-control commit not only deviant acts but also analogous acts that provide immediate gratification such as skipping school, smoking, drinking and driving fast. Generally, there is fairly consistent support for their theoretical propositions (Gottfredson and Hirschi 1999: 175). However, they take no account of larger social forces that affect the family from outside and often have a transformative effect on the nature and role of the family in American life. In addition, studies have shown that low self-control is not the only cause of delinquency and, regardless of the level of self-control, factors such as associating with delinquent peers and neighborhood dislocation continue to be significant (Vito et al. 2007: 190). Finally, no account is taken of changes in gender roles or of racial inequality (Lilly et al. 2011: 120).

Although they are both control theories, social bonding and self-control theory are not compatible. Social bonding sees involvement in crime as ebbing and flowing as a person's bonds to society strengthen or weaken in later life, whereas self-control theory sees criminality as being established in childhood and deviance as stable through the life course. Self-control theory denies any empirical relationship between social bonding and crime because self-control accounts for both the bond and the level of crime (Cullen and Agnew 1999: 164).

Sampson and Laub (1999) criticize Gottfredson and Hirschi for their belief that because problem behaviors occur in early childhood they are irreversible and must always constitute a source of criminality that will become worse into adulthood. Sampson and Laub argue that change may always affect antisocial conduct – some problem children will grow up to become delinquents and others will not, some adults will remain criminals and others not (quoted in Cullen and Agnew 1999: 164). While Gottfredson and Hirschi fail to account for changes in behavior, Sampson and Laub (1999: 189) suggest that the answer lies in taking a life-course perspective that sees a person's life as following a certain "trajectory" involving continuities in behavior but at the same time experiencing life-course events which they call "transitions" that promote changes in behavior called "turning points." Thus, change is a key element of their explanatory framework.

Sampson and Laub see the establishment of social bonds such as marriage or schooling as significant interventions that can direct persons away from crime and into a conforming life. They argue that most criminological studies have neglected to examine the informal social control processes from childhood through adulthood (1999: 192). As they put it, they bring both childhood and adulthood back into the picture of age and crime and develop "a theory of age-graded informal social control and criminal behavior" (p. 188). For Sampson and Laub, high-quality social bonds are especially salient and quality associations such as a fulfilling marriage and a rewarding job denote commitment. Thus obligations and commitments facilitate social control (Cullen and Agnew 1999: 165). The dominant social control institutions in childhood and adolescence are the family, school, peer groups and the juvenile justice system. During the time of young adulthood institutions of higher education or vocational training, work and marriage become more significant (Sampson and Laub 1999: 192). Changes that strengthen social bonds to society during adulthood will lead to less crime and deviance, and conversely changes that have the effect of weakening social bonds will generate more crime and deviance.

John Hagan's *power-control theory* of delinquency pursues the articulation between gender and control theory, looking at gender in terms of husbands and wives and in relationships between parents and children (Cullen and Agnew 1999). Hagan sees crime also as a form of gratification – as a form of risk-taking – and therefore more attractive to those who value risk-taking. Hagan sees risk-taking as gendered. In a traditional patriarchal family, boys suffer fewer controls than girls who are socialized to be feminine and become home-makers, and so develop stronger risk preferences and have a higher involvement in crime. Where the family exercises gender equity, male and female children are likely to be subject to the same level of control and thus have similar involvement in delinquency, as their risk preferences are comparable. Thus, power relations between parents shape control over children as the family tries to reproduce gender relations.

It is not clear how Hagan's approach would be applied to a single-parent family, especially one headed by a mother in a disadvantaged community. Hagan himself suggests that his perspective best explains less serious "common" delinquency, leaving open the issue of violent and serious crime. Nevertheless, Hagan does draw attention to the key issue of gender-based power relations between parents as a causal factor in delinquency (Cullen and Agnew 1999: 165). Empirical support has also been forthcoming, but the theory is silent on how structural conditions affect parenting (see studies cited in Lilly et al. 2011: 129).

Labeling

The usual reaction to a violation of the law is to demand the apprehension of the offender, a trial and the imposition of punishment, if convicted. The logic is that the state intervenes to pursue offenders on behalf of society and ensures they are punished. Labeling theorists challenge this set of assumptions, arguing that state intervention, which has the effect of labeling offenders as "criminals," has adverse effects. The public, and especially the media, employ stereotypes and react to all offenders as though they were all of poor character and bound to recidivate. Early on, even before labeling theory, prisons, as a form of societal reaction to crime, were recognized to constitute a site for learning and reinforcing criminality.

Unlike other theories of delinquency, labeling theory does not focus on the offender; nor does it ask whether the cause of delinquency arises within or outside of the offender. Instead, it focuses on the behavior of those who label, react to, or in other ways try to control offenders (Cullen and Agnew 1999: 269). Labeling theory argues that these acts instigate the processes that trap persons into a criminal career. Labeling, or societal reaction, therefore has the effect of creating the very act it intends to prevent and produces a self-fulfilling prophecy. Contrary to Reckless' containment theory, labeling theory contends that a delinquent self-image follows rather than precedes the delinquent act (Shoemaker 2005: 210).

Frank Tannenbaum is often noted as an early source of labeling theory. His work *Crime and the Community* (1938) refers to the "dramatization of evil," meaning the events of arrest and public opprobrium and scorn that constitute the process he describes in almost Foucaultian terms as follows:

> [T]he process of making the criminal, therefore, is a process of tagging, defining, identifying, segregating, describing, emphasizing, making conscious and self-conscious; it becomes a way of stimulating, suggesting, emphasizing, and evoking the very traits that are complained of.
>
> (Tannenbaum 1938: 20)

According to Tannenbaum, the best approach to dealing with delinquent juveniles is "a refusal to dramatize the evil. The less said about it the better" (p. 20). In this sense, he can be seen as establishing a foundation for schemes such as juvenile justice diversion where juvenile offenders are diverted out of the justice system, or where the police issue cautions or warnings rather than bringing formal charges. It is argued that at some point many youth engage in minor acts of delinquency but most cease to be delinquent if left alone, and consequently non-intervention is the best strategy. An alternative to this approach is to condemn delinquent acts but not to impose overly harsh sanctions because harsh sanctions weaken the emotional ties between the juvenile and his or her family and teachers, impose strain, and may cause the juvenile to associate with delinquent others (Agnew 2009: 152–153).

In 1952, Edwin Lemert originated the terms "primary" and "secondary" deviance in criminology. He argued that while primary deviance might occur for many reasons, individuals regard it as exterior to their identity, whereas in secondary deviance the deviance becomes an organizing mechanism for a person's life and identity (Lemert 1972: 63). Lemert contended that a key element in the shift from primary to secondary deviance is the "reactions of others." Continual negative reactions from others are amplified and prompt stigmatization so that a deviant person comes to accept his or her deviant status. He proposed that the sequence of events from primary to secondary deviance would be: (1) primary deviation; (2) social penalties; (3) further primary deviation; (4) stronger penalties and rejections; (5) further deviation, perhaps with resentment against those imposing penalties; (6) the community stigmatizes the deviant; (7) the deviance is enhanced in reaction to the stigmatization; and finally (8) acceptance of the deviant status (Lemert 1972).

By the mid-1960s, especially with the work of Howard Becker, the insights of Tannenbaum and Lemert became incorporated into the school of criminological theory known as "labeling" or "societal reaction" (Cullen and Agnew 1999: 270). Theorists of labeling basically focus on three issues:

1   Labeling asks why certain behaviors are designated as criminal and others not – in other words, labeling theorists regard criminal conduct as socially constructed because what counts as "criminal" changes over time and across cultures and societies. Thus, what constitutes crime and deviance is always problematic. It is not the harm that is caused that makes an act criminal; rather, it is whether the act is deemed criminal by the state. For example, Howard Becker (1963) explained how the Federal Bureau of Narcotics served as a "moral entrepreneur" in designating possession of marijuana as criminal, and Kathleen Tierney (1982) revealed how gender-based violence did not become worthy of criminal intervention until the 1970s when feminist organizations made it visible and demanded action to counter it. This issue raises questions about how the powerful in society use resources, including the law, to secure and maintain their dominant positions. It is argued that powers are exercised along class, race and gender lines. Conflict and Marxist theories of criminality address these questions.

2   Even when crimes have been socially constructed, not all who violate are detected and designated to be criminal – thus criminality depends not only on a person's actions but on how others react to that person. As Becker describes it, "deviance is not a quality of the act the person commits, but rather a consequence of the application by others of rules and sanctions to the offender" (Becker 1963: 8–9). Thus, he contends that agents of the criminal justice system enforce the law selectively in the interests of powerful groups against persons who tend to be young, male, unemployed, lower class, uneducated, minority residents of high crime areas (Vito et al. 2007: 193).

3   Labeling theorists focus on the consequences of the societal reaction to labeling – once a person has earned the designation of "criminal," it is argued that this label becomes the defining feature of that person.

In a well-known longitudinal study of delinquency in a small town, concerned with official and unofficial labeling and delinquent self-images, William Chambliss (1973) looked at two juvenile gangs – the "Saints," comprising eight juveniles from upper middle-class families and the

"Roughnecks," comprising six youths from lower class families. While no member of the Saints had ever been arrested they were just as involved in delinquency as the Roughnecks who had been arrested many times. The Saints enjoyed a good reputation in the community and their deviance was seen as youthful pranks, but the Roughnecks were viewed by police, school officials and others in the community as "trouble" and "a bad bunch of boys" (Chambliss 1973: 27–28). Both gangs tended to live up to their reputation in the community – the Saints failed to see themselves as delinquents but just as a group out for a good time, while the Roughnecks openly showed hostility to the community and even sought out others with similar self-identities. This qualitative study seems to show that labeling does produce or at least contribute to delinquent self-images. In Chambliss' view, the community's bias against the lower class resulted in the Saints' actions being labeled as pranks and the Roughnecks as delinquent. In contrast, quantitative studies have failed to confirm changes in identity following official labeling (Shoemaker 2005: 217).

One of the issues faced by labeling theorists is to be able to differentiate behavior caused by the pre-labeling factor from behavior that occurs in response to labeling. Howard Becker's response to this issue was to identify three situations of delinquent behavior: the pure deviant – a recognized deviant, the falsely accused deviant – those who actually conform to norms but are thought by others to be deviant; and the secret deviant – a person who violates norms but is not noticed or thought to be doing so (Shoemaker 2005: 212).

Labeling theorists apply symbolic interactionism to argue that a person's identity is formed by the reactions of others – their interactions determine that person's identity and he or she comes to accept the notion of having been criminalized. Not only is one's social identity transformed but also one's social relationships. Thus, once stigmatized, a person begins to associate with others bearing the same label and discards conventional relationships (Cullen and Agnew 1999: 272).

Most recently a focus on informal reactions and the notion of reintegrative shaming have given new life to labeling theory (Cullen and Agnew 1999: 273). Reintegrative shaming and Sherman's (1993) defiance theory represent attempts to theorize how the quality of forms of sanctioning affects reoffending.

Generally, the societal reaction element in labeling has been taken to refer to the formal justice system and to formal criminal sanctions, but Matsueda (1992) has argued that informal sanctions such as the reactions and appraisals of parents or friends can exacerbate deviance. Appraisals, it is argued, can be a reflection of a youth's own perception that others identify him or her as delinquent, which in turn causes the youth to act upon those assessments and to create a delinquent self. Matsueda adopts a symbolic

youth, crime and justice

interactionist approach centering on the notion that social order is the outcome of an ongoing process of social interaction in which shared meanings, expectations of behavior and what he terms "reflected appraisals" are accumulated and applied to behavior (Matsueda 1992). Thus, symbolic interactionists contend that our self-concept – the way we view ourselves – is an outcome of how others view and treat us. It follows that if others such as parents and teachers treat you as intelligent, you will come to view yourself in that way and act on the basis of that self-concept. The same logic applies if you are treated as a bad person (Agnew 2009: 154).

John Braithwaite's (1989) theory of reintegrative shaming (see Chapter 8) argues, consistent with labeling theory, that shaming a delinquent can worsen crime – as when a community stigmatizes the delinquent. However, when the shaming is not stigmatizing but reintegrative and the community of law-abiding persons accepts the offender back into it, this has the effect of reinforcing social bonds and encouraging pro-social influences. According to Braithwaite, societies with low crime rates are those which shame "potently and judiciously" and where reintegrative shaming is an effective crime control measure, stigmatization "pushes offenders toward criminal subcultures" (p. 18). He acknowledges that his theory of reintegrative shaming builds on earlier theories including the notion of stigmatization from labeling theory.

Sherman's defiance theory aims to answer the question "Under what conditions does each type of criminal sanction reduce, increase, or have no effect on future crimes?" (1993: 445). Sherman's concept of defiance is explained as "the net increase in the prevalence, incidence, or seriousness of future offending against a sanctioning community caused by a proud, shameless reaction to the administration of a criminal sanction" (p. 459). Thus, where offenders are treated unfairly or disrespectfully by police or the criminal justice system, or at least perceive they have been so treated, the outcome is likely to be defiance. This minimizes the legitimacy of sanctions and is likely to promote recidivism. Sherman argues that other factors increase the risk that unfairness and disrespect will promote increased offending. First, when an offender lacks social bonds to the community there is no effective restraint; second, offenders are more likely to be defiant if they perceive they have been personally stigmatized; and third, offenders are more likely to want to exact revenge on society when they reject or deny the stigmatization imposed on them. Empirical studies show mixed support for this theory (Lilly et al. 2011: 159).

Critics of labeling point out that the theory has no empirical support and relies on the idea of societal reaction, especially as expressed by the criminal justice system, as a key element in offenders adopting a criminal career. However, numerous studies have shown that during the life course, deviance emerges early in life and before interventions take place (Cullen and Agnew 1999: 272). In addition, labeling theory takes no account of structural factors or inequality that might affect behavior. Radical criminologists argue that labeling does not go far enough in analyzing the social construction of crime because it does not connect the criminal justice system to the economic order. They contend that criminal labeling has developed owing to inequalities associated with the capitalist system which criminalizes the poor but never the rich (Lilly et al. 2011: 148). Another criticism of labeling is that while it rejects the determinism of psychological, biological and social factors as causes of crime it simply replaces them with the notion that social reaction drives a person to crime and leaves no room for voluntary acts. Generally, owing to the deficiencies noted above, some regard labeling as an approach or a "sensitizing concept" and not as a fully evolved criminological theory (Muncie 2009: 129).

Nevertheless, recognizing the stigmatizing effect of societal reaction is an important insight into what makes a career criminal (Cullen and Agnew 1999: 274). For example, being stigmatized as criminal can result in a breakup of pro-social relationships, peers and friends begin to distance themselves, and persons in that condition may associate with subcultural groups, further reinforcing antisocial values. Where imprisonment is the penalty, a person loses employment and perhaps family connections are strained, and upon release employment prospects are diminished so that often only menial, low-paying jobs are available. This can result in crime being seen as a more profitable option. Thus, conferring a status of permanent criminal can severely impact a person's future prospects and become a self-fulfilling prophecy (Lilly et al. 2011: 146). There is also an association between labeling and racial profiling – that is, whether minorities experience higher levels of scrutiny by law enforcement through traffic stops because of their race and ethnicity – the so called "driving while Black" issue. Here, the research suggests that social control and labeling are being applied to minorities, perhaps owing to racial prejudice or other institutionalized practices associated with stereotyping.

Research indicating that state intervention, while not an actual cause of crime, can be a risk factor for criminality is demonstrated in a study of more than 95,000 adults convicted of felony and facing probation. A Florida law in this case actually explicitly created the labeling that gives judges power to withhold the designation of felony offender. For those who are not designated a felon, no civil rights are lost and they may indicate on employment applications that they have not been convicted of a felony. However, those formally determined as felony offenders are subject to all the constraints associated with that term. Researchers found that those adjudicated as felons were significantly likely to recidivate compared to those not so adjudicated, thus providing support for the labeling theory (Chiricos et al. 2007: 570).

As noted above, the logic of labeling in relation to state intervention is that if state intervention does cause crime, such intervention should be limited. This has been attempted through decriminalization of conduct otherwise ruled to be criminogenic, such as juvenile status offenses and deinstitutionalizing juvenile offenders. Abortion has been decriminalized and the personal possession of marijuana in small quantities is treated as a minor offense (Lilly et al. 2011: 154).

Criminology and gender

Until the latter part of the 20th century females were largely ignored in criminology and most studies used data collected from males to explain male offending. Similarly, theories of crime attempted to explain only why boys and men were engaged in crime. With the advent of the women's movement the situation changed, and there is now a much greater focus on women's and girls' criminality. As Muncie (2009: 135) observes, feminist theorizing about female crime initially took the form of critiques about the neglect and distortion of female experiences with criminality. Feminists also attempted a reconceptualization of the social world to explain women's offending. The principal questions in addressing gender and crime and in understanding the feminist perspective on crime were identified as and remain: Why do women commit so few crimes as compared to men? – the gender ratio problem; and, Do theories that were devised to explain men's criminality also explain female offending? – the generalizability problem (Daly and Chesney-Lind 1988: 497). Generally, while sex is a physical, biological attribute with a predominantly fixed state of being, gender "involves a dynamic process of definition of appropriate characteristics and actions associated with being feminine or masculine" (Morash 2006: 9). Conceptions of femininity and masculinity are not fixed but vary across cultures (p. 9).

The feminist perspective in the relationship between feminism and criminology takes different forms but feminisms are commonly categorized as: *liberal feminism*, *socialist feminism* and *radical feminism*. The existence of these perspectives demonstrates that there is no single feminist criminology (Muncie 2009: 136). *Liberal feminism* was most influential at the start of the feminist movement. Its focus is on equal opportunity and gender discrimination, and it stresses the use of affirmative action and amendments to laws as change agents. It tends to ignore race and class, and uses traditional positivist methodologies to study crime, and is most at home with mainstream criminology (Walklate 2007: 89). Liberal feminists apply sex role theory in arguing that women are socialized to certain roles and subjected to a greater degree of social control than men. However, this does not explain why women commit crime despite effective socialization into "feminine" roles that would preclude delinquency. Deconstructing so-called "natural" gender roles and showing how they were in fact socially constructed is a key element of this style of thinking about gender (Muncie 2009: 136). *Socialist feminism* sees gender inequity as a function of the capitalist society which nurtures both social class divisions and patriarchy so that the powerful are males and capitalists, and the powerless are women and the working class. The interaction between sex, class and race is also a central concern (Walklate 2007: 87). *Radical feminism* highlights patriarchy and sees women's subordination as an outcome of male aggression and the control of female sexuality. Crime is then seen as an expression of men's need to control women. This perspective focuses more on men's oppression of women than on other social conditions that might engender women's subordination, and can be credited with placing men's violence toward women high on the criminological agenda (p. 87). According to this perspective, much criminality is accounted for by the structure of the patriarchal society (Muncie 2009: 136). However, radical feminism is criticized for its essentialism because it implies or assumes a unitary male personality (Messerschmidt 1993).

In light of the disputes between the various feminist perspectives on gender and crime, some scholars have taken an anti-criminological position. They argue that feminist criminologists have, for example, adopted terms such as "crime" and "deviance" uncritically, and that there is a need to be critical of the discipline of criminology itself (Muncie 2009: 137). For example, Carol Smart has taken this approach, describing attempts to alter criminology as simply "revitalizing a problematic enterprise" (Smart 1990: 70).

Like other scholars, James Messerschmidt has argued that criminological theories provide an incomplete understanding of crime because they fail to bring gender into their analysis. The question of how gender is organized as an ongoing affair has been addressed in important ways by Connell (1987) and Messerschmidt (1993). The main issue in terms of the gender gap in offending can be expressed as a question: What is it about men that induces them to commit crime? If this approach is followed the focus shifts to masculinity, and by exploring masculinity men are brought into a comprehensive feminist theory of gendered crime (Messerschmidt 1993). Proposing three social structures underlying gender relations (and following Connell (2002: 53)): the gender division of labor, gender relations of power and sexuality, Messerschmidt contends that these social structures are forms of interaction that constrain and channel social action and that "crime operates subtly through a complex series of class, race and gender practices" (pp. 62–63). Gender is conceptualized as a situated accomplishment and therefore men accomplish masculinity in specific social situations in a variety of ways. It follows that masculinity must be seen as "structured action – what men do under specific constraints and varying degrees of power" (Messerschmidt quoted in Evans and Jamieson 2008: 169). For some men, then, crime becomes a resource for doing gender – for accomplishing masculinity – when other resources are unavailable and, through analyzing masculinities, it becomes possible to explain why men perform varieties of crime (p. 170). Thus, men employ crime to show others that they are "real men." Messerschmidt (1993: 119) provides an account of the variety of ways in which masculinity is expressed in the context of crime in three locations – the street, the workplace and the home, specifically the pimp on the street, the sharp business practice of the business executive and modes of violence in the home. These accounts show how men demonstrate manliness to others and to themselves.

Masculinity theory has been criticized for focusing on structure and for not explaining how a minority of men from a particular race or class background accomplish masculinity through crime while a majority do not. The notion that subjective elements should be taken into account finds expression in work on the "seductions of crime" (Katz 1988) which highlight the gratification and excitement of the drama of crime. Thus, it is argued that a complete picture of delinquency should incorporate a psychosocial criminology (Muncie 2009: 138).

In responding to issues about women's and girls' criminality, it is important to understand how women's and girls' deviance has been viewed by criminologists in the past and how feminist theories about the operation of gender relations inform theories about women's and girls' offending. In *The Female Offender* (1895), Cesare Lombroso argued that female criminals were those who had failed to develop proper feminine traits. They were more masculine and stronger than ordinary women and could "think like a man" (quoted in Lilly et al. 2011: 233). However, women were less inclined toward crime than males due to their sedentary nature and their role as caretaker of children. Thus criminal women were seen as abnormal and as excelling in cunning, spite and deceitfulness, and their criminality was often seen as "a preoccupation with sexual matters" (Lilly et al. 2011: 233; see also Chesney-Lind and Shelden 2004: 100). Lombroso, with his focus on biological characteristics and sexuality, laid the foundations for later work that followed similar reasoning.

In *The Unadjusted Girl* (1923), W.I. Thomas also focused on sexuality, arguing that nearly all female delinquency was an outcome of sexual problems (quoted in Chesney-Lind and Shelden 2004: 101). Thomas believed that female delinquency began with a desire to experience new events and excitements, and that girls learned they could achieve this by manipulating their sexuality (Shoemaker 2005: 248). Otto Pollak's *The Criminality of Women* (1950) again targets female biology as an explanation for female offending and therefore is in the tradition of Lombroso (Smart 1977). He suggests that "precocious biological maturity" (Pollak 1950: 124) was a significant factor in criminality and argues that women offenders are more deceitful than men (a trait acquired in childhood) and therefore much of their criminality remains undetected. He contends that women in fact instigate crimes and manipulate men into performing them, showing their inherent evilness. According to Pollak, this ability to manipulate men is a function of the fact that women conceal their "positive emotion" during sex while men do not. In relation to the treatment of female offenders by the justice system, Pollak claimed that the chivalrous attitude of men (based on a misconception of their being gentle and passive) led to women receiving more lenient treatment than men (Smart 1977).

How is it possible to understand men's overrepresentation in criminal behavior? Many argue that the cause is parenting practice and that if parents raised boys as they do girls there would be a dramatic fall in male offending (Morash 2006). In 1975, Freda Adler's *Sisters in Crime* and Rita Simon's *The Contemporary Woman and Crime* claimed that the gender ratio would shrink because the women's movement would provide more opportunity for women to engage in both legal and illegal enterprises. According to Adler, women's violent crime rate would be affected while Simon contended that only the rate of property crime would increase (quoted in Morash 2006: 16). Thus, according to their perspectives, feminism would drive women's criminality higher. This was the so-called "liberation hypothesis" (see Chapter 4) and it was criticized by feminists for linking female crime causally with the women's movement when there existed no empirical evidence that holding feminist views would increase women's competitiveness (Morash 2006: 16). Subsequent studies have shown that women's criminality has not in fact changed radically and that they are still much less likely to commit violent crime, although their involvement in property crime has increased (Steffensmeier 1980).Nevertheless, women and girls continue to demonstrate far less criminality than men and boys. After Adler and Simon's work the focus shifted away from "women's liberation" to the theme of male dominance in a patriarchal society and its effect on women's criminality, and to illuminating gender power differences (Lilly et al. 2011: 240). By 1988, Daly and Chesney-Lind were ready to state the essential features of feminist theory, which at that time included the following (Daly and Chesney-Lind 1988):

- gender is a complex, social, historical and cultural product related to biological sex differences;
- gender and gender relations order social life in fundamental ways;
- gender relations are founded on men's superiority and their social, political and economic dominance over women;

- knowledge production is gendered and reflects men's views and perspectives;
- women should not be invisible or viewed as appendages to men.

Since the 1990s feminist criminologists have been exploring what is called the "gendered pathways" approach to explaining female criminality. In a number of respects the pathways perspective is similar to the life course analysis approach and it maps female experiences looking at causes of crime (Lilly et al. 2011: 249). It differs from life-course theory in that it pays attention to sexual relationships and victimization, especially with intimate male partners and sexual exploiters, while life-course analysis focuses on structural, neighborhood and family contexts that can influence boys' delinquency (Morash 2006: 169). In terms of explaining why some women and girls commit crimes, Gelsthorpe and Morris (2002: 290) argue that criminal justice practice should focus not only on the immediate events associated with a crime but also "on the broad social and individual factors which may contribute to and which, so to speak, put women on the pathways to crime." For example, studying girls who have fled their homes in response to abuse or neglect has shown how they often become street people and encounter homelessness, drug abuse and unemployment, and become sex workers in order to survive (Chesney-Lind and Pasko 2004). Consequently, recourse to delinquency may be an outcome of strategies which girls pursue to escape or survive physical and sexual abuse. Status offenses, such as running away from home, evoke social control responses that criminalize what are essentially responses to victimhood (Evans and Jamieson 2008: 3).

Studies that have examined the gender gap using variables from mainstream crime theories show mixed results. The assumption in such studies is that male and female offending is caused by the same factors and typically studies can account for some, but not all of the gender gap. Generally, social learning variables such as delinquent peers, school performance and traditional gender beliefs and masculinity best explain gender differences in offending (Vito et al. 2007: 228).

In relation to the generalizability issue, studies have generally shown that variables from mainstream crime theories also explain female offending, but this does not mean that they represent a complete explanation. Feminists point out, for example, that studies conducted by males may overlook factors that are uniquely female. In particular, it should be noted that victimization – and especially sexual victimization – is heavily implicated in female offending (see Chapter 4 for a discussion on the sexual abuse of incarcerated girls). In a typology of victimized street women Daly (1994) identifies the following commonalities: generally, have experienced high levels of abuse with the outcome that they live on the street; were often abused and neglected children who are more likely to be addicted to drugs and alcohol and become violent; were battered women as a result of gender violence at the hands of abusive partners but sometimes resisted and retaliated against the abuser.

A key question in the debate about gender and crime is as Walklate (2007: 103) describes it: "how much there is to be learned about crime, its causation and the process of criminalization, by rendering the question of gender more explicit." She observes that theorizing masculinity has provided insights into causal processes but she asks under what circumstances does gender constitute a key explanatory variable? She calls for reflexivity and a critical perspective in work on gender to establish the extent to which gender matters more or less than other variables in criminological projects.

As Akers (1994: 172) suggests, there is not yet a fully developed feminist explanation of the generalizability and the gender ratio questions discussed above. An adequate feminist explanation of female delinquency is still a work in progress. While the basic patriarchal structure of society is a key element in understanding female crime, as Chesney-Lind has noted (1989: 19), the ways in which social control agencies act to reinforce gender differences (as described in Chapter 4) should also be examined.

Recap

Understanding why crime occurs is a necessary precursor to developing strategies to counter it. Thus, theoretical perspectives serve a practical purpose in that they help to shape and order data about criminality and society into understandings and explanations that policy makers can act upon.

No single theory can explain all types of delinquency. This chapter has explored the dominant mainstream theories of delinquency, namely *strain*, *social learning*, *control* and *labeling*, all of which offer explanations of youth crime. The role played by gender in juvenile crime has come to be recognized as a key element in understanding criminality but a full appreciation of the functioning of gender is still lacking. At its core, the issue is whether criminality is a freely chosen course of action or whether juveniles are pushed into crime by external factors. Social learning theory argues that youth become delinquent as a result of their association with others; control theories envisage that all youth would offend unless a control prevents that from happening, and strain and control theories put the importance of external structural variables at the center of explanations for delinquency. Labeling theory argues that society labels persons as deviant, and that those who are selected accept that label and become deviant. Strain theories focus on crime as the outcome of constraints faced in achieving socially valued goals where illegitimate means employed to achieve goals proved unattainable using legitimate means.

youth, crime and justice

In considering gender and criminology, feminist scholars first drew attention to the fact that females had been generally ignored in studies and that most research had used data collected from males to explain male offending. Thus feminists initially promoted studies on women and girls and the place of gender within criminality as a discrete topic within the project of criminology. Subsequently, two key research issues were identified: Why do women commit so few crimes as compared to men? – the gender ratio issue; and, Do theories that were developed to explain men's criminality also explain female offending? – the generalizability issue. The explanatory power of gender as a factor in criminality generally remains as yet undetermined and feminist explanations of girls' delinquency are still incomplete.

References

Adler, Freda. 1975. *Sisters in Crime*. New York: McGraw-Hill.

Agnew, Robert. 2009. *Juvenile Delinquency: Causes and Control*. New York: Oxford University Press.

Akers, Ronald. 1994. *Criminological Theories: Introduction and Evaluation*. Los Angeles, CA: Roxbury.

Akers, Ronald. 1998. *Social Learning and Social Structure: A General Theory of Crime and Deviance*. Boston, MA: Northeastern University Press.

Becker, Howard S. 1963. *Outsiders: Studies in the Sociology of Deviance*. New York: Free Press.

Berkowitz, Leonard. 1993. *Aggression: Its Causes, Consequences and Control*. New York: McGraw-Hill.

Braithwaite, John. 1989. *Crime, Shame and Reintegration*. Cambridge: Cambridge University Press.

Burgess, Robert and Ronald Akers. 1966. "A Differential Reinforcement Theory of Criminal Behavior." *Social Problems* 14: 128–146.

Chambliss, William. 1973. "The Saints and the Roughnecks." *Society* 11: 24–31.

Chesney-Lind, Meda. 1989. "Girls' Crime and Woman's Place: Toward A Feminist Model of Female Delinquency." *Crime and Delinquency* 35: 5–29.

Chesney-Lind, Meda and Lisa Pasko. 2004. *Girls' Troubles and Female Delinquency in The Female Offender: Girls, Women and Crime*. Thousand Oaks, CA: Sage.

Chesney-Lind, Meda and Randall G. Shelden. 2004. *Girls, Delinquency and Juvenile Justice*. Belmont, CA: Wadsworth.

Chiricos, T., K. Barrick, W. Bales and S. Bontrager. 2007. "The Labeling of Convicted Felons and its Consequences for Recidivism." *Criminology* 45: 547–581.

Cloward, Richard A. and Lloyd E. Ohlin. 1960. *Delinquency and Opportunity*. New York: Free Press.

Cohen, Albert K. 1955. *Delinquent Boys*. New York: Free Press.

Colvin, Mark. 2000. *Crime and Coercion*. New York: St. Martin's Press.

Connell, Robert W. 1987. *Gender and Power: Society, the Person and Sexual Politics*. Cambridge: Polity Press.

Connell, Robert W. 2002. *Gender*. Cambridge: Polity Press.

Cullen, Francis T. and Robert Agnew (eds). 1999. *Criminological Theory: Past to Present*. Los Angeles, CA: Roxbury Publishing.

Daly, Kathleen. 1994. *Gender, Crime and Punishment*. New Haven, CT: Yale University Press.

Daly, Kathleen and Meda Chesney-Lind. 1988. "Feminism and Criminology." *Justice Quarterly* 5(4): 497–538.

Elliott, Delbert S., Suzanne Ageton and Rachel Canter. 1979. "An Integrated Theoretical Perspective on Delinquent Behavior." *Journal of Research in Crime and Delinquency* 16: 3–27.

Evans, Karen and Janet Jamieson. 2008. *Gender and Crime: A Reader*. New York: Open University Press.

Gelsthorpe, Loraine and Allison Morris. 2002. "Women's Imprisonment in England and Wales: A Penal Paradox." *Criminology and Criminal Justice* 2(3): 277–301.

Gottfredson, Michael and Travis Hirschi. 1990. *A General Theory of Crime*. Stanford, CA: Stanford University Press.

Gottfredson, Michael and Travis Hirschi. 1999. "A General Theory of Crime." In Francis T. Cullen and Robert Agnew (eds) *Criminological Theory: Past to Present*. Los Angeles, CA: Roxbury Publishing, pp. 175–186.

Greenberg, David F. 1977. "Delinquency and the Age Structure of Society." *Contemporary Crises* 1: 189–223.

Hirschi, T. 1969. *Causes of Delinquency*. Berkeley: University of California Press.

Hirschi, Travis. 1999. "Social Bond Theory." In Francis T. Cullen and Robert Agnew (eds) *Criminological Theory: Past to Present*. Los Angeles, CA: Roxbury Publishing, pp. 167–174.

Hirschi, Travis. 2009. *Causes of Delinquency*. Princeton, NJ: Transaction Publishers.

Katz, Jack. 1988. *Seductions of Crime*. New York: Basic Books.

Lemert, Edwin M. 1952. *Social Pathology*. New York: McGraw-Hill.

Lemert, Edwin M. 1972. *Human Deviance, Social Problems, and Social Control*. Englewood Cliffs, NJ: Prentice Hall.

Lilly, Robert J., Francis T. Cullen and Richard A. Ball. 2011. *Criminological Theory: Context and Consequences*. Thousand Oaks, CA: Sage.

Matsueda, Ross L. 1992. "Reflected Appraisals, Parental Labeling and Delinquency: Specifying a Symbolic Interactionist Theory." *American Journal of Sociology* 6: 1577–1611.

Merton, Robert K. 1938. "Social Structure and Anomie." *American Sociological Review* 3: 672–682.

Merton, Robert K. 1968. *Social Theory and Social Structure*. New York: Free Press.

Messerschmidt, James. 1993. *Masculinities and Crime: Critique and Reconceptualization of Theory*. Totowa, NJ: Rowman and Littlefield.

Morash, Merry. 2006. *Understanding Gender, Crime and Justice*. Thousand Oaks, CA: Sage.

Muncie, John. 2009. *Youth and Crime*. London: Sage.

Pollak, Otto. 1950. *The Criminality of Women*. New York: Barnes.

Sampson, Robert and John Laub. 1999. "Crime and the Life Course." In Francis T. Cullen and Robert Agnew (eds) *Criminological Theory: Past to Present*. Los Angeles, CA: Roxbury Publishing, pp. 187–198.

Sherman, Lawrence. 1993. "Defiance, Deterrence and Irrelevance: A Theory of the Criminal Sanction." *Journal of Research in Crime and Delinquency* 30: 445–473.

Shoemaker, Donald J. 2005. *Theories of Delinquency*. New York: Oxford University Press.

Simon, Rita James. 1975. *The Contemporary Woman and Crime*. Washington D.C.: U.S. Government Printing Office.

Smart, Carol. 1977. "Criminological Theory: Its Ideology and Implications Concerning Women." *British Journal of Sociology* 28(1): 89–100.

Smart, Carol. 1990. "Feminist Approaches to Criminology or Postmodern Woman Meets Atavistic Man." In Allison Morris and Loraine Gelsthorpe (eds) *Feminist Perspectives in Criminology*. Buckingham: Open University Press.

Steffensmeier, D.J. 1980. "Sex Differences in Patterns of Adult Crime, 1965–1978." *Social Forces* 57: 1080–1108.

Sykes, Gresham M. and David Matza. 1999. "Techniques of Neutralization." In Francis T. Cullen and Robert Agnew (eds) *Criminological Theory: Past to Present*. Los Angeles, CA: Roxbury Publishing, pp. 85–91.

Tannenbaum, E. 1938. *Crime and the Community*. New York: Columbia University Press.

Thomas, W.I. 1923. *The Unadjusted Girl*. New York: Harper and Row.

Tierney, Kathleen J. 1982. "The Battered Women Movement and the Creation of the Wife Beating Problem." *Social Problems* 29: 207–220.

Vito, Gennaro J., Jeffrey R. Maahs and Ronald M. Holmes. 2007. *Criminology: Theory, Research and Policy*. Sudbury, MA: Jones and Bartlett.

Walklate, Sandra. 2007. *Understanding Criminology: Current Theoretical Debates*. Maidenhead: Open University Press.

chapter 3

Juvenile Institutions

History and development of juvenile corrections

Historical contingencies, social forces and punishment discourses have shaped the birth and development of juvenile institutions in the U.S. The contours that converge in the institutionalization of juveniles begin in the colonial period between 1607 and 1775 when imported English laws were applied prescribing the death penalty for a wide range of crimes. However, many colonies adopted a more flexible approach to punishment based on the pace of social change, economic growth and population changes (Preyer 1982: 327). Colonies shared a common belief in the value of the family, the community and the church as key resources in the fight against sin and criminality (Rothman 1990: 16). The family was the central mode of juvenile social control to the extent that early laws even provided the penalty of death for children who disobeyed their parents (Krisberg 2005: 23, 24).[1] However, harsh laws imposing the death penalty or other punishments were often unenforced by magistrates uneasy about sending children to adult jails (Schlossman 1995: 326). The close-knit community life of this period enabled easy identification of criminals and promoted a wariness of strangers. Two critical social issues were maintaining community cohesion and order and obedience to God. Crime was seen as a sin and a crime against God because it violated community norms. Like sin, crime was thought to be the outcome of a depraved human condition and because all men were born to corruption, the causes of crime did not need investigation (Rothman 1990: 15, 17).

Puritan conceptions about punishment saw it as a cleansing process that would integrate the offender back into the community. An admission of wrongdoing and a display of contrition would often be sufficient to defer or minimize a fine or other punishment (Cahn 1989: 127). Abiding by the English model, punishment did not differentiate between child and adult and often took a public form, designed to shame the wrongdoer. Modes of punishment included fines, whipping and banishment. Only jails and workhouses employed confinement as punishment but in the case of jails, detention was usually for those awaiting trial and for debtors (Barnes 1972: 114). A jail sentence seldom exceeded 90 days and often lasted for only 24 hours (Colvin 1997: 47). The local jail did not adhere to any particular architectural design and resembled any house within the community with offenders confined in groups to rooms, simulating a family environment. Workhouses, also known as houses of correction, reproducing the European model of the mid-16th century, were often used in the colonial period as adjuncts to jails (Blomberg and Lucken 2000: 33).

The period from 1776 to 1825 was one in which the new ideas generated by the Enlightenment began to affect the discourse of punishment in the U.S. As well, the old communal lifestyle was replaced by labor mobility, a population explosion and the expansion west. Towns and then cities were created; for example, between 1790 and 1830 the population of Massachusetts doubled, that of Pennsylvania tripled and the population of New York increased fivefold (Blomberg and Lucken 2000: 36). The Enlightenment discourse of the rational man, of the capacity of science to define the universe for man, and of a more benevolent God, contributed to new punishment discourses that sought to break away from old inherited models. The republican focus on liberty set up a contrast with confinement as deprivation of liberty. Ideas about individualism and individual merit may have promoted the concept of a process of rehabilitation to be conducted within confinement (Hirsch 1992: 53). Crime began to be seen as a product of the environment rather than as something inherent in man. Thus, constructing a discrete setting for an offender would enable reform to occur (Rothman 1990: 71). By the second decade of the 19th century most states had changed their laws to replace the death penalty with incarceration (p. 61). Punishment began to be linked with work and labor, and modes of punishment took the modern forms of the death penalty, fines and incarceration (Hirsch 1992: 42, 58).

In explaining how confinement, principally in the form of the penitentiary, came to be the conventional mode of punishing crime in the U.S. and elsewhere, David Rothman argues that U.S. reformers believed that the penitentiary would instill in prisoners the necessary self-discipline they lacked as the products of dysfunctional families. In addition, fears about disorder due to social change in the new republic necessitated a political response and confining those considered dangerous would protect the new republic from being torn asunder. Rothman points to the emphasis on order, discipline and regularity in facilities for the insane, the criminal, the delinquent and the poor as illustrative of a shared apprehension of social disorder (Rothman 1971: xxxviii). Michael Ignatieff argues that the U.S. adopted the English model of the penitentiary with its factory-like routines and rules, and notes how the penitentiary incorporated the hierarchical social order that many feared would not be sustained in the new republic (Ignatieff 1978: 84). In contrast to Ignatieff's contention that fears of class warfare constituted the rationale for incarceration, Rothman suggests that the fear was more one of moral dissoluteness (Rothman 1971: xliii). Michel Foucault locates the emergence of the penitentiary in technologies of power that sought to punish and discipline those considered dangerous to society (Foucault 1977). A Marxist perspective on the birth of the penitentiary came in 1939 when Rusche and Kirchheimer attempted to link the birth of the prison with conditions of labor by arguing that the penitentiary was a means of controlling surplus labor (Rusche and Kirchheimer 1939). Melossi and Pavarini affirm the economic rationale for incarceration, suggesting that it represented a response to economic dislocation in a society where being poor came to be seen as synonymous with criminality (Melossi and Pavarini 1981: 119).

During the period from 1825 to 1860 the House of Refuge was created as part of a series of reforms intended to minimize juvenile delinquency (Krisberg 2005: 27).[2] This was a time of high levels of immigration, revolutionary movements in Europe and perceived increases in crime and disease in the U.S., all fueling fears of social unrest among elite conservative reformers who saw themselves as the guardians of the nation's moral condition. The poor and the deviant were seen as threats to class privileges. At that time children were detained in adult jails and workhouses but the reformers believed this practice would only increase their chances of becoming adult criminals. The reformers called for prisons for juveniles, described in a report of the Society for the Prevention of Pauperism as more like "schools for instruction, than places of punishment" where youth would undergo "a course of discipline, severe and unchanging. . . . A system should be adopted that would provide a mental and moral regimen" (quoted in Krisberg 2005: 27).

On January 1, 1825 the New York House of Refuge opened, and within a year similar Houses were opened in Boston and Philadelphia. All accepted both delinquents and destitute children, thus establishing the conjunction of juvenile offenders with neglected and dependent children still found today. The Fifth Annual Report of the New York Society for the Reformation of Juvenile Delinquents, founder of the New York House of Refuge, explicitly welcomes the new enlarged powers, reporting: "If a child be found destitute; or abandoned by its parents, or suffered to lead a vicious or a vagrant life; or if convicted of any crime, it may be sent to the House of Refuge" (quoted in Sutton 1988: 45).

A House of Refuge was characterized by a regime of strict discipline, obedience to authority, regimentation and a dedication to the principle of work. Like contemporary juvenile institutions, the daily schedules in the Houses of Refuge allocated blocks of time to "productive" activity erasing any casual or random movement. Serving indeterminate sentences until the age of majority, many were released to undertake forms of apprenticeship and, according to Mennel (1973 quoted in Sutton 1988: 47), about 40 percent of those placed there escaped from the Refuge or from their apprenticeships. Houses of Refuge firmly established incarceration as the appropriate response to multiple forms of youth deviance (Sutton 1988: 47). They failed to achieve their moral purposes for a range of reasons including that harsh forms of discipline and punishment were employed; youth detained there came to comprise the most experienced criminal delinquents; and reform efforts declined as detainees from the immigrant classes began to populate them (Rothman 1971: 262).[3]

Taking children away from their parents to commit them to Houses of Refuge required a legal justification, and this became available in 1838 when *Ex parte Crouse* established the right of the courts to remove infants from their parents by applying the *parens patriae* doctrine. Mary Ann Crouse's father tried to secure her release from the Philadelphia House of Refuge under a writ of habeas corpus. Her mother committed her because she believed this would prevent her from becoming a pauper, yet she had committed no crime. The Pennsylvania Supreme Court decided that "the right of parental control is a natural, but not an unalienable one" and asked whether "the natural parents, when unequal to the task of education, or unworthy of it, be superseded by the parens patriae or common guardian of the community?" (*Ex parte Crouse*, 4 WHART.9 [PA. 1838]). The Pennsylvania Supreme Court denied the claim for habeas corpus. As Rendleman notes (1971: 69), in *Crouse* the Court applied *parens patriae* to justify schemes that parted poor or incompetent parents from their children. The doctrine served as a convenient mechanism under which the state, through the courts, was enabled to act against the poor rather than punish delinquency (p. 70). Once placed in a House of Refuge, the protection of the criminal law ceased to apply (Mennel 1973: 73). Thus, the Refuge was able to exercise the discretionary authority of the family supplemented by the formal law (Sutton 1988: 47).

Between 1850 and 1890 a new group of reformers, ideologically analogous to those who created Houses of Refuge, and who have come to be known as the Child Savers (Platt 1977), established private philanthropic societies to save children from criminality. The Child Savers "viewed the urban masses as a potentially dangerous class that could rise up if misery and impoverishment were not alleviated" (Krisberg 2005: 31). They believed that children who revealed criminal tendencies through acts such as truancy needed to be regulated in the interests of society because they would otherwise become criminals (Platt 1977: 32). These middle- and upper class reformers therefore devised new forms of social control to protect their powers and privileges (p. xx). Their core convictions identified the institution of the family as a reformatory for delinquents and therefore, to take one example, gathering up and placing delinquents with farming families in the newly opened west was a favored strategy. It was thought that the city corrupted children, and that country life would deter criminality and ensure children's socialization as good citizens.

The child savers' emphasis on the authority of parents in the home, the attractions of rural life and the independence of the nuclear family was intended to counteract the influence of urbanism and the new industrialization. Drawing on their middle-class values, child savers were not so much interested in criminal acts as they were in creating norms to regulate youthful behavior in terms of education, recreation, attitudes to family and personal morality. The child savers "were most active and successful in extending governmental control over a wide range of youthful activities that had been previously ignored or dealt with informally. Their reforms were aimed at defining and regulating the dependent status of youth" (Platt 1977: 99). Their interventions blurred the difference between delinquency and dependency so that formal legal distinctions were not made between those who were delinquent and those who were dependent or neglected, or those whose behavior was offensive but did not rise to the level of criminality (pp. 135, 138). The logic underpinning this perspective was that parental neglect caused a child to become unruly, and "unruly children turn into adult paupers and criminals who in turn neglect their children" (Sutton 1988: 65).

By the middle of the 19th century state and municipal governments had taken over the administration of private institutions for children and by 1876, of the 51 Houses of Refuge or reform schools (as the newer institutions were known, implying a focus on formal schooling), nearly three-quarters were operated by state or local governments (Krisberg 2005: 33–34). By 1890, except for the south, almost every state had a reform school holding children under indeterminate sentences until they reached the age of majority or had been reformed, a decision resting within the discretion of the reform school officials. Many schools operated a cottage system, grouping the youth into units of 40 or fewer, each group housed in their own cottage. The Civil War enlarged reform school populations and strained their capacity. When state funding was reduced, schools resorted to the contract labor system to raise revenue, leading to criticism that exploiting the labor of children rather than securing their reformation had become their main purpose (p. 34).

During the Progressive Era from 1880 to 1920, reform schools continued to experience financial constraints. Criticism of the contract labor system caused some states to legislate to exclude children under the age of 12 from being placed in reform schools and even to abolish contract labor altogether (Krisberg 2005: 37). Doubts about the efficacy of reform schools and legal challenges to the doctrine of *parens patriae* raised the issue of procedural protection for delinquent children. In 1899 Illinois enacted the first juvenile court law in the country following the efforts of a new wave of Child Savers, members of wealthy Chicago families. The new juvenile court would entertain cases of both delinquent and dependent and neglected children. The court had the power to institutionalize children and placed institutions for dependent youth under the control of a state board. By 1925, all but two states had established special courts for juveniles.

Throughout the 1930s and 1940s the numbers committed to juvenile institutions increased. The creation of the centralized California Youth Authority just before World War II provided a model for other states and under it, criminal courts sent youth offenders aged from 16 to 21 to the Authority which was responsible for determining the appropriate disposition. Its mission favored training and treatment over retribution (Krisberg 2005: 54, 55) and all delinquent youth were to be sent to "diagnostic centers" before placement to identify individual problems and needs, and to match them with the available treatment (Schlossman 1995: 345). These treatment technologies reflected the state of social and behavioral sciences at that time.

By the 1950s and 1960s, psychologically directed treatment approaches had begun to appear in juvenile institutions. Also at this time, community-based correctional facilities such as group homes, partial release programs and half-way houses were introduced with the aim of reducing the numbers sent to institutions. In the 1960s, the President's Commission on Law Enforcement and the Administration of Justice (1967) and the National Commission on the Causes and Prevention of Violence (1969) both concluded that incarceration had failed to deter crime or rehabilitate criminals (Schlossman 1995: 346). The President's Commission called for diversion and deinstitutionalization (McGarrell 1988: 8). The move against institutionalization was exemplified in Massachusetts when in 1972 it closed almost all its training schools for delinquents, effectively deinstitution-alizing its juvenile justice system and sending most juveniles to group homes, foster homes and private treatment facilities (Krisberg 2005: 56; Welch 2004: 211). In 1974, the passing of the *Juvenile Justice and Delinquency Prevention Act* gave political endorsement to deinstitutionalization (Krisberg 2005). However, the zeal to deinstitutionalize did not endure, and by the 1980s a punitive shift against both adult criminals and juvenile delinquents had occurred. Increased rates of juvenile crime were experienced from the late 1980s until the mid-1990s with a trend toward longer periods of incarceration and increases in the transfer of juveniles to adult courts (Austin et al. 2000: ix). Even though this trend of increased juvenile crime has now been reversed, most states continue to rely on institutionalization.

Contemporary juvenile corrections

According to Thomas Bernard (1992: 3; Bernard and Kurlychek 2010: 3), juvenile justice policies repeat themselves in a cycle. The cycle begins when justice officials and the general public believe juvenile crime to be at a very high level. Because of this perception, punishments are severe and many minor offenders are released because there are no lenient punishments available. It is believed that imposing harsh punishments will exacerbate existing minor criminality (Bernard 1992: 4). At this point policy makers and the public acknowledge that the choice between harsh punishment and no punishment is a concern because harsh punishment increases juvenile crime, as does taking no action at all. At this stage in the cycle, the solution is seen as lenient treatment for offenders and there is general optimism that crime rates will decline. Even so, there is a perception that the level of juvenile crime is high and policy makers now blame lenient punishments for the high crime rates. Therefore, policy responses for serious offenders are made tougher, as are responses to average or typical offenders, so that all categories receive harsh punishment. This process advances to a stage where there are many harsh punishments and few lenient ones. At this stage, policy makers and the public perceive crime to be at a high level and thus must choose between harsh punishment and taking no action (p. 4). The cycle has thus returned to its starting point. According to Bernard, a proper justice policy can only be established by breaking through the cycle of juvenile justice (p. 6). The key issue then in juvenile justice policy reform is that harsh punishments are blamed for high crime rates and are therefore replaced by lenient treatments. However, lenient treatments are then blamed for high crime rates and replaced by harsh punishments (p. 22).

Bernard (1992) argues that the cycle of juvenile justice derives from the fact that juvenile crime rates are seen as high irrespective of justice policy. Nevertheless, many perceive that high rates of juvenile crime are a recent occurrence and that in the good old days juvenile crime was low and would be again if appropriate policies were in place (p. 49). This constituency generates pressure to reverse existing justice policies and replace them with new policies. However, only a limited number of policies are possible and therefore the juvenile justice system cycles back and forth between harsh and lenient punishments. It is impossible to break this cycle with justice policy interventions because every policy suffers the same constraints: once it is implemented many will believe that juvenile crime is exceptionally high, that it was not previously a serious problem, and would not now constitute a serious problem if proper policies were now in place.

In the following case study we can see an example of the response to a perception that there are too many harsh penalties.

SUPREME COURT BANS LIFE WITHOUT PAROLE FOR JUVENILES CONVICTED OF MURDER

On June 25, 2012, the Supreme Court ruled that state laws that mandatorily sentence juveniles convicted of murder to life in prison without parole are unconstitutional. The Court held by a five-to-four majority decision that a sentence of life without parole for juveniles violates the Eighth Amendment's prohibition on cruel and unusual punishment. The ruling could affect nearly 2,500 juvenile prisoners who must now be permitted an opportunity to have the length of their sentence determined.

This decision reflects recent Supreme Court rulings on juvenile sentencing. In 2010 the Court declared juveniles found guilty of non-homicides could not receive life without parole, and in 2005 the Court banned the death penalty for juveniles.

The Supreme Court had already established that children are constitutionally different from adults for purposes of sentencing. The Court found that juveniles have diminished culpability and greater prospects for reform, and they are less deserving of the most severe punishments. Previous Supreme Court cases relied on three significant gaps between juveniles and adults. First, children have a "lack of maturity and an underdeveloped sense of responsibility," leading to recklessness, impulsivity and heedless risk-taking. Second, children "are more vulnerable . . . to negative influences and outside pressures," including from their family and peers; they have limited "control over their own environment" and lack the ability to extricate themselves from horrific, crime-producing settings. Third, a child's character is not as "well formed" as an adult's; his traits are "less fixed" and his actions less likely to be "evidence of irretrievable depravity."

Each of the two cases coming before the Court involved a boy aged 14 who was convicted of murder and sentenced to mandatory life imprisonment without the possibility of parole. In one case the boy Jackson accompanied two other boys to a video store to commit a robbery; on the way to the store he learned that one of the boys was carrying a shotgun. Jackson stayed outside the store for most of the time of the robbery but after he entered it one of his co-conspirators shot and killed the store clerk. Jackson was charged as an adult with capital felony murder and aggravated robbery, and a jury convicted him of both crimes. The trial court imposed the mandatory penalty of life imprisonment without the possibility of parole.

In the other case, Miller, together with his friend, beat Miller's neighbor and set fire to his trailer after an evening of drinking and drug use. The neighbor died. Miller was initially charged as a juvenile but his case was removed to adult court, where he was charged with murder in the course of arson. A jury found Miller guilty, and the trial court imposed a statutorily mandated punishment of life without parole.

Source: Adapted from *Miller vs. Alabama. U.S. Supreme Court.* No. 10–9646. Argued March 20, 2012 – Decided June 25, 2012. http://www.supremecourt.gov/opinions/11pdf/10-9646g2i8.pdf

The following case study is another example of Bernard's cycle illustrating the response when the perception is that there are too many harsh penalties.

STATES PROSECUTE FEWER TEENAGERS IN ADULT COURTS

The *New York Times* reported on March 5, 2011 that many in the juvenile justice field now agree that young delinquents have not been handled properly by the adult court system. This reaction comes a generation after reportedly record levels of juvenile crime prompted a punitive response – punish more juveniles as if they were adults.

New York led the move to crack down on juvenile crime after a 15-year-old shot and killed two people in the New York subway in 1978. The shooter received a five-year sentence – the then maximum for a juvenile – and this caused outrage in the community, resulting in legislators changing the law to reduce the age of adulthood to 13 years in murder cases and 14 for all other major felonies. For other crimes the age was fixed at 16 years – the lowest in the nation.

One recent case in Manhattan's adult criminal court illustrates the issue of treating juveniles as adults. It involved a 17-year-old admitted shoplifter who after being found guilty was offered the choice of a residential drug treatment program or a one- to three-year prison sentence. The defendant knew that his mother would not be able to afford the treatment program (a cost of US$600 a month) and he chose prison. Had he been dealt with in the juvenile court he could have been ordered into a treatment program, the costs of which would have been met by the taxpayers of the state.

Changes in treating juveniles as adults include Connecticut prohibiting 16-year-olds from being sent to adult court – and Illinois transferring offenders charged with minor crimes back into its juvenile court system. In January 2011, Massachusetts brought forward legislation to raise the age at which juveniles could be tried as adults and now Wisconsin and North Carolina plan to follow suit. These changes follow research studies showing that the older adolescents still lacked the capacity for sound decision making and that they would benefit from having access to treatment – something that is not generally available to them in adult prisons.

These changes have also been influenced by the decision of the Supreme Court in *Roper v. Simmons* where the Court prohibited the death penalty for defendants younger than 18 years owing to the factors that differentiate them from adults – lack of maturity, susceptibility to peer pressure and a less than fully developed character.

As well as the judicial determination about youth capacity, states have paid attention to the additional costs of prosecuting juveniles as if they were adults. An analysis by the well-respected Vera Institute of Justice found that transferring about 31,000 16- and 17-year-olds to North Carolina's juvenile system would cost about US$71 million annually but would also generate US$123 million in benefits in the form of fewer arrests over the long term and fewer people in jails and prisons.

Source: Adapted from Secret, Mosi. 2011. "States Prosecute Fewer Teenagers in Adult Courts." *New York Times*, March 5, 2011. http://www. nytimes.com/2011/03/06/nyregion/06juvenile.html?pagewanted=all.

Contemporary juvenile institutionalization arrangements are located within the policy framework of lenient and harsh punishments. They commonly comprise juvenile detention centers (known in many jurisdictions as "juvenile halls") and longer term institutional facilities, often called "training schools." In 2008 there were 757 juvenile detention centers in the country, most operated by state or local government. Almost three-quarters had 50 beds or fewer and only 10 percent accommodated more than 100 youth (Livsey et al. 2009). These facilities are often overcrowded and understaffed (Holmand and Ziedenberg 2006).

Each year about 600,000 juveniles are placed in detention centers often for less than 24 hours but with an average stay of 15 days (Krisberg 2005). The decision to detain in a center is usually made by intake officers who may use structured risk assessment instruments (RAIs) to make detention decisions. These tools are used in an attempt to calculate the risk of the juvenile committing another delinquent act before his or her case is adjudicated, and points are generally allocated to youth based on factors such as the current charge, prior offense history, legal status and evidence of failure to appear (Barton et al. 1994: 81; Krisberg 2005: 74–75). Placement in a detention center may involve an alleged minor offender sharing accommodation with youth who have criminal backgrounds and detention centers may be subjected to gang violence. They are not treatment centers and few services are provided. Nevertheless, they constitute a much more acceptable detention location than adult jails where youth are exposed to violence and possible sexual abuse.

The 1974 *Juvenile Justice and Delinquency Prevention Act* was in part designed to end the practice of committing youth to jails and police lock-ups.[4] At that time it was estimated that almost 500,000 juveniles were entering adult jails each year and later amendments to this law required the complete relocation of youth out of adult jails. This was not fully implemented because states were empowered to decide who constituted a "juvenile" for detention purposes. Thus, an estimated 7,600 youth under the age of 18 were held in adult jails on June 30, 2000 (quoted in Sickmund 2004: 18). The law also required that adults and juveniles be separated in adult jails (so-called "sight and sound separation") but this also does not always occur in practice. Nevertheless, by the late 1980s juvenile placements in adult jails had been reduced to about 65,000 a year (Krisberg 2005: 77).

Reliance on the sanction of detention for juvenile offenders has been constant. In 1989, 21 percent of all cases involved detention; in 1994 this had dropped slightly to 18 percent and by 1998 had risen to 19 percent (Welch 2005). Beginning from the late 1980s the so-called "war on drugs" was associated with a high rate of juvenile detention for drug offenses (p. 207). Juvenile detention practices and the nature of those facilities vary widely. Some institutions resemble adult prisons while others appear more residential in design, continuing the cottage design pioneered during the progressive period. Others take the form of wilderness camps or boot camps, the latter emphasizing discipline and structure.[5] Boot camps, a reinvention of the Houses of Refuge but modeled on armed forces disciplinary practices, no longer enjoy a reputation as an effective remedy for delinquency (Armstrong and Kim 2009: 75). Private facilities play a significant part in juvenile institutionalization, although they held only 29 percent of juvenile offenders in residential placement in October 1999 (Sickmund 2004: 2). As between states, practices vary; for example, Mississippi places 99 percent of juveniles in public facilities compared to Massachusetts where 64 percent are located in private facilities (Welch 2005: 208).

Within juvenile institutions, tools for order maintenance and internal punishment for rule violations include isolation and the use of restraints. Isolation is the removal of a youth to a room or to a specially constructed site for behavioral control, and restraints refers to the use of devices to induce a calming effect or to prevent injury. Researchers have noted a lack of consistency in isolation practices among juvenile facilities, with some having no criteria or only vague rules. Isolation can mean simply confining a juvenile to his or her room, or to an isolation room or to a separate facility often known as "adjustment" or "security" units. Studies have indicated that prolonged isolation, such as for adult prisoners in maximum security units, can result in impulsivity, perceptual distortion, affective unrest and paranoia (Mitchell and Varley 1990: 251, 252). As for restraints, while some facilities use so-called "soft" restraints with leather or soft coverings, many make use of handcuffs which have been employed to spread-eagle youth or to "hog tie" them, handcuffing wrists to ankles behind the back (Mitchell and Varley 1990: 254). Using handcuffs to bind a youth's arms and legs to a bed frame is a practice known as "four-pointing" and was widely employed in Arizona until it became the subject of a lawsuit. This practice was used for a wide range of behaviors including when youth were acting in a disruptive manner for more than 15 minutes. It was common for youth to be four-pointed naked for hours, or wearing only underclothing (Bortner and Williams 1997: 7, 8).

Recently, following the *Prison Rape Elimination Act* of 2003, data have been collected on sexual victimization in juvenile facilities. Reports from youth who claim to have been sexually victimized in juvenile facilities indicate that an estimated 12 percent of youth in state facilities and in large non-state facilities were subjected to one or more incidents of sexual victimization by another youth or a staff member between 2008 and 2009 (Beck et al. 2010: 1). However, victimization rates vary by facility with some facilities experiencing a rate of 30 percent or more. Incident prevalence is biased toward staff with reports showing about 2.6 percent of youth describing an incident involving another youth and 10.3 percent an incident involving staff (p. 1).

Youth who have been convicted in adult courts of criminal offenses may be committed to adult prisons. In 2008 a total of 3,650 juveniles under the age of 18 comprising 3,531 males and 119 females were held in state prisons (West and Sabol 2009). In 2000, the standing population of inmates younger than 18 held in state prisons was 70 percent greater than in 1985 (Sickmund 2004: 20). Research reveals that juveniles in adult prisons are exposed to a much greater risk of harm than youth in juvenile facilities (Austin et al. 2000: 7). In a qualitative study of violent youth in an adult prison, Eisikovits and Baizerman (1982) found that the youths' daily concern was for their survival among an adult population. To exist in that environment required that they learn the practices of the mainstream inmate culture and "fit in," but survival also meant coping with inmates exercising authority over them. While they had previously been leaders of their peers on the streets they were now marginalized. One youth captures the initial experience of incarceration:

> "And they threw the door behind me. I was very scared. Big place. At other institutions I have been, they weren't prisons. There was no bars. . . . All I saw was 100 people running around all over the galleys and on the flag, and they looked like dangerous people. They looked to me the kind of people that would kill you if you looked at them twice. I didn't know what's coming down, who I could trust or anything" – 16 year old.

> (Eisikovits and Baizerman 1982: 13)

After "fitting in" the youth "settle down," which the authors explain as the youth realizing that fear and violence are part of everyday life: "'Everyone has that fear of getting stabbed. Everyone tells you: Get off my back or I'll stab you. After a while you just don't worry' – 17 year old" (Eisikovits and Baizerman 1982: 15). In the same way that youth adopted violence on the streets so they take on violence in the prison (p. 15).

Generally, four methods are employed to house juveniles in adult prisons: place them in administrative segregation until they reach 18; house them in a separate facility within the prison that accommodates only those under 18; accommodate them with others under 18 in one or more units that also hold adults; and integrate them into the general inmate population by housing them in the same way as adults (Levinson and Greene 1999: 61).

In 2007, 86,814 juvenile offenders were held in public or private residential placement, a reduction over the 2006 figure of 92,854 (Sickmund et al. 2008). These facilities are often called "training schools" but some closely resemble adult prisons. There has been a steady decline in placements since 2000. As between the states, in 2007, the residential placement rate per 100,000 juveniles in the general population varied from the highest of 513 in South Dakota to the lowest of 69 in Vermont (Sickmund 2010). Almost half of all offenders in residential placement were held in the six states of California, Texas, Florida, Pennsylvania, Ohio and New York (Sickmund 2010). The 2003 Census revealed that minorities made up 61 percent of the juvenile custody population with black youth accounting for 38 percent of all offenders in custody. In all states except Vermont, the custody rate for black juvenile offenders exceeded the rate for whites (Snyder and Sickmund 2006). Blacks made up about 12.3 percent of the national population in 2000.

In 2003, females comprised only 15 percent of juveniles in residential placements with private facilities housing nearly four in ten female offenders (Snyder and Sickmund 2006). The female share of offenders held for simple assault, technical violations and all status offense categories exceeded 20 percent (Snyder and Sickmund 2006).

"Waiting for the outs": experiencing juvenile corrections

There are few recent qualitative studies of the experience of juvenile detention, no doubt due to the difficulty in securing research permission. Qualitative research adds an important dimension to the understanding of juvenile institutions as carceral sites where modes of disciplining youth and treating them for delinquency are deployed. The dynamics of staff and resident relations reveal contestations, acts of resistance and the operation of power relations. These enhance our knowledge about our attempts to erase delinquency from the "docile bodies" of incarcerated youth (Foucault 1977). In addition, exploring how masculinity is performed within a juvenile institution also adds to our understanding of youth criminality, institutional discipline and power relations. Examining the practice and discourse of treatment reveals how some youth adopt the language of treatment to secure their release from confinement. Within institutions, the nature, purpose and effect of institutional discipline and application of modes of treatment for delinquency are particular themes that have emerged from qualitative research.

Treatment

Commonly, treatment for delinquency is based on notions of psychological individualism, and treatment programs are classified as cognitive-behavioral and cognitive behavioral skills. These programs usually include training in self-control, anger management, problem solving, empathy, moral reasoning and changing attitudes and beliefs. Techniques such as group discussion and role play are employed to advance cognitive development (Guerra et al. 2008: 84). Studies of treatment and corresponding treatment regimes help to reveal how many are constituted by a set of programs which all residents are required to undertake regardless of their personal circumstances (Banks 2009; Reich 2010).

In the maximum security unit of one juvenile facility in Rhode Island there is a high level of security for the 20 or so youth held there at any one time (Reich 2010). The unit houses residents who have committed serious violent crimes or, more likely, who exhibited behavioral issues in the main facility where they refused to participate in the regime of points and levels (pp. 11, 12). Having involved themselves in crime to perform masculinity, these youth now construct masculinity within the unit "through a competitive struggle for distinction" (p. 14).

Building on Connell's notion of hegemonic masculinity and Messerschmidt's approach to masculinity as a "situated accomplishment" where young men commit crime as an assertion of masculinity outside of institutional channels, Reich's (2010) analysis proposes that the juvenile institution conducts a game, which Reich names the "Game of Law." Playing the "Game of Law" enables residents to win social power by acquiescing to the authority of those in power. Thus, residents perform "insider masculinity" by earning "points" and achieving "levels,"[6] thereby securing privileges for displaying obedience, responsibility and respectability. Specifically, in undertaking treatment programs residents acquire "life skills," confess to "thinking errors"[7] and learn not to be a victim but rather to accept responsibility for their actions (p. 31). Successfully completing treatment means gaining points, ascending levels and securing privileges.

Reich argues that in this institution, rehabilitation has been conflated with management practices so that exhibiting obedience and rejecting disorder (and thereby gaining points and achieving levels) is to successfully play the "Game of Law" and secure release from confinement. Staff believe that instilling obedience in the residents through treatment will produce disciplined workers and husbands for the social world outside the facility, a world in which they will need to accept that they are subordinates and where they will need to display proper male attitudes (Reich 2010: 39, 119). Thus, in the social world outside the facility, residents can apply the obedience they have learned inside and submit themselves to the "tracking practices of the state – clean drug tests, attendance at drug treatment or drug testing centers" (p. 125).

What do residents learn in this facility? In light of the staff preoccupation with order, residents acquire life skills such as: "I learned to control my swearin' and my negative attitudes" (Reich 2010: 156), but change happens only within the facility and does not endure on the "outs": "when you're here, you think everything's changing but on the streets nothing's changing. Everything's the same" (p. 156). Shaping the residents for life on the outside means inscribing ways of behaving that are right for the facility but lack relevance in the social world to which a resident will return.

In this institution delinquency is thought to be the exclusive outcome of defective personalities who make faulty choices and commit "thinking errors." However, this approach offers only a partial perspective because it excludes consideration of the immediate social situation, which may overwhelm personal traits. Accordingly, when youth are released from confinement they will confront the same social situation that contributed to their delinquency. For this reason some treatment approaches attempt to take account of the fact of a return to the community. For example, one model program in a juvenile facility in Arizona aimed to be relevant to life on the outside and to discourage youth from simply conforming to institutional life, pleasing staff and securing release through obedience and conformity. Internally, the program aimed to establish a "respectful, thera-peutic community" (Bortner and Williams 1997: 14, 177).

Nevertheless, as the authors note, in this facility youth accustomed to institutions and their practices knew that "learning to play the game better" meant advancing through the system of levels and securing more privileges (Bortner and Williams 1997). As one resident remarked:

> "I'm just learning to play the game better. . . . Because, I mean, to a certain extent you learn things, you know, behaviors like not going off. But some things you learn are that you'll get things easier and you get more things if u don't yell. . . ."

"They want us to go and voice our opinions, but if we do, then we'll never get out of the program."

(Bortner and Williams 1997: 109)

In *Asylums* (1968), Goffman revealed how the concepts and language of treatment define the institutional reality of the mental hospital:

Everything that goes on in the hospital must be legitimated by assimilating it or translating it to fit into a medical-service frame of reference. Daily staff actions must be defined and presented as expressions of observation, diagnosis and treatment. To effect this translation, reality must be considerably twisted, somewhat as it is by judges, instructors, and officers in other of our coercive institutions.

(Goffman 1968: 334)

In the same way, in the Arizona facility, residents perceived staff as adopting treatment concepts and treatment language to sustain their power over residents in disputes over decision making. For example, one resident noted that staff would cut off debate with residents, asserting that residents' responses constituted "criminal thinking." In addition, during group discussions within the treatment regime, residents complained that staff classified resident accounts and narratives as irregular thinking. Thus, as one resident put it:

"They wanted us to speak our mind, and what they want us to do is to tell 'em what is on our mind. And once we start doing that, they start interruptin' us and sayin' 'This is "criminal thinking" and "delinquent thinking."'"

(Bortner and Williams 1997: 123)

Similarly, Nurse (2010) found that residents in juvenile facilities in Ohio criticized anger management classes, contending that the subject was mostly common sense. Residents noted that if they followed staff instructions and expressed emotion they would be required to take anger management classes. The dominant discourse of treatment, deployed through staff knowledge, ensures that all other discourses are silenced. As one resident put it:

"'Cause every time you talk to somebody . . . you're angry. You need anger management. Blah, blah, blah, blah. Motherfucker, you never been mad before? . . . Somebody died in my family. Oh, oh, oh, oh. You know what? You have emotional stress problems. You got real issues. You need to go to this treatment. What the fuck kinda shit's that?"

(Nurse 2010: 67)

Eisikovits and Baizerman (1982) found that violent youth in juvenile facilities in a large Midwestern state concentrated their efforts on securing early release and this meant mastering the processes associated with being changed. For these youth, buying into the treatment model meant gaining control of time and changing the indeterminate to the determinate. Owning time was achieved by learning to do treatment to such an extent that the researchers found that youth were reading from a script and using the language of treatment in group discussions where youth must be responsive and articulate a problem (p. 15).

Thus, youth show a problem to staff in the treatment process and score points by managing it. The more adept a youth becomes at the treatment game the fewer are the controls exercised over him within the institution. Remarkably, some youth gained such an addiction to treatment, especially within the group, that on release they committed delinquent acts with the aim of being confined within a predictable environment (in contrast to the streets) that they had learned to master (Eisikovits and Baizerman 1982: 17).

In a qualitative study of treatment and the language of treatment in a juvenile institution (comprising both a detention center and a long-term institution) in Alaska, Banks (2009) suggests that treatment in this institution possesses a ritual quality and that the language of treatment is reified to become the dominant and, in fact, the master discourse. The language of treatment, drawn from the discipline of psychology, is a discourse of science to be mastered by both residents and staff. It encodes understanding within the institution and defines and shapes conditions for release. It requires acts of self-examination, confession and disclosure and, as Foucault puts it, "explanation of oneself, revelation of what one is" (Foucault 1988: 126). Sites for practicing and perfecting treatment language within the institution include group work, counseling sessions and the writing of autobiographies and assignments. Testing and examination are constants in the process of learning the dominant discourse.

The treatment process is ritualistic because all residents must undertake the same treatment programs regardless of their needs (Banks 2009). This quality of invariance is a prime characteristic of ritual. As Bell puts it, "one effect of invariance is generally understood to be the molding or shaping of persons according to enduring guidelines and conditions" (Bell 1997: 150). Staff and residents both acknowledged that treatment programs had no substantive impact on residents who were mandated to acquire and articulate this discourse solely because it represented the institutional reality of this juvenile facility.

The ritual of treatment is performed by residents undertaking and successfully completing a series of programs that require residents to accept personal responsibility for their delinquency and to recognize the need to modify their behavior.[8] Behavioral change is scripted in manuals and program guides and administered by largely untrained staff. The script includes a set of "terms to know" that embody the language of treatment, examples of which are: "thinking errors" are "tools used by people to avoid responsibility, stay in denial, and manipulate," and "open to feedback" means "hearing what people say about your attitude and behavior, and thinking about what they said" (Banks 2009: 80, 81).

While institutional mandates prescribe treatment for behavior modification, staff strive to achieve a different goal. Their concern is "moving the kids through" the treatment process so that the next delinquent group can be accommodated (Banks 2009: 7) and not in "facilitat[ing] a significant change in the delinquent pattern of behavior which resulted in institutionalization" (p. 24). No staff explained treatment in terms of rehabilitation or reformation and many expressed their function as imparting information, knowledge and education (p. 164).

It is only by learning the language of treatment through examination and testing that residents are able to secure their release because speaking the lingo verifies a transformation from delinquency to normality. Residents earn points for completing treatment assignments and ascend through five steps to the last, pre-release, with each step requiring a stipulated number of points. Before entering the treatment phase itself a resident must be able to recite treatment goals, have met with at least 10 staff and written "concerns" on a "concerns sheet" and participated in a "move-up group" where personal and treatment goals are addressed. Above all, residents require treatment team approval to ascend to the treatment level. Promotion to the status of pre-release is dependent on an oral presentation to a "PR Move-up Committee" (Banks 2009: 77, 78). Treatment goals include learning the social graces; for example, one staff entry in respect of a resident reads: "Treatment Goals – courtesy – i.e. he says please, thank you, chews food with mouth closed" (p. 166).

Staff, too, locate themselves within the discursive framework of the language of treatment and construct institutional reality according to its terms. Records indicate that staff focus almost exclusively on whether residents meet the standards of interaction which staff expect, regardless of a resident's personal issues and background. Residents' narratives attesting to their guilt must be framed by the language of treatment, and other narratives implicating social, cultural and economic factors that may have figured in their delinquency are excluded (Banks 2009: 198).

Residents whose behavior is keyed according to the institutional reality are designated "fast track" and are expected to complete the program quickly (Banks 2009: 172). Those classified as "lazy" who failed to "open up" and "show their real selves" (p. 178) had failed to acquire the attributes valued by staff and were given additional testing and examination. For example, one resident's record read:

"I spoke with G about his lack of effort towards meeting/getting to know staff. He will now be making journal entries about the staff he is getting to know. At this point he will be expected to try to meet with one staff each day and write something about them in his journal. I will be checking his journal daily so if he is keeping up with his 'meet the staff' please don't reward him with extra points. ... This kid is an institutionalized mentality he feels all he has to do is follow the rules and everything will be ok. No behavioral problems – he will need higher expectations with treatment work. .... If he does have some problems then maybe we will see the real G."

(Banks 2009: 179)

Confessing or "opening up" was a key element in the treatment regime and staff were ready to bring pressure to bear, to "turn up the heat on this guy," to have a resident "expose his values" and not give just "surface compliance all the way." However, residents "opening up" could prove problematic because staff might use confessional material illegitimately. Thus, as one resident reported:

"I can't speak my mind or I'll get in trouble. They encourage us to say what I want but they take points away anyway. For example, they ask 'what was your crime?' I didn't want to say but they said 'go ahead you can be honest. You won't lose points.' Then they said I was glorifying it and took points for glorifying crime but I wasn't."

(Banks 2009: 187)

Residents adopt treatment language and its norms of conduct and thought and confess to "thinking errors," but they must be wary of being seen as "treatment wise." Where staff so designate a resident they have concluded that he or she shows no genuine commitment to the "minimum" treatment goals associated with successful cognitive treatment for delinquency. In such cases, staff raise the level of expectations as in the case of one resident described as "sneaky and highly manipulative" who was written up as "treatment wise" (Banks 2009: 175). The resident was confronted by a staff member about an essay that contained "no thinking errors – not complete truth," and the record reveals that staff "want to keep him on the unit and make him as uncomfortable as we can – maybe this will get him moving in tx" (p. 175). Thus, residents must master the treatment language and speak and display it appropriately in group sessions and in their writings, and not be seen to be subverting or destabilizing it.

In some juvenile facilities youth are exposed to victim awareness courses where victims of actual crimes narrate their personal encounters with crime. Among a group of residents in Ohio institutions there was agreement that victim awareness was popular because it was "less boring than their other activities." One resident became sufficiently empowered to deploy the discourse of victim awareness in court as follows:

SAM: I had victim awareness and I did pretty good. Even though I got minimal participation. I don't even know how I got it. I just, like, did. . . .
ANNE: So did you find that helpful?
SAM: Yeah. It worked in court when I talked about it.

(Nurse 2010: 68, 69)

In an uncritical account of a treatment program in a Texas juvenile facility journalist John Hubner reveals how psychologists in the Capital Offenders Group break down "students" in a "resocialization course" that resembles the "tough love" approach favored in the facility in Alaska (Hubner 2005). Students must "open up" by narrating "Life Stories" and "Crime Stories." In the Life Stories group (the words are always capitalized), says Hubner in the "resocialization dialect"[9] that students learn (Hubner 2005: 3), students narrate their background and upbringing in endless group sessions, revealing narratives of personal sexual and physical abuse and then, with their peers in the group, perform role plays (considered a questionable practice within the discipline of psychology) where they are essentially revictimized by being required to relive the most painful events of their childhood. However, the resocialization process disregards their revealed victim status because students are obliged to show that they "take responsibility" for their acts and, in effect, deny their own narratives.

Students are examined, tested and scrutinized for displays of "empathy" without which they will never successfully complete the program. As the author writes, "A boy who cannot convince a set of tough-minded therapists he has empathy is most likely on his way to prison" (Hubner 2005: 83). Exactly how empathy is assessed or measured is never discussed by the author, but the therapists are convinced that "fronting" or faking empathy is all but impossible because students "can't hide from the group" (p. 9). Nevertheless, as Hubner points out, students learn the resocialization dialect and memorize and internalize treatment language. In performing role plays in a group, students may even be rehearsing "impression management" (Goffman 1959: 203) for a presentation of the self as empathetic.

In this Texas institution, like Alaska, confession and "opening up" are key elements of the discursive framework and unfold within power relationships. As one therapist in the facility puts it:

"You want to get to the feelings behind the anger. You want to ask 'What are you thinking? What are you feeling?' That's the toughest part, getting in touch with the feelings behind the anger. It's painful. Kids don't want to do it. But those feelings are deep down inside and they are going to come out and hurt somebody – a wife or someone else – unless they get dealt with. Feelings will continue to have power until they are expressed."

(Hubner 2005: 46)

Active "resocialization" in this facility functions regardless of a youth's past or existing emotional trauma, victimization in childhood, or cultural specificity that has inscribed other, more circumspect modes of displaying the self. Confession and revelation forced by power tactics from technical experts and, arguably, unethically from peers in group settings, is intended to destroy autonomy and reshape youth into empathetic bodies.

In Texas, students in the Capital Offenders Group receive determinate sentences. Where the treatment staff at this facility determine that a youth has successfully completed treatment programs they may recommend a release on parole. A Special Services Committee meets each week empowered to recommend release on parole, or transfer to a state adult prison to serve the entire sentence. It may also direct a youth that if he or she does not "change" the outcome will be transfer to a state prison (Hubner 2005: 87). As noted above, to a considerable extent, the disposition this Committee issues rests on whether a youth has displayed an adequate measure of empathy. Thus, where empathy is tested for and found to be absent, the Committee produces a reality, a "ritual of truth" (Foucault 1977: 194), from the field of learning of psychology, stating that a youth has not been normalized sufficiently to return to the social world.

Discipline and control

Relations of power within juvenile institutions between staff and juveniles and forms of agency and modes of resistance within power relations have been analyzed in qualitative studies. Emergent themes include: how, congruent with Foucault's insights, the institutional disciplining process extracts time and labor and controls activities through timetables that "intensify the use of the slightest moment" (Foucault 1977: 154); issues of legitimacy, when residents call into question unfair or arbitrary exercise of power by staff; forms and modes of resistance by residents within power relations that reveal the active nature of agency within a juvenile institution; and how rewards and privileges are used to preserve order and security, and come to subsume all other activities, including treatment.

In a Rhode Island juvenile facility the "Game of Law" as explained by Reich requires that order and discipline take precedence. Youth earn rewards for obedience in the form of points and levels, and are thus enabled to perform "insider masculinity" by competing against each other (Reich 2010: 31). Empowering residents to sustain order in this manner gives them a sense of control over their own lives even in this "total institution." Thus, the internalization of the disciplinary regime promotes modes of self-control that staff conflate with rehabilitation. As one staff member describes it:

> "So that's why I think that, you know, discipline is an important part out here, 'cause (if) we don't discipline them, we just let them do what they want to do, then it's just like hanging around, you know what I mean? It's just like no rehab."
>
> (Reich 2010: 133)

Within the system of points and levels staff exercise a high degree of discretion to value or to devalue the efforts of residents by imposing micro-penalties (Reich 2010: 131). In this facility "playing by the rules" is highly valued because it "conditions" residents' behavior:

> "You have to condition them. In some units here we have conditioned a lot of these kids. . . . From walking with their hands behind their back, you know what I mean, knowing where they have to line up when they get outside the door."
>
> (Reich 2010: 134)

Power relations are exercised to produce disciplined, docile and conditioned residents who play by the internal rules in the facility. Of course, this is helpful to staff in managing the facility. By continuously monitoring and surveilling the time and activity of residents, staff construct a social world within the facility where, for staff, maintaining order and discipline becomes the only measurable output. In preserving order, staff must still, however, negotiate with residents, make alliances with some and employ force with others (Reich 2010: 147). Residents regard the disciplinary regime as arbitrary, "like an extremely strict household" (p. 164) where manners are taught, and where residents become "stubborn" and "a lot more resistant to authority" (pp. 164, 165).

In Arizona, residents complained that they lost points if they questioned program rules. They believed that some staff simply "made up rules on the spot" (Bortner and Williams 1997: 134). In the Arizona facility within the model program described by Bortner and Williams, there was to be a participatory process between staff and residents, mutual respect and collective decision making. The required degree of reflection and interaction left little free time and youth were always involved in "goal-directed activities and all-encompassing group discussions" (p. 18). Issues of order and discipline were to be resolved through "Therapeutic Crisis Intervention" where "Life Space Interviews" were to be conducted. Disruptive activity would be addressed in "Huddle-ups" made up of youth and staff and lasting for 10 or 15 minutes. Where activity might lead to harm to others, or where weapons, contraband or escape implements or plans were found, large groups called "marathons" would be convened (p. 22).

The model program also incorporated a level system where points were allocated for behavior and progress. Four levels applied inside the facility and two to release on parole, and higher levels earned privileges such as extra telephone time. At the end of each staff shift every youth was ranked on a scale of one to four points. The previous disciplinary unit was renamed the "Behavioral Management Program" and facility security became the "Crisis Management Team" (Bortner and Williams 1997: 25–26).

Despite the array of mechanisms available to tame disruptive conduct, some youth still resisted the program but in one case resistance faded once the youth appreciated that his release was contingent upon cooperation. He concluded a 'behavioral contract' which the youth described as:

"I've gotta be respectful to staff. I can't sag my pants. I gotta obey staff immediately. I gotta – I can't be intimidating. If I do, I gotta go to [the disciplinary unit]."

(Bortner and Williams 1997: 89, 90)

Thus, when youth challenge the program, staff are ready and willing to abandon its model conflict resolution processes of huddle-ups and marathons in favor of authoritarian contracts about respect, obedience and wearing clothing in a non-threatening manner. In fact, the model processes were subverted by staff and marathons "ended up being used to maintain general control or to punish an entire unit." An example is the first marathon when a youth carved gang graffiti on a television set and all 24 residents were required to attend a three-day marathon session (Bortner and Williams 1997: 103). Consequently, in this facility, discourses of self-examination and treatment clash with those of discipline and order.

Arbitrary and capricious decision making on the part of staff raises issues of legitimacy within power relations. Bottoms (1999: 255) notes, in relation to prisons, that one aspect of legitimacy is that staff "act fairly" so that their authority is assented to. When rules are grounded in shared values they are likely to be regarded as legitimate. In this Arizona facility and in the Alaska institution described by Banks (2009), residents noted that staff violated program precepts about consistent decision making and resident participation in decisions, demonstrating illegitimacy in the exercise of power. In Arizona, when asked how decisions were made in the unit, one resident responded:

"The staff do it and the supervisors. They make all the decisions. They said we was gonna make our decisions and our rules up, but they do it."

(Bortner and Williams 1997: 116)

"Acting fairly" includes communicating correct information to residents. However, in Arizona, while youth were told that the model treatment program could be completed within three months, staff failed to explain to the youth that they believed that to "consistently meet behavioral expectations" would in fact take much longer (Bortner and Williams 1997: 121).

In Alaska, staff agreed that there were "a lot of inconsistencies" when it came to deducting points from residents and thought that if staff discussed how rules were to be implemented, a more consistent overall approach would be followed by all staff. As residents described it:

"Some staff are rule bound, some give slack. The rule bound focus on how much supplies e.g. shampoo, hand cream etc. you get. You lose points for petty stuff."

(Banks 2009: 99, 100)

Staff techniques of power intended to train residents included staff inattention to residents' needs and requests, regarded by residents as a form of unfairness. In Alaska, staff would respond to resident requests with claims of "being busy" but in fact would not be performing any tasks. Similarly, staff trained residents not to give opinions which staff regarded as questioning their authority by responding to opinions with comments such as "who's got the keys to this place" and "don't tell me how to do my job" (Banks 2009: 102, 103). In the Ohio institutions described by Nurse, residents claimed unfairness when they were sometimes permitted to keep more than the officially sanctioned number of photographs in their rooms and staff would suddenly undertake a sweep of all rooms and confiscate them as contraband (Nurse 2010: 82).

Forms of resistance within power relations were identified by Banks in the Alaska juvenile facility as acts "performed within and in opposition to a framework of power and discipline represented by the nature of the institution itself, its rules, regulations and expectations, and through staff implementation of those rules, regulations and expectations" (Banks 2009: 69). Drawing on the theoretical work of Foucault, Garland, Matthews and others, Banks identifies points of resistance and narratives and strategies of resistance beginning with the experience of admission to the facility for those in detention who may spend up to 22 1/2 hours a day locked in a room. Resistance here takes the form of what staff term "acting out" explained by residents in this way:

"It gets to you being shut in a room all day. I get up sometimes; knock on the door to talk to someone. Staff get angry. They yell 'no knocking!' I don't care. I just bang harder."

(Banks 2009: 13)

"[T]his place is an angry place – you get angry – it gets you mad . . . – I'm tired of staff – sometimes you get tired and use your body as a punching bag – that's when you lose your mood and start acting out because you have to sit in your room all day. . . . I want to act out every day – I can't help it any more."

(Banks 2009: 113)

Sometimes, residents simply refuse to acknowledge staff power and resist staff demands through a strategy of total non-cooperation. The record of one resident in Alaska reveals this form of resistance: "sleeps all day – won't answer the simplest direct question and blatantly ignores staff instructions" and later, "trying to get any attention and once he's out of his room he won't go back or lock his door – he doesn't care about points," and later still, "he continues to present as almost a non-entity." In "this writer's presence he remains expressionless – facially and tonally – and almost every word he utters requires extraction." When a resident responds to staff power in this manner staff designate him a 'nonentity' and exclude him (Banks 2009: 115, 116).

When a resident conducts daily contestations with staff, bringing about multiple rule violations and consequent loss of points, he incurs "micro-penalties" as he resists institutional training. In the Alaska facility one resident was unwilling to obey institutional norms and reacted to being institutionalized with fear and acts of self-mutilation. His record reveals a series of acts noted by staff as worthy of micro-penalties in the form of points losses, including acts that arguably amount only to horseplay among teenagers such as " snapping towel," "bumping into others," "towel fighting with roommate" and "horseplay around desk." His lack of social skills was also penalized; for example, points were lost for "rude farting," "goofy in line," "coughing in people's faces" and "feet on furniture" (Banks 2009: 120). In contrast to this activity, other actions of this resident represent a confluence of techniques of resistance, including: "pounding in room," "excessive knocking," "pounding on window," "slamming door about phone call" and "penciling walls." The exercise of power in this case produces a set of normalizing judgments covering horseplay, social skills and forms of "acting out" (pp. 120, 121).

Subtle forms of resistance are also explored by Banks, often charac-terized by staff as "manipulative behavior" or lying. The record of one resident reveals: "watch this guy with meds. He has twice lost points for 'fooling around' and not swallowing his meds – starts problems and then sits back to watch the action – he lies lots and says 'I joke'" and later, "constantly trying to manipulate us. Uses subtle power thrusting techniques on a regular basis" (Banks 2009: 123). Here, staff draw on their field of knowledge and assign this resident's activity a truth in treatment terms (p. 123).

Other forms of resistance identified by Banks include "The Stand-off" where a resident and staff member confront each other, with the resident willing to accept the consequences of challenging staff power and "Resistance Through Making Formal Complaints" where a resident uses grievance procedures to make formal complaints, seen by both staff and resident as resistance (Banks 2009: 127–132).

Modes of resistance through physical aggression toward staff, and acts of self-mutilation[10] are explicit statements of resistance and rejection. The record shows that one resident was resisting all forms of confinement and instruction, and staff concluded that "his needs were not being met." According to his file, one need he had was contact with his family but this was denied (Banks 2009: 134). Staff regarded self-mutilation as "attention seeking and a cry for help" (p. 137). Residents who self-mutilated explained their action as having the aim of upsetting staff and relieving boredom, and noted that "when I get angry mutilation doesn't hurt" (p. 136). While staff perceive residents who show physical aggression and who self-mutilate through the lens of the dominant treatment discourse, the residents themselves challenge the fact of their confinement and its associated tedium and monotony, and express their need for familial contact. However, their discourse is marginalized by staff who focus on their need for control.

Foucault's insights into disciplinary technologies include the strategy of rigorously dividing time into minutes and seconds, and the general ordering of time through the use of timetables and schedules (Shumway 1989: 125). The purpose is to extract moments from time and use them productively. Thus, discipline aims to intensify the use of the slightest moment. This strategy is exemplified in the model treatment program in Arizona where "daily routines" provided for activities commencing weekdays from 5.30 a.m. until 10 p.m. (Bortner and Williams 1997). Residents participated in intensive group sessions, counseling and educational programs. "Recreation, 'responsibility time' (for chores and personal hygiene), and free time (for relaxation, letter writing and television)" were monitored with television time being very limited (p. 18). Each day began and ended with "affirmation groups" where residents announced or reviewed daily goals (p. 18).

In the Alaska facility staff controlled residents' time through the daily routine which allowed only limited periods of recreation and for those in detention, by linking time spent there to expected standards of conduct. Residents in detention who were not undertaking treatment programs had little to do, and for them boredom was a major concern. In their rooms, time seemed 'not to move' in contrast to movement around the facility where they described staff as pushing and rushing residents. In the treatment unit residents were constantly working, and as one staff member put it, "they're not here to sleep and do nothing. We try to keep them to a schedule" (Banks 2009: 85). In contrast, one resident observed: "if they think you're sleeping they take points – they say there doesn't have to be proof" (pp. 85–87).

Recap

This chapter has traced the birth and development of the juvenile institution and revealed how confinement came to be accepted as the principal regime for the treatment and punishment of juvenile offenders. Over time, social forces coalesced to endorse the notion that juvenile treatment and punishment should be modeled on the family unit where previously there had been no distinction made between adult and juvenile punishment. Jails constituted the early forms of confinement but labor and discipline came to be associated with punishment and confinement. Fears about social order and moral dissoluteness combined with technologies of power were associated with the dangerousness of the poor and the marginalized to inspire an emphasis on discipline and regularity.

The early House of Refuge was to be a school for the poor and to provide a regime of morality to minimize their dangerousness. From the outset, destitute and delinquent children were not differentiated – a notion that continues today with criminal delinquency and the criminalization of status offenses. While the House of Refuge firmly established incarceration as the appropriate response to multiple forms of youth deviance it did not succeed in reforming delinquents. The Supreme Court permitted the *parens patriae* doctrine to be invoked to separate children from their poor or incompetent parents, and then a new school of moral reformers – the Child Savers – acted to ensure that society would not be overthrown by the poor urban masses. Now the institution of the family became the model reformatory for delinquents owing to middle-class fears that unruly children might become adult paupers and criminals, who in turn would employ their defective parenting skills in producing a new generation of delinquents. As Houses of Refuge became reformatory schools and training schools and states took over the business of confining and reforming delinquents, social forces provoked an authoritarian and punitive response.

Studies of the lived experience of juvenile confinement and detention humanize the process and reveal that treatment and punishment regimes often say less about delinquents and more about how staff construct their role as reformers. The qualitative studies discussed in this chapter underscore how juveniles learn the language of treatment and how completing treatment successfully means gaining points, ascending levels and securing privileges. Management practices merge with treatment practices so that exhibiting obedience and rejecting disorder means playing the game successfully and getting out. Treatment regimes reveal how many are constituted by a set of programs which all residents are required to undertake regardless of their personal circumstances; shaping the residents for life on the outside means inscribing ways of behaving that are right for the facility but lack relevance in the social world to which a resident will return. In a return to the House of Refuge, instilling discipline and obedience in residents is seen in some institutions as the desired outcome of reform. For many residents the most effective use of time is mastering the processes associated with "being changed." For these youth, "buying into" the treatment model means gaining control of time and changing the indeterminate to the determinate. Researchers found that youth were "reading from a script" and using the language of treatment in group discussions where youth must be seen as "responsive" and must articulate a problem. The more adept a youth becomes at the "treatment game" the fewer are the controls exercised over him or her within the institution.

In one institution, treatment possesses a ritual quality and the language of treatment is reified to become the dominant and, in fact, the master discourse. Drawn from the discipline of psychology, treatment is a discourse of science to be mastered by both residents and staff. It encodes understanding within the institution and defines and shapes conditions for release. It requires acts of self-examination, confession and disclosure. It is only by learning the language of treatment through examination and testing that residents are able to secure their release because speaking the lingo verifies a transformation from delinquency to normality. These studies attest to the superficiality and pointlessness of many contemporary youth treatment programs.

Notes

1 The Massachusetts Body of Liberties of 1641 provided this penalty for children over 16 years of age who "curse or smite their natural father or mother," but Krisberg notes that there is little evidence that this penalty was actually imposed (Krisberg 2005: 24).
2 Several similar institutions already existed in England and Europe and shaped the U.S. model of the House of Refuge (Schlossman 1995: 327).
3 Sutton (1988: 47, 48) suggests that Rothman's analysis of the reasons for failure is simplistic and points to conflict among reform groups as a contributing factor. His extensive exploration of this topic is at pp. 49–89.

4 The 1974 *Juvenile Justice and Delinquency Prevention Act* provides that "juveniles . . . charged with or who have committed offenses that would not be criminal if committed by an adult or offenses which do not constitute violations of valid court orders, or alien juveniles in custody, or such non-offenders as dependent or neglected children, shall not be placed in secure detention facilities or secure correctional facilities" (Sickmund 2004: 17).

5 In 2004 there were 118 ranch or wilderness camps and 51 boot camps (Livsey et al. 2009).

6 The facility applies four levels and points are aggregated to achieve each level until level 4 is attained. Privileges for each level include: phone calls, receiving visits and later "lights out" at each level, personal blankets and a walkman (Reich 2010: 129, 130).

7 Thinking errors were posted on the facility walls and include: "Acting Helpless: Feeling sorry for yourself . . . acting like you're the victim" and "Overreacting: Having a strong emotional reaction, especially anger, when criticized or confronted; using anger to control others" (Reich 2010: 126).

8 The programs included "Criminal Responsibility, Substance Abuse Issues, Anger Management and Independent Living Skills" (Banks 2009: 21).

9 Tellingly, Hubner writes that students memorize a language "they will eventually internalize" (Hubner 2005: 4).

10 Only one study has been published on the prevalence of self-mutilation among youth in juvenile facilities. The researchers found that 10.4 percent of male juveniles engaged in at least one such act during their incarceration (Penn et al. 2003). This compares to a rate of self-mutilation of only 1.2 to 2.8 percent in the general population. Factors associated with self-mutilation in adolescents include depressed mood, substance abuse, anxiety and anger. Relief and escape from such upsets are commonly given as reasons for this behavior (Penn et al. 2003: 763).

References

Armstrong, Gaylene and Bitna Kim. 2009. "The Rise and Fall of Juvenile Boot Camps." In Rick Ruddell and Matthew O. Thomas (eds) *Juvenile Corrections*. Richmond, KY: Newgate Press, pp. 75–91.

Austin, James, Kelly Johnson and Maria Gregoriou. 2000. *Juveniles in Adult Prisons and Jails: A National Assessment*. Washington D.C.: Bureau of Justice Assistance.

Banks, Cyndi. 2009. *Alaska Native Juveniles in Detention: A Qualitative Study of Treatment and Resistance*. Lewiston, NY, Queenston, Ontario and Lampeter, UK: The Edwin Mellen Press.

Barnes, Harry E. 1972. *The Story of Punishment: A Record of Man's Inhumanity to Man*. Mont Clair, NJ: Patterson Smith.

Barton, William H., Ira. M. Schwartz and Franklin A. Orlando. 1994. "Reducing the Use of Secure Detention in Broward County." In Ira M. Schwartz and William H. Barton (eds) *Reforming Juvenile Detention: No More Hidden Closets*. Columbus, OH: Ohio State University Press.

Beck, Allen J., Paige M. Harrison and Paul Guerino. 2010. "Sexual Victimization in Juvenile Facilities Reported by Youth, 2008–2009." U.S. Department of Justice, Office of Justice Programs, Bureau of Justice Statistics Special Report, January 2: 1–47.

Bell, Catherine. 1997. *Ritual: Perspectives and Dimensions*. New York: Oxford University Press.

Bernard, Thomas J. 1992. *The Cycle of Juvenile Justice*. New York: Oxford University Press.

Bernard, Thomas J. and Megan Kurlychek. 2010. *The Cycle of Juvenile Justice*, 2nd Edition. New York: Oxford University Press.

Blomberg, Thomas and Karol Lucken. 2000. *American Penology: A History of Control*. New York: Aldine de Gruyter.

Bortner, M.A. and Williams, L.M. 1997. *Youth in Prison: We the People of Unit Four*. New York: Routledge.

Bottoms, A.E. 1999. "Interpersonal Violence and Social Order in Prisons." *Crime and Justice* 26: 205–281.

Cahn, Mark. 1989. "Punishment, Discretion and the Codification of Prescribed Penalties in Colonial Massachusetts." *American Journal of Legal History* 23: 107–113.

Colvin, Mark. 1997. *Penitentiaries, Reformatories and Chain Gangs: Social Theory and the History of Punishment in Nineteenth Century America*. New York: St. Martin's Press.

Eisikovits, Zvi and Michael Baizerman. 1982. "Doin' Time: Violent Youth in a Juvenile Facility and in an Adult Prison." *Journal of Offender Counselling, Services and Rehabilitation* 6(3): 5–20.

Foucault, Michel. 1977. *Discipline and Punish. The Birth of the Prison*. London: Penguin Books.

Foucault, Michel. 1988. "The Dangerous Individual." In L.D. Kritzman (ed.) *Michel Foucault: Politics, Philosophy, Culture: Interviews and Other Writings 1977–1984*. New York: Routledge, pp. 125–151.

Goffman, E. 1959. *The Presentation of Self in Everyday Life*. New York: Doubleday.

Goffman, Erving. 1968. *Asylums*. Harmondsworth: Penguin.

Guerra, Nancy G., Tia E. Kim and Paul Boxer. 2008. "What Works: Best Practices with Juvenile Offenders." In Robert D. Hoge, Nancy G. Guerra and Paul Boxer (eds) *Treating the Juvenile Offender*. New York: The Guilford Press, pp. 79–102.

Hirsch, Adam. 1992. *The Rise of the Penitentiary: Prisons and Punishment in Early America*. New Haven, CT: Yale University Press.

Holman, B. and J. Ziedenberg. 2006. *The Dangers of Detention: The Impact of Incarcerating Youth in Detention and other Secure Facilities*. Washington D.C.: Justice Policy Institute.

Hubner, J. 2005. *Last Chance in Texas: The Redemption of Criminal Youth*. New York: Random House.

Ignatieff, Michael. 1978. *A Just Measure of Pain: The Penitentiary in the Industrial Revolution, 1750–1850*. New York: Pantheon Books.

Krisberg, Barry. 2005. *Juvenile Justice: Redeeming Our Children*. Thousand Oaks, CA, London and New Delhi: Sage.

Levinson, Robert B. and John J. Greene. 1999. "New Boys on the Block: A Study of Prison Inmates under the Age of 18." *Corrections Today* 61(1): 60–64.

Livsey, S., M. Sickmund and A. Sladky. 2009. *Juvenile Residential Facility Census 2004 Selected Findings*. Washington D.C.: Office of Juvenile Justice and Delinquency Prevention.

Melossi, Dario and Massimo Pavarini. 1981. *The Prison and the Factory : Origins of the Penitentiary System*. Totowa, NJ: Barnes and Noble.

McGarrell, Edmund. 1988. *Juvenile Correctional Reform: Two Decades of Policy and Procedural Change*. Albany, NY: State University of New York Press.

Mennel, R.M. 1973. *Thorns and Thistles: Juvenile Delinquents in the United States 1825–1940*. Lebanon, NH: University Press of New England.

Miller vs. Alabama. U.S. Supreme Court. No. 10–9646. Argued March 20, 2012 – Decided June 25, 2012. http://www.supremecourt.gov/opinions/11pdf/10-9646g2i8.pdf (accessed June 25, 2012).

Mitchell, Jeff and Christopher Varley. 1990. "Isolation and Restraint in Juvenile Correctional Facilities." *Journal of American Academy of Child and Adolescent Psychiatry* 29(2): 251–255.

Nurse, Anne M. 2010. *Locked Up. Locked Out: Young Men in the Juvenile Justice System*. Nashville, TN: Vanderbilt University Press.

Penn, Joseph V., Christainne L. Esposito, Leah E. Schaeffer, Gregory K. Fritz and Anthony Spirito. 2003. "Suicide Attempts and Self-Mutilative Behavior in a Juvenile Correctional Facility." *Journal of American Academy of Child and Adolescent Psychiatry* 42(7): 762–769.

Platt, Anthony M. 1977. *The Child Savers: The Invention of Delinquency*. Chicago, IL: The University of Chicago Press.

Preyer, Kathryn. 1982. "Penal Measures in the American Colonies: An Overview." *American Journal of Legal History* 26: 326–353.

Reich, Adam D. 2010. *Hidden Truth: Young Men Navigating Lives In and Out of Juvenile Prison*. Berkeley, CA: University of California Press.

Rendleman, Douglas R. 1971. "Parens Patriae: From Chancery to the Juvenile Court." *South Carolina Law Review* 23: 205–259.

Rothman, D.J. 1971. *The Discovery of the Asylum*. New York: Aldine de Gruyter.

Rothman, David. 1990. *The Discovery of the Asylum: Social Order and Disorder in the New Republic*, Revised Edition. Boston, MA: Little Brown and Company.

Rusche, Georg and Otto Kirchheimer. 1939 (reprinted 1968). *Punishment and Social Structure*. New York: Russell and Russell.

Schlossman, S. 1995. "Delinquent Children: The Juvenile Reform School." In N. Morris and D.J. Rothman (eds) *The Oxford History of the Prison: the Practice of Punishment in Western Society*. Oxford: Oxford University Press, pp. 325–349.

Secret, Mosi. 2011. "States Prosecute Fewer Teenagers in Adult Courts." *New York Times*. March 5. http://www.nytimes.com/2011/03/06/nyregion/06juvenile.html? pagewanted=all (accessed June 23, 2012).

Shumway, D.R. 1989. *Michel Foucault*. Charlottesville: University Press of Virginia.

Sickmund, Melissa. 2004. *Juveniles in Corrections*. OJJDP National Report Series Bulletin.

Sickmund, Melissa. 2010. *Juveniles in Residential Placement 1997–2008*. OJJDP Fact Sheet.

Sickmund, M., T.J. Sladky and W. Kang. 2008. "Easy Access to the Census of Juveniles in Residential Placement." Washington D.C.: US Department of Justice, Office of Juvenile Justice and Delinquency Prevention, January 11: 2010.

Snyder Howard N. and Melissa Sickmund. 2006. *Juvenile Offenders and Victims: 2006.* National Report.

Sutton, John R. 1988. *Stubborn Children: Controlling Delinquency in the United States, 1640–1981.* Berkeley, CA: University of California Press.

Welch, M. 2004. *Corrections: A Critical Approach.* New York: McGraw-Hill.

West, Heather C. and William J. Sabol. 2009. *Prison Inmates at Midyear 2008 – Statistical Tables.* U.S. Department of Justice, Office of Justice Programs, Bureau of Justice Statistics. March. NCJ 225619.

chapter 4

Gender and Juvenile Justice

Offenses committed by girls have always made up a minor component of the overall rate of crime committed in the U.S. and in other countries. In fact, so negligible has been their criminality that until quite recently girls were almost invisible in juvenile justice. The study of girls' criminality serves as a lens into how gender has shaped the lives of girls who come into contact with the law. Beginning with gendered laws that punished girls who violated expectations of proper conduct by, for example, running away from home because of ill-treatment or sexual abuse, the juvenile justice system created a framework of status offenses that empowered the court to control girls' sexuality. In seeking the causes and identifying the circumstances of girls' criminality, research into pathways and life course reveal that sexual and physical abuse have often been the determinants of the lives of girl offenders.

Gender stratification can be seen as the product of a patriarchal society in which gender relations are founded on the organizing principle of male superiority. As James Messerschmidt notes, "in most, (but clearly not all) situations, men are able to impose authority, control and coercion over women" (1993: 71). The reality of girls' lives reveals a sexual double standard and an expectation that they will adhere to a role considered appropriate for girls. In other words, social conformity is gendered. In North American cultures, for example, girls are socialized to be nice, non-aggressive and empathic, and to be concerned about others (see Zahn-Waxler (2000) for an in-depth discussion). Generally, gender distinctions arise out of different socialization practices; thus, gender is socially constructed. While socialization is accomplished through interaction with parents and teachers and within power relations, children themselves are not without agency. As Thorne (1993: 3) notes, theorists now contend that "children participate in their own socialization." There are stages in the gender socialization process which arguably begin by the age of 2. Katz (1979: 9) suggests that these comprise: learning the appropriate behavior for a male or female child; acquiring concepts about what is appropriate conduct for a female or male adult; and behaving in ways deemed appropriate for male and female adults during the life span.

Early and late adolescence are the periods when changes occur. For example, youth rely more on peers than on parents or teachers for information and opinions. It is when girls approach puberty that parental monitoring and supervision is enhanced, sometimes resulting in oppositional incidents. As Thorne (1993: 156) puts it, "parents in gestures that mix protection with punishment, often tighten control of girls when they become adolescents, and sexuality becomes a terrain of struggle between the generations." Parents begin to apply a sexual double standard that encourages males to explore their sexuality but sanctions female sexuality (Chesney-Lind and Irwin 2008: 75). It is at this time that adolescent subcultures and the media begin to significantly influence girls' sexuality, requiring that they be both sexually alluring and chaste as well as sexually responsible (Durham 1998: 385).

To explain delinquency among girls necessitates an examination of gender stratification and a critical mapping of the extent of social control exercised by the juvenile justice system, noting how that system continually reinforces female subordination by labeling and relabeling girls as deviant. Yet even before coming under the control of the juvenile justice system girls are controlled by multiple institutions and structures, and the daily scrutiny to which they are subjected is far more intense than that applied to boys (Cain 1989: 1). Feminists have suggested that informal controls over girls, especially the focus on sexuality and sexual reputation, are reproduced by the juvenile justice system. Thus, when girls are perceived as having violated the norms of behavior expected of them, they are seen as having violated the informal rules of femininity as well as the formal law (Brown 2005: 134).

Prevailing discourses propose rationales for the increased social control of girls, especially their sexuality. For example, the so-called "liberation hypothesis" has been advanced, contending that as an outcome of feminist advocacy and action, girls are becoming "mean girls" or are achieving equality with boys in committing acts of violence. This discourse has raised questions about whether researchers such as Prothrow-Stith and Spivak (2005: 44, 48) are correct in claiming that "girls are beginning to show up in a new role, a new behavior – the ones doing the killing."

These discourses can assume the form of a moral panic (see Chapter 7) where rational explanations are disregarded in favor of incarcerating "the new violent girl" (Chesney-Lind and Jones 2010: 4). Underlying these moral panics are the same gender stereotypes that have always condemned girls for alleged "immorality" now perhaps supplemented by racial fears because today four out of ten girls and young women under 25 years of age are of color – a visible indicator of social change (Males 2010: 15).

Possible explanations for apparent increases in girls' violence that pinpoint policy changes in policing domestic violence incidents, as well as changes in punishing girls for bullying in schools, are ignored in the interests of publishing sensationalist commentaries that feed fears and reinforce gender and racial stereotypes. As Worrall notes (2004: 44), more girls who offend are now brought within the control of the criminal justice system rather than by systems that provide welfare. Girls' bad behaviors are being redefined and relabeled as criminal and there has been a shift away from welfarism toward criminalization. The criminal justice system and the media appear to complement each other's roles in controlling women. As Chesney-Lind and Eliason (2006: 43) explain:

> Popular media masculinize and demonize a few women, effectively casting them out of the "protected" sphere of femininity, while cele-brating the presumed passivity of the rest of womanhood. The criminal justice system steps in, both ratifying and enforcing the gender order, along with the racial, sexual and class order, through its processing and punishment regimes.

When processed through the juvenile justice system, adjudicated delinquent and placed in custody for a status offense, delinquent girls suffer the inadequacies of poor or non-existent treatment and programming because institutional regimes of treatment fail to meet their specific needs. These and related topics will be explored in this chapter. Throughout, it will be seen that constructions of gender underpin all explanations, theories and propositions about girls' criminality.

Controlling girls: gender and history

From the very beginnings of colonization, the family unit constituted the means of juvenile social control and imposed discipline and order upon children. Early laws even provided the penalty of death for children who disobeyed their parents. For example, the 1641 *Body of Liberties* of Massachusetts provided that children over 16 years of age who "curse or smite their natural father or mother" could suffer the death penalty, subject to various defenses (Krisberg 2005: 23, 24). As noted in Chapter 3 the establishment of Houses of Refuge enabled parents who could not control their children to commit them to custody, and *Ex parte Crouse* affirmed the right of Mary Crouse's mother to have her daughter committed even though she had committed no crime.

The "child savers" elevated the role and importance of the family and parental authority as well as of normative conduct (Platt 1977: 98). Middle-class women began to concern themselves with the morality of working-class girls and women while urban growth and industrialization brought about social change. Delinquent children and dependent children could be taken into custody for a variety of non-normative acts. For example, in Illinois in 1879, the Industrial School for Girls Law authorized any "responsible" resident to petition the courts to enquire into a girl's dependency and, if satisfied that her parents were not fit to have custody, to commit her to the school until she reached the age of 18. Dependency was defined by the law to include: begging and receiving alms for selling; wandering through streets and alleys or other public places; living with or associating with thieves; or being found in a house of ill repute or a poor house (p. 111). Parents who were unable to control their daughters applied to the court to restrain them. As Odem (1995: 5) suggests, contextually, it is helpful to envisage the court system in such cases as "a complex network of struggles and negotiations among working-class parents, teenage daughters, and court officials."

In the Progressive era, from the 1890s to the 1920s, female delinquency came to be seen as a serious social problem, female stereotypes flourished, and girls' "immorality" was broadly defined, especially in relation to immigrant girls who met with punitive punishment (Schlossman and Wallach 1978: 68). "Social purity" became the goal and, between 1910 and 1920, 23 girls' reformatories were opened, representing a dramatic increase in government intervention in girls' delinquency (p. 70). "Immorality" became designated as the catch-all charge for the social control of girls. The label did not mean that a girl had had sexual relations; rather, that she displayed signs of having had intercourse or was suspected of having a propensity to engage in sex in the near future. The acts regarded as evidence of such immorality included being away from home, coming home late at night, attending dance houses, masturbating, using obscene language and riding in vehicles without a chaperone (p. 72). Girls ran away from home for many reasons, including, for example, that a girl "was tired of restrictions placed on her by her parents and planned to leave home and seek employment and make her own way in the world" (*Oakland Tribune*, February 9, 1912 quoted in Odem 1995: 50).

During this period young women began to work outside the home in factories, offices and retail stores. While domestic service had previously been the principal means of employment for young women, the percentage of women employed as domestic servants fell dramatically. For example, between 1870 and 1910 it decreased from 61 percent to 26 percent (Odem

1995: 21). In the new workplaces young women met and interacted with young men, and from the 1880s onwards were able to enjoy the commercialized amusements available in the cities such as dance-halls, amusement parks and movie houses. These entertainments predominantly attracted the young and unmarried of both genders without chaperones (D'Emilio and Freedman 1988: 195). By the 1920s, this new order of pleasure was causing problems in working-class and immigrant families where demands that a girl's wages be handed over to her family, or that she always be chaperoned, were liable to provoke rebellion (D'Emilio and Freedman 1988: 199). Middle-class women reformers, believing their notion of sexual purity and innocence to be under challenge, sought to impose the ideals of middle-class morality on working-class girls. Thus, girls who flirted with men, attended dance-halls, wore makeup and fancy clothes or had sex outside marriage were considered "wayward" and in need of moral protection (Odem 1995: 25).

In the field of girls' delinquency, Knupfer (2001: 35) explains how the discourses of psychology and psychiatry promoted the "medicalization of heterosexuality" following the establishment of the first juvenile court in Chicago in 1899. Judges began to call for testing and diagnoses of the suspect behavioral problems of alleged delinquents. Interrogations and elicited confessions by professionals produced medical histories, case studies and records from which were built diagnoses and treatment plans for these delinquents. According to Knupfer (2001: 36), these accounts established norms of appropriate sexual conduct so that those who deviated from them were faced with technologies of control in the form of hospitals, industrial schools, clinics and reformatories.

Psychologists and psychiatrists investigated the etiology of immorality and explained it as an outcome of feeble-mindedness (immigrant and poor girls were most often classified in this way), or, where girls had aggressive personalities as evidenced by acts such as running away, destruction of property and bad habits of a sexual nature, as "psychopathic" (Knupfer 2001: 40). Psychopathic girls were described as suffering "mania, hallucinations, and insanity" as well as being "cunning" and stubborn (p. 40). Another category was constituted by "hysterical" girls who exhibited aggression and a set of associated symptoms that included delusions, stupor, amnesia and anxiety, believed to be the outcome of repressing sexual desires (p. 41). The notion that these girls may have been demonstrating independence rather than aggression was not entertained. Immorality in the juvenile court was heavily gendered. For example, in 1912, a three-year study revealed that 80 percent of girls were brought before the court on a charge of immorality as compared to only 2 percent for boys (p. 92). In its decision making the juvenile court followed a "maternalist ideology," and "motherhood, marriage and home" comprised its guiding precepts and reform program (p. 97).

Gender also figured in decisions about institutionalization. In 1912, Sophonisba Breckinridge and Edith Abbott, Directors of the Department of Social Investigation, Chicago School of Civics and Philanthropy, published *The Delinquent Child and the Home* (quoted in Odem 1995: 100). They contended that delinquency could be explained as the outcome of the harsh economic and social conditions of the working class (quoted in Odem 1995: 103). They, like other reformers, continued to promote the notion that delinquent girls had a greater need for institutionalization than delinquent boys owing to the relative seriousness of the girl's offense. As the authors explained it, the delinquent girl "is in a peril which threatens the ruin of her whole life, and the situation demands immediate action . . . the delinquent boy, on the other hand, is frequently only a troublesome nuisance who needs discipline but who, as the probation officer so often says is 'not really a bad boy'" (quoted in Odem 1995: 115). These reformers believed that removing a delinquent girl from her degrading family life and placing her in an institution was her only hope for the future.

In the immediate postwar period the female delinquent was viewed as challenging the authority of the family through acts of revolt, alienation and violation of the law. In the period from 1945 to 1965 the majority of girls' crimes continued to be status offenses, the dominant acts being "ungovernability," running away from home, sexual offenses and truancy (Devlin 1998: 88–89). It was thought that girls were becoming "tough," "hardened" and "vicious" while boys' delinquency could be dealt with by a firm hand and through the courts, embracing the "back to the woodsheds movement" (p. 93). On the other hand, girls' conflicts with the law were depicted as more difficult to control yet still requiring an authoritative approach (p. 93). Yet repression seemed not to be the solution to girls' delinquency. For example, the *Saturday Evening Post* ran a series on delinquency under the title "The Shame of America" which included the story of Florence, a case study against parental authoritarianism. Florence's father required her to be circumspect in her conduct; she was not permitted to attend dances, even high school-sponsored dances, and was not allowed to wear lipstick. In response, she ran away from home, became involved with several men and learned about "beer joints and narcotic peddlers," finally ending up in a state training school for girls as "incorrigible." The *Saturday Evening Post* argued that "heavy use of rod not only failed to keep Florence on the straight and narrow path but obviously had driven her from it" (quoted in Devlin 1998: 93).

Nowadays, youth can be policed proactively for antisocial behaviors because of the assumed risk that such behaviors can escalate into serious delinquency. Over the past two decades policing strategies have emphasized situational crime prevention and zero-tolerance tactics that target minor forms of criminality as a technique to deter serious crime. This strategy has involved making arrests or 'charging up,' in particular in relation to crimes of violence, meaning that charges laid are more serious than before. For example, domestic violence has come to be regarded as a public crime, and is no longer a private family affair. Violence, in all its forms, is seen as an act that will not be tolerated, and modes of behavior that were formerly regarded as merely antisocial are now perceived to be manifestations of violence and have been criminalized as such. These modes and techniques of crime control aim to reduce and manage risk and to collectively form a culture of crime control (Garland 2002; Steffensmeier et al. 2005: 363). In terms of gender, such strategies have resulted in an increased interest in girls' violence, especially within schools where a wide range of hidden criminality in the form of bullying and relational violence has been "revealed." Thus, expansive definitions of conduct seen as constituting violence have redefined disorderly behaviors and transformed them into simple assaults, and upgraded simple assaults to aggravated assaults. Given that girls tend to commit milder forms of violence, net-widening and charging-up techniques have impacted them adversely through heavier sanctions (Steffensmeier et al. 2005: 365).

The punitive attitude toward delinquent youth has included the readiness to treat girls as adults and to have them tried in adult courts and, when convicted, to be incarcerated in adult prisons. Accordingly, between 1992 and 1995, 41 states enacted laws that facilitated trying juveniles as adults and, as of June 30, 2007, 116 females under the age of 18 were in custody in state prisons (Sabol and Couture 2008: 9). However, little is known about this population. A study of 22 girls incarcerated in a women's prison in the southwest noted the absence of comparative research addressing the differences between juvenile institutions holding girls in custody and women's prisons (Gaarder and Belknap 2002). However, the researchers reported limited access to education, health professionals, vocational work and social activity, even relative to the adult women who were incarcerated there (p. 508).

Girls offending

Male offenders dominate the juvenile justice system. In 2003, the 14,590 female juvenile offenders in custody comprised only 15 percent of all offenders in custody. Of the 15 percent of female juveniles in custody, 14 percent had been adjudicated delinquent and 40 percent were in custody for status offenses (Snyder and Sickmund 2006: 206). However, the proportion of female offenders in custody varies between states, ranging from no more than 10 percent of those in custody in Colorado, Maryland, New Jersey and Rhode Island to at least 25 percent in Hawaii, Nebraska, North Dakota, South Dakota and Wyoming (p. 207). In 2003, female offenders were more likely than males to be in custody for simple assault, technical violations and status offenses, indicating that despite the rhetoric about violent girls, it is boys, not girls, who are detained for the serious violent offenses of aggravated assault, robbery and murder (p. 210).

Between 1991 and 2003 the detained population of juveniles increased for both males and females. Yet there is a striking contrast, because while among males the increase was 23 percent for those committed and 29 percent for those detained, among females the increases were 88 percent and 98 percent respectively (Snyder and Sickmund 2006: 208). Status offenders accounted for a large proportion of female offenders in custody in 2003 but the proportion of female offenders in custody for status offenses had fallen from 33 percent in 1991 to only 13 percent in 2003. In contrast, for males, the status offender proportion has remained steady at between 3 percent and 6 percent (p. 206). Running away from home and prostitution are the only two categories of conduct for which more girls than boys are arrested, although running away far outstrips prostitution in its incidence. In 2003, for example, almost 50,000 girls were taken into custody as runaways, while fewer than 1,000 were arrested for prostitution (Chesney-Lind and Irwin 2008: 80).

Girls are increasingly arrested for crimes of violence. The Ten Year Arrest Trend from 1997 to 2006 shows that girls' arrests for the category "other assaults" increased by 18.7 percent while boys' arrests for the same category of offense decreased by 4.3 percent over this period (FBI 2007: Table 33). For females the increase in "person offenses" cases from 1985 to 2002 was 202 percent. The juvenile female arrest rate for cases of "simple assault" for the period 1980 to 2003 far outpaced the increase for males – the rate for females increased by 269 percent compared to 102 percent for males (Snyder and Sickmund 2006: 142, 161). How are these apparent increases in cases involving female violence to be explained? Do they indicate that girls are becoming more violent, or can the data be explained in other ways?

As noted in Chapter 7 in the discussion of girl gangs and girl violence as moral panics, while the statistical data reveal a dramatic increase in girls' violence, accepting statistical evidence at face value is problematic because the statistics may not so much be depicting "facts" about criminality as indicating changes in policing practices and criminal justice policies (Alder and Worrall 2004: 3). Chesney-Lind argues that increases in girls' violence can be explained by changes in policy and practice involving arrests for incidents of domestic violence, and by an increased intolerance for violence in schools post-Columbine. These policies, she argues, have resulted in more referrals of girls to court for violations of zero-tolerance policies (Chesney-Lind 2010: 60). Her view is supported by the fact that self-report delinquency data reveal a trend of decreases in self-reported

youth, crime and justice

school-aged youth violence. Accordingly, the Centers for Disease Control (CDC) *Youth Risk Behavior Survey* conducted biannually reveals that while 34.4 percent of girls surveyed in 1991 reported having been in a physical fight in the preceding 12 months, in 2009, only 22.9 percent reported similarly for the previous year (CDC, 1991–2009). Victimization data reveal a similar trend, suggesting that the shifts in girls' arrests do not relate to actual changes in behavior and are not indicative of girls becoming more violent.

In relation to incidents of domestic violence, due to legislative changes, the police have implemented domestic violence policies that have resulted in increased arrests. While domestic violence laws were originally targeted to address the needs of female victims, legislation has since expanded the types of relationships included so that now the police are required to respond to heterosexual and same-sex relationships, and to take account of others in households including siblings, parents, teenagers and so on (Buzawa and Hirschel 2010: 33). Laws now authorize the police to arrest without warrant for misdemeanor charges in domestic violence incidents and to arrest on a presumptive basis (p. 34). Data reveal that other forms of family violence make up a large proportion of the incidents reported to the police. For example, over the past 25 years, surveys have shown that each year up to 33 million siblings violently assault their brothers and sisters, and over a million parents each year are victims of assaults by their children aged 15 to 17 (p. 35). Other studies tend to indicate that the proportion of non-adult partner violence being brought to police attention has been increasing (p. 35). Thus, overall, not only has there been an increase in the extent of domestic violence coming to the attention of the police, but there is an increased likelihood of being arrested as a result of a reported incident of domestic violence (p. 35).

Research has shown that juveniles involved in cases of domestic assault are more likely to be arrested than adults (Buzawa and Hirschel 2010: 36). Further research indicates that female juvenile offenders are more likely to be impacted by domestic violence policies and practices because their acts are likely to be classed as misdemeanors as compared to male acts of violence (p. 36). Chesney-Lind (2002) has suggested that in practice the police may often act to uphold the parents' authority where a domestic assault involves parent and child by making an arrest where previously they may have proceeded by way of a non-criminal status offense classifying the juvenile as an "incorrigible" or as a "person in need of supervision." Thus, it is argued that status offenses have, in effect, been revived and reclassified as assaults, imposing a greater degree of social control than previously existed. Consequently, the disproportionately increased arrest rates for female juvenile offenders may be explained, in part, by the dramatic increase in domestic violence arrest rates (Chesney-Lind 2002).[1]

According to Feld, the notion that females who would previously have been dealt with as status offenders are now subjected to "bootstrapping" and relabeling as delinquents may be credited to the deinstitutionalization mandates of the *Juvenile Justice and Delinquency Prevention Act* of 1974 (2009: 241). The 1974 Act banned states from confining status offenders with delinquents in secure facilities and withheld funds from states that took no action to remove them. The intention of the legislation was that programs within the community would be developed to take status offenders who would be diverted into those programs. However, a 1980 amendment to the Act, added at the request of the National Council of Juvenile and Family Court Judges, permitted states to confine status offenders for violating "valid court orders." This gave the judges the power to bootstrap status offenders under a delinquency label and to place them in custody for contempt of court for violating conditions of probation. The outcome of the deinstitutionalization policy was a substantial reduction in the number of status offenders held in custody in secure facilities but with no commensurate increase in community sanctions into which to divert status cases. In the absence of any incentive to offer community services, this in turn was an impetus to continue to confine status offenders by relabeling them as delinquents (Feld 2009: 244, 245). There is a considerable overlap between a status offense and a delinquent act because, for example, a runaway girl may also engage in delinquency, or the acts of an "unruly" girl may also constitute an assault. After analyzing the use of the contempt powers of the juvenile courts for violation of court orders, Bishop and Frazier (1992) found that differential treatment by gender as well as the bootstrapping of girls perpetuated gender bias. Thus, the courts and other actors in the juvenile justice system demonstrate their reluctance to give up their power to discipline "unruly" girls.

It is significant that the rate at which the police arrested girls for the offense of simple assault in 2005 was almost four times the arrest rate in 1980, yet by comparison arrests of juvenile males only doubled over the same period (Feld 2009: 250). After comparing arrest data covering boys and girls from the FBI Uniform Crime Reports with victim self-reports and juveniles' self-reports, no systematic changes in girls' rates or prevalence compared to that of boys were found, despite the dramatic increase in girls' arrests for violence (Steffensmeier et al. 2005). As Steffensmeier et al. (2005: 387–390) point out,

> the rise in girls' arrests for violent crime and the narrowing of the gender gap have less to do with underlying behavior and more to do with . . . net-widening changes in law and policing toward prosecuting less serious forms of violence . . . and less biased or more efficient responses to girls' physical or verbal aggression on the part of law enforcement, parents, teachers, and social workers.

youth, crime and justice

In their review of all assault cases from 2,819 jurisdictions in 19 states for the year 2000, Buzawa and Hirschel (2010) examined whether age and gender had any effect on police responses to calls for assistance. They found that juveniles were more likely to be arrested than adults, with juvenile females having the highest arrest rates for aggravated and simple assault. Juveniles were far more likely to be arrested for assaulting adults, and adults were far less likely to be arrested for assaulting juveniles (p. 46). This research clearly raises questions about how the police determine the appropriate course of action when a juvenile is said to have assaulted an adult.

As is pointed out in Chapter 7, the discovery of girls' "relational" aggression and its relationship with the mix of behaviors that constitute bullying has resulted in increased monitoring and surveillance of girls' conduct in schools. This has been justified on the basis that relational aggression is a form of serious bullying. It is now argued that girls are as aggressive as boys when relational aggression is taken into account. The kinds of behaviors included within the relational mirror stereotypical labels that have been associated with women for centuries, namely the devious, cunning and manipulative female figure. Chesney-Lind and Jones (2010: 112) argue that this approach to girls' aggression provides "new ways to devalue and demonize girls" and suggests "the need to police their behavior even more assiduously." School zero-tolerance policies for bullying and all forms of aggression mean that girls are now more likely to be referred to law enforcement for incidents that would formerly have been dealt with internally. Schools are now being required to adopt anti-bullying prevention and education policies, and 32 states had introduced bills with such provisions as of May 2003 (p. 118).

Physical aggression has been shown to be normative in pre-school years and then as declining (Vaillancourt and Hymel 2004). Verbal and social modes of aggression emerge later and become increasingly normative with age. Studies have consistently shown that boys engage in greater levels of physical aggression than girls but gender differences in verbal forms of aggression have not been clearly established (p. 61). Thus, despite the claims now being made that girls are just as violent as boys, a number of studies have found no difference between boys' and girls' performance of relational aggression, and moreover, some studies have found boys to be more relationally aggressive than girls (Chesney-Lind and Jones 2010: 113). As well, research has failed to demonstrate a progression from relational aggression to actual violence (pp. 116, 117). As always, context is vital to explaining and understanding girls' behaviors in school where relational aggression is said to have occurred, and the circumstances and gender arrangements need to be fully examined in each case (p. 123).

Pathways to delinquency

Traditional theories of crime causation tend to be based on male models of crime and male conduct, and fail to explain the experiences of delinquent girls (Belknap 2001; Chesney-Lind and Shelden 2004). The "Life Course Development Model" contends that offending behavior is age associated and related to the various developmental stages of the life course (Laub and Lauritsen 1993: 235). The stage of adolescence is perceived as a time of risk for delinquent behavior owing to stresses such as peer pressure and puberty. While life-course approaches to delinquency do address concepts such as "poor family functioning," they fail to adequately account for childhood victimization such as neglect, and parental physical and sexual abuse, as well as for experiences of discrimination and oppression based on race and sex.

The "pathways to crime" approach to girls' offending seeks to identify the childhood experiences that place girls at risk of offending. Studies adopting the pathways approach indicate that childhood sexual and physical abuse and child neglect are often associated with the likelihood of criminality (Belknap and Holsinger 1998; Daly 1992: 11). The pathways perspective recognizes that girls' criminality is associated with their social conditions as well as with their role as females within a patriarchal society where the intersecting oppressions of gender, race, class and sexuality exist. The "blurred boundaries" theory of victimization and criminalization is a prominent feature of recent models of etiology of women's crime but it has also been critiqued because it may not capture the complexities and meanings of agency and responsibility involved in women's violations of the law (Daly 1992: 48). Of course, not all sexually or otherwise abused girls become delinquent and not all delinquent girls are survivors of sexual and other forms of abuse. However, there is no doubt that childhood abuse, in its various forms, is disproportionately represented in girls adjudicated as delinquent.

How does race influence girls' pathways to offending? Studies seem to suggest that black girls are more likely to engage in serious forms of delinquency than other racial groups (Holsinger and Holsinger 2005: 214). Research also indicates that black girls are socialized to become self-sufficient and to be more independent than white girls and consistent with this, black girls report more assertiveness and self-confidence than white girls and seek to project an image of power through their distinct style of dress (Holsinger and Holsinger 2005: 218). Based on samples of white and black girls, researchers found that black girls reported experiencing less abuse, less drug use and fewer incidents of suicide or self-injury than white girls. Even so, physical abuse was reported in 70 percent and sexual abuse in 46 percent of black girls sampled, compared to 90 percent and 62 percent for white girls (p. 227). For black girls in the study, correlates of delinquency were abuse, drug and alcohol use, family experience and antisocial personality (p. 232). For white girls, the strongest correlates were antisocial personality, mental health and drug use (p. 232). According to Holsinger and Holsinger, these differential pathways to violence and self-injurious conduct reflect racial differences in self-esteem and socialization, with black girls socialized to be self-reliant and therefore likely to act in more assertive ways, while white girls, raised to be dependent and accepting of traditional gender roles, are more likely to internalize problems, leading to self-criticism, low self-esteem and mental health issues (p. 236).

The association between childhood abuse and victimization and girls' delinquency has been confirmed in many studies. In most cases girls have been victims themselves before they offend (Girls Incorporated 1996). Substantial numbers of girls in the juvenile justice system report a history of victimization as children through physical or sexual abuse (Dembo et al. 1993). In examining the linkages between victimization and delinquency some argue that behaviors such as running away from home, prostitution and gang membership operate as strategies of resistance and coping mechanisms in girls' lives.

Girls' violence: definitions and explanations

As Worrall puts it, "No longer 'at risk' and 'in moral danger' from the damaging behavior of men, 'violent girls' now exist as a category within penal discourse" (2004: 41). Violence and aggression are terms that carry different meanings for different people, and a range of competing discourses define and elaborate their meanings. Laws generally specify forms of violence on a scale of seriousness ranging from a simple assault to aggravated assault and finally to murder. However, when criminal files are examined to explore the actual events and conduct that constitute an offense, they sometimes appear not to meet the popular perceptions of that particular mode of criminality. For example, Chesney-Lind and Paramore (2001: 142) show that when the police reported an increase in juvenile robbery in the city and county of Honolulu over two separate periods of time, the acts that constituted robbery comprised a pattern of acts involving largely youthful victims, the majority of whom were at least casually acquainted with the offenders. The median value of items stolen from all victims in 1991 was US$10 and in the second period of robberies, in 1997, the median value dropped to only US$1.25 (p. 157). In the majority of robberies no weapon was involved and most robberies did not result in serious injuries to the victims. The robberies followed a similar pattern – they were characterized by slightly older youth bullying and hijacking younger youth for small amounts of cash and sometimes for jewelry. The authors suggest that there was no surge in robberies but rather that the redefinition of thefts that occurred within school grounds to "robbery" had a substantial effect on the increase in the number of arrests of juveniles for robbery (p. 162).

Definitions of what is considered violence are also subjective, and in deciding what amounts to aggression or violence it is important to know how juvenile girls themselves explain these terms. In this way we can share their knowledge of acceptable and non-acceptable behaviors. For example, among girls living in group homes owing to violent behaviors in Nova Scotia, Canada, all defined violence in terms of physical acts that involved striking another with some part of their body (Brown 2010). They did not include relational forms of violence within their definitions of this term. All the girls living in group homes had experienced violent behaviors as children, thus blurring the boundary between victimization and perpetrating violence, and all developed survival strategies of fighting back. As Brown (2010: 181) puts it:

> The girls did not cross a line one day, moving from victim to perpetrator. Their use of violence was not retold according to a catalyst event. The move was seamless, between being witness to and living in an environment of violence to using violence to protect or express oneself.

Thus the lived experience of girls adds a context to violence and to the "violent" girl, and expectations of appropriate feminine behaviors ought to take account of the different environments to which girls are subjected and in which they are brought up. Differing race and class backgrounds also function to define what is regarded as "violence." Thus, it has been suggested that the concept "violent girls" is merely a construct of white middle-class culture and that girls of color are constructed as always-already "violent," regardless of how they present themselves (Batacharya 2004: 61).

Girls' violence is often closely linked to their environments. Those who experience violence as part of their daily life in distressed inner cities must develop survival skills if they are not themselves to be subjected to gender-specific violence. The experience of violence for a black inner city girl will be different to that of a white middle-class girl living in the suburbs. As Nikki Jones (2010: 203) explains, black inner city girls develop "situated survival strategies" growing up in neighborhoods where the ruling ethic is "the code of the street" under which black men practice hegemonic masculinity, relying on physical domination in their daily interactions (p. 205). For black girls the challenge of growing up in such circumstances is a gendered challenge and they are assessed not only according to normative gender expectations that apply to all girls regardless of color, but also according to expectations of how black women and girls ought to behave (p. 206). These girls must navigate the streets and learn how to manage potential threats of violence at the risk of violating expectations of appropriate femininity that place considerable constraints on how they may act. For example, they are expected to avoid physical violence and employ forms of relational aggression but in the environment of the inner city "sometimes you do got to fight" and, if you do, you risk being judged as "street" or "ghetto" (p. 207). Naming girls as such adds a gendered dimension because good and decent girls are "young ladies" but "ghetto chicks" are young girls whose "behaviors, dress, communication and interaction styles" violate both mainstream and black middle-class expectations of appropriate femininity (p. 207).

The "situated survival strategies" described by Jones comprise modes of interaction and routinized activities that center upon securing one's personal well-being as a black adolescent girl living in the inner city. Threats to their personal safety necessitate developing strategies that physically separate girls from the streets. In contrast to girl fighters who hang out on the streets, they will stay at home, read and do school work, and generally avoid social interactions that may cause conflict (Jones 2010: 209). They will also isolate themselves from their peers, so they do not form close friendships that would require them to come to the aid of their peers in forms of physical violence. Thus, girls have "friends" and "associates" and will fight for the former but not the latter (p. 209). In this way the code of the streets impacts adolescent black girls' development by circumscribing relational connections and networks. Miller (2008) describes similar survival strategies in the black inner city of St. Louis where she noted two survival themes adopted by girls: avoiding public spaces in the neighborhood, especially at night; and relying on the company of others, especially males, for protection, including networks of family and friends in an area. As one resident, Jackie, explained:

> "I stay in the house. . . . I don't go outside at all when I'm at home. When I'm around my grandma's house I go outside sometimes. I know mostly everybody over there. But when I'm at home I don't go outside unless I'm going to the store, but I don't talk to nobody."
>
> (Miller 2008: 60, 61)

The views and experiences of teenage girls of violence in Scotland are presented by Michele Burman (2004: 81), "to grasp how violence is understood by them and how it is both encountered and mobilized in their daily lives." Interestingly, when asked to explain "violence" in an abstract sense, these girls offered an explanation that related violence to harmful physical actions such as fighting, punching, kicking and using weapons to injure another. However, in recounting their own experiences of being violent or suffering violence they broadened their definition to include a more diverse range of behaviors including verbal threats, self-harm, offensive name calling and bullying as well as intimidation. Most thought that these relational forms of violence were experienced as more hurtful and damaging than actual physical violence, especially when they were encountered within existing friendships (p. 85). Ongoing verbal abuse directed mainly at other girls over long periods of time was the most common conflict situation reported, and such behaviors engendered feelings of humiliation, anger and powerlessness in the target of the abuse (p. 88). Despite their definitions of violence the girls did not apply that term to describe acts of physical violence occurring between siblings in the home which, while prevalent, were never considered to qualify as acts of "violence" but rather as "not serious" and wholly "natural" events. Thus, context and relationships rendered this form of violence non-violent, and in general terms all definitions and explanations of violence were shaped by context and the relationships involved (p. 90). Thus, girls more easily characterized events that occurred outside the home, not involving family members, as violence. All the girls were prepared to use violence themselves if warranted by the situation, but generally they regarded its use as a last resort. Instances where violence was acceptable included a response to verbal attacks to prevent continued harassment, and situations where they felt compelled to "stick up" for themselves. Girls exercised agency then, taking the conceptualization of girls' violence beyond simply a response to gendered forms of victimization (p. 97).

Emphasizing the need to examine the social contexts in which violence emerges as a strategy for girls living in the central city neighborhoods of St. Louis, Miller and White (2004: 187) find that girls employ violence differently than males, shaping its use according to gender, the situation and their motives and goals. For example, in robberies the girls employ physical aggression when robbing other girls but do not use weapons and have no male assistance. In contrast, when robbing men, girls use weapons but make no physical contact with their male victims, simply pretending to be sexually interested in them to get the males to lower their guard (2004: 177). In performing robbery on the streets girls are operating in a male-dominated environment and make technical choices about modes of robbery that reflect the gender stratification of the environment in which men are perceived as strong and women as weak. As Barrie Thorne puts it (1993: 109), in terms of gender relations, "An emphasis on social context shifts analysis from fixing abstract and binary differences to examining the social relations in which multiple differences are constructed and given meaning."

For those living in the environment of the black inner cities, violence takes on an added dimension because it becomes an integral part of life. Studies of the impact of this level of violence on youth who grow up witnessing and experiencing violence reveal that it is related to increases in aggression, increases in emotional and psychological trauma, that it breeds an intense vigilance, and that there is an increased risk of being victimized (Miller 2008: 34). In addition, "repeated exposure to high levels of violence may cause children and adolescents to become uncaring toward others, and desensitized toward future violent events" (Farrell and Bruce 1997: 3). Sexual harassment and its possible consequences in one of the poorest sections of the black inner city of St. Louis were explained by one informant to Miller (2008: 36) as follows:

> "if [girls] look good, somebody might try to touch 'em or something. And they might not want them to touch them and they might say something to 'em. And the dudes in my neighborhood, they might try to beat them up 'cause the girl wouldn't let them touch em" (Dwayne).

In this inner city neighborhood many youth believe that girls could be subjected to significant personal danger if they dressed in a provocative way that draws attention to them. Victim blaming has become a way to psychologically distance themselves from violent events. Here, the public spaces are male dominated and sites for possible sexual conquest if young women are present. Mirroring the "situated survival strategies" described by Jones (2004), the rules of this neighborhood include "staying out of others people's business" and developing a "level of desensitization and callousness" to restrain any possible personal attempt to intervene when girls saw others being attacked by young males in public spaces (Miller 2008: 41, 44). In schools, where they are constantly in contact with young men and could not avoid them by staying in their homes, girls try to ward off sexual harassment by attempting to stand up for themselves but these efforts are seen by male youth as forms of disrespect and as challenges to their sexual entitlements and could provoke situations of personal danger (p. 111). The sexual double standard they experience is epitomized by male conventions which stipulate that to qualify as a "real girlfriend" girls must police their own sexual desires and also resist young men's advances (p. 156).

Girls' violence and the "liberation hypothesis"

According to this hypothesis, the supposed increase in girls' violence is explained as the outcome of the feminist agenda and feminist advocacy. In the struggle for equality with men, it is argued that feminists have now made girls resemble boys and have taken them away from their proper roles as wives, mothers and daughters. In response, feminists counter that it is patriarchy that drives girls to be violent and that girls employ violence to counter gender oppression. Both approaches assume that girls are naturally non-aggressive and non-violent. Many popular books propagate the liberation hypothesis, for example, *See Jane Hit: Why Girls Are Growing More Violent and What We Can Do About It* (2007) by James Garbarino. His overall approach is to argue that freedoms now enjoyed by girls have altered their behavior. The following exemplifies this approach to girls' violence:

> Girls in general are evidencing a new assertiveness and physicality that go far beyond criminal assault. . . . We would welcome the New American Girl's unfettered assertiveness and physicality. . . . But I believe that the increasing violence among troubled girls and the generally elevated levels of aggression in girls are unintended consequences of the general increase in normal girls getting physical and becoming more assertive. All this, the good news of liberation and the bad news of increased aggression, is the New American Girl.
>
> (Garbarino 2007: 4)

In 2005 a similar contention about girls' violence was published in *Sugar and Spice and No Longer Nice: How We Can Stop Girls' Violence* by Deborah Prothrow-Stith and Howard R. Spivak. The adverse effects of women's liberation were described as follows:

> Girls continue to break down barriers and diminish the differences between their level of achievement and that of boys in many areas, and violent behavior is no exception. . . . Girls have become a part of the epidemic of youth violence.
>
> (Prothrow-Stith and Spivak 2005: 1, 2)

This concern about women and girls enjoying more freedom and the dire consequences that result is not a new theme. Commentators who examined arrest data to establish whether more women and girls are being arrested have tried to link any increases to the agenda for women's rights. However, they failed to undertake a thorough evaluation of arrest data to seek explanations of what was actually being measured and so ignored changes in policing policy and practice as possible causal factors. In the 1960s and 1970s studies boldly asserted a connection between the "emancipation" of women and criminality. For example, a 1969 report submitted to the U.S. National Commission on the Causes and Prevention of Violence stated, "It is also the case that the 'emancipation' of females in our society over recent decades has decreased the differences in delinquency and criminality between boys and girls, men and woman as cultural differences between them have narrowed" (Mulvihill et al. 1969: 425).

The most celebrated example of this "liberation of women" discourse was the publication in 1975 of *Sisters in Crime: The Rise of the New Female Offender* by Freda Adler who proposed that the newly liberated women of the 1960s were becoming more criminogenic than women of previous generations. In relation to girls, Adler claimed that they had adopted male roles and were thus more involved in drinking, stealing, gang activity and fighting. She claimed that appropriating the male role and departing from the "safety of traditional female roles" at the point of the onset of adolescence created increased risk factors for criminal behaviors (Adler 1975: 95). Adler relied on interviews and FBI arrest data to make her argument but her contention that there were substantial percentage increases in girls' arrests from 1960 to 1970 ignored the fact that while boys' arrests had increased by 82 percent and girls' arrests by 306 percent during that period, the actual numbers of arrests in rates per 10,000 for 10- to 17-year-olds showed an increase for boys of 49.33 and for girls of 27.30. Critical assessments of Adler's assertions followed, including research that tried to specifically address her contention that women's liberation had resulted in more women and girls becoming involved in crime. These studies did not support Adler's arguments and consequently there exists no convincing empirical support for this "liberation hypothesis" (Sprott and Doob 2009: 17).

Programming inadequacies in the treatment of girl offenders

The domination of the juvenile justice system by male offenders means that most treatment programs have historically been designed for boys and not girls. In the 1990s in the U.S. 35 percent of delinquency programs served only males and 42.4 percent served primarily boys (Girls Incorporated 1996). Only 2.3 percent of programs served females and 5.9 percent primarily served girls (Girls Incorporated 1996). Girls have always constituted a minor proportion of youthful offenders in custody and detention, and as a result gender-specific programming has been absent and girls have been "out of sight, out of mind." In many cases, programs designed for boys have simply been expanded to include girls. Establishing gender-specific programs for girls is problematic in light of the low numbers, short custody terms and the fluctuations in demand. Nevertheless, girls in the juvenile justice system do exhibit different needs than boys in the form of an increased likelihood of mental health problems, greater experience of victimization and differences in how aggression is manifested (Antonishak et al. 2004: 171). The most promising gender-specific programs are both individualized and comprehensive. Thus, a focus on developing healthy relationships may be appropriate for a girl with issues of relational aggression while a girl who persistently runs away may need programming on family issues and victimization (p. 174).

In 1998 the U.S. Office of Juvenile Justice and Delinquency Prevention issued recommendations for gender-specific programming, specifying, for example, respectful staff, a safe supportive environment, educational services that ought to be applied generally, and for special services aimed at improving girls' self-esteem, body image, feelings of empowerment and interpersonal relationships (OJJDP 1998). The *Juvenile Justice and Delinquency Prevention Act 1992* calls for the development and adoption of policies "to prohibit gender bias in placement and treatment and establishing programs to ensure that female youth have access to the full range of health and mental health services, treatment for physical or sexual assault and abuse, self defense instruction, education in parenting education in general, and other training and vocational services." Despite legal provisions intended to specifically address the needs of delinquent girls, research reveals that some juvenile justice staff persist in rejecting gender-specific treatment approaches. For example, Gaarder and others (2004) found that four out 14 juvenile probation officers in one Arizona county insisted that all juveniles had similar needs and no gender-specific approaches were warranted. Some of the staff believed that girls who did not adhere to feminine standards of behavior should be treated as if they were boys, describing these girls as follows:

> "They're not your typical girls . . . you know, the fingernails, the makeup, the Ms Prissy. They're just like the boys. They go out and they prove themselves like they're not feminine. You know they don't want anybody to think . . . well I'm helpless. I can take care of myself. So they play the role as portraying to be something that they're not."
>
> (Gaarder et al. 2004: 567)

Schaffner (2006: 160) stresses the need for programming for girls to reflect what are regarded as normative standards by contemporary youth and not to focus on topics such as getting out of prostitution that involve only a tiny minority of girls. She argues that staff should be in tune with contemporary mores and be aware of gender and gender issues so that girls are not faced with "middle-aged, middle-class adults who delivered gender programming [and] bombarded girls in lock up with humiliating harangues." Similarly, Gaarder and others (2004: 555) found that probation officers in Arizona lacked any knowledge of culturally and gender-appropriate treatments, and often referred girls to treatment services that did not match their needs.

Gender-specific – also known as gender-responsive – programming draws on a feminist perspective and stresses the unique experience of being a girl in the U.S. It is one approach to the treatment of girls who have been adjudicated delinquent. Another perspective is to ask "what works" and advocates of this approach argue that the principles of effective intervention that reduce recidivism can be identified from quantitative studies that are not gender specific. This approach is associated with the work of Canadian psychologists (Hubbard and Matthews 2008: 226). In a comprehensive review of these two treatment strategies Hubbard and Matthews (2008) identify how the strategies diverge as well as the contentions put forward by the opposing advocates. For example, the "what works" approach suffers from the fact that most of the research relied on has not involved girls. In the case of the gender-responsive approach, research has tended to be qualitative and is therefore criticized on the basis of lack of generalizability. Thus, it becomes clear that as much as anything the two approaches reflect long-standing contentions about the value of qualitative versus quantitative research. At a more fundamental theoretical level the gender-specific approach is rooted in feminist arguments that girls' delinquency must be related to issues of racism, sexism, class and gender, and that societal and justice system factors play a significant role in their marginalization. The "what works" perspective is much more of a traditional theoretical approach, drawing on long-standing criminological theory such as strain as well as social learning and the cognitive-behavioral approach in psychology. It is essentially a positivist approach as compared to a feminist analysis (p. 232).

The two schools of thought diverge sharply in considerations of the most effective therapeutic approach for delinquent girls. "What works" advocates favor the cognitive-behavioral model that has been applied to boys and has come to be regarded as the most effective treatment mode in a number of countries. By contrast, a gender-specific approach asks why these psychological models should necessarily be applied to girls when the antisocial attitudes to which they are targeted are characteristic of only one gender. Of course, psychological approaches are also individualistic and take no account of social or structural issues, and therefore can be criticized for pathologizing girls' responses to their social circumstances (Hubbard and Matthews 2008: 232). Gender-specific advocates take issue with the concept of risk and how it is applied to girls (p. 234). For example, they argue that girls "may be high need" (p. 234) but not high risk given that their low crime rates are indicative that they are no danger to society. Advocates also argue that a focus on high risk usually means placing girls in detention and this works to exacerbate problems such as depression, sexual abuse and disruptions in relationships that contributed to their contact with the law in the first place (p. 234).

The gender-specific approach assumes that treatment staff must be aware of girls' individual trauma resulting from incidents of abuse, must comprehend the role that trauma plays in a girl's life, and create services that appropriately address those circumstances. This includes reinforcing survival and coping skills, and focusing on treatment goals that enhance decision making (Hubbard and Matthews 2008: 238, 239). In terms of girls' trauma, for example, the Female Detention Project found that 81 percent of girls studied reported experiencing some kind of trauma, such as sexual or physical abuse, witnessing violence or being abandoned (Chesney-Lind 2010: 64). Moreover, girls were misdiagnosed with "Oppositional Defiant Disorder" and not "Post-Traumatic Stress Disorder" with the outcome that they were not receiving appropriate treatment (p. 65).

Hubbard and Matthews (2008: 251) conclude their review of these two approaches with a balanced statement that recognizes the merits of each as follows:

> [T]he two major contributions of the gender-responsive group include their (a) explication of how the social context of being a girl in the United States facilitates girls' delinquency and (b) research and discussions on the need for gender-responsive treatment to reflect the differences in the socialization of girls and boys. The major contributions of the what works literature include (a) their empirical basis for program development and (b) their success in translating this research into practical applications for correctional and juvenile justice agencies.

Girls in the juvenile justice system struggle against cultural and gender stereotypes promoted and reinforced by juvenile justice officials. For example, research has consistently shown that girls are perceived by juvenile justice officials as being "more difficult" to manage than boys (Gaarder et al. 2004). A recent study of probation files in Arizona showed probation officers rendering value judgments such as "fabricating reports of abuse, acting promiscuously, whining too much, and attempting to manipulate the court system." Girls were viewed as "harder to work with," as being "too needy" and as having "too many issues" (Gaarder et al. 2004: 556).

Schaffner (2006: 158) reports that when she asked juvenile detention and probation staff to compare boys with girls, staff regularly regarded girls as "less good than or not as good as boys" and provided the following views:

> "Girls are more emotional than boys. . . . Everything is a big ol'drama trauma with them! That's why we handle 'em a little differently" (middle-aged, African American, middle-class woman, guard).

"Girls are just harder to work with. . . . The boys will follow the rules; they are quieter. The girls never listen; they just tangle with you on everything" (young, white, working-class woman, guard).

(Schaffner 2006: 158)

Why are girls regarded as so challenging? The sexualization theory of female offending sees differential treatment as the outcome of a double standard of behavior where the deviant behavior of women is regarded as a symptom of problematic sexuality requiring welfare rather than punishment. Thus, as Worrall argues, the same concern to protect exists alongside unease that a girl is dangerous and "out of control" (2001: 152).

Other issues concerning the needs of girls in custody identified by researchers include the lack of mental health services and an absence of prenatal care and health services for pregnant girls in New York City; girls experiencing sexual abuse while being detained in California; and a lack of female staff, limiting gender-specific programming and resulting in reduced outdoor recreation for girls in Florida (Chesney-Lind 2010: 65).

Recap

As this account of the interaction between girls and the juvenile justice system has shown, enduring gender stereotypes, expanded definitions of girls' violence and the continuing criminalization of victimized girls mark the increased attention paid to girls and their delinquency. Girls' vulnerability to arrest has been enhanced by expansive redefinitions and relabeling of what constitutes "violence" and especially by the discovery of new pathologies concerning relational violence and bullying in schools. Law-enforcement policies and practices have contributed to this vulnerability because it has been more convenient for police called to domestic violence incidents to take a girl into custody than to remove a parent or both parents from the home. Thus, changes in the gendered nature of offending have adversely affected girls. From one perspective therefore, the increased focus on girls' criminality has enhanced the surveillance, monitoring and social control exercised over girls to their obvious detriment. Nevertheless, studies of the gendered forms of violence to which black girls are subjected in the inner cities (as opposed to the usual focus on girls in gangs, prostitution and drug dealing) and the debate over gender-responsive treatment for delinquent girls emerge as positives in the debate over girls' criminality. The pathways approach to girls' offending has revealed the blurred nature of the boundary between victimization and offending, and the structural factors that impact many girls' lives expose the limitations of pathologizing girls' criminality.

The fact remains that girls are far less likely to be involved in serious crime, and the majority of girls processed through the juvenile justice system commit ordinary crimes and simple assaults. Gender typing seems to be largely maintained in schools and the sexual double standard applied to girls, but not to boys, has lost none of its power. Similarly, girls continue to be punished for not conforming to expected "feminine" standards of behavior so that overall there seems to have been little change in the core elements of gender so far as girls are concerned despite claims made by the liberation hypothesis. There is a need to address not only gender differences in the type and frequency of crime but also to better understand how gender is performed in the context of offending. The history of the juvenile justice system in relation to girls has been one of sexism and paternalism, and this continues to make it a problematic site for gender-specific services.

Note

1 In the various editions of *Girls, Delinquency and Juvenile Justice*, Chesney-Lind and Shelden add a note to the effect that the authors learned from sources inside the juvenile justice system "that some police and probation officers are suggesting to parents the following: When a girl threatens to run away, the parent should stand in her way; if she runs into the parent or pushes the parent out of the way, then the parent can call the court and have the girl arrested on 'simple assault' or 'battery' or some other 'personal' crime that would fit into the FBI category 'other assaults'" (Chesney-Lind and Shelden 2004: 30).

References

Adler, Freda. 1975. *Sisters in Crime: The Rise of the New Female Offender*. New York: McGraw-Hill.

Alder, C. and A. Worrall (eds). 2004. *Girl's Violence: Myths and Realities*. Albany, NY: State University of New York Press.

Antonishak, Jill, N. Dickson Reppucci and Carrie Freid Mulford. 2004. "Girls in the Justice System: Treatment and Intervention." In Marlene M. Moretti, Candice L. Odgers and Margaret A. Jackson (eds) *Girls and Aggression: Contributing Factors and Intervention Principles*. New York: Kluwer Academic/Plenum Publishers, pp. 165–180.

Batacharya, Sheila. 2004. "Racism, 'Girl Violence,' and the Murder of Reena Virk." In Christine Alder and Anne Worrall (eds) *Girls' Violence: Myths and Realities*. Albany, NY: State University of New York Press, pp. 61–80.

Belknap, Joanne. 2001. *The Invisible Woman: Gender, Crime and Justice*. Belmont, CA: Wadsworth Publishing.

Belknap, Joanne and Kristi Holsinger. 1998. "An Overview of Delinquent Girls: How Theory and Practice Have Failed and the Need for Innovative Changes." In Ruth T. Zaplin (ed.) *Female Crime and Delinquency: Critical Perspectives and Effective Interventions*. Gaithersburg, MD: Aspen Publishing.

Bishop, Donna M. and Charles E. Frazier. 1992. "Gender Bias in Juvenile Justice Processing: Implications of the JJDP Act." *Journal of Criminal Law and Criminology* 82: 1162–1186.

Brown, Marion. 2010. "Negotiations of the Living Space: Life in the Group Home for Girls Who Use Violence." In Meda Chesney-Lind and Nikki Jones (eds) *Fighting for Girls: New Perspectives on Gender and Violence*. Albany, NY: State University of New York Press, pp. 175–199.

Brown, Sheila. 2005. *Understanding Youth and Crime: Listening to Youth?* Maidenhead, Berkshire: Open University Press.

Burman, Michele. 2004. "Turbulent Talk: Girls Making Sense of Violence." In Christine Adler and Anne Worrall (eds) *Girls' Violence: Myths and Realities*. Albany, NY: State University of New York Press, pp. 81–104.

Buzawa, Eve S. and David Hirschel. 2010. "Criminalizing Assault: Do Age and Gender Matter?" In Meda Chesney-Lind and Nikki Jones (eds) *Fighting for Girls: New Perspectives on Gender and Violence*. Albany, NY: State University of New York Press, pp. 33–55.

Cain, Maureen (ed.). 1989. *Growing Up Good: Policing the Behaviour of Girls in Europe*. London: Sage.

Centers for Disease Control and Prevention (CDC). 1991–2009. *Youth Risk Behavior Survey*. Atlanta, GA: Department of Health and Human Services.

Chesney-Lind, Meda. 2002. "Criminalizing Victimization: The Unintended Consequences of Pro-Arrest Policies for Girls and Women." *Criminology and Public Policy* 1(2): 81–90.

Chesney-Lind, Meda. 2010. "Jailing 'Bad' Girls: Girls' Violence and Trends in Female Incarceration." In Meda Chesney-Lind and Nikki Jones (eds) *Fighting for Girls: New Perspectives on Gender and Violence*. Albany, NY: State University of New York Press, pp. 57–79.

Chesney-Lind, Meda and Michele Eliason. 2006. "From Invisible to Incorrigible: The Demonization of Marginalized Women and Girls." *Crime, Media and Culture* 2(1): 29–47.

Chesney-Lind, Meda and Katherine Irwin. 2008. *Beyond Bad Girls: Gender, Violence and Hype*. New York: Routledge.

Chesney-Lind, Meda and Nikki Jones (eds). 2010. *Fighting for Girls: New Perspectives on Gender and Violence*. Albany, NY: State University of New York Press.

Chesney-Lind, Meda and Vickie Paramore. 2001. "Are Girls Getting More Violent?: Exploring Juvenile Robbery Trends." *Journal of Contemporary Criminal Justice* 17(2): 142–166.

Chesney-Lind, Meda and Randall G. Shelden. 2004. *Girls, Delinquency and Juvenile Justice*. Belmont, CA: Wadsworth.

Daly, Kathleen. 1992. "Women's Pathways to Felony Court: Feminist Theories of Lawbreaking and Problems of Representation." *Southern California Review of Law and Women's Studies* 2: 11–52.

Dembo, Richard, Linda Williams and James Schmeidler. 1993. "Gender Differences in Mental Health Service Needs Among Youths Entering a Juvenile Detention Center." *Journal of Prison and Jail Health* 12(2): 73–101.

D'Emilio, John and Estelle Freedman. 1988. *Intimate Matters: A History of Sexuality in America*. New York: Harper & Row.

Devlin, Rachel. 1998. "Female Juvenile Delinquency and the Problem of Sexual Authority in America 1945–1965." In Sherrie A. Inness (ed.) *Delinquents and Debutantes: Twentieth-Century American Girls' Cultures*. New York and London: New York University Press, pp. 83–108.

Durham, M.G. 1998. "Dilemmas of Desire: Representations of Adolescent Sexuality in Two Teen Magazines." *Youth and Society* 29: 369–389.

Farrell, Albert D. and Steven E. Bruce. 1997. "Impact of Exposure to Community Violence on Violent Behavior and Emotional Distress among Urban Adolescents." *Journal of Clinical Child Psychology* 26(1): 2–14.

Federal Bureau of Investigations (FBI). 2007. *Crime in the U.S. 2006*. Washington D.C.: U.S Government Printing Office.

Feld, Barry C. 2009. "Violent Girls or Relabeled Status Offenders? An Alternative Interpretation of the Data." *Crime and Delinquency* 55: 241–265.

Gaarder, Emily and J. Belknap. 2002. "Tenuous Borders: Girls Transferred to Adult Court." *Criminology* 40(3): 481–517.

Gaarder, Emily, Nancy Rodriguez and Marjorie S. Zatz. 2004. "Criers, Liars and Manipulators: Probation Officers' Views of Girls." *Justice Quarterly* 21: 547–578.

Garbarino, James. 2007. *See Jane Hit: Why Girls Are Growing More Violent and What We Can Do About It*. Harmondsworth: Penguin.

Garland, David. 2002. *The Culture of Control: Crime and Social Order in Contemporary Society*. Chicago, IL: The University of Chicago Press.

Girls Incorporated. 1996. *Prevention and Parity: Girls in Juvenile Justice*. Washington D.C.: U.S. Department of Justice, Office of Juvenile Justice and Delinquency Prevention.

Holsinger, Kristi and Alexander Holsinger. 2005. "Differential Pathways to Violence and Self-Injurious Behavior: African American and White Girls in the Juvenile Justice System." *Journal of Research in Crime and Delinquency* 42(2): 211–242.

Hubbard, Dana J. and Betsy Matthews. 2008. "Reconciling the Differences Between the 'Gender-Responsive' and the 'What Works' Literatures to Improve Services for Girls." *Crime and Delinquency* 54: 225–258.

Jones, Nikki. 2004. "'It's not Where you Live it's How you Live': How Young Women Negotiate Conflict and Violence in the Inner City." *Annals of the American Academy of Political and Social Science* 595(1): 49–62.

Jones, Nikki. 2010. "'It's About Being a Survivor . . .'": African American Girls, Gender, and the Context of Inner City Violence." In Meda Chesney-Lind and Nikki Jones (eds) *Fighting for Girls: New Perspectives on Gender and Violence*. Albany, NY: State University of New York Press, pp. 203–218.

Katz, P. 1979. "The Development of Female Identity." In C. Kopp (ed.) *In Becoming Female: Perspectives on Development*. New York: Plenum Press.

Knupfer, Anne Meis. 2001. *Reform and Resistance: Gender, Delinquency, and America's First Juvenile Court*. London: Routledge.

Krisberg, Barry. 2005. *Juvenile Justice: Redeeming our Children*. Thousand Oaks, CA, London and New Delhi: Sage.

Laub, John H. and Janet L. Lauritsen. 1993. "Violent Criminal Behavior Over the Life Course: A Review of the Longitudinal and Comparative Research." *Violence and Victims* 8: 235–252.

Males, Mike. 2010. "Have Girls Gone Wild?" In Meda Chesney-Lind and Nikki Jones (eds) *Fighting for Girls: New Perspectives on Gender and Violence*. Albany, NY: State University of New York Press, pp. 13–32.

Messerschmidt, James W. 1993. *Masculinities and Crime: Critique and Reconceptualization of Theory*. Lanham, MD: Rowman and Littlefield.

Miller, Jody. 2008. *Getting Played: African American Girls Urban Inequality and Gendered Violence*. New York: New York University Press.

Miller, Jody and Norman A. White. 2004. "Situational Effects of Gender Inequality on Girls' Participation in Violence." In Christine Alder and Anne Worrall (eds) *Girls' Violence: Myths and Realities*. Albany, NY: State University of New York Press, pp. 167–190.

Mulvihill, Donald J., Melvin M. Tumin and Lynn A. Curtis. 1969. *Crimes of Violence: A Staff Report Submitted to the National Commission on the Causes and Prevention of Violence*. Washington D.C.: Government Printing Office.

Odem, Mary E. 1995. *Delinquent Daughters: Protecting and Policing Adolescent Female Sexuality in the United States 1885–1920*. Chapel Hill: The University of North Carolina Press.

Office of Juvenile Justice and Delinquency Prevention (OJJDP). 1998. *Guiding Principles for Promising Female Programming: An Inventory of Best Practices*. Washington D.C.

Platt, Anthony M. 1977. *The Child Savers: The Invention of Delinquency*. Chicago, IL: The University of Chicago Press.

Prothrow-Stith, Deborah and Howard R. Spivak. 2005. *Sugar and Spice and No Longer Nice: How We Can Stop Girls' Violence*. San Francisco, CA: Jossey-Bass.

Sabol, William J. and Heather Couture. 2008. *Prison Inmates at Midyear 2007*. Department of Justice, Bureau of Justice Statistics. Washington D.C.: Government Printing Office.

Schaffner, Laurie. 2006. *Girls in Trouble with the Law*. New Brunswick, NJ, and London: Rutgers University Press.

Schlossman, Steven and Stephanie Wallach. 1978. "The Crime of Precocious Sexuality: Female Juvenile Delinquency in the Progressive Era." *Harvard Educational Review* 48(1): 65–94.

Snyder, Howard N. and Melissa Sickmund. 2006. *Juvenile Offenders and Victims: 2006 National Report*. Office of Juvenile Justice and Delinquency Prevention, Department of Justice. Washington D.C.

Sprott, Jane B. and Anthony N. Doob. 2009. *Justice for Girls? Stability and Change in the Youth Justice Systems of the United States and Canada*. Chicago, IL: The University of Chicago Press.

Steffensmeier, Darrell, Jennifer Schwartz, Hua Zhong and Jeff Ackerman. 2005. "An Assessment of Recent Trends in Girls' Violence Using Diverse Longitudinal Sources: Is the Gender Gap Closing?" *Criminology* 43(2): 355–405.

Thorne, Barrie. 1993. *Gender Play: Girls and Boys in School*. New Brunswick, NJ: Rutgers University Press.

Vaillancourt, Tracy and Shelley Hymel. 2004. "The Social Context of Children's Aggression." In Marlene M. Moretti, Candice L. Odgers and Margaret A. Jackson (eds) *Girls and Aggression: Contributing Factors and Intervention Principles*. New York: Kluwer Academic/Plenum Publishers, pp. 57–73.

Worrall, Anne. 2001. "Governing Bad Girls: Changing Constructions of Female Juvenile Delinquency." In Jo Bridgeman and Daniel Monk (eds) *Feminist Perspectives on Child Law*. London: Routledge Cavendish, pp. 151–168.

Worrall, Anne. 2004. "Twisted Sisters, Ladettes, and the New Penology: The Social Construction of 'Violent Girls.'" In Christine Alder and Anne Worrall (eds) *Girls' Violence: Myths and Realities*. Albany, NY: State University of New York Press, pp. 41–60.

Zahn-Waxler, C. 2000. "The Development of Empathy, Guilt and the Internalization of Distress." In R. Davidson (ed.) *Anxiety, Depression and Emotion: Wisconsin Symposium on Emotion*, Volume II. New York: Oxford University Press, pp. 222–265.

youth, crime and justice

chapter 5

Race and Juvenile Justice

"Race" is a social construct used in the U.S. to establish categories of persons for specific purposes. It is used primarily to refer to differences in skin color but it is considered a crude measure of difference in terms of distinguishing categories such as black and white (Lauritsen 2005: 84, 85). Since 1790, a census of the population has been conducted every ten years and this has necessitated the creation of racial categories to which persons of various ethnic backgrounds may be assigned. The U.S. Department of Commerce Economics and Statistics Administration employs five race categories as follows:

White: people having origins in any of the original peoples of Europe, the Middle East or North Africa, including those who indicated their race as white or as Irish, German, Italian, Lebanese, Arab, Moroccan or Caucasian representing 72 percent of the population;

Black or African-American: people having origins in any of the Black racial groups of Africa (including people who identify themselves as Black, Negro or African-American or reported as African-American Kenyan, Nigerian or Haitian) and representing 13 percent of the population;

American Indian and Alaskan Native: people having origins in any of the original peoples of North, Central and South America who maintain tribal affiliation or community attachment (or reported their enrollment) or principal tribe such as Navajo, Blackfeet, Inupiat, Yup'ik or Central

American Indian groups or South American Indian groups and representing 0.9 percent of the population;

Asian: people having origins in any of the original peoples of the Far East, Southeast Asia or the Indian subcontinent including Cambodia, China, India, Japan, Korea, Malaysia, Pakistan, the Philippine Islands, Thailand, and Vietnam and representing 5 percent of the population;

Native Hawaiian and Other Pacific Islanders: people having origins in any of the original peoples of Hawaii, Guam, Samoa or other Pacific Islands and representing 0.2 percent of the population;

Some Other Race: for those persons not able to identify with any of the above categories – most people responding with this category identified themselves as "Hispanic" or "Latino," multiracial, mixed, interracial, who represent 3 percent of the population. "Hispanic or Latino" refers to a person of Cuban, Mexican, Puerto Rican, South or Central American, or other Spanish culture or origin regardless of race (U.S. Census Bureau 2010). Federal agencies are required to use a minimum of two ethnicities: Hispanic or Latino and Not Hispanic or Latino. According to the U.S. Census Bureau, "Hispanic origin can be viewed as the heritage, nationality group, lineage, or country of birth of the person or the person's parents or ancestors before their arrival in the United States. People who identify their origin as Hispanic, Latino, or Spanish may be any race."

(Humes et al. 2011: 1, 3–4)

This chapter will focus on the categories described as Black or African American and American Indian and Alaskan Native. Although the Hispanic category is substantial, making up the largest minority group in the country for criminal justice purposes, there is no routine collection process that differentiates Hispanics from Whites, Blacks or other groups. This applies also to Hispanic delinquency, where the Office of Juvenile Justice and Delinquency Prevention (OJJDP) bulletins and reports fail to disaggregate Hispanics from Whites (Cintron 2006: 29).

How does race impact juvenile justice? In 2007, the U.S. juvenile justice system handled an estimated 1.7 million delinquency cases (Knoll and Sickmund 2010: 1). That year, white youth accounted for 64 percent of cases, black youth 33 percent and American Indian youth 1 percent. The racial disparity varied according to offense category with white youth accounting for 72 percent of drug cases – the highest of all offense categories for whites (p. 2). White youth were involved in 56 percent of cases compared to 41 percent of black youth – the highest offense category for blacks. American Indian youth accounted for a very small proportion of cases across all offense categories. Black youth comprise about 15 percent of the 10- to 17-year-old population at risk for delinquency (Knoll and Sickmund 2010: 2).

Are there racial disparities within the juvenile justice systems in the U.S.? When decision points within the juvenile justice system are linked to groups of youth the outcome reveals the existence of racial disparities. Thus, the rate at which black youth were referred to the juvenile court for delinquency was about 140 percent greater than the rate for white youth (Knoll and Sickmund 2010: 2). Cases were brought to the court for formal processing at a rate 12 percent higher for black youth than for white youth. In terms of adjudication, the rate for black youth was about 8 percent less than for white youth. In relation to waiver to the criminal court, the rate was 9 percent greater for black youth than for white youth. The rate ordered for residential placement after adjudication was 27 percent higher for black youth than for white youth and the rate ordered for probation was 14 percent less for black youth than for white youth (p. 2).

Pope and Feyerherm have shown that "there is substantial support for the statement that there are race effects in operation within the justice system, both direct and indirect in nature" (1990: 335), and the OJJDP, in a research study concerning the processing of minority youth, noted that over the past three decades the body of literature that focuses on the problem of selection bias in the juvenile justice system suggests that the processing decisions of many juvenile justice systems "are not racially neutral" and that "Minority youth are more likely than majority youth to become involved in the system" (quoted in Pope and Feyerherm 1990: 335).[1]

Race effects may be direct or indirect, and may be felt at various decision points within the system and may accumulate as youth move through the system (Pope and Feyerherm 1995: 2, 8). The same study observed that disproportionate representation of minorities may be explained by selection bias and by the nature and volume of offenses committed by minority youth. In the latter case structural factors associated with "the urban underclass may, in part account for the increasing number of minorities coming into contact with the juvenile justice system" (p. 8).

In considering therefore how race impacts juvenile justice for blacks and American Indians and Alaskan Natives it is crucial to gain an understanding of the social, cultural, political and economic history, and the contemporary circumstances relevant to these categories of persons. Factors such as the political economy of crime, poverty and welfare, crime control, moral panics about youth, the current punitive populism concerning punishment and, in cultural terms, the perceived "otherness" of those included in these race categories (Nunn 2002: 690–714) intersect to form a complex multifaceted foundation for minority criminality. This chapter will therefore devote considerable attention to the social, economic and cultural landscape of these minority groups.

A host of studies over the past 30 years or so have examined bias in the juvenile justice system and many have located bias at various decision points while others have not. Some studies, especially the most recent, have employed sophisticated and complex quantitative methodology but very few studies have used qualitative research methods. The outcome has been a plethora of highly technical studies finding bias (or not) but unable to explain how it may have occurred. Qualitative methods have been employed in only a few cases to supplement the technical data with meaningful explanations. The focus of this chapter will be on explaining bias, where this is possible, and on contextualizing minority juvenile criminality so that it is grounded in the lived experiences, lifestyles and living conditions of those minorities.

The chapter also explores the actual workings of the juvenile justice system and will show how bias connects to the various decision points within the system. It is only by fully understanding the operation of the system that it is possible to develop explanations for bias.

African Americans: the urban underclass

Representations of black criminality inevitably include images of the inner city, peopled almost entirely by blacks, black gangs and references to "the underclass." It is indisputable that black ghettos have formed in some cities, concentrating blacks into areas of poverty and high unemployment, and perpetuating physical decay, crime and social disorder. It is therefore crucial to understand how this came about in order to appreciate fully the context in which much black criminality originated and now occurs. As Bourgois (1995: 17) notes in relation to the Puerto Rican crack sellers in the Barrio of Spanish Harlem, New York, "the self-destructive daily life of those who are surviving on the street needs to be contextualized in the particular history of the hostile race relations and structural economic dislocation they have faced."

The segregation of blacks in some inner cities has developed urbanized black ghettos. It is argued that residential segregation has been imposed on blacks over the past 50 years through the deliberate acts, public policies and institutional arrangements of whites (Massey and Denton 1993). Within 16 large metropolitan areas that contain one-third of all blacks there exists segregation of such intensity that a black person living in such an area is likely never to have contact with any group other than blacks. Growing up in such an environment means having little or no contact with the culture and norms of the rest of American society. Adapting to and coping with the demands of segregation has promoted a culture that is opposed to mainstream American middle-class values, that is alienated and often hostile to the dominant culture, and that places little or no value on education, work, schooling and marriage (Massey and Denton 1993: 8). This so-called "street culture" may constitute "an alternative forum for autonomous personal dignity," and many of its aspects have been acquired and appropriated by mainstream culture which has presented street culture as a form of pop culture (Bourgois 1995: 8). Consequently, both cultural and structural factors have contributed to the crisis facing black males. The level of black isolation is unique among racial groups and there are few signs of change because it has become structural in nature (Massey and Denton 1993: 2). Social isolation within the inner city black ghetto, explained as "the lack of contact or of sustained interaction with individuals and institutions that represent mainstream society" (Wilson 1987: 60) means that with no access to networks that might produce regular employment, alternatives like welfare and the illicit economy come not only to be relied upon, but to be regarded as constituting a way of life (p. 57).

Following riots in the late 1960s in the black ghettos, the Kerner Commission, established by President Lyndon Johnson to identify the causes of the violence and to propose solutions, reported in May 1968 as follows:

> Segregation and poverty have created in the racial ghetto a destructive environment totally unknown to most white Americans. What white Americans have never fully understood – but what the Negro can never forget – is that white society is deeply implicated in the ghetto. White institutions created it, white institutions maintain it and white society condones it.
>
> (The Kerner Report 1968)

By the end of the 1970s, despite the admonitions of the Kerner Commission, the discourse on race and poverty (incorporating images of black families forever caught up in a cycle of unemployment, headed by unmarried mothers and dependent on government for economic survival) had been worked into a concept called the urban underclass (Massey and Denton 1993: 4). Scholars argued that this persistent black poverty was the outcome of the structural transformation of the economy of the inner city. The relevant causal factors were the decline in manufacturing and the rise of the service economy offering limited poorly paid work. The effect was increased black joblessness and fewer men able to provide for a family. Marriage became therefore less attractive to women and female-headed households multiplied. Blacks were disproportionately affected by these massive changes in the economy because they were located in cities and occupations that were most affected. As Wilson (1987: 39) explains:

Urban minorities have been particularly vulnerable to structural economic changes, such as the shift from goods-producing to service-producing industries, the increasing polarization of the labor market into low-wage and high-wage sectors, technological innovations, and the relocation of manufacturing industries out of the central cities.

Segregation has promoted poverty because blacks have been unable to relocate out of the inner city ghettos to neighborhoods that are safe, possess higher home values and have good schooling. Barriers to mobility are also barriers to social advancement and improved life chances (Massey and Denton 1993: 14).

How did black isolation in ghettos come about? In 1870, 80 percent of blacks still lived in the rural south but by 1970 80 percent of blacks lived in urban areas, with nearly half living outside the south (Massey and Denton 1993: 18). The migration to northern cities was joined by immigrant groups entering the country in their millions between 1880 and 1920, but for these groups the cities were a means of integration, assimilation and advancement (p. 18). Before 1900, blacks in northern cities were not segregated from whites and rarely made up more than 30 percent of residents in a locality. In fact, typically the black residents of a northern city in the 19th century lived in a neighborhood that was almost 90 percent white and in the south before 1900 segregation levels were lower even than in the north (pp. 23, 24).

After 1900, two events occurred that impacted integrated living: industrialization and the movement of blacks from the farms to the cities. Large factories located in manufacturing districts and collectively employing thousands became the pattern of industrialization in the north. The density of housing increased in those areas where workers were accommodated. Primarily, European migrants met the high demand for labor, but during the 1880s and 1890s some 150,000 blacks migrated to the north (Massey and Denton 1993: 27). Between 1910 and 1920, some 525,000 blacks left the south and the migration reached 877,000 in the 1920s, raising concerns among the whites about integration and causing a surge of racial violence in the cities between 1900 and 1920 (p. 29). Blacks were attacked and those not living in black neighborhoods had their houses burned or looted (p. 30). Intolerance for integrated living developed, and blacks living in white areas were forced to relocate to black locations, constituting the preparatory stages for black ghetto formation, so that by World War II a black ghetto had been established in every northern city. For example, Chicago's isolation index (the measure of the segregation of the activities of multiple populations) rose from only 10 percent in 1900 to 70 percent by 1930, New York's changed from 5 percent to 42 percent and Cleveland, from 8 percent to 51 percent (p. 31).

It is argued that whites employed violence to constitute and sustain the black ghettos. Following the violence between 1900 and 1920, whites began to target violence along the boundary of the ghetto to ensure that middle-class blacks trying to escape the housing pressures and poor living conditions of the ghetto did not remain in areas populated by whites (Massey and Denton 1993: 34). This was accomplished through harassment and warnings, and actions such as realtors buying out black home owners. Mobs of whites would, if necessary, attack and damage black-occupied houses, and if that failed they used bombs to dislodge the black occupiers. After the 1920s less physical methods were employed, including organizational techniques such as forming neighborhood improvement associations whose real agenda was preventing black entry into white areas (pp. 34–35). They protected white areas from black intrusion by seeking zoning restrictions and lobbying local authorities to close hotels and rooming houses that accommodated black workers. The most effective tool, however, proved to be implementing restrictive covenants that bound property owners to refuse to allow blacks to own or lease their property. It was not until 1948 that the Supreme Court decided these were unenforceable (p. 36).

Realtors developed a policy of containing blacks by ensuring that entire blocks were filled before permitting them to move to the next. When blacks moved into white areas, this provoked white intolerance, and a racial turnover of the area from white to black began (Massey and Denton 1993: 38). The effect was to ensure that the poorest black families were located toward the center of the ghetto, with the least attractive housing and the fewest amenities and services, with the middle-class blacks occupying the outer areas to the ghetto boundary (p. 39).

The Depression prompted some 400,000 blacks to move to the north despite a lack of employment there, but by the 1940s the demands of the wartime economy for labor meant that black migration from the south soared and population densities within the northern ghettos increased greatly (Massey and Denton 1993: 43). The postwar period was characterized by the development of the suburbs, by the white middle class vacating the inner cities and by highway construction that permitted rapid movement to the cities by car and truck (p. 44).

Economic trends for young black men have been unfavorable since the end of World War II (Wilson 1987: 82). The old centralized manufacturing districts declined, as production could now be easily located away from the inner city. In the south agriculture became industrialized, and this, together with the postwar economic boom and a high demand for labor, prompted almost three million blacks to leave the south in the 1950s and 1960s (Massey and Denton 1993: 45). Between 1950 and 1970 the percentage of blacks in northern cities rapidly increased, for example, from 14 percent to 33 percent in Chicago. By 1970, Newark was 54 percent black and Washington 71 percent (p. 45).

The population influx into the ghettos increased their size as whites rapidly moved out to the suburbs. By 1980, an average 71 percent of northern whites resided in suburbs compared to only 23 percent of blacks (Massey and Denton 1993: 67). Even then a pattern had emerged so that once a suburb had an appreciable black presence it tended to attract more blacks than whites, leading to a racial turnover and the creation of a new black enclave (p. 70).

Individual and collective discrimination in housing by whites was supplemented by federal government public policy beginning in the 1930s with the move to promote home ownership. Institutions tasked with lending money for mortgages adopted risk management practices that "redlined" neighborhoods of the lowest quality, thus ensuring that older inner city areas were undervalued and funds diverted away from black areas. Private banks followed the federal loan approach, and the Federal Housing Administration (FHA) and the Veterans Administration (VA) pumped vast amounts of loan money into the suburbs for new housing to the detriment of the inner cities (Massey and Denton 1993: 52, 53). These federal policies meant that by the late 1950s many cities were in decline as whites moved out to the suburbs and became home owners. Federal assistance to the cities was provided in 1949 and 1954 with funding allocated to local authorities to clear slum areas and redevelop them with public housing. By 1970 public housing had become largely occupied by blacks (p. 57).

Even in the early 1970s, cities still contained manufacturing and heavy industries that provided strong employment for blacks, and, until the 1973 recession, black income levels were increasing and the rate of black poverty had reached its lowest level.[2] Despite the *Fair Housing Act 1968* banning discrimination in housing and renting, segregation continued, and by the end of the 1970s the country was experiencing high unemployment and falling incomes with increased rates of black poverty. The designation of the urban underclass was assigned to the ghetto population during the 1970s (Massey and Denton 1993: 61). *Time* magazine of August 19, 1977 explained "The American Underclass" as follows:

> Behind [the ghetto's] crumbling walls lives a large group of people who are more intractable, more socially alien and more hostile than almost anyone had imagined. They are the unreachables: the American underclass.

As Michael Katz (1989: 185) puts it:

> [T]he concept of the underclass captured the mixture of alarm and hostility that tinged the emotional response of more affluent Americans

youth, crime and justice

to the poverty of blacks increasingly clustered and isolated in post-industrial cities.

Two images captured the concept of the underclass: black teenage mothers and black unemployed youth. In the case of the latter, incarceration appeared to be the dominant policy approach as rates of incarceration in the U.S., especially for blacks, climbed far above those in other western industrialized states.

In the 1970s, many jobs in manufacturing were eliminated owing to increased foreign competition, wages were reduced and the real value of welfare payments lowered. Full-time employment in manufacturing fell from 27 percent in 1947 to 26 percent in 1969 and to 19 percent in 1984 (Katz 1989: 128). Black poverty rates increased as a result and by the end of the 1970s a typical poor black family lived in a neighborhood where at least one-third of the families were poor (Massey and Denton 1993: 125, 130).[3] By the late 1980s, due to the decline in manufacturing, fewer than half of working-age blacks with less than a college education were working full time (Wilson 1993: 25–34). This compares to early 1970 when 70 percent of such men were working in paid employment.

Segregation interacts with poverty to create conditions that are unable to sustain access to retail goods and services. Lack of income and low consumer demand condemns the inner city ghettos to rudimentary services. Crime and social disorder are strongly predicted by high rates of poverty (Massey and Denton 1993: 135). Where blacks are unable to access job networks and do not interact with those in regular and stable employment, they become isolated from society. These conditions become normative for young blacks who come to expect poor educational performance, joblessness, single parenthood and welfare dependency (p. 140). The concept of the "underclass" underpins notions about the character and circumstances of poor urban blacks. The term implies that this group is crime-ridden, prone to violence, mired in unending economic deprivation and composed of the most immobile and socially isolated persons. The traits most associated with this group are "violence, aggression and idleness" (Young 2004: 27).

Discussing the environment in Spanish Harlem in New York City and the Puerto Rican crack dealers, Bourgois (1995: 24) comments on the manner in which violence is integrated into that lifestyle:

Regular displays of violence are essential for preventing rip-offs by colleagues, customers, and professional hold up artists. Indeed, upward mobility in the underground economy of the street-dealing world requires a systematic and effective use of violence against one's colleagues, one's neighbors, and, to a certain extent, against one's self.

In seeking to explain the links between the conditions of segregation, poverty, the oppositional culture of the inner city ghettos and black crime, Alford Young (2004) investigated the life-worlds and social conditions of a group of young black men all aged 20 to 25, living in a community within the black ghetto of the Near West Side of Chicago. There, "People . . . live in a virtually all black, low income social environment" (p. 99). For most of the men in the group, "daily life consists of little more than being in the streets and interacting with others in public space" (p. 39). Not being required to manage daily commitments meant that there was no necessity to plan or organize the day, leading to "an entirely different way of thinking about time" (p. 42). Thus, for these men, work was an abstract concept, "because they knew of few men in their age group who went to work everyday" (p. 53). Despite this, all the men adhered to the traditional individualism and moralism associated with the attainment of the American Dream, and none saw structural factors as a constraint to individual effort and initiative (p. 141).[4] In this ghetto, like the Barrio of Spanish Harlem, New York City, men seeking work may face the constraint that street culture radically contradicts the obedient interactions that are expected of low-level employees in offices of service providers, especially when contrasted with the comfortable masculinity of the factory floor (p. 142).

Unemployment in the black ghetto community is explained by declining industries. For example, the city of Chicago lost 38 percent of its factories between 1967 and 1982. Jobs in manufacturing declined from 390,000 to 172,000 between 1958 and 1982 (Young 2004: 52). Overall, between 1970 and 1987 Chicago lost nearly 250,000 jobs in manufacturing. This was offset to an extent by an upsurge in service sector employment which increased from 620,000 jobs in 1970 to 1.12 million by 1987, but those jobs were not necessarily high paying (p. 53). For the black ghetto community, however, the issue was the decrease in employment in manufacturing and manual skill jobs which they considered within their capabilities and actively sought.

In the ghetto, concerns about personal safety dominate and no young black man can be sure he will complete the day unharmed or without causing harm to another himself. The possibility of random and unpredictable violence is always present and has to be countered by minding one's own business and looking out for oneself on the streets (Young 2004: 44). Gang membership becomes therefore a form of security that enables daily interactions. Violence is an ever-present topic of discussion, and men express their apprehensions and fears in the same way that others in employment discuss their work (p. 50). In his research in the Barrio of New York among the Puerto Rican crack cocaine sellers, Bourgois notes that most of the inhabitants of the Barrio are involved in illegal enterprises and in lifestyles encompassing violence and "internalized rage" (Bourgois 1995: 9).

youth, crime and justice

In their personal interactions with others, over half of the group studied by Young (2004) did not know or have any regular interaction with any person who had a college degree, and over 60 percent knew no more than two others in white-collar employment. Less than one-third of the group experienced regular social contact with persons who were not black and their highest level of exposure and interaction was with unemployed blacks who had not completed high school (p. 56). An absence of interracial and interclass exposure was normative for this community. Gaining upward mobility from those with whom they associated was an unlikely event, and they knew few persons who had advanced their lives and moved up the class or social scale. Daily discourse was described as:

> "There aint nothing we talk about like everyday. We just, we just be hanging out, just kicking it. We talk about females, or if a tournament going on we'll talk about the tournament or something like that, basketball, that's all."
>
> (Young 2004: 56)

Over half of the group had been involved in crime, mostly petty thieving and "hustling" or in selling drugs, the latter bringing an even higher probability of violence into their lives. Almost the entire group of 26 men had been taken to the local police precinct and for them detention by law enforcement was a common occurrence. Often they were just detained and all were aware that a criminal conviction would constitute a severe constraint to employment (Young 2004: 95). Incarceration was worse than living on the Near West Side, as one man who was employed in a factory and therefore much better off than the others explained:

> "Man, me getting out [of prison], you know, in one full piece, I still got my eyes. A lot of people when I was there, you see their eyes, its one eye you know. Motherfuckers done try to tear their eye out of their head. I've seen that. You knows, fingers, limbs, you know."
>
> (Young 2004: 97)

Poverty, and its acceleration, remains a core and acute structural issue in the black inner city ghettos. As Wilson (1987: 55) explains:

> It is the growth of the high- and extreme-poverty areas that epitomizes the social transformation of the inner city, a transformation that represents a change in the class structure in many inner city neighborhoods as the nonpoor black middle and working classes tend no longer to reside in these neighborhoods, thereby increasing the proportion of truly disadvantaged individuals and families.

Increasing poverty is instanced by a study examining the concentration of poverty in 239 metropolitan areas. Researchers found that while a quarter of poor blacks in the 239 areas resided in high poverty neighborhoods in 1970, by 1990 the figure had increased to one-third (Jargowsky 1997). This compares to 2.9 percent of poor whites in 1970 increasing to 6.3 percent in 1990 (p. 37). Concentrated disadvantage, characterized by highly disadvantaged neighborhoods experiencing high rates of poverty, unemployment and family disruption, has been shown to lead to more criminal activity. In comparing highly impoverished to extremely impoverished neighborhoods, while property crime rates were not significantly different, the patterns for violent crime showed a marked increase in the case of extremely impoverished neighborhoods (Wilson 1987). Krivo and Peterson conclude that "Wilson is correct in arguing that extreme disadvantage provides a distinctly different structural context for crime" (1996: 631).

There is no doubt that segregation in inner cities, the loss of employment due to deindustrialization, the growth of the service economy, and poverty in black inner city ghettos has brought about an increase in youth violence, especially in homicide involving guns, by young black men (see Chapter 7). As a result of media representations of the black underclass, the juvenile court has come to be seen as a site for sanctioning violent minority youth. At the same time, the discourse of youth violence has promoted the notion of the juvenile "superpredator" (see Chapter 7), and punitive penal policies have challenged the notion that juveniles are to receive treatment and not punishment, as if they were already adults.

Bias and the operation of the juvenile justice system

Minority youth are overrepresented in the juvenile justice system. Whether or not this disproportionality reflects discriminatory decision making within the justice system is open to argument. Despite significant research over decades there is still no definitive answer to the question: Why do minority youth enter and process through the juvenile justice system at such disproportionate rates? Two explanations have been suggested: "differential offending" and "differential treatment" (Bishop 2005). The former argues that minority overrepresentation is attributable to race differences in the incidence, seriousness and persistence of delinquency, and the latter contends that overrepresentation can be located in inequalities and unfairness, both deliberate and unintended, within the juvenile justice system (p. 23). Two terms are commonly employed in discussing this topic: *disparity* and *discrimination*. *Disparity* denotes between-group differences in outcomes due perhaps to differences in offending, the differential impact of laws and policies, or from racism within the system. An example of disparity due to the differential impact of laws and policies is the "War on Drugs" where, by the early 1990s, arrest rates for blacks were four to five times higher than for whites (Miller 1996: 85) because the police targeted low-level dealers in minority neighborhoods. *Discrimination* describes a situation where extra-legal or illegitimate factors cause disparate outcomes (Bishop 2005: 24, 25).

There is no doubt that policies and practices that are claimed to be race neutral can in practice produce discriminatory outcomes. The question is: How does this come about? An example may be seen in how decisions are made by the juvenile court. The juvenile court, in exercising its dual functions of social control and social welfare, calls for an examination of the family and lifestyle circumstances of a youth in order to design individualized measures of treatment. Thus, variables like family supervision, performance at school and unemployment within the family, inform the court's dispositions. These factors tend to be correlated with race, and inevitably, therefore, more black youth will be likely to enter the juvenile justice system and receive harsher dispositions (Bishop 2005: 64). A similar argument applies to resources, where minority families will have less capacity to provide support to a child in contact with the law because they have reduced resources compared to most whites. Thus, a clear link exists between structural factors like living conditions, employment and poverty, and race disparities in juvenile justice processing. It is also easy to understand how racial stereotyping can provide a short cut to assessing a black youth when there is insufficient information about an offender's dangerousness or likely response to treatment. The end result is that stereotypes are created and maintained that typically describe blacks as more criminogenic and more dangerous than whites in similar situations (pp. 64, 65).

Identifying and locating bias in decision making in the juvenile justice system necessitates a full understanding of the relevant decision points and the conditions and factors that influence decisions. Comprehending how decisions are arrived at may in turn assist in providing explanations for bias and discrimination within the system. While the states do have diverse justice systems, there are nevertheless common features and shared decision points as an alleged delinquent moves through the system. Overall, the police refer 85 percent of all delinquents to the juvenile court for allegations of delinquency (Butts et al. 1995). Most police referrals are for misdemeanor charges, with about one-third for property offenses and only about 8 percent for violent crimes (Feld 1999: 114).

The police, parents, school or probation officers refer cases to the local prosecuting authority or to the juvenile court intake unit and thus initiate the system. Prosecutors or intake staff will typically divert almost half of all refer-rals informally, using procedures such as dismissal, warning, cautioning or counseling, or referral to another agency (Feld 1999: 115, 116). The next stage is that prosecutors or intake staff will file a delinquency petition which puts the case formally before the juvenile court. Between one-fifth and one-quarter of all juveniles are held in secure detention by the court for some period between referral of their case to intake staff and final disposition (Butts et al. 1995).

A youth appears for a first hearing before the court and when a petition has been filed the court will typically allocate a lawyer. The youth may admit to or deny the allegations at the first hearing, called the arraignment. In many cases an admission of guilt is made and the court proceeds to enter a disposition without appointing defense counsel for the youth. When a lawyer has not been assigned to the case, an appointed public defender will confer with the youth before an admission or denial of the allegations is made. Sometimes, but rarely, a youth may be represented by a private lawyer (Feld 1999). In common with the adult system, most cases are resolved without a trial. The system allows prosecutors, probation staff and the court judge to informally determine the outcome of most cases at the pre-trial stage or after negotiations with the youth's lawyer (Feld 1999: 116). About 2 percent of youth who have been formally charged are transferred to adult court. Most youth are sentenced to probation by the juvenile court (53%), while 29 percent are placed in residential homes or juvenile institutions (Butts et al. 1995: 9).

Police arrests

What disparities arise in police arrests? For persons under 18, a total of 1,906,600 arrests were made in the U.S. in 2009, 17 percent lower than in 2000 (Puzzanchera and Adams 2011: 4). Arrests for violent crime were as follows:

> 47% involved white youth, 51% involved black youth, 1% involved Asian youth, and 1% involved American Indian youth. For property crime arrests, the proportions were 64% white youth, 33% black youth, 2% Asian youth, and 1% American Indian youth.
>
> (Puzzanchera and Adams 2011: 6)

The proportion of black arrests far exceeds the proportion of black youth in the population (about 16 percent). Black youth are disproportionately arrested for offenses of violence. In 1999, blacks comprised 49 percent of persons arrested for murder and manslaughter compared to 47 percent for whites. Thus, juvenile policies that "get tough" on violent juvenile offenders are sure to have a disproportionate effect on minority youth. Between 1965 and 1992 black youth were arrested for violent crimes at a rate of about five times greater than that of white youth and, in the case of homicide, at a rate of more than seven times that of white youth (Maguire and Pastore 1994: 447). Beginning in 1986, when youth homicide rates began to sharply increase, arrests of black and white youth began to diverge so that between 1986 and 1993 arrests of white youth for homicide increased about 40 percent while those of black youth increased 278 percent (Sickmund et al. 1997: 13). The sharp increase in homicide rates is accounted for by the use of firearms by youth. Almost all of that firearm use occurred within the black population located in the inner cities and has been attributed to the emergence of the crack cocaine industry (Blumstein 1995). Within cities, homicide rates are highest in the inner city neighborhoods populated by poor blacks (Feld 1999: 206).

How do minorities become disproportionately of interest to the police? The police exercise considerable discretion in deciding whether or not to arrest youth and seldom keep records of encounters that do not result in arrest. Thus, accountability for what might be considered discriminatory acts is lacking, even though the police are the principal gatekeepers of the juvenile justice system. Importantly, any bias exercised by the police is likely to be amplified through the system at later stages (Bishop 2005). In terms of operational activity, studies have shown that patrols are dispropor- tionately deployed in areas with the highest number of service calls and the highest reported crime rates. Naturally, these tend to be areas populated by minorities (Bishop 2005: 39). The overall effect is to increase surveillance over minorities, especially youth, resulting in likely increases in arrest. In addition, subjecting minority neighborhoods to more intensive surveillance may well antagonize black youth who perceive police activity as harassment. This in turn can lead to additional conflict and more arrests (p. 63). In a focus group conducted by Conley (1994), an incarcerated black youth explained the reaction of black youth to heavy police surveillance as:

"Cops is more scared of Blacks. Because we just don't be caring, you know. The cops are everywhere. They've been messing with you so long, it's like, you know, fuck it, I don't care anymore."

. . .

"They [the police] going to be riding down the street real slow and if they know, they will call your name out on the loud speaker – that's messing with you."

(Conley 1994: 141)

The same effect can be observed where the police institute "crackdowns" and "sweeps" targeted at high crime areas populated by minorities.

Generally, observational studies show that the police concentrate their focus on minority ghettos, on persons with a lower socio-economic status, and are more likely to initiate contacts in racially mixed and minority neighborhoods and to stop and question minorities, especially minority youth, particularly where their demeanor renders them "potential troublemakers" in the view of law enforcement (see, e.g., Conley 1994; Piliavin and Briar 1964; Smith 1986 quoted in Bishop 2005: 40–42). If taken into custody, studies show that blacks are more likely to be referred for formal processing through the juvenile justice system than whites in the same situation (see, e.g., Bell and Lang 1985; Kurtz et al. 1993 quoted in Bishop 2005: 44). Generally, because minority populated areas have the highest crime rates they will be exposed to higher levels of police activity, resulting in more police arrests. In these "dangerous" areas, stereotypes based on class and race prevail and even encourage the police to adopt a more aggressive approach (Bishop 2005: 45).

Intake

Probation officers or caseworkers usually conduct this part of the process. They review police reports, consider any prior offenses, and interview youth to decide on detention and formal processing. Research studies indicate that first offenders and those accused of minor offenses are dealt with informally and diverted out of the system, but those same studies show racial disparities in outcomes (see, e.g., Dean et al. 1996; Leiber 1994; Leiber and Jamieson 1995; Leiber and Stairs 1999 quoted in Bishop 2005: 48). Significant practical constraints can operate to disadvantage minority youth when diversion out of the system is being considered. For example, policies in a juvenile court may mandate that when parents cannot be contacted for a face-to-face meeting, a juvenile will not be diverted. It may be difficult for minority parents to meet this requirement because they are less likely to possess a phone, to be able to access transportation easily and to be able to take time off work (Bishop 2005: 48). Stereotyping and applying criteria for diversion that minorities cannot easily satisfy create conditions that operate against minority youth. Thus, single-parent families, perceived inadequate parental supervision, poverty and living in neighborhoods regarded as "bad" may all apply more readily to minority youth. However, court personnel tend to defend such decision making by arguing that this kind of selective processing actually benefits minority youth by enabling them to receive services they could not otherwise afford (Bishop 2005: 50).

Secure detention

The juvenile court exercises wide discretion over whether or not a juvenile will be detained because state statutes authorizing detention typically do not provide any criteria or standards to regulate this decision. The Supreme Court has approved the preventive detention of juveniles who pose a "serious risk" of committing any crime (*Schall v. Martin* 467 U.S. 283[1984]), a much less restrictive standard than that applying to an adult. Many juveniles are detained even though they do not constitute a threat to themselves or to others, and studies show that juvenile courts detain disproportionately greater numbers of minority youth (Feld 1999: 147; Snyder and Sickmund 1995). For example, the proportion of white youth detained between 1985 and 1989 decreased 12.6 percent and the proportion of non-white youth increased 41.5 percent (McGarrell 1993). In the sense that pre-trial detention increases the chance of a post-adjudication sanction (because the court, in detaining the juvenile, has already predicted a greater risk of criminality), this form of detention has a significant impact on the processing of juvenile cases involving minority youth (Feld 1999: 138). Decisions about detention appear to be linked to family background as in intake decisions, so the availability of family supervision is an important factor (Bishop 2005: 52).

Waiver to adult court

Basically, three legislative approaches are employed to send alleged juvenile offenders for trial in the adult court. These are: judicial waiver, offense exclusion and prosecutorial discretion (Feld 1999: 209). The most common is judicial waiver and involves the juvenile court conducting a hearing to determine whether a youth can be treated, or whether he or she constitutes a danger to public safety. Offense exclusion operates to exclude juveniles from the jurisdiction of the juvenile court based on their age and the seriousness of the offense. When the prosecutor is empowered to exercise a discretion to waive the juvenile, that decision is generally not reviewable (p. 210). Several studies have shown that in the case of judicial waiver, judges tend to render arbitrary and discriminatory decisions (p. 216). For example, one study in Philadelphia reported that judges more readily waived black youth with white victims than youth exhibiting other victim offender racial patterns (p. 217). An analysis of judicial waivers in four states found:

■ Blacks were more likely to be waived to adult court than whites for offenses of violence, or involving property or drugs.

- In Pennsylvania, black youth were more than twice as likely to have their case waived than whites.
- For blacks, Arizona had waiver rates that were 55 times those of California.

(U.S. General Accounting Office 1995: 59)

Laws that target violent offenses for likely judicial waiver or for offense exclusion will indirectly identify larger proportions of black youth than white youth, and expose black youth to the more severe adult sanctions.

Legal representation

In the case of *In re Gault* (387 U.S. 1 [1967]) the United States Supreme Court stated that a juvenile had a right to be represented by counsel in delinquency adjudication proceedings when the consequences were that the juvenile could be committed to a state institution. Studies have shown that between 15 and 95 percent of juveniles are legally represented, so the right to counsel has not been fully implemented (see, e.g., Aday 1986; Clark and Koch 1980 quoted in Guevara et al. 2004: 345). In practice, lawyers paid out of public funds tend to be overworked and inexperienced and to commonly represent black youth. Black juveniles generally possess significantly fewer resources than whites and are usually unable to hire a private attorney who may be more experienced and provide proper representation (Guevara et al. 2004: 345). Studies show that juveniles who are represented by private attorneys receive better outcomes than those represented by public defenders (see, e.g., Carrington and Moyer 1990; Clark and Koch 1980 quoted in Guevara et al. 2004: 345).

Adjudication

At the point of adjudication in the process, the court decides whether to dismiss a case or to make a finding of delinquency. Here, unlike other decision points, studies show that whites are considerably more likely than minority youth to be adjudicated delinquent. One explanation for this may be that after earlier stages in the process minority cases may in fact be weaker than whites and at this stage the court acts not so much on family background evidence as on evidence relevant to proof of the offense (Bishop 2005: 53).

Juvenile court dispositions

Judges considering an appropriate disposition for youth tend to depend on predisposition reports prepared by probation officers. A range of relevant issues will be discussed in the report including facts relevant to punishment, prior record and treatment issues such as alcohol and drug use (Bishop 2005: 53, 54).

A larger proportion of minority juveniles live in urban jurisdictions than do white juveniles. When this is linked to the tendency of urban juvenile courts to be more process oriented and formal, the outcome is more severe sentencing for juveniles, including minorities, coming before these urban courts (Feld 1999: 134, 135). Studies have also shown that due to the greater availability of detention facilities in urban areas, youths held in pre-trial detention tend to receive more severe sentences than those who are left at liberty (p. 265). Thus, the urban association between minorities and crime puts them at risk of more severe sentencing.

Studies also reveal that the primary variables in sentencing decisions are the current offense and the prior record of a juvenile (Feld 1999: 267). After controlling for these factors research reveals that there is discrimination based on race in disposition decisions (Bishop 2005: 54; Feld 1999: 268). Minority youth are more likely to be detained than whites in similar situations, and offense type may also result in a more severe sentence, for example, where the offense involves drugs. The importance of the delinquent's family has also been revealed in interviews with court officials in three eastern communities (Bishop 2005: 55). All officials interviewed believed the family situation should be considered at disposition and 87 percent said bias existed against blacks from dysfunctional families living in lower class neighborhoods. This meant that those living in such neighborhoods were more likely to be removed from their homes. While officials may well believe that removing such youth from their homes is more likely to benefit them, this kind of disposition cannot of course impact upon the structural conditions that cause or contribute to the impoverishment of a neighborhood, such as long-term unemployment and underemployment. Other explanations of bias are associated with conflict theory and contend that minority youth from inner city ghettos are viewed as especially threatening and therefore as requiring confinement (pp. 55, 56).

When researchers examined predisposition reports of probation officers in three counties in a western state they discovered significant differences in the assessments of the cause of offending as between black and white delinquents (Bridges and Steen 1998). Among the black youth, offending was more frequently linked to character defects, such as lack of remorse and failure to accept responsibility for acts, than for whites. In contrast, when assessing white offenders, external factors such as family issues, peer delinquency and performance at school were stressed, suggesting that they were less likely to offend. Probation officers therefore applied racial stereotypes and recommended more lenient sentences for whites than for blacks (Bridges and Steen 1998).

In 1988 the *Juvenile Justice and Delinquency Prevention Act* was amended to create the concept of disproportionate minority confinement (DMC), explained as arising where the proportion of juveniles detained who are members of minority groups exceeds the proportion of such groups represented in the general population. In 1992, the OJJDP applied the DMC initiative requiring that states ensure equitable treatment for juveniles on the basis of factors that include race, and that they assess the reasons for DMC in juvenile facilities and develop strategies to correct it (Penn 2006: 49). A review of the states reporting on DMC found that minorities were overrepresented in every state and at all decision points. There was a variance between states as to the greatest overrepresentation at particular decision points. Minority overrepresentation therefore existed across the entire country, and in many cases was greater in states with small minority populations (Leiber 2006: 148, 149). Police decision making was also found to be a contributor to minority overrepresentation, including length of time held at the police station, use of secured holding place and placement in detention. Interviews with justice personnel revealed racial stereotyping and convictions about middle-class values that impacted case processing, including beliefs about crime, the family and respect for authority. These values were translated into the operational ideology of the court. Specifically, blacks were considered to be more criminal, to be residing with a single parent who could not provide adequate supervision, and to lack respect for law and authority as judged by eye contact, dress and demeanor (pp. 151, 152).

Racial amplification

Research has shown that decisions at different stages in the juvenile justice process amplify racial disparities affecting minority youth as they proceed through the system with the outcome that they receive more severe dispositions than do white youth. Consequently, it is crucial in looking at disproportionate minority representation to see the system as a series of decision points that produce an outcome in the aggregate and to not focus only on the final decision made at the stage of disposition (Feld 1999: 268). Accordingly, for example, increases in referral rates of black youth in 17 states resulted in corresponding increases in detention and residential placement (McGarrell 1993).

Qualitative research has revealed two factors that explain the impact of race on dispositions. When determining the appropriate individualized disposition, the court may have regard to the factors of "parental sponsorship" and "residential space availability" (Feld 1999: 271). The capacity of parents to provide supervision influences processing decisions. For example, in a single-parent home – and black households predominate in having only one parent – the court is obviously less likely to find the expected degree of supervision. Juvenile court personnel in one qualitative study informed researchers that "delinquent youth from single parent families and those from families incapable of (or perceived to be incapable of) providing good parental supervision are more likely to be referred to court and placed under state control" (Bishop and Frazier 1996: 409). The relative importance of family support is difficult to exaggerate. A delinquency intake supervisor explained its effect as follows:

> "Our manual told us to interview the child and the parent prior to making a recommendation to the state's attorney. We are less able to reach poor and minority clients. They are less responsive to attempts to reach them. They don't show. They don't have transportation. Then they are more likely to be recommended for formal processing. Without access to a client's family, the less severe options are closed. Once it gets to court, the case is likely to be adjudicated because it got there. It's a self-fulfilling prophecy."
>
> (Bishop and Frazier 1996: 407–408)

It seems that black youth will suffer a disadvantage even where both parents live in the home because parental sponsorship will still be found to be inadequate (DeJong and Jackson 1998: 501).

The term "residential space availability" relates to the capacity and willingness of parents to afford the cost of private treatment and this can affect case processing and dispositions. As Bishop and Frazier (1996: 408) explain,

> Youths from affluent families may take advantage of these [private] treatment options and avoid formal processing. Minority youths who are less affluent can only obtain comparable services by being adjudicated delinquent and then committed to residential facilities.

Thus, if parents possess the wherewithal they can in effect buy their child out of the juvenile justice system. As one Florida juvenile judge observed:

> "Minorities and low income kids get more [juvenile justice system] resources. If parents can afford [an expensive private treatment facility], the child gets probation. If not, he gets committed. Income is significant

in that a lot of early interventions are directed to middle income groups. If a child needs constructive activity, a middle class family can afford it. Maybe there is institutional bias."

(Bishop and Frazier 1996: 408–409)

There is much still to be revealed and explained about disproportionate minority representation in the juvenile justice system. The factors that influence assessments and decisions made within the system have barely been explored, and qualitative research studies that focus on the dynamics of decision making and investigate attitudinal issues, especially the prevalence of stereotyping, are essential. As well, attention needs to be paid to the effect of structural factors and structural inequalities as well as the links between those factors and the responses of the juvenile justice system (Bishop 2005: 68). For example, a recent study relates social and economic conditions to black and white youth homicide arrest rates from 1967 to 1998 (Messner et al. 2001). Researchers found that increases in child poverty were linked to arrest rates for homicide for juveniles, both black and white, in that homicide rates rose during periods of increased child poverty (Messner et al. 2001).

Minorities and gangs

Gangs have functioned in Europe since the 15th century and have been an element in American youth culture since the 19th century (McShane and Williams 2006). In the U.S., gangs have almost always been linked to groups of new immigrants and have commonly been constituted as a means of self -protection, often drawn from other similar groups. Gangs have always been linked to minorities, the marginalized, the poor and the powerless (p. 112). As urbanization and industrialization created city neighborhoods, often poor and disorganized, gangs developed when youth were drawn into groups reflective of a particular neighborhood. Hence, the early immigrant communities of Poles, Irish and Italians, for example, fashioned gangs in ethnic neighborhoods, and these were later followed by African American, Chicano and Puerto Rican gangs born in the ghettos of the inner cities. The decline of the inner city economy and the replacement of full employment with welfare and the illicit economy have impacted black, Chicano and Puerto Rican communities and gangs. As Jackson puts it, linking economic change and the growth of gangs:

> [D]emographic and economic transition seem to have some influence on crime and the presence of youth gangs in U.S. cities, even in the presence of controls for possibly competing explanations; opportunity

factors related to the ease and profit of crime, age structure, racial and income heterogeneity, and economic and relative deprivation.

(Jackson 1991: 393)

Similarly, Klein notes:

Uneducated, underemployed young males turn to the illegal economies enhanced by gang membership, including selling drugs in some instances. Older males who in earlier decades would have "matured" into more steady jobs and family roles hang on to the gang structure by default.

(Klein 1995: 196–197)

Similar research into the involvement of American Indian youth in gangs has revealed that structural conditions such as poverty, lack of employment, discrimination and the diminution of cultural identity make gangs an attractive option for American Indian youth (Donnermeyer et al. 1996: 167). In a study of youth gangs in Hawaii comprising Hawaiians, Samoans and Filipinos, researchers found that gangs offered a social outlet to youth living in marginalized and chaotic neighborhoods which suffered from high rates of crime, boredom and a lack of resources (Joe and Chesney-Lind 1999). Family life in those communities was affected by severe financial constraints that led to tension and often violence. The gang provided "a safe refuge and a surrogate family" (p. 220). In the case of African American gangs, it has been suggested that these youth are drawn into gangs to gain a sense of belonging, identity, power, security and discipline (Shelden et al. 2004: 54).

Minority youth in inner city high crime areas are often the targets of police surveillance and anti-gang laws because, where gangs exist, law enforcement perceives an association with violence, robbery, drug dealing and lower level antisocial activity such as graffiti (McShane and Williams 2006: 116). Street gangs are located in low-income ethnic minority neighborhoods emerging from situations of urban neglect, social isolation and economic dislocation. Members of street gangs are socialized in street culture and learn how to secure protection, loyalty and adaptation to the routines provided by the gang. The gang dominates for youth who lead unstructured lives because other institutions which might supply it have become fragmented and rendered largely ineffective (Vigil and Yun 2002: 165). Generally, the policy approach to gang activity has been to design special anti-gang laws and to adopt a punitive strategy. Consequently, the social and structural problems associated with the minority neighborhoods where youth form gangs have been largely ignored, and issues of identity, protection and status that give rise to gangs have not been addressed in any meaningful manner (McShane and Williams 2006: 122).

American Indians and Alaskan Natives

When Europeans came to what is now the U.S., there were about 10 to 12 million indigenous people living on the land, divided into autonomous nations (Ross 1998: 11). In April 2000, American Indians and Alaskan Natives accounted for 4.1 million or 1.5 percent of the population of the U.S. (Perry 2004: 1). Some states have significant populations of indigenous peoples; for example, Alaska, 15.6 percent, New Mexico, 9.5 percent, Oklahoma, 7.9 percent, Montana, 6.5 percent and Arizona 5 percent (U.S. Census Bureau 2006). As at 2006, there were 562 federally recognized Native American nations and Alaskan Native villages and about another 150 tribal entities that lack federal recognition (Nielsen and Robyn 2009: 74).

Only brief histories of these indigenous groups are possible here. North America experienced three general stages of American Indian and European relations. During the first stage, from initial contact until the end of the Revolutionary War, both groups cohabited more or less cooperatively. The Europeans were dependent on indigenous peoples for food, shelter, trade links and knowledge of the land and its resources (Miller 1989). The second stage comprised a period of coercion and force by the European colonists and lasted until World War II. This period was characterized by military expeditions against American Indians, the spread of disease among them, and general social dislocation in terms of their ways of life and cultures. The population suffered a huge loss, reaching a low point of about 237,000 by 1990 (Shoemaker 1999: 3). Also during this period missionaries and reformers attempted to induce indigenous peoples to adapt to European ways and values. Alcohol was traded or given to tribes and the reservation system applied so that they were located on unproductive land. Their children were taken and placed in boarding-schools so that they would acculturate, and Indian agents were empowered to make numerous decisions affecting their daily lives. American Indians were perceived as naked savages or naïve children, and social Darwinist discourses promoted notions of biological and intellectual inferiority.

During the third stage, up until today, relations between indigenous peoples and the dominant culture have been characterized by confrontation over land and the environment, over political and social rights and over the maintenance of cultural traditions and practices (Shoemaker 1999). Marginalization and social disorganization have led to states of poverty for many American Indian peoples with about 32 percent of Native American children under 18 living in poverty compared to 11 percent of white non-Latino children (Ogunwole 2006: 16). Poor levels of education and unemployment have endured along with high rates of suicide, domestic violence and alcohol abuse (Nielsen and Robyn 2009: 75–76). Between 1990 and 2001 the suicide rate for American Indian juveniles (59.5) was almost twice the non-Hispanic rate and three times the rate of other racial or ethnic groups (Snyder and Sickmund 2006: 27).

In 2007, American Indian youth and Alaskan Native youth accounted for only 1 percent of the U.S. juvenile population, and only 1 percent of delinquency cases handled in 2007 involved American Indian youth (Knoll and Sickmund 2010: 2). In addition, American Indian youth made up only a very small proportion of cases across all offense categories with the highest rate in property offenses (p. 2). The single most significant category for American Indian youth is alcohol-related arrests. In 2001 the arrest rate for alcohol violations – driving under the influence (DUI), liquor law violations and drunkenness – was double the national rate (Perry 2004: 17). American Indian youth aged 17 or under had an alcohol violation arrest rate of 681 compared to 362 for youth of all races (p. 17). For Alaska, data show that in 2009, 30 percent of all charges brought against juveniles involved Alaskan Native juveniles (State of Alaska 2009), even though Alaskan Natives make up about 23 percent of all Alaskan youth in the 10- to 17-year-old population group (Schafer et al. 1997: 10).

In a report on the disproportionate representation of minorities in the juvenile justice system in Alaska, Schafer and others (1997) found that minority youth were disproportionately referred to the juvenile justice system and that race was significantly associated with at least some post-referral decisions. As compared to white youth, referrals associated with minority youth were more likely to result in a petition to the court for assault, burglary, theft and drug use. In virtually every offense category where the intake decision resulted in a petition to court, the mean number of prior referrals was higher for minority than for white youth. In relation to alcohol, the researchers concluded that "the extraordinary number of referrals of Natives for possession/consumption of alcohol suggests that referring agencies view this behavior differently for Native youth than for white or black youth" (Schafer et al. 1997: 22). During the period 1992 to 1995 Alaskan Natives made up 55 percent of all referrals for possession or consumption of alcohol. Schafer et al. note that "the referral data for minor consuming cannot be assumed to reflect behavior patterns among Alaska's young people. . . . Referrals for this offense probably reflect local perceptions and local concerns" (1997: 10).

In 2001, slightly fewer than 14 percent of American Indians arrested for violent offenses were under the age of 18, a rate similar to that of all violent crime arrestees (15%) (Perry 2004: 16). For violent crimes other than murder, American Indians aged 17 or under were less likely to be arrested than were youth of all races (p. 16). Ten of the 70 jails located in tribal areas are designated as juvenile facilities and on June 28, 2002, juvenile facilities were supervising 180 juveniles being held for the Federal Bureau of Prisons (p. 27). The 10 facilities had a total capacity of

341 juveniles and so were operating at 54 percent of capacity on June 28, 2002 (p. 27).

As noted above, in relation to American Indian youth, disproportionate representation in the juvenile justice system is associated with the use of alcohol. Historically, European traders introduced indigenous peoples to alcohol and, as Axtell puts it, "Having, as with the mirror, no counterpart to alcohol in their culture, the Indians had to fashion their own rules for its use, but too often fell prey to its power" (Axtell 2001: 136). In their analysis of indigenous alcohol use in Australia, New Zealand and Canada, Saggers and Gray note that alcohol issues are linked to colonial histories and that indigenous stereotypes such as that of "the drunken Indian" are refuted by the complexity of indigenous drinking patterns, including the fact that many drink moderately and that rates of abstention from alcohol are higher among indigenous peoples (Saggers and Gray 1998: 13). Drinking patterns and forms are fashioned by the social and cultural context, as explained by Mandelbaum (1965: 28):

> Alcohol is a cultural artifact; the form and meanings of drinking alcoholic beverages are culturally defined. . . . The form is usually quite explicitly stipulated, including the kind of drink that can be used, the amount and rate of intake, the time and place of drinking, the accompanying ritual, the sex and age of the drinker, the roles involved in drinking, and the role behavior proper to drinking.
>
> (Mandelbaum 1965: 28)

The notion that indigenous peoples are biologically inferior and therefore unable to drink alcohol in the same way as Europeans is derived from ideas of European superiority associated with social Darwinism. Studies have shown, however, that there is no firm evidence that ethnicity is a determinant of alcohol use or consumption, although clearly there are individual biochemical and physiological factors that influence individual responses to alcohol (Saggers and Gray 1998: 70). Similarly, the supposed genetic predisposition to alcohol use remains unproved, and researchers have suggested that explanations for alcohol dependence among non-indigenous peoples cannot be applied to indigenous peoples (Levy and Kunitz 1974). For example, heavy drinkers among indigenous populations are able to control or even abstain from drinking with little difficulty in a way that non-indigenous peoples are not. Researching this issue among the Navajo, Levy and Kunitz report that:

> [M]ost of the individuals in this study who did become aware that alcohol consumption is more costly than it is worth were apparently able to stop drinking with little difficulty. . . . This indicated to us that

excessive drinking amongst most Navajos does not originate in the same pathological motives as it does among Anglo alcoholics. The behaviors are labeled the same because they look the same, and often produce the similar end results.

(Levy and Kunitz 1974: 193)

After reviewing the explanations put forward for indigenous excessive alcohol use, Saggers and Gray conclude that it may be regarded as having many distinct causes but that the suggested reasons for drinking are themselves "a function of relationships between indigenous and non-indigenous societies within the broader web of political and economic relationships" (1998: 88).

Comparative racial disparities

As Michael Tonry points out, it is difficult to take a comparative view of racial disparities in other countries because many states do not maintain official records of race or ethnicity, usually for ethical reasons, especially when such data can create or support stereotypes that are damaging to minority groups (Tonry 1997: 5). Nevertheless, those countries where data are collected reveal that racial disparities are not unique to the U.S. For example, England experiences a 7:1 Afro-Caribbean/white difference in stopping and searching, 3.5:1 in likelihood of arrest and 6:1 in likelihood of imprisonment (Muncie 2009: 295). In Canada, in 1986, the native non-native difference was 16:1, and in Australia, in 1993, the Aborigine/non-Aborigine difference was 12:1 (Tonry 1997: 6).

According to Tonry, despite the absence of detailed data, some findings are so definitive among states that they are generalizable. Thus, "In every country, crime and incarceration rates for members of some minority groups greatly exceed those for the majority population" (Tonry 1997: 12). For example, in the Netherlands, the greatest disparities are experienced by immigrants from Morocco and Surinam, and in Sweden, the greatest disproportionality in arrests affects immigrants from Arab states, South America and Eastern Europe. In France, the highest rates of imprisonment affect people from Algeria, Morocco and Tunisia (p. 12). As noted above in relation to disparities affecting blacks in the U.S., in other countries "Minority groups characterized by high crime and imprisonment rates are also characterized by various indicators of social and economic disadvantage" (p. 13). However, there are exceptions to this statement. In England, immigrants from Asia, while disadvantaged, have lower imprisonment rates than the equally disadvantaged Afro-Caribbeans (p. 13). In the Netherlands, Turks and Moroccans both arrived in the country at about the same time and both are comparatively less well-off than the Dutch, but the imprisonment and crime rates for Turks are similar to those of the Dutch, while the rates for Moroccans are far higher (p. 14). These exceptions remain unexplained.

Additional disparities in England include the fact that: members of the black and minority ethnic community, if arrested, are less likely to be cautioned than whites and more likely to be prosecuted; Afro-Caribbeans are more likely to be charged with indictable-only offenses; are more likely to be denied bail; and, if found guilty, are more likely to be given a custodial sentence and for longer terms than whites; and are less likely to be granted probation (Muncie 2009: 295). A Research Report on Differential Treatment in the Youth Justice System in England compiled for the Equality and Human Rights Commission in 2010 found:

> [S]ome evidence that at some stages of the youth justice system there may be discrimination against ethnic minorities, in that differences between ethnic groups could not be accounted for by features of the offence or criminal history of the suspects or defendants.
>
> Taking offence and criminal history into account, mixed race offenders and suspects were more likely than whites to be prosecuted than to be reprimanded or warned.
>
> Black and mixed race defendants were also more likely to be remanded in custody than white defendants.
>
> At court, black defendants had a higher chance of being acquitted than whites. At the sentencing stage, mixed race teenagers were more likely than others to be given a community sentence rather than a (less serious) first-tier penalty such as referral orders and fines.
>
> The use of custody appears not to differ between ethnic groups, after taking all relevant factors into account – although those who are remanded in custody are more likely to get a custodial sentence, and black defendants are, as discussed, more likely to be remanded. In general, differences between areas in the way in which they treated suspects and defendants – regardless of ethnicity – were greater than differences between ethnic groups in the treatment they received.
>
> (May et al. 2010: 10–13)

May et al. (2010) differentiate reactive and proactive policing. The former relates to reports to police by victims and witnesses and the latter to reports to police uncovering offenses in the course of their duties. The researchers found that overall, reactive policing accounts for a larger flow of youth into the juvenile justice system than proactive policing with two out of three arrests being the result of reactive activity (p. 12). However, reactive policing still accounts for a substantial flow of cases and this kind of policing relies heavily on police discretion. The researchers note distinct differences in policing styles in the geographic areas under study. One style of interaction with the public could be characterized as professionalized "rule of law" and the other as adversarial. In the latter, the public brought their own stereotypes and prejudices to the interaction, reflecting tensions over a period of time between those sections of the community and the police (pp. 12–13). The authors noted that the professionalized "rule of law" style of policing was obviously to be preferred to the adversarial model and that:

> Those officers who pursued adversarial tactics regarded these as justified, in that they targeted young people who they judged to be involved in offending. In making this assessment they tended not to take account of the damage done to police/community relations in persistently targeting youth from minority groups who saw themselves as unfairly over-policed.
>
> (May et al. 2010: 14)

In Belgium, public concern over youth crime relates to offending by minorities, especially Moroccans and undocumented Eastern Europeans. A study of police arrest data revealed an overrepresentation of youth from these locations and a more sophisticated study showed that the likelihood of being arrested was more than three times higher for Moroccan youth than for boys of Belgian origin (Put and Walgrave 2006: 122). In France, it is estimated that in the age range of 18 to 24 those with a North African father are 9.27 times more likely to be prosecuted than those whose father was born in France (Gendrot 2006: 60). In the Netherlands, data suggest that minorities are significantly overrepresented in the juvenile justice system with more than half of the population of youth detention centers being foreign born. Youth from the Netherlands Antilles show a disproportionate representation in police and youth interactions, followed by Africans (Beljerse and Swaaningen 2006: 71).

Recap

The social construct of "race" in the U.S. and data published for different "races" enables an examination of whether or not racial disparities exist within the various state juvenile justice systems. This kind of analysis is not possible in other countries where law often prohibits keeping records of "race" or ethnicity because a focus on "race" promotes the development of the kinds of stereotypes often associated with young blacks, Puerto Ricans and American

Indians in the United States. Nevertheless, the limited comparative data reveal that racial disparities occur in many juvenile justice systems worldwide.

Research in the U.S. has shown that when decision points within the juvenile justice system are linked to groups of youth, the outcome reveals the existence of racial disparities. Thus, studies show substantial support for the statement that there are direct and indirect race effects in operation within the justice system. As well, disproportionate representation of minorities may be explained by selection bias, and by the nature and volume of offenses committed by minority youth. In the latter case, structural factors associated with the notion of the urban underclass may partly account for the increasing number of minorities coming into contact with the juvenile justice system.

In considering how race impacts juvenile justice for blacks and American Indians and Alaskan Natives, it is crucial to gain an understanding of the social, cultural, political and economic history, and the contemporary circumstances relevant to these categories of persons. In addition, this chapter has contextualized minority juvenile criminality so that it is grounded in the lived experiences, lifestyles and living conditions of those minorities. The discussion in this chapter has revealed how segregation interacts with poverty to create conditions that foster youth criminality. In the black inner city ghettos, lack of income, rudimentary services, loss of employment due to deindustrialization, the growth of the service economy and poverty have brought about an increase in youth violence, especially in relation to homicide using guns.

Despite significant research over decades there is still no definitive answer to the question: Why do minority youth enter and process through the juvenile justice system at such disproportionate rates? Analyzing the various decision points within the system, namely arrest, intake, secure detention, waiver to adult court, legal representation, adjudication and dispositions, illuminates how racial disparities can arise. Research illustrates the importance of seeing the system as a series of decision points that produce an outcome in the aggregate instead of focusing only on the final decision made at the stage of disposition.

Notes

1   Franklin Zimring notes that the issue of minority overrepresentation in the juvenile justice system is but one aspect of a broader pattern revealed throughout law enforcement in the U.S. (Zimring 2005: 174).
2   The poverty rate as a whole fell from 30 percent in 1950 to 17 percent in 1965 and declined to about 11 percent in the mid-1970s. It then began to rise, reaching 14 percent by 1995 (Gilens 1999: 20). In 2008 the U.S. Census declared a poverty

rate of 13.2 percent. By race, the rates for 2008 were 8.6 percent for non-Hispanic Whites, 24.7 percent for blacks and 24.2 percent for American Indian and Alaskan Natives (DeNavas-Walt and Smith 2009: 15).

3 Martin Gilens points out that since the 1960s poverty and race have become closely linked in public discourse so that contemporary images of the poor include "the teenage ghetto gang member" and blacks constitute the minority most associated with poverty and welfare (Gilens 1999: 67, 69).

4 Similarly, the Puerto Rican crack dealers with whom Bourgois associated for more than three years in the Barrio of Spanish Harlem subscribed to the notion that their marginality in the Barrio was the outcome of their own personal failings and not the fault of society (Bourgois 1995: 54).

References

Aday, D.P. 1986. "Court Structure, Defense Attorney Use, and Juvenile Court Decisions." *The Sociological Quarterly* 27(1): 107–119.

Axtell, James. 2001. *Natives and Newcomers: The Cultural Origins of North America*. New York: Oxford University Press.

Beljerse, Jolande uit and Rene van Swaaningen. 2006. "The Netherlands: Penal Welfarism and Risk Management." In John Muncie and Barry Goldson (eds) *Comparative Youth Justice*. London: Sage, pp. 65–79.

Bell, D. and K. Lang. 1985. "The Intake Dispositions of Juvenile Offenders." *Journal of Research in Crime and Delinquency* 22(4): 309–328.

Bishop, Donna M. 2005. "The Role of Race and Ethnicity in Juvenile Justice Processing in Our Children." In Darnell F. Hawkins and Kimberly Kempf-Leonard (eds) *Their Children: Confronting Racial and Ethnic Differences in American Juvenile Justice*. Chicago, IL: The University of Chicago Press, pp. 23–82.

Bishop, Donna M. and Charles S. Frazier. 1996. "Race Effects in Juvenile Justice Decision-Making: Findings of a Statewide Analysis." *Journal of Criminal Law and Criminology* 86: 392–413.

Blumstein, Alfred. 1995. "Youth Violence, Guns and the Illicit Drug Industry." *Journal of Criminal Law and Criminology* 86: 10–36.

Bourgois, Philippe. 1995. *In Search of Respect: Selling Crack in El Barrio*. New York: Cambridge University Press.

Bridges, George S. and Sara Steen. 1998. "Racial Disparities in Official Assessments of Juvenile Offenders: Attributional Stereotypes as Mediating Mechanisms." *American Sociological Review* 63: 554–570.

Butts, Jeffrey A., Howard N. Snyder, Terrence A. Finnegan, Anne L. Aughenbaugh and Rowen S. Poole. 1995. *Juvenile Court Statistics 1994*. Washington D.C.: U.S Department of Justice, Office of Juvenile Justice and Delinquency Prevention.

Carrington, P.J. and S. Moyer. 1990. "The Effect of Defence Counsel on Plea and Outcome in Juvenile Court." *Canadian Journal of Criminology* 32: 621–637.

Cintron, M. 2006. "Latino Delinquency: Defining and Counting the Problem." In E.B. Penn, H.T. Greene and S.L. Gabbidon (eds) *Race and Juvenile Justice*. Durham, NC: Carolina Academic Press, pp. 27–40.

Conley, Darlene J. 1994. "Adding Color to a Black and White Picture: Using Qualitative Data to Explain Racial Disproportionality in the Juvenile Justice System." *Journal of Research in Crime and Delinquency* 31(2): 135–148.

Dean, C.W., J.D. Hirschel and R. Brame. 1996. "Minorities and Juvenile Case Dispositions." *Justice System Journal* 18: 267–285.

DeJong, C. and K. Jackson. 1998. "Putting Race into Context: Race, Juvenile Justice Processing and Urbanization." *Justice Quarterly* 15: 487–504.

DeNavas-Walt, Carmen and Jessica C. Smith. 2009. "Income, Poverty and Health Insurance Coverage in the United States: 2008." Washington, D.C.: U.S. Department of Commerce Economics and Statistics Administration, U.S. Census Bureau.

Donnermeyer, J.F.R., W. Edwards, E.L. Chavez and F. Beauvais. 1996. "The Involvement of American Indian Youth in Gangs." *Free Inquiry in Creative Sociology* 24(2): 167–174.

Feld, Barry C. 1999. *Bad Kids: Race and the Transformation of the Juvenile Court.* New York: Oxford University Press.

Gendrot, Sophie. 2006. "The Politicisation of Youth Justice." In John Muncie and Barry Goldson (eds) *Comparative Youth Justice.* London: Sage, pp. 48–65.

Gilens, Martin. 1999. *Why Americans Hate Welfare: Race, Media, and the Politics of Antipoverty Policy.* Chicago, IL: The University of Chicago Press.

Guevara, Lori, Cassia Spohn and Denise Herz. 2004. "Race, Legal Representation and Juvenile Justice: Issues and Concerns." *Crime and Delinquency* 50: 344–371.

Humes, Karen R., Nicholas A. Jones and Roberto R. Ramirez. 2011. Overview of Race and Hispanic Origin: 2010. *2010 Census Briefs.* Washington, D.C.: U.S. Department of Commerce Economics and Statistics Administration, U.S. Census Bureau.

Jackson, P.G. 1991. "Crime, Youth Gangs and Urban Transition: The Social Dislocations of Postindustrial Economic Development." *Justice Quarterly* 8: 379–398.

Jargowsky, Paul A. 1997. *Poverty and Place: Ghettos, Barrios and the American City.* New York: Russell Sage Foundation.

Joe, Karen and Meda Chesney-Lind. 1999. "'Every Mother's Angel': An Analysis of Gender and Ethnic Variations in Youth Gang Membership." In Meda Chesney-Lind and John M. Hagedorn (eds) *Female Gangs in America.* Chicago, IL: Lake View Press, pp. 210–231.

Katz, Michael B. 1989. *The Undeserving Poor: From the War on Poverty to the War on Welfare.* New York: Pantheon Books.

Kerner Report, The. 1968. National Advisory Commission on Civil Disorders 1967. New York: Bantam Books. http://faculty.washington.edu/qtaylor/documents _us/Kerner%20Report.htm (accessed July 15, 2004).

Klein, Malcolm W. 1995. *The American Street Gang.* New York: Oxford University Press.

Knoll, Crystal and Melissa Sickmund. 2010. *Delinquency Cases in Juvenile Court, 2007.* OJJDP Fact Sheet, June. Washington, D.C.: U.S. Department of Justice.

Krivo, Lauren J. and Ruth D. Peterson. 1996. "Extremely Disadvantaged Neighborhoods and Urban Crime." *Social Forces* 75: 619–650.

Lauritsen, Janet L. 2005. "Racial and Ethnic Differences in Juvenile Offending in Our

Children, Their Children: Confronting Racial and Ethnic Differences." In Darnell F. Hawkins and Kimberly Kempf-Leonard (eds) *American Juvenile Justice*. Chicago, IL: The University of Chicago Press, pp. 83–104.

Lieber, R.J. 1994. "Comparison of Juvenile Court Outcomes for Native Americans, African Americans and Whites." *Justice Quarterly* 11: 257–279.

Leiber, Michael J. 2006. "Disproportionate Minority Confinement (DMC) of Youth: An Analysis of State and Federal Efforts to Address the Issue." In Everette B. Penn, Helen Taylor Greene and Shaun L. Gabbidon (eds) *Race and Juvenile Justice*. Durham, NC: Carolina Academic Press, pp. 141–185.

Leiber, M.J. and K.M. Jamieson. 1995. "Race and Decision Making within Juvenile Justice: The Importance of Context". *Journal of Quantitative Criminology* 11: 363–388.

Levy, J.E. and S.J. Kunitz. 1974. *Indian Drinking: Navajo Drinking and Anglo-American Theories*. New York: Wiley-Interscience.

Maguire, Kathleen and Ann L. Pastore (eds). 1994. *Sourcebook of Criminal Justice Statistics 1993*. Washington D.C.: U.S. Department of Justice, Bureau of Justice Statistics.

Mandelbaum, D.G. 1965. "Alcohol and Culture." *Current Anthropology* 6: 281–293.

Massey, Douglas S. and Nancy A. Denton. 1993. *American Apartheid: Segregation and the Making of the Underclass*. Cambridge, MA: Harvard University Press.

May, Tiggey, Tracey Gyateng and Mike Hough. 2010. *Differential Treatment in the Youth Justice System*. London: Equality and Human Rights Commission.

McGarrell, Edmund F. 1993. "Trends in Racial Disproportionality in Juvenile Court Processing: 1985–1989." *Crime and Delinquency* 39: 29–48.

McShane, Marilyn and Frank P. Williams III. 2006. "Reducing Minority Youth Gang Involvement." In Everette B. Penn, Helen Taylor Greene and Shaun L. Gabbidon (eds) *Race and Juvenile Justice*. Durham, NC: Carolina Academic Press, pp. 111–123.

Messner, S., L. Raffakovich and R. McMillan. 2001. "Economic Deprivation and Changes in Homicide Arrest Rates for White and Black Youths, 1967–1998: A National Time Series Analysis." *Criminology* 39: 591–614.

Miller, J.R. 1989. *Skyscrapers Hide the Heavens: A History of Indian–White Relations in Canada*. Toronto: University of Toronto Press.

Miller Jerome. 1996. *Search and Destroy*. New York: Cambridge University Press.

Muncie, John. 2009. *Youth and Crime*. London: Sage.

Nielsen, Marianne O. and Linda Robyn. 2009. "Stolen Lands, Stolen Lives: Native Americans and Criminal Justice." In *The Criminology and Criminal Justice Collective of Northern Arizona University*. Englewood Cliffs, NJ: Prentice Hall, pp. 74–85.

Nunn, Kenneth B. 2002. "The Child as Other: Race and Differential Treatment in the Juvenile Justice System." *De Paul Law Review* 51: 679–714.

Ogunwole, Stella U. 2006. *We the People: American Indians and Alaska Natives in the United States*. U.S. Census Bureau. Washington D.C.: U.S. Government Printing Office.

Penn, Everette B. 2006. "Black Youth: Disproportionality and Delinquency." In Everette B. Penn, Helen Taylor Greene and Shaun L. Gabbidon (eds) *Race and Juvenile Justice*. Durham, NC: Carolina Academic Press, pp. 47–64.

Perry, Steven W. 2004. *American Indians and Crime: A BJS Statistical Profile, 1992–2002*. Washington D.C.: U.S. Department of Justice, Bureau of Justice Statistics.

Piliavin, I. and S. Briar. 1964. "Police Encounters with Juveniles." *American Journal of Sociology* 70(2): 206–214.

Pope, C. and W. Feyerherm. 1990. "Minority Status and Juvenile Justice Processing: An Assessment of the Research Literature (parts I and II)." *Criminal Justice Abstracts* (June and September): 327–335; 527–542.

Pope, C. and W. Feyerherm. 1995. *Minorities in the Juvenile Justice System*, 2nd Edition. Washington D.C.: U.S. Department of Justice, Office of Juvenile Justice and Delinquency Prevention.

Put, Johan and Lode Walgrave. 2006. "Belgium: From Protection towards Accountability?" In John Muncie and Barry Goldson (eds) *Comparative Youth Justice*. London: Sage, pp. 111–127.

Puzzanchera, Charles and Benjamin Adams. 2011. "Juvenile Arrests 2009." *Juvenile Offenders National Report Series Bulletin*, December. Washington D.C.: U.S. Department of Justice, Office of Justice Programs, Office of Juvenile Justice and Delinquency Prevention.

Ross, Luana. 1998. *Inventing the Savage: The Social Construction of Native American Criminality*. Austin: University of Texas Press.

Saggers, Sherry and Dennis Gray. 1998. *Dealing with Alcohol: Indigenous Usage in Australia, New Zealand and Canada*. Cambridge: Cambridge University Press.

Schafer, N.E., Richard W. Curtis and Cassie Atwell. 1997. *Disproportionate Representation of Minorities in the Alaska Juvenile Justice System Phase I Report*. Justice Center, University of Alaska, Anchorage. http://justice.uaa.alaska.edu/research/1990/9501juv/9501_02a.pdf (accessed July 15, 2004).

Shelden, Randall G., Sharon K. Tracy and William B. Brown. 2004. *Youth Gangs in American Society*. Belmont, CA: Wadsworth.

Shoemaker, Nancy. 1999. *American Indian Population Recovery in the Twentieth Century*. Albuquerque: University of New Mexico Press.

Sickmund, Melissa, Howard N. Snyder and Ellen Poe-Yamagata. 1997. *Juvenile Offenders and Victims: 1997 Update on Violence*. Washington D.C.: Office of Juvenile Justice and Delinquency Prevention.

Snyder, Howard N. and Melissa Sickmund. 1995. *Juvenile Offenders and Victims: A National Report*. Washington D.C.: U.S. Department of Justice, Office of Juvenile Justice and Delinquency Prevention.

Snyder, Howard N. and Melissa Sickmund. 2006. *Juvenile Offenders and Victims: 2006 National Report*. Washington D.C.: U.S. Department of Justice, Office of Justice Programs, Office of Juvenile Justice and Delinquency Prevention.

State of Alaska, Health and Social Services. 2009. *Juvenile Justice, Race % as Reported at Referral for Each Region and Office FY2009*. http://www.hss.state.ak.us/djj/information/stats_fy2009/race_office.htm (accessed July 15, 2004).

Time magazine. 1977. "The American Underclass." August 19.

Tonry, Michael. 1997. "Ethnicity, Crime and Immigration." In Michael Tonry (ed.) *Crime and Immigration: Comparative and Cross National Perspectives*, Vol. 21. Chicago, IL: The University of Chicago Press, pp. 1–29.

U.S. Census Bureau. 2006. *United States Census 2006*. Washington, D.C.: U.S. Department of Commerce, U.S. Census Bureau.

U.S. Census Bureau. 2010. *United States Census 2010*. Washington, D.C.: U.S. Department of Commerce, U.S. Census Bureau.

U.S. Department of Justice. 2001. *Sourcebook of Criminal Justice Statistics 2000*. Washington D.C.: U.S. Department of Justice.

U.S. General Accounting Office. 1995. *Juvenile Justice: Juveniles Processed in Criminal Court and Case Dispositions*. Washington D.C.: U.S. General Accounting Office.

Vigil, James Diego and Steve C. Yun. 2002. "A Cross-Cultural Framework for Understanding Gangs: Multiple Marginality and Los Angeles." In C. Ronald Huff (ed.) *Gangs in America*. Thousand Oaks, CA: Sage, pp. 161–174.

Walker, S., C. Spohn and M. DeLone. 2004. *The Color of Justice: Race, Ethnicity and Crime in America*. Belmont, CA: Wadsworth.

Wilson, William Julius. 1987. *The Truly Disadvantaged: The Inner City, The Underclass and Public Policy*. Chicago, IL: The University of Chicago Press.

Wilson, William Julius (ed.). 1993. *The Ghetto Underclass: Social Science Perspectives*. Thousand Oaks, CA: Sage.

Young, Alford A. 2004. *The Minds of Marginalized Black Men: Making Sense of Mobility, Opportunity and Future Life Chances*. Princeton, NJ: Princeton University Press.

Zimring, Franklin. 2005. *American Juvenile Justice*. New York: Oxford University Press.

chapter 6

Youth Culture and Delinquency

This chapter is concerned with youth culture or subculture, deviance and delinquency. Its focus is on aspects of youth culture that link to deviance and delinquency. Youth culture has been explained as:

> Youth culture is historical and contemporary, it creates the opportunity for young people to forge roles and make identities. It enables degrees of differing participation at different ages and at different periods in young people's lives. Youth culture is foreground and background for all young people's lives. It is both established by young people and made by others for young people.
>
> (Blackman and France 2001: 181)

It is first necessary to explain deviance and youth culture or subculture and relate them to sociological theories of crime. Sociology researches and studies social organization, collective behavior and the relationship of the individual to the group, and it is within this framework that sociological theories of crime have been constructed. Criminologists are interested in subcultures that constitute elements within broader social themes in society when those subcultures are associated in some manner with delinquent acts. Subcultures are to be distinguished from counter-cultures and cultures.

In the U.S., the study of youth subcultures, after initially being a field of sociology investigated most notably by the "Chicago School," came to be subsumed under the topic of deviance within the discipline of criminology. The U.S. preoccupation with youth and gangs produced studies of gangs in the 1950s and 1960s. In the British tradition, on the other hand, a distinct body of sustained research and theory into youth subcultures evolved from the late 1960s under the leadership of Stuart Hall and his sociology colleagues at the University of Birmingham, Center for Contemporary Cultural Studies. Each of these approaches to youth subculture will be explored here.

Sociological theories of crime and delinquency examine crime in social terms and within the production and persistence of social order. During the 1920s and later, the Sociology Department of the University of Chicago established a research tradition in the social mapping of cities that focused on uncovering social problems within the urban landscape. Using the techniques of the social anthropologists, the Chicago School explored customs, practices, behaviors and cultures of urban communities and found, for example, in regard to delinquency, that "to a very great extent . . . traditions of delinquency are preserved and transmitted through the medium of social contact with the unsupervised play group and the more highly organized delinquent and criminal gangs" (Shaw and McKay 1942: 260). This research laid a foundation for the development of many fields within criminology, including the study of subcultures (Downes and Rock 1998: 19). The Chicago School considered the origins of juvenile delinquency to be of strategic importance because it was during youth that patterns of criminal conduct were laid down (Faris 1967: 72). The Chicago sociologists wanted to explain the social and cultural context of deviance as opposed to treating deviance in pathological terms. In-depth qualitative analyses of cultural life became the main feature of the Chicago School and, in terms of deviance, Thrasher's The Gang (1927) and Cressey's The Taxi-Dance Hall (1932) represent examples of this kind of research. Subcultures were seen to be "relatively distinct social subsystem[s] within a larger social system and culture" (Fischer 1975: 1323).

According to Williams (2007: 575), with the passing of the hippie movement in the 1970s, youth subculture, as a field of study, shifted from sociology to criminology, specifically to the study of deviance. Within criminology, certainly in the U.S., research on youth subculture is often directed at gangs, violence and delinquency. For example, Albert Cohen formulated his now classic "general theory of subcultures" in Delinquent Boys: The Culture of the Gang (1955), and Cloward and Ohlin responded with Delinquency and Opportunity: A Theory of Delinquent Gangs (1960). The developing field of "cultural criminology" has, however, recently begun to engage more closely with culture, including youth subcultures, and to explore activities and practices such as graffiti and skateboarding, which have developed their own subcultures. These will be discussed below.

Deviance and youth

Within criminology, deviance refers to an alleged violation of an established social norm, and studying deviance informs us about the dominant social order and the organization of so-called deviant lifestyles (Rubington and Weinberg 1999: 1). Various theories offer definitions of what constitutes deviance. For example, Downes and Rock suggest that it is "banned or controlled behavior which is likely to attract punishment or disapproval" (1998: 26). A key element in deviance studies is the notion that deviance is socially defined; that is to say, an act is deviant if people say it is. Consequently, identifying a departure from social norms that amounts to deviance, influencing others to also regard the author of that act as deviant and acting on the basis of that perspective, gives rise to a set of social reactions and interpretations.

Deviance can be studied as objectively given or as subjectively problematic. The former approach involves identifying societal norms and seeing any deviation from them as constituting deviance. The principal difficulty with this approach that renders it problematic is that U.S. society comprises multiple groups, cultures and modes of thinking, therefore making it difficult to agree on a set of norms and identify deviants. As well, this approach tends to ensure that agencies which enforce social controls will select certain categories of acts and denote them as deviant. The objective approach focuses on the characteristics of the deviant or on the conditions that give rise to deviant acts. The subjective approach to deviance assumes that people and groups will interact and communicate using symbols such as style of dress and body language. Thus, labeling a person or group as deviant is to identify a symbol that stigmatizes and differentiates that person or group as deviant. Youth cultures are especially susceptible to labeling as deviant because they have become very significant, not only in relation to patterns of consumption, but also because young people have become a very distinctive group, one which is regularly labeled as linked to disorder and deviant activity (Smith 2010: 41). The youth market, the role of youth as producers of new cultural forms and the relative cultural and social autonomy of youth create tensions and social contradictions (Austin 1998: 240). Sociologists who follow this subjective, interactionist approach focus on the perspective and reactions of the person labeled as deviant, on those who label a person deviant, and on the social interaction between the two (Rubington and Weinberg 1999: 2). The classic interactionist text is Howard Becker's (1963) *Outsiders: Studies in the Sociology of Deviance*. He explains labeling deviance in the following terms:

> [S]ocial groups create deviance by making the rules whose infraction constitutes deviance, and by applying those rules to particular people

and labeling them as outsiders. From this point of view, deviance is not a quality of the act the person commits, but rather a consequence of the application by others of rules and sanctions to an "offender." The deviant is one to whom that label has successfully been applied: deviant behavior is behavior that people so label.

(Becker 1963: 9)

Thus, according to Becker, the elements that define deviance will be: the nature of the act (does it violate a rule); and the societal response to that act resulting from the interaction between the person performing the act and those responding to it. Deviant behavior is therefore a product of labeling and delinquent subcultures are drawn into a process of "deviance amplification" because they commit further deviant acts following the initial negative societal response. This effectively reinforces the marginalization and stigmatization already conferred. Both Becker and Erving Goffman noted that groups taking an oppositional stance toward society were much more likely to be labeled deviant. As Goffman uncompromisingly states:

These are the folk who are considered to be engaged in some kind of collective denial of the social order. They are perceived as failing to use available opportunity for advancement in the various approved runways of society; they show open disrespect for their betters; they lack piety; they represent failures in the motivational schemes of society.

(Goffman 1968: 170–171)

The labeling perspective confronted the progression of social control into areas of moral uncertainty or into fields where the deviance was relatively harmless. The focus of labeling was directed more at the line between deviance and mere difference. Accordingly, labeling theory questioned the value of criminalizing prostitution and marijuana use as well as homosexuality (Sumner 1994: 204). Goffman (1968) argued that minor deviance occurred every day and was normal in a society with numerous groups and value systems, and Lemert (1952, 1972) maintained that secondary deviance was the outcome of social control agencies exercising their institutional power to label deviance as serious.

Youth subcultures

In Britain, studies of working-class youth at the Center for Contemporary Cultural Studies at the University of Birmingham in the late 1960s and 1970s adopted a subcultural approach.[1] The cultural studies perspective saw the rise of youth cultures as distinctive within British culture and as "a metaphor for social change," and attempted to link youth subcultures to a general social and cultural historical analysis (Hall and Jefferson 1993: viii). Working-class youth were seen as constantly seeking out ways to challenge their oppression and to create spaces within which to realize their identity. This was exemplified by a collapse of the hegemony of the dominant class in the late 1960s and the 1970s. It was at this point that youth began to see themselves as distinctly different from the parent generation. This generational divergence was to be found in different sets of institutions and experiences from those of their parents. The institutions concerned were education, work and leisure.[2]

Culture was seen by the Birmingham researchers as:

> The "culture" of a group or class is the peculiar and distinctive "way of life" of the group or class, the meanings, values and ideas embodied in institutions, in social relations, in systems of belief, in mores and customs, in the uses of objects and material life.
>
> (quoted in Hall and Jefferson 1993: 10)

Subcultures were explained as more localized structures within larger class-cultural networks but also as sharing some things in common with the "parent" culture and as having a relation to the dominant culture, this being termed "the overall disposition of cultural power in the society as a whole" (Hall and Jefferson 1993: 6). Thus, divergent delinquent subcultures exist within a working-class parent culture and are subservient to the dominant middle-class culture. Subcultures must be identifiably different from their parent culture and are associated with certain activities, values, places and "focal concerns." While they may be tight or loose groupings the Birmingham researchers' focus was on tightly bound groups, differentiated by age and generation called "youth subcultures" (Hall and Jefferson 1993: 6–7). These may be regular features of the parent culture such as the "culture of delinquency" or may appear only at certain times when they are denoted and labeled, command public attention and then fade away.

The work of Phil Cohen (1972) was influential in developing the theoretical underpinnings of the Birmingham youth subculture project. Cohen argued that it was necessary to differentiate between subculture and delinquency, and in trying to separate the two concepts he identified subcultures as a property of the working class, produced by a dominated and not by a dominant culture. For Cohen, place was vital and he perceived subcultures as lying at the heart of working-class communities (1972: 23). In this sense, therefore, subculture describes forms of solidarity that are seen as opposing dominant societal norms.

Sociologists at the Center researched aspects of working-class youth cultural practices from the 1960s onwards, including, teddy boys, mods, rockers, hippies and punks, drawing on the cultural Marxism of Gramsci (1971) and Althusser (1971) (quoted in Bennett and Kahn-Harris 2004: 1). Participation in youth subcultures was seen as a form of resistance to cultural hegemony and as reflecting class struggles. Applying Gramsci's arguments about hegemonic struggles in late capitalist societies, the Birmingham sociologists contended that negotiating space for subcultural formations on the street corner and for leisure was an element of the class struggle and challenged authority. Spaces and sites for subcultural formation and practices included street corners, dance venues and weekend vacation locations. Youth were seen to be negotiating with or opposing the dominant ideology or subverting dominant meanings by appropriating and transforming them.

The style adopted by a subcultural group was seen in symbolic terms and analyses of subcultural formations applied poststructuralist semiotics rather than adopting an ethnographic approach along the lines of the Chicago School (Hall and Jefferson 1993). The task of the researcher was interpretive – to interrogate meaning, to analyze style, consumption practices and forms of leisure, and to explore the lived aspects of youth culture. Thus Hebdige (1979) in his semiotic interpretation of British white working-class styles argued that they constituted divergent responses to black culture and racial politics.

Hall and Jefferson (1993) argue that the dominant society initially reacted to these emergent youth subcultures with "confused perplexity" and then came to see them as symbolizing social change. While social change was regarded as beneficial in terms of overall affluence and prosperity, it also eroded the traditional order of things and consequently produced social anxiety (p. 56). As youth subcultures redrew moral boundaries and transformed class relations through their styles, events and actions, the resulting social anxiety was displaced on to scapegoat groups, giving rise to the moral panics described in Chapter 7. The Birmingham researchers conducted textual analyses of the media to reveal how moral panics were the outcome of media representations of youth.

The Chicago School also recognized the importance of place to specific subcultural activities. An example can be found in the case of the taxi-dance hall, which Cressey (1932) explored as a social setting where young women danced for a commission with varieties of patrons. Typically, youth subcultures cover wide geographical spaces such as the skinhead culture that emerged in both Britain and the U.S., albeit in different modalities. Similarly, punk, straightedge and goth subcultures are also transnational lifestyles (Williams 2007: 583).

As Williams points out (2007: 587), subcultural studies tend to celebrate youth subcultures, sometimes as heroic movements, while criminology still describes and explains youth cultures in terms of deviance and delinquency.

Hebdige describes the contrast as "two image clusters – the bleak portraits of juvenile offenders" and "the exuberant cameos of teenage life" (1983: 295). Critics assert that this concern with spectacular or highly visible styles seen through the semiotic lens fails to capture aspects of gender, class, race and ethnicity that might also be incorporated into youth cultural practices. According to McRobbie (1980), this romanticizing of youth subcultures can be attributed to some academics who, disappointed at the collapse of other counter-hegemonic movements such as student radicalism and trade unionism, looked to other groups, namely skinheads and mods, to pursue the insurgent movement for change.

Criticisms of the theoretical framework of the Birmingham Center include that it privileged class and therefore failed to take account of other key dimensions of youth identity including gender and black culture. An early critique from McRobbie and Garber (1976) noted that female cultural styles were not acknowledged as legitimate cultural forms. While the concept of youth subcultures has endured it has been suggested that it is now used in an arbitrary fashion and is in need of a critical evaluation because it has "become little more than a convenient 'catch-all' term for any aspect of social life in which young people, style and music intersect" (Bennett 1999: 599). It is clear that since the 1980s youth styles have multiplied and become mixed so that it is now more difficult to identify youth subcultures that cohere in discrete formations. As Muggleton (2000: 47) notes, "Subcultural fragmentation . . . hybrids and transformations . . . and the coexistence of myriad styles" are said to characterize the 1980s and 1990s. Subcultural studies has also been taken to task for lack of geographical specificity and, given its specific focus on British white working-class youth, its incapacity to inform other national contexts (Bennett and Kahn-Harris 2004: 9). It has also been pointed out that subcultural studies fails to recognize the importance of the media in contributing visual and other resources to the formation of subcultural identities (pp. 9–10).

Other critiques of the subculture approach to youth deviance note that some subcultures have attracted only a minority of adherents from the relevant age group and that members do not always adopt the subculture as a lifestyle, but more as a part-time leisure activity (Martin 2004: 31). The Birmingham researchers are also accused of failing to base their case studies on ethnographic methodologies. Hall and Jefferson respond that empirical studies into the life-worlds of subcultural participants are still uncommon (1993: xii).

Nevertheless, some researchers have noted "important continuities" in the work of the youth subcultures group despite the configuration of new concepts. New articulations have challenged the notion that participating in "rave" culture can be generalized to denote an entire lifestyle. Carrabine and Longhurst (2002) argued that youth in fact inhabit the rave culture space only intermittently and participate in additional cultural practices over time. What is required, therefore, is an account based on a precise and nuanced explanation of how youth interact with various cultural formations (pp. 185–186). The subcultures concept has continued to be employed, notwithstanding its numerous critiques (Hall and Jefferson 1993: xi).

The class and culture theorization as well as the prominence given to class were critiqued from the beginning. Hall and Jefferson (1993: xv) acknowledge that since the 1960s and 1970s societies have become more individualistic, and that in fact the nature of class itself may well have changed. However, they insist that class divisions continue to exist and exert huge influences on "life-chances and opportunities in every sphere of life – influences which are transmitted across the generations and become embedded in the social order" (pp. xv–xvi).

The extensive critique of subcultural theory since the 1990s has prompted a fresh approach to the study of youth culture in the form of "post-subcultural theory." This approach takes as its starting point the argument that subcultural divisions have collapsed in the face of new cultural productions such as clubbing and rave which have dissolved divisions like race, class and gender. There is now a "Supermarket of Style" through which youth may move swiftly and fleetingly, and an increasing fluidity in youth participation in cultural practices, bringing out fresh conceptual thinking and new designations for youth culture such as "neo-tribes" (Bennett 1999), "lifestyle" (Miles 2000) and "scene" (Bennett and Kahn-Harris 2004: 13; Stahl 2003). For postmodernists, subcultures construct cultural practices through consumption, identity formation, agency, locality and the appropriate global commodities (Blackman 2005: 8). For some, subcultural style is now constituted only through consumption, and class, gender, ethnicity and even age are deemed immaterial (Muggleton 1997: 199).

Post-subcultural studies of youth tend to focus on music and dance cultures, or on issues of style, and to minimize class and structural issues such as social inequalities. Shildrick and MacDonald argue that this has led to the creation of a distorted and incomplete account of contemporary youth subcultures (2006: 126, 128). Hall and Jefferson acknowledge the postmodern turn, and while applauding its capacity to uncover new knowledge, caution that it is still necessary to investigate, interrogate and explain the wider social and cultural processes such as the new market societies, the commercialization of culture, and the development of mass consumption and globalization and how they relate to youth subcultures (1993: xx, xxi).

The interaction between youth cultures and deviance

Youth is a complex, culturally constructed category. Often described as a symbol of hope for the future, youth are also thought to constitute a threat to the social order. Hedonistic pleasures and consumerism by both youth and adults are said to characterize the current phase of modernity. Conspicuous consumption is now thought to offer a better explanation for deviance than subcultural rebellion (Hall et al. 2008). Questions that arise include: How do leisure, lifestyle, consumption and the pursuit of pleasure constitute youth cultures? What is the public reaction to youth cultural production? What interactions occur between youth cultures and deviance? Why and how are certain youth cultural practices considered deviant, and what processes, persons and institutions are involved in signifying deviance?

Negative labels and characterizations of youth are easily found such as "Generation X" (Coupland 1991) and "Generation Me" (Twenge 2006), the former signifying cynicism, self-centeredness and a preoccupation with materialism (Howe and Strauss 1993), the latter indicating a generation that is narcissistic and "has never known a world that put duty before self" (Twenge 2006: 1). In Britain, the centrality of consumption in the lives of young people is considered evidence of "a growing contempt for the collective and a ubiquitous preference for low level criminality as the means to gratify hedonistic drives" (Hall et al. 2008: 13).

Cultural criminology

Cultural criminology, as a still evolving field of criminological study, attempts to capture the nexus between crime and culture. Cultural criminology explores the convergence of the criminal and the cultural in society. It pays attention to popular culture constructions and attempts to transfer the insights of cultural studies to criminology by investigating subcultures labeled as deviant (Ferrell and Websdale 1999: 3, 5). Case studies in cultural criminology share commonalities in identifying forms of "contested power relations and the emergence of social control, at the intersection of culture, crime and deviance" (p. 12).

Cultural criminologists attempt to document the lived realities of subcultures judged to be deviant and then to deconstruct their alleged deviance to offer alternative understandings and images of deviance, crime and social control. In this task, they employ the interactionist perspective and the sociology of deviance, especially labeling, and incorporate perspectives from a range of disciplines, including media studies, urban studies, anthropology and postmodern theory (Ferrell et al. 2008: 5).

Cultural criminologists attempt to understand crimes that contain emotional or expressive elements, that provide an adrenaline rush, where individuals willingly accept risks, such as graffiti writing and illicit motor bike racing, in an interplay of emotion, risk, deviance and identity (p. 72).

A key organizational concept in cultural criminology is the analysis of urban spaces (Ferrell et al. 2008: 80). Public space is now subjected to "regimes of control" designed to fend off the unwanted and the marginalized. Often, this includes youth subcultures or simply groups of youth gathering for social purposes. As Rose (2000: 330) expresses it:

> The civilizing public spaces of nineteenth century liberalism and twentieth century social architecture – public parks, libraries, playgrounds, the streets themselves – are increasingly abandoned, desolate and dangerous. They are replaced by an archipelago of secured spaces – shopping malls, arts centers and gourmet restaurant strips. Access to each is guarded, the internal space is under electronic surveillance and private security policing, its architecture and design so organized as to eliminate or expel those who have no legitimate – that is to say – consumerized – reason to be there.

Contesting the use of public space is a common theme in each of the youth subcultures explored in this chapter.

Having outlined developments in the study of youth subcultures and deviance, specific subcultures are now explored, namely the acid house and rave subculture, writing graffiti and skateboarding. The aim is to delineate the nature of each subculture, explain the cultural processes in play, interrogate public reactions and establish the link between a subculture and deviance.

Acid house parties and the rave subculture

The term *acid house* is derived in part from the expression "house music" first used in Chicago in the late 1970s. In Chicago dance clubs of that time, some DJs mixed sounds to produce an up-tempo type of disco music at about 124 beats per minute (bpm) (Rietveld 1998: 17) and this began to be marketed as dance music in areas away from the central leisure areas of the city. This music moved across to New York City where dance participants used cocaine and ecstasy. The Chicago house scene began to be regarded as troublesome and police finally placed a ban on after-hours house parties in about 1987, effectively stifling any further development of house music in that city. However, house music crossed the Atlantic and by 1988 had become an active feature of youth culture in clubs in Britain, the

Netherlands, Germany, Belgium and Italy, where the music mixes became more "techno." Eventually the music was exported back to the U.S. as "techno-rave" (Rietveld 1998: 24, 26).

In Britain and Europe the dance experience and associated music was termed "acid house party" or "rave." It began as an underground scene and melded with a club concept exported back to Europe from the Spanish resort island of Ibiza where Europeans on vacation had created a club scene. By the end of 1987, large London warehouse parties had started using the Ibiza model (Rietveld 1998: 52, 55). By mid-1988, the new dance experience had started to clash with the 2 a.m. British closing time for clubs. Many dancers had become accustomed to the freedom of longer clubbing hours in Spain, and crowds in Britain spilled out on to the streets still charged up on ecstasy. The limits on night-club hours were later eased with the aim of moving raves into properly licensed club premises (Critcher 2000: 151).

By the end of the summer of 1988 the media were reporting on hedonistic dancing at acid house parties as the latest dance craze, but by October, following two deaths from ecstasy, media reports were encouraging a moral panic (see Chapter 7) about acid house parties, casting drug dealers as the folk devils (Critcher 2000: 148). By this time, acid house parties were being commercially organized beyond urban surveillance with up to 10,000 people attending (Rietveld 1998: 58, 59). House music had become a national phenomenon in Britain with parties of up to 20,000 held in venues ranging from film studios to aircraft hangars and fields (Hill 2002: 89).

Responding to media moral panics, legislators passed the *Entertainments (Increased Penalties) Act 1990*, dubbed the "Acid House Bill" which increased penalties for party organizers and effectively reduced the number and scale of the parties (Hill 2002). The fine for organizing an unlicensed party was increased from a maximum of £2,000 to £20,000 and six months' imprisonment. In July 1990, following this legislation, a mass arrest of 836 persons took place in the north of Britain but only one person was charged with an offense. Complaints were leveled at the police, and police action came to be bitterly resented by participants (p. 98). Unlike previous moral panics where only limited police action had been taken against teds, mods and rockers and punks, the reaction to acid house was exceptional even to the extent of enacting this special legislation (p. 99).

Political elites' response to acid house echoes a theme in which popular culture is seen as threatening social order and therefore social control is deployed to label it deviant (Hill 2002: 90, 91). Notions of noise as a form of subversion (as exemplified by rock-and-roll music earlier), fear of the mob and of disruption to the social orderliness of the countryside through traffic convoys, and party venues themselves, as well as the use of drugs and the disregard for licensing laws and health requirements, converged to provoke police and political action against house parties (pp. 93–96). The "authoritarian populism" of the Thatcher years in Britain refused to tolerate this threat to social discipline. In response, the police formed a special unit to raid parties, erected road-blocks, and used check-points to frustrate party organizers. However, the scale of the phenomenon resulted in frequent clashes between the police and organizers such as that described in this report in the *Daily Mail* of October 2, 1989:

> The drugs crisis took a menacing twist yesterday when guards at an acid House party routed the police. A private army of security men attacked with baseball bats, CS gas and vicious dogs. They left 16 officers injured. A superintendent, fearing for the lives of his men, ordered a retreat and had to release two prisoners. At one stage there were fears about an officer being taken hostage and the field where the event was held became a no-go area, leaving more than 10,000 revellers free to shatter the peace of a suburban weekend.
>
> (quoted in Hill 2002: 97)

In 1994 the *Criminal Justice and Public Order Act* criminalized trespassing, traveling in convoys (the means by which most participants traveled to raves) and gatherings of 100 or more persons where amplified music was played during the night (Critcher 2000). The music was defined as "wholly or predominantly characterized by the emission of repetitive beats" (*Criminal Justice and Public Order Act 1994*, section 63 (1) (b)). For the first time in law, a category of music became an element in a criminal offense. Police were empowered to control traffic within a five-mile radius of a rave, to stop vehicles at road-blocks and to arrest those who failed to leave the location of a rave after being asked to do so by police. Police were reluctant to invoke the Act (p. 150) but, in any event, by 1993, warehouse raves had ceased and raves were being staged lawfully in clubs. The move into clubland caused media attention to wane (pp. 148, 149).

In a final legislative assault on raves, the 1997 *Public Entertainments (Drug Misuse) Act* facilitated elimination of the unlicensed rave and regulated clubbing. Local authorities were empowered to revoke night-club licenses where police affirmed that drug taking or drug dealing was believed to be occurring on the club premises (Critcher 2000: 150). Interestingly, no special action was taken in regard to the use of ecstasy which became simply another recreational drug, perhaps because any action would have been ineffective given its widespread use; at the height of its popularity, at least 10 percent of 16- to 25-year-olds were regular ecstasy users and in 1996, the British government reported that based on seizures of the drug, a million ecstasy tablets were being consumed each week (p. 157).

Although for some the experience of participating in a rave was itself sufficient to transport them, acid house parties were associated with the drugs MDMA (ecstasy), poppers, speed, acid, cocaine and cannabis (Rietveld 1998: 176). Like LSD and cocaine, ecstasy is a mood enhancer and its effects last for about four hours. It is totally prohibited from use under U.K. law. Ecstasy enhances the production of serontonine, a neurotransmitter which affects one's mood, causing a kind of euphoric feeling. Within the social space of the house party, the user can lose identity in the dancing and music, often dancing alone, trancelike, in an altered mind state, while also feeling empathically connected to other dancers in a kind of community. Combining ecstasy and house music was so effective for clubbers that the two became synonymous (pp. 180, 181). Deaths linked to the use of ecstasy were reported in Britain but most deaths resulted from heat stroke and not the drug itself (Saunders and Doblin 1996). One respondent in the northeast of Britain described the feeling of using ecstasy at a rave as follows:

> "It's brilliant. You feel a bit like when you are really in love. Like a warm feeling inside; excited but not nervous or horrible. Really nice feeling. It makes you feel lovely – you really love the people you are with and you tell them" (Sally).
>
> (Merchant and MacDonald 1994: 20)

During the 1990s, house music and its attendant parties migrated to cities around the world from Sydney, Australia to Cape Town, South Africa to Tokyo, Japan (Rietveld 1998: 210). In Toronto, where the rave scene has been active since the early 1990s, party venues included sites ranging from a roller-skating rink to an ethnic community hall. The age range of participants in one study was from 15 to more than 40 years with the median age being 22. The décor at parties included psychedelic murals, banners, lights and children's toys, and, while liquor was available, the areas licensed for alcohol consumption were underused (Weber 1999: 319–321). Crowd sizes ranged from 300 to 5,000 people, mostly white and middle class. Summarizing the rave experience, one 22-year-old male explained a rave as:

> "A party where tons of people go to take E [ecstasy] and dance. It's a place where fags and freaks can go and pretend that they are normal for that night. Everyone is really friendly and fights are rare. People are too wrapped up in their trip to be pissed off."
>
> (Weber 1999: 323)

The convivial atmosphere of the rave meant that people "apologize when they bump into you" and the expressions "community" and "family" were used to describe the "vibe" dancers experienced. Raves were unlike the club experience where the atmosphere was more hostile owing to the availability of alcohol and where men constantly approached women. As well, raves in

Toronto were described in terms of a form of escapism from boredom, "a mini vacation" and a site where participants could act "like small children" and be carefree (Weber 1999: 324, 326). Raves were now being branded through rave culture items like fanzines, flyers as collector's items, famous clubs and special clothing (p. 331).

POLICE INJURED DURING VIOLENT CLASHES AT ILLEGAL RAVE IN LONDON

On October 30, 2010 riot police in London surrounded a disused building to break up a suspected illegal rave. Several police were injured and bottles and bricks were thrown at them, and at least seven arrests were made for public order-type offenses.

Police were called to the disused building in central London at about 11.20 p.m. on October 30. Most of the party goers returned to the eight-storey building after clashes with police to continue their rave. The police adopted a watching strategy as the rave continued into the morning with loud music, pointing to the huge number of people inside and the fact that they were heavily outnumbered. Hundreds of ravers spilled out into the street wearing Halloween costumes, some drinking beer in the street or holding water bottles. One raver, a man aged 24, said, "We're rebelling but we're not harming anyone, we don't cause damage."

Police finally took possession of the building at 4.15 p.m. on Sunday, October 31 and declared the rave over.

Some observers drew parallels to the raves that occurred during the Thatcher years – as then, the ideology of the current Conservative government is committed to a reduction in the size of the state and Britain is experiencing a sustained recession. They argue that illegal raves may make a come-back in a backlash against this Conservative government.

Others, following a more practical approach, pointed out that recessions tend to produce empty buildings suitable for illegal raves and in such circumstances the underground club scene can thrive. They note that organizing a rave is easy using the Internet, especially given the social networks that are now available.

Source: Adapted from the *Guardian* (October 31 and November 6, 2010)

In his analysis of raves in Perth, Western Australia, Moore found a community of rave participants of all social classes, mainly single and aged between 16 and 28 with most being regular users of a range of drugs comprising cannabis, acid, ecstasy and speed. Rave participants attended raves and dressed in street fashions, and comprised discrete identifiable groups of: gays and lesbians; "grungies" denoting a subculture of being unemployed and poor and favoring grunge music, dressing in old or torn clothing and wearing studs and facial rings; and ravers who enjoyed techno music (Moore 1995: 195).

Australia continues to import youth cultures or subcultures from Britain due mainly to the large population of children of British migrants. In Perth, raves became commercialized through the creation of production companies and some raves held in quarries, warehouses and open fields commanded audiences of 3,000 people. Locating a rave in Perth required attending a pre-rave party where maps giving directions were distributed. In Britain the rave venue would be secret and tickets issued with a phone number to call a computer message giving the meeting details (Critcher 2000: 147).

The Perth rave site was often divided into three areas: a large dance area occupying most of the floor space; an area selling water to counter the dehydration caused by drugs and long hours of dancing in hot temperatures,[3] chewing-gum and lollipops to ease the jaw grinding associated with drug use; and an outside "chill-out" area with rest and toilet facilities where dancers could cool down, smoke and chat to others. The lighting in the dance area comprised strobes and multicolored lasers, and smoke would be periodically pumped out. Raves usually began around 10 p.m. and, if police permitted it, ran until between 8 a.m. and 10 a.m. (Moore 1995: 197–199). As a rave participant, Moore conveys the atmosphere of the dance as follows:

> "About 4.00 am I stopped dancing on a platform at the rear of the dance floor to marvel at the scene in front of me. Perhaps 1,500 people dancing feverishly, lasers flashing, music pumping, sweat dripping, air thick with a sweaty humidity, most ravers standing in irregular lines with their friends to their right and left facing the front of the dance floor."
>
> (Moore 1995: 202)

Perth raves, like others, possessed a quality of community and togetherness. Dancers were "alone together" and it was possible to "feel the flow of people" in a "highly social" but largely non-verbal environment. There was an absence of aggression and the kind of "predatory sexuality" that characterizes regular night-clubs (Moore 1995: 207, 208). As Moore (1995: 211) puts it:

youth, crime and justice

> [T]he ravers [go] through what is socially defined as a "special" event, a demarcated, time-out cultural space in which many of the routines for behavior are suspended in favor of new ones. In this ritual space, both the personal and group boundaries become permeable and temporarily re-drawn.

In contrast to the many scholarly studies of rave culture in Britain, Canada and Australia, similar studies in the U.S. are absent. *Village Voice* reporter Frank Owen found that in a Manhattan rave club participants were working and lower middle class, and suggests that the first rave scene in the U.S. was located in Brooklyn/Staten Island where rave promoters modeled their club raves on the large U.K. rave scene (Owen 2003: 42, 74). Rave was said to be a culture of childhood, with dancers dressing in oversized clothing, women wearing their hair in pigtails and both genders sucking pacifiers (Tomlinson 1998: 200).

In the U.S., radio stations do not broadcast much rave music because it is mainly instrumental and tends to extend beyond the length acceptable for radio. As well, rave music lacks a "star system" and MTV refuses to show rave videos. The result is that rave has not enjoyed mainstream consumption in the U.S.

In Britain, some researchers see raves as working-class events while others believe them to be more inclusive according to location, with more upmarket raves in some parts of London and more working-class raves in other locations. Some argue that raves have served to democratize youth culture by involving persons from diverse social backgrounds (Merchant and MacDonald 1994: 24). Others draw on associations with the Thatcher years and its focus on entrepreneurialism to interpret this subculture. As Collin (1998: 7) explains, "Ecstasy culture seemed to ghost the Thatcher narrative – echoing its ethos of choice and market freedom, yet expressing desires for a collective experience that Thatcher rejected and consumerism could not provide."

Raves and rave culture may have had less to do with resistance to state hegemony, as in the case of skinhead and punk subcultures, and more to do with survival or avoidance of the authoritarian populism of the Thatcher years. Nevertheless, there was resistance to the policing of raves and this continues in the form of attacks on police attempting to bring them under some degree of control. Above all, a rave was "a totally hedonistic experience . . . significantly different from its conventional leisure equivalents, at least initially" uniting music, dance and drugs in a way never before experienced in Britain and moving drug use to the center of youth leisure (Critcher 2000: 147, 157).

In this sense therefore raves are about having fun and feeling good, and in general do not represent a challenge to authority beyond resistance to attempts to curtail them. Some researchers argue that reordering the status of rave drugs as licit rather than illicit and normalizing their use can be justified on the basis that these drugs are recreational and largely non-addictive. Parker and others (1998: 157) argue that the drugs are purely an artifact of leisure and that British culture accepted and facilitated their use. Together, the drug ecstasy and house music formed:

> the largest youth cultural phenomenon that Britain had ever seen, Ecstasy culture had become the primary leisure activity for British youth, seamlessly integrated into the fabric of the weekend ritual.
>
> (Collin 1998: 267)

Moreover, because ecstasy is a criminalized product, the increase in youth drug use, including ecstasy, since the 1980s means that mainstream youth culture has become coupled with law-breaking in a way never before experienced.

What kind of statement is made by rave culture? Critcher (2000: 158, 160) suggests that raves exemplify leisure values as "a continuation of the time out of Saturday night when the values of the weekend take over from those of the weekday" and "a case study in the moral regulation of leisure." Similarly, Malbon (1999: 164) proposes that a rave is about "the here and now," a statement of identity through the association of one's self with the dancers and an expression of emotion and vitality. Presdee agrees, suggesting that rave is "a fascination with sensation and the sensory mechanisms of the body. . . . All life must be fun, immediate, ahistorical. The aim is to escape into sensation and stand free of logic." Thus, for Presdee, "the body and its adornment become the primary site of defiance" (Presdee 2000: 121, 122).

As noted above, traditional displays of sexual availability seem to form almost no part of rave culture. McRobbie observes that the rave culture softens the edges of white working-class masculinity as males using ecstasy transform into sociable bodies and join with females in a virtually sexless experience governed by the sheer pleasure of the dance culture (McRobbie 1993: 407).

Redhead (1993: 65) suggests that "Within popular culture the attempt to evade surveillance can be of vital importance," an insight equally valid for graffiti artists and skateboarders. Clearly, rave organizers took quite elaborate steps to keep rave venues secret and in the early period acid house parties were held in locations well away from normal zones of surveillance. Like the "sneaky property crimes" of adolescents described by Katz (1988: 76) that "prove they can be deviant in society and get away with it," ravers have also projected a form of resistance to authority showing that they too could get away with it. However, like skateboarding and, to some extent, graffiti, raves have been brought under control by being appropriated by commercial interests, branded and enclosed in spaces where they can be monitored, controlled and inspected.

Writing graffiti

Writing graffiti on public spaces dates back at least to the days when man first began to draw on the walls of caves. Graffiti is but one of a number of ways of marking the social world. Other modes in any urban landscape include logos, images and symbols, all of which leave a sign (Halsey and Young 2002: 181). According to Jeff Ferrell (1993: 5), urban graffiti is of two types: graffiti writing and graffiti. The latter relates to gang-type graffiti, latrinalia and racist and neo-Nazi inscriptions and the like, and is not to be confused with graffiti writing, some of which has earned the status of an art form. Opponents of graffiti tend to confuse this boundary, sometimes deliberately, and to distort or ignore this differentiation in attempts to link graffiti with vandalism. For Ferrell, in the Denver graffiti world writers shared an aesthetic, an artistic style, rendering writing not a crime constituted by trespass and vandalism but a "crime of style" (p. 53).

Graffiti is associated with adolescence and youth and has become recognized as a youth subculture. Because the writing of graffiti is considered a criminal act, youthful graffiti writers are usually classed as delinquents, even though writing graffiti is clearly a less than heinous act of deviance. Graffiti writing enjoys a problematic status as both damage to public property and an art form. While it may be regarded as antisocial conduct, it may not be motivated by that intent (Halsey and Young 2002: 171). It has been suggested that the rationale for graffiti writing may be "to acquire fame, to command respect," and because "there is nothing else to do" (Feiner and Klein 1982: 52). Fame is acquired by writing the three main forms of graffiti: "tagging," "throw ups" and "pieces." Respect is gained not only for the quantity and quality of writing but also for undertaking the risks associated with writing, as explained by one writer:

> "You might do a piece and it might not be all that good, but because you've done it in a certain depot or certain night or because the yard is considered hot [risky] and you've still gone in there, you still get respect" (Acrid).

> (MacDonald 2001: 84)

Similarly, the size of a piece of writing is related to the degree of respect because a larger piece indicates a longer time spent in danger (MacDonald 2001: 84). However, simply possessing the status and identity of a writer brings an adolescent writer respect:

"I mean, as an adolescent you've got to just wait until you grow up for people to take notice of what you're doing. So with graffiti you can start at any age and people will look up to you. However small you are, people will look up to you with some respect" (Mear).

(MacDonald 2001: 189)

Studies reveal that some graffiti writers regard themselves as subversives and "outlaws," and as contesting the dominant culture's hegemony. While writers acknowledge that they engage in acts categorized as deviant, they insist that their activity does not warrant police attention (Brewer and Miller 1990: 362). Austin (1998: 242) argues that graffiti writers are resisting the "conflictual class hierarchy of urban names – a hierarchy that works to circulate the names of 'the famous' within the public sphere/public space while ignoring others." An interactionist analysis of graffiti writers looks for meanings in the labels attached to the subculture and may see the individual commitment to graffiti as an outcome of the solidarity that seems to exist among writers. Ferrell contends that graffiti writing is a form of "anarchist resistance" because "Working together, graffiti writers construct an alternative, street-wise aesthetic that subverts the pre-packaged imagery of the culture industry and city hall" (1993: 173). This "cultural resistance" is resistance with creativity because graffiti is art – the art of the streets, not that of the public monument, the corporation or the advertising industry. Accordingly, Ferrell argues that graffiti is employed to resist the cultural domination of urban spaces by the culture industry (pp. 173, 175).

The following section will explore studies of graffiti in New York and Denver where moral panics about graffiti have revealed the politics associated with attempts to eradicate it. As well, a comparative study from Australia helps illustrate how local authorities strategized against graffiti. The motivations of graffiti writers will be examined, as well as studies that have unpacked the meaning or social significance of the subculture. The gendered nature of graffiti writing will be explored in light of persuasive arguments that male writers "do masculinity" while doing graffiti.

Graffiti as art

The original graffiti writers did not emerge from the art world (Lachmann 1988: 242), but some graffiti is now regarded as an art form. In the 1970s and 1980s, graffiti was commodified and sold by the art world as a form of primitive art and advertising agencies now hire graffiti writers to paint large outdoor murals. The commodification and marketing of graffiti writing has produced specialist stores selling clothing, graffiti equipment and fanzines. There are now organized conventions and a multitude of websites and networks for graffiti writers.

According to Rahn (2002: 9), describing the graffiti subculture in Montreal, Canada, some practitioners of graffiti culture have attempted to resist commercialization by developing the notion of "keeping it real." This notion includes perpetuating the illicit nature of writing to an extent that a writer who paints licitly will be criticized for not "keeping it real." Thus, while some writers wish to preserve the street culture association between hip-hop graffiti and other elements of hip-hop, others favor promoting graffiti as an international art form. One "old school" writer regarded hip-hop graffiti as a means of expressing his anger against authority and saw writers as a collective, with each member gaining personal power to take on the "system" from that union (p. 175). Younger writers suggested that graffiti's transformation into a mainstream licit art form was the "natural course of events" and planned to enjoy the resulting profits while at the same time maintaining an identity as subversives. Nevertheless, the advance of branding and marketing has changed the nature of graffiti writing and its status as an "outlaw" activity. As Rahn puts it:

> As graffiti culture becomes increasingly packaged as a lifestyle, it becomes sanitized of any political awareness and sold as a consumer good. Youth buy into representations of hip-hop because it suggests danger and transgression, without learning the codes and beliefs driving the community.
>
> (Rahn 2002: 177)

Despite the appropriation of graffiti by the art world, writers continue to maintain that graffiti is a public art form, that writing in public is "the original way to do graffiti" and that graffiti on canvas is "like a watered down version" (MacDonald 2001: 167). In his account of the graffiti world in Denver, however, Ferrell notes that the best writers associate closely with alternative gallery owners and that the alternative arts scene functions as a kind of support network (Ferrell 1993: 40).

GRAFFITI WRITING

Graffiti writing is an international subculture; by the mid-1980s the hip-hop graffiti style had reached Canada, Amsterdam, London, Paris, Copenhagen and Vienna (Ferrell 1993: 10). Writers across countries share a common argot. It is therefore useful to set out some commonly used terms in graffiti writing.

"Grafitti"
The word is derived from the Italian verb graffiare meaning "to scratch" and encompasses forms of writing from cave paintings to "latrinalia" (writings on walls of mostly public bathrooms) and all other forms of public writing that convey messages (Castleman 1982: xi).

"Getting up"
The term has been used since the mid-1970s and describes the need for graffiti artists to write prolifically. Thus, where a writer is "getting up" other writers will applaud that and tend to ignore any deficiencies in style. What counts is whether the work is "out there" and "around" (Castleman 1982: 20). Thus, "getting it up" and "getting it out there" describe the desire of writers to have the widest possible exposure of their work (Rahn 2002: 15).

"Style"
The goal of every writer is to have good style, and style is judged in public displays of writing and the content of sketchbooks in which designs are tried out (Castleman 1982: 21, 25). The term "wild style" describes almost any style judged to be unreadable. Wild style comprises very complex configurations of lettering and is attempted only by very accomplished writers (Rahn 2002: 14).

"Biting"
This is the practice of borrowing or "biting" the style of other writers. This habit is frowned upon and may lead to confrontations between the biter and those who are bitten (Castleman 1982: 24). Accusing a writer of biting another's style questions the willingness or ability of that writer to produce innovative work (Ferrell 1993: 86).

"Tags" and "tagging"
A tag is the most basic and simple form of graffiti and consists of the name of the writer presented in a stylized way, as if it were a logo. Tags are written quickly and often, in order to gain the recognition of other writers (Castleman 1982: 26). If a tag is painted large with styles and colors it is called a "piece" and taggers who develop painting styles of some complexity identify themselves as writers (Rahn 2002: 4, 5). Taggers may use spray paint but most use markers of all kinds (p. 10). Painting or tagging a surface is termed "hitting," and an area covered by a large number of tags or pieces has been "hit up." A very prolific writer is said

to "kill" (p. 22). Most graffiti writers do not advance beyond tagging to painting murals. Taggers compare themselves to advertisers, contending that rather than paying for space they purchase it through their boldness and style (Lachmann 1988: 236). Gangs recruit taggers to design a gang tag that can be displayed on their clothing. Gaining employment with a gang is a mark of distinction for a tagger. Gangs will infest territory they wish to claim by tagging it with their gang logo or tag (p. 239). In Denver, writers avoided tagging areas that possessed their own aesthetics such as sculptures and granite walls (Ferrell 1993: 74).

"Throw ups"

This describes a spray-painted two- or three-letter name in one or two colors, using large, simple lettering formed into a single unit that can be quickly written in public in a few minutes. The term is also used to refer to other forms of writing that lack style (Castleman 1982: 29, 31). A spray-painted work containing only letters in one or two colors can be quickly thrown up on a wall and typically uses large, simple lettering. Some writers disparage throw ups as being too close to tagging (Rahn 2002: 14). In terms of style, the status of a throw up is between a tag and a piece (Ferrell 1993: 84).

"Pieces"

Short for "masterpieces" and comprises the names formerly painted on the outsides of subway trains (Castleman 1982: 31). A "large piece" represents the standard in hip-hop graffiti ranging in size from six feet long and four feet high and may take hours or days to execute. Complex letter arrangements and sometimes cartoon images are used (Rahn 2002: 14). A mural is a piece. Writing a piece is called piecing.

"Top-to-bottoms"

On a subway car, this term describes the names and drawings that extend from the bottom of a subway car to its top but not extending the full length of the car (Castleman 1982: 31).

"Backgrounding," "going over," "crossing out," "dog out," "line out"

In the case of subway graffiti, this describes a code that prohibits writers from crossing out each other's pieces. Once a piece has been gone over it is considered to be destroyed (Castleman 1982: 43). This is done by putting a line through another writer or crew's name. A "cross-out war" describes a dispute between writers who are lining out each other's names (MacDonald 2001: xi).

"Racking up"
Refers to the tradition in graffiti writing that materials employed in the actual writing be acquired through stealing. Racking up describes the act of stealing. Writers may rack as a team (Castleman 1982: 47).

"Toy" and "toys"
Used by writers to refer to anything lacking significance, including writers lacking style and the capacity to use spray paint or markers effectively. It can also refer to writers who lack the bravado necessary for the task of subway painting or who are police informers. A writer who fails in getting up is most likely to be judged a toy (Castleman 1982: 76). A toy's work is termed "wack" as lacking skill and clearly inferior (Rahn 2002: 5). A young, inexperienced or artistically incompetent writer is a toy (MacDonald 2001: xii).

"Writers' corners"
A gathering place on the street for graffiti writers where they can meet, gossip and perhaps join together to write. In New York, police pressure effectively put an end to these gathering places (Castleman 1982: 85, 87).

"Crew"
An informal association of graffiti writers capable of executing large pieces. A single writer may be associated with a number of crews and crews may paint as a collective or acknowledge their relationship by citing the names of their crew around the edges of a piece. A crew is commonly mis-categorized as a gang, but crews are formed to paint, not engage in violence (Rahn 2002: 5). Crews can range in size from a few to two dozen writers who may live in the same neighborhood or attend the same school. Being a member of one crew does not preclude joining another (Brewer and Miller 1990: 355).

"Black book" or "piece book"
A book or portfolio containing a writer's ideas for sketches for pieces in which other writers can sign or sketch their tags. Writers bring these books to gatherings to display their skills (Brewer and Miller 1990: 353; Rahn 2002: 14). Piece books may also contain photographs of a writer's work (Ferrell 1993: 68).

> **"Burner"**
> A piece that shows off the superior artistry, style, skill and originality of a writer. The term "burning" refers therefore to the artistic aspects of hip-hop graffiti (Brewer and Miller 1990: 358). To "burn" is to paint exceptionally well (MacDonald 2001: xi).
>
> **"Battling"**
> In "battling," one writer faces off against another, responding to a challenge, and attempts to paint a stylistically superior piece in the judgment of non-battling and battling writers (Brewer and Miller 1990: 358).
>
> **"Bomb," "cane," "destroy," "kill"**
> To completely cover something with graffiti (MacDonald 2001: xi).
>
> **"Selling out"**
> To renounce illegal graffiti writing and work commercially for cash (MacDonald 2001: xii).

Subway graffiti in New York

In his descriptive account of graffiti writing in the New York subway (the first substantive account of this subculture), Castleman (1982) notes that graffiti writing began to appear on the subway in the late 1960s when the name Taki 183 could be seen on subway stations all over Manhattan. As the number of graffiti writers grew, designs began to appear on subway trains, both inside and outside, as writers tagged throughout the subway (pp. 54–55). By late 1973 the first entire subway car had been painted, and subsequently, whole car murals appeared containing cartoons, caricatures and outdoor scenes (p. 60). Most of the New York subway writers began to write at the age of about 11 and retired after reaching 16 when they became subject to adult penalties.[4] The average age was about 15 with a minority of female writers (pp. 67–68). Female writers generally avoided the dangers of the train yards and focused on train tagging and painting on walls. The characteristics of these writers included: a significant interest in the art and practice of writing graffiti; enjoyment in using its distinctive discourse, exaggerating their abilities to other writers or outsiders; and the ability to run fast to elude police, and to move quickly in a variety of subway environments that call for climbing, sliding and vaulting (pp. 69–70). Writers believed that their writing beautified the city and constituted a public service (p. 71), and that writing inscribed an identity. As one writer put it:

"A lot of people found. . . . [s]ecurity and comfort in dealing with their name. It was strengthening who they were to themselves. . . . Writing your name identifies who you are. The more you write your name, the more you begin to think about and the more you begin to be about who you are. Once you start doing that, you start to assert your individualism and when you do that, you have an identity."

(Castleman 1982: 76)

Challenging graffiti

Ferrell (1993: 12, 15) asserts that during the 1970s and 1980s urban corporate and political leaders constructed graffiti writing as a social problem, designed elaborate campaigns to eradicate it (producing, for example, the *Denver Graffiti Removal Manual* (Clean Denver 1988)), and formed national networks for that purpose.

Castleman (1982) chronicles the "politics of graffiti" in New York from 1972, when elected officials, private citizens, the media and other anti-graffiti organizations developed strategies to rid the subway system of graffiti and its writers. Previously, graffiti was confined to low-income residential areas, and there was no media interest and no public protest (Ley and Cybriwsky 1974: 492). Only when writers began to display on the subway and its facilities did graffiti become a public concern. The "wars against graffiti" began under Mayor John Lindsay in the 1970s and continued under Mayor Ed Koch in the early 1980s (Austin 1998: 245).

Media interest in subway graffiti began in 1971 when the *New York Times* investigated tagging by Taki 183 but it was not until spring 1972 that the *Times* published an editorial denouncing the "wanton use of spray paint to deface subways" (quoted in Castleman 1982: 136). The editorial followed a call from the city council president to wage "an all-out war on graffiti" because "it pollutes the eye and mind" (p. 136) and for an anti-graffiti day when the people of New York would scrub walls and the subway clean of graffiti. Subsequently, the Mayor, disturbed by the "'unsightly appearance" of the subway and other public places (p. 136), joined in the emergent campaign, proposing that anyone caught with an open spray can in a city building or facility be fined and jailed.

A committee of the city council submitted an anti-graffiti bill to the council in mid-September 1972 that called for serious punishment for perpetrators, made it illegal to carry an aerosol can of paint into a public facility, and banned writing on public property. As punishment, the bill proposed that graffiti writers be sentenced to remove graffiti under the supervision of city officials. The media described the graffiti as "sometimes obscene and always offensive" and termed the writers "youthful vandals," thus linking graffiti writers to the worst forms of delinquency (Castleman 1982: 136).

The Mayor then established a graffiti task force to execute "tough new programs" and the anti-graffiti legislation was approved by the city council (Castleman 1982: 137–138). Private citizens, acting as moral entrepreneurs, became involved in the campaign, voluntarily cleaning buildings and trains while the Mayor's task force announced that 426 graffiti writers had been convicted and sentenced to spend a day in the train yards scrubbing away graffiti. The transit authority called for more arrests, complaining that there was the possibility of a "grand design" epidemic where large designs would cover half or more of a train's outside area. The graffiti task force responded to what had now become a moral panic with a US$24 million project to reduce the defacement to an acceptable 10 or 20 percent (p. 140).

At this point the moral panic was challenged by a long article in the *New York Magazine* of March 26 asserting that the city's fight against graffiti had "Gotten Completely Out of Hand" (Goldstein 1973). It named the writers as members of a "genuine teenage street culture" who were deploying a new form of art. Nevertheless, the Mayor continued to rail against "the demoralizing visual impact of graffiti" (Castleman 1982: 141, 142).

In waging the war against graffiti, the courts took the view that graffiti writing could not be taken seriously and that they lacked the time and facilities to handle such prosecutions (Castleman 1982: 144). After 1975 media interest in graffiti in the city declined, but in 1981 the Mayor's office again announced a program to combat graffiti by using fences and guard dogs to keep the writers out of the yards. For the first time the Mayor's office claimed that the public was frightened by graffiti (pp. 146–147) and the MTA Chairman announced that graffiti symbolized a loss of control of the subway, thus enhancing its reputation as a place of danger (p. 176). When reports surfaced about the viciousness of the guard dogs the *New York Times* reversed its stand, now calling the graffiti "always striking and sometimes cheerful" where previously the writers had been denounced as "animals," "youthful vandals" and "a public menace" (quoted in Castleman 1982: 150).

The New York City Transit Police Department claimed that graffiti writing was a "slippery slope" to later criminal activity, and described writing as "a school for crime" (Castleman 1982: 167). Lachmann's police and prosecutor informants in New York challenged this view, with one district attorney claiming that "the link between graffiti and real crime is just in our rhetoric" (Lachmann 1988: 236). The MTA continued to claim that the public saw graffiti as "a form of deterioration like garbage, noise, dirt and broken doors" (Castleman 1982: 177). According to Lachmann's informants, police in New York City would beat graffiti writers rather than arrest them and this constituted an effective constraint for writers (Lachmann 1988: 244).[5]

In Australia, an examination of the measures adopted by municipal governments in South Australia revealed the following typology: removal of the graffiti, criminalization, welfarism and acceptance (Halsey and Young 2002). Removal was accomplished through contractors or volunteer groups. Criminalization involved mandatory reporting of all incidents to the police, prosecuting writers and viewing graffiti as a police problem. Welfarism was an outreach strategy to writers aimed at diverting them away from writing into other activities. A strategy of acceptance essentially co-opted graffiti writing by transforming it into forms of mainstream art such as commissioning murals and providing art classes for writers. The authorities hoped that tagging would diminish as writers who possessed only limited tagging skills became upgraded to mural artists. It was thought that linking graffiti writing, as an element of hip-hop culture, to skateboarding parks where graffiti would be tolerated, would help minimize the extent of graffiti in public areas. Moreover, graffiti would then be more appropriately sited contiguous to another youth subculture (p. 178).

Denver's war against graffiti

In his account of anti-graffiti movements and politics in Denver, Ferrell (1993) notes that in the early days of graffiti writing there was little public or political concern. However, by late 1987 a political and corporate crack-down on graffiti began in Denver with a "graffiti task force" and undercover detectives actively pursuing writers (pp. 102, 103). It proved effective, as writers who were jailed stopped tagging and piecing after their release. Commentators linked the crack-down to the Mayor facing a recall election and his using a war on graffiti to boost his support (p. 106).

A principal agent in the anti-graffiti campaign was the organization known as "Keep Denver Beautiful" which argued that a survey conducted in 1987 had shown that "65 per cent of Denver residents deemed graffiti a major problem in Denver and in their own neighborhoods" (Ferrell 1993: 107). In April 1988, the Denver Post announced the crack-down with a front-page story that identified elements of the campaign as requiring convicted persons to perform public service and pay graffiti cleaning costs, education programs, police talks to public schools to "discourage vandalism" (p. 107), a new graffiti removal manual for householders and alternative sites for those wishing to paint murals on walls. In early 1989 the Denver Police joined the campaign with a 24-hour graffiti hotline, rewards for information on writers and increased coordination between state agencies (p. 109).

Ferrell identifies the property owners and business interests in the city as the principal promoters of the anti-graffiti campaign, including a paint supplier who donated cover-up paint. Thus, corporate interests joined with political power in an exercise that deployed and coordinated their joint interests (Ferrell 1993: 112).

GRAFFITI WARS

In February 2010 it was reported that law enforcement, judges and politicians throughout the country were stepping up their fight against graffiti artists – but this may have served only to make the artists even bolder. The fight included some stiff penalties. For example, in December 2010, Texas Judge Saldana sentenced an 18-year-old to eight years in prison on three counts of graffiti and one count of possession of marijuana.

In March 2009, Hert, 22, the second most wanted graffiti writer in Pittsburgh, arrived at the Allegheny court-house, only to be informed by the police that they held warrants for his arrest on 69 misdemeanors and four felony counts of criminal mischief arising from damage caused by his alleged vandalism involving spraying his tag on public and private buildings and on railroad assets. Detective Daniel Sullivan said, "He was the number two tagger in the city, hitting more than 100 pieces of property" and causing an estimated US$212,000 in damage. Sullivan added, "graffiti crime is increasing at a significant rate" but noted that enforcement is complicated by the commercialization of the graffiti culture.

Hert's arrest signals a crack-down on graffiti artists through increased prosecutions. For example, Graffiti Tracker, a company based in Omaha, Nebraska, which investigates graffiti acts under contracts with law enforcement or sells police software, now has over US$1 million in contracts with law enforcement in 45 cities, towns and municipalities. Pittsburgh itself has created a "vandal squad" dedicated to catching graffiti artists. In Pittsburgh damage exceeding US$5,000 can be charged as a felony.

But graffiti artists are unconcerned by this crack-down. Taggers claim that writing graffiti is a victimless crime but Judge Nauhaus of Pittsburgh's Allegheny County strongly disagrees, arguing that "The victims in these situations own the property." To this, Manhattan graffiti artist KET responds, "Wealthy building owners think that having something on the wall hurts their property values and makes people fearful but young people think that writing on the wall is a form of expression; it's artistic and it's beautiful." KET claims that law enforcement wears down graffiti artists until they run out of money and "then you got to take a shitty deal and do prison time or get a permanent record. And then you become a criminal by their standards, and they can immediately toss you in jail if you ever get out of line."

Source: Adapted from The Crime Report. 2010. "Art Crime: Graffiti Wars." Monday, February 22. http://www.thecrimereport.org/archive/art-crime-graffiti-wars/

In 1989, the state passed legislation with harsh new penalties for gang-related graffiti which potentially could apply to non-gang graffiti writers who operated in organized groups and could arguably constitute "a gang." In other measures the city applied zoning ordinances to force property owners to remove graffiti (Ferrell 1993: 119). In the courts, once a writer was convicted, the sentence included a mandatory graffiti cleaning. Writers cleaned alley walls and dumpsters guarded by Sheriff's officers in a shaming ceremony designed to humiliate writers, in furtherance of a moral panic where "deviants must not only be labeled but also be seen to be labeled" (p. 121).

The outcome of these efforts was mixed. Initially, the police were reluctant to take graffiti seriously but later changed their attitude, so that by January 1989 a police crack-down began with increased arrests in an effort characterized by the Chief of Police as saving Denver from a "nightmare of painted obscenities and satanic symbols" (Ferrell 1993: 125). Denver police joined with local residents in a "Graffiti Stoppers" program and offered rewards, as expressed in the media, for "turning in graffiti vandals." Local resident volunteers cleaned graffiti under a program called "Adopt-A-Spot" (p. 128). In 1988, in an attempt to lure writers away from public graffiti writing, the Mayor publicized an "artway" for legally sanctioned graffiti which comprised a construction site walkway (p. 131).

Ferrell (1993) explains that the business and political elites of the city presented the anti-graffiti campaign as an issue of public interest so that, in the end, the campaign was constructed as if it came from the community. Economic and property issues were reconfigured as a social problem and in turn were transformed into a moral panic. The supposed disgust of the community or the neighborhood with graffiti was in fact that of political and business interests. The community willfully excluded graffiti writers and admirers of graffiti, youth and other marginal groups from the supposed majority will (pp. 134, 135). This moral panic promoted constructions like "graffiti vandals" who "attack" and "rob," and claims about "victims of graffiti vandalism," and spread a sort of "free-floating fear" among the general public (p. 140).

According to Ferrell, associating graffiti with lack of control within the city, with chaos and with vandals who rob and attack victims is intended to render graffiti threatening and frightening and to marginalize graffiti writers in a "war" against their activities (1993: 143). Moreover, attacking all forms of graffiti, even pieces which satisfy aesthetic principles because it challenges authority, calls into question "the politics of public space" and "public art" (p. 143). Ferrell poses the question: "Is there not a place in public for art that comes from the community as opposed to corporate and public art forms that perhaps fail to directly engage the community in the same way?" (p. 185).

According to Ferrell, the overall effect of the war against graffiti in Denver was to increase the profile of graffiti writers because media accounts publicized their work and the alternative media sprang to their defense. This increased visibility led in turn to a demand for writers' services in the form of commissions from a range of business interests (1993: 146). In an odd reversal, therefore, the crack-down on graffiti led to greater activity within the graffiti subculture, even adding to the thrills of writing as writers resisted the crackdown. The very activity at which the war was targeted – tagging – in fact multiplied because of the moral panic (p. 149).

Hip-hop

Graffiti is associated with hip-hop culture. According to Rahn (2002) and Ferrell (1993), the term "hip-hop" originates in the culture of the behop musicians of the 1940s. It emerged in the 1970s as it became associated with break dancing, DJ-ing and MC-ing (now called rapping) so that by the 1980s, these various forms constituted the elements of hip-hop culture. In the 1970s, hip-hop developed in the South Bronx area of New York City as an African American and Afro-Caribbean youth culture or subculture (Rahn 2002: 1–2) and moved out into the inner cities of Philadelphia, Chicago, Los Angeles and Washington D.C. Graffiti is an integral part of the hip-hop culture, having also originated in the Bronx.

Traditions and commercialization

There is said to be a conflict between old school and new school thinking about graffiti. Rahn (2002: 43) describes the two schools as follows:

> The old school is like the original New York 1970s attitude that you paint your tag because you want to prove that you're alive. You're living in this shitty society where you're not a part of anything, you're nothing. You go out and write your name up on a wall because you want people to know that you were there. You paint on a train and the train travels

all around the city and people know that there's life in the boroughs. The thing is, that's come a long way since then, you know. The graffiti attitude that "you're up," your tag has to be everywhere.

Concerning the motivation for writing graffiti, one 24-year-old writer of the old school explained that he wrote:

"to take back a part of what belongs to me anyway. The city belongs to everyone who lives in it and everyone has a right to have a say, but unfortunately we live in such a half or half-assed democratic society where it doesn't matter; nobody counts anyway. All the politicians say, 'Screw them. I want to do what I want.' I attack what they claim is so precious to them and hit them where it hurts and ruin their little glass city, which they have erected somehow."

(Rahn 2002: 67)

In Denver too, Ferrell reports a disconnect between working on the streets and in the yards with its attendant risks, and doing murals for AIDS campaigns for cash. The latter is pejoratively called "signpainting" by some writers because writers are required to adopt the vision of the commissioning agency and to compromise their style to execute a "throwaway" (Ferrell 1993: 93).

The thrill of graffiti writing

In 1961 Matza and Sykes asked the question, "What makes delinquency attractive in the first place?" In response, they suggested that delinquents are in it for the fun, and that "thrills" and "kicks" are a product of the fact that an activity involves breaking the law (Matza and Sykes 1961: 713). Normally, this moment would be represented by leisure time and in activities like sports, recreation and vacations. As Matza and Sykes note, most societies provide space for events like carnivals, parades and processions where thrill seeking is permitted for a time and deviance excused (p. 713). Terming the search for adventure, excitement and thrills a "subterranean value," they argue that it does not constitute deviance, "but it must be held in abeyance until the proper moment and circumstances for its expression arrive" (p. 716). However, there are some groups that do not observe the constraints placed upon thrill seeking and are consequently judged deviant. Building on this argument, Presdee (2000: 33) proposes that in contemporary late modernity the search for thrills actually spills over into the "unbearable rationality of modern life" so that "acts of carnival become a daily need for social survival."

Graffiti writers compete for mastery of public space and occupy it with their names, expressing their bravado and fearlessness. Philadelphia graffiti writer Cool Earl explained:

> "I started writing . . . to prove to people where I was. You go somewhere and get your name up there and people know you were there, that you weren't afraid."
>
> (Ley and Cybriwsky 1974: 494)

Most old school writers agree that the principal characteristics of graffiti were "the thrill of the act," being "subversive" and the peer response to their writing. In contrast, the new school writers are more concerned with the aesthetics of graffiti. They perceive their efforts as art and regard graffiti as synonymous with mural art, seeing the thrill experienced from performing an illicit act as only ancillary to the artistic expression (Rahn 2002: 140, 170). According to Rahn, the thrill or seduction of graffiti comes from violating norms embodied in the law against graffiti writing. Thus, a writer feels empowered as he or she does graffiti and transgresses the law. This notion of the thrill associated with graffiti writing is also explored by Lachmann, who found that subway graffiti writers in New York delighted in their contest with the police, comparing their skills like stealth and speed and smartness to the police who, in their view, were big and strong and used brute force. This "superior attitude" about their craft extended to stealing paint, even though their patrons gave them money to buy it. Echoing this superiority, one study notes that writers like to convey a "tough street image" and cast themselves as "modern outlaws," appropriating names that signify their outlaw status such as "Menece to Society" (sic), "Crime Over Night" and "Instant Destruction" (Brewer and Miller 1990: 361).

Graffiti writers told Ferrell (1993: 28), for example, that it was the illegal tagging or piecing that thrilled them, a blending of the illegality of the act with the creative act of painting itself. As one writer, Voodoo, described the experience of piecing:

> "Right before you hit the wall, you get that rush. And right when you hit the wall you know that you're breaking the law and that gives that extra adrenalin flow. And that's what really got me going. It's like, it's kind of almost like a drug. . . . Yeah it's like being a jewel thief. It's not like you're really breaking the law, it's like a jewel thief, its real kind of a romantic criminal act."
>
> (Ferrell 1993: 82)

The relative lack of seriousness attached to graffiti writing under the criminal law was said to provide a safe means of experiencing the thrills of law-breaking, an exhibition of bravery and a way to express contempt for authority (Lachmann 1988: 235, 236). Thus, celebrating the illicit nature of the subculture with other writers and more serious criminals enabled writers to share in the "seductions of crime" (Katz 1988). Comparing the thrills of the illicit to the monetary gains of the licit, one writer, Teck, explains:

> "I made a fair amount of money doing legal art for TV commercials and other film endeavors. In actuality all of this paled to the thrill of being chased through back streets and narrowly escaping the beam of police headlights. Living precariously against the grain took precedence in my daily routine."
>
> *(Urb* magazine 1994 quoted in MacDonald 2001: 73)

In his discussion of adolescents and what he terms "sneaky property crimes," Katz suggests that such crimes are "especially attractive to adolescents as devices for proving that they can be deviant in society and get away with it" (1988: 76). Such crimes include shoplifting, vandalism and joyriding, and Katz believes the special salience of such crimes for adolescents is that they allow them to be "privately deviant in public places" (p. 77). One dimension of the thrill of sneaky property crimes is that they constitute a kind of game – a ludic experience where this kind of deviance can be tried again and again because it is fun (p. 67). The ludic dimension resonates with accounts of graffiti writers' enjoyment in "gaming" the police, in escaping surveillance and in returning again and again to public spaces to write their names.

Gender and graffiti

Explaining the gendered nature of graffiti subculture in Montreal, one female writer complained of being excluded from the male writers' "boys club" and noted that there seemed to be few women who became recognized on their own merits and not because they were associated with or were mentored by male writers. However, she also thought that the new school was more accepting of women and more likely to treat them as equals (Rahn 2002: 153). In New York, the subway graffiti writers interviewed by Lachmann in 1988, who were overwhelmingly male, believed that writing should be confined to males.[6] They maintained a "bravura conception" of the subculture defined by the dangerousness associated with executing designs in subway yards:

> "You got to get into the yards by going under or over those barbed-wire fences. They have dogs loose. Women gets scared and can't keep up."
>
> (Lachmann 1988: 235)

youth, crime and justice

In a wide-ranging exploration of masculinity in graffiti writing, MacDonald (2001: 96–150) contends that doing graffiti writing enables male writers to "construct and confirm their masculine identities" and that writing as a subculture provides "a space for the construction of masculinity" (p. 96). MacDonald's informants believed that the risks and dangers associated with writing rendered only males capable of undertaking it – it was "men's work." Thus, as one female writer explained when asked why more women did not write graffiti:

> "Because it's a dirty job, a dirty hard job. You have to carry paint in the dark, crawl through God knows what and hide behind disgusting things and scale big fences. Basically it's men's work. It's that, you know, most girls are raised to be little feminine things. . . . It just takes some qualities and girls are just way too feminine and they don't have nearly as much guts to do such daring things like that."
>
> (MacDonald 2001: 99–100)

The elements of a writer's masculinity are "resilience, bravery and fortitude" and graffiti writing may be seen as an initiation rite on the road to manhood (MacDonald 2001: 101, 102), with writers deploying cunning and courage to break into train yards and cross electrified train tracks (p. 106).

The argot of graffiti writing is replete with masculinist militaristic terminology such as "bomb," "hit," "battling" and "burner" (Brewer and Miller 1990: 361). Warfare and combat characterize graffiti discourse as writers fight authorities and sometimes other writers for control of public spaces. Sometimes the police seize control and sometimes writers are able to occupy urban territory in an ongoing contest between controlling deviance and doing masculinity through the thrills of illicit behavior. Male writers construct females who enter the subculture as possessing stereotypical feminine traits that greatly impede any attempt to do graffiti correctly. Consequently, they must prove they are not women to meet the standards set by males (MacDonald 2001: 131). A further constraint for female writers is that they often enter the subculture because they are girlfriends of male writers. Thus, a girl can be labeled as not being authentically committed to the subculture but rather to her boyfriend's passion for it (p. 135). MacDonald summarizes her view on gender in graffiti:

> This subculture must be acknowledged for what it is. Not a site for "youth" but a site for "male" youth – an illegal confine where danger, opposition and the exclusion of women is used to nourish, amplify and salvage notions of masculinity.
>
> (MacDonald 2001: 149)

MacDonald (2001) seems to be suggesting that graffiti writing constitutes a form of hegemonic masculinity because she identifies it as possessing the traits associated with that form, such as toughness, heterosexuality, power and competition. Theoretical work on masculinity has led to an understanding that there exist complex and multiple masculinities but this aspect is not explored by MacDonald (Heidensohn and Gelsthorpe 2007: 388). Is MacDonald suggesting that graffiti writers who possess these traits are signifying their masculinity or that these traits are a causal factor in their deviance? The issues of class and race remain unexplored in her discussion. Do all graffiti writers accomplish masculinity in the same way and, if not, to what degree is the particular version of hegemonic masculinity they invest in determined by their social structural position?

Graffiti writers insist that they write graffiti for other writers and not for society generally, thus enhancing their identity as outsiders, nonconformists and even subversives. Writers delight in being able to translate graffiti into meaningful messages while the rest of society stands baffled. The very incomprehensibility of writing empowers the writers. Not only does graffiti seem untranslatable to outsiders; it also conveys a sense of fear, suggests disorder and poses a threat (MacDonald 2001: 157, 158).

Writers ensure that their secret world of writing remains hidden from society. With its argot and rules and the confidentiality associated with membership, writers remain mysterious figures. Usually their work is the only visible sign of their presence. Like a secret society, writers identify other writers through observation and reading cues such as "the way they watch the trains," "the hip-hop way they dress" and a "barely concealed effort not to look at walls." Once mutually identified, writers are said to possess an immediate affinity and solidarity (MacDonald 2001: 161, 162).

Skateboarding

Like writing graffiti, skateboarding is a distinct youth subculture with its own design styles, argot, clothing, music, magazines and cultural practices, including codes of conduct. In addition, like graffiti, skateboarding calls into question how public space should be used and what rights, if any, members of youth subcultures enjoy over sites that are supposedly open to all. In many cities skateboarding is illegal but skateboarders, similar to graffiti writers, sometimes challenge the law, offering various justifications for disregarding it.

Much of the literature associated with skateboarding is concerned with its impact on public space as well as how skate parks have evolved to divert skaters out of public spaces and into discrete enclosures. Questions include how and why skateboarders insist on skating the streets when parks are available, sometimes for their exclusive use. As skateboarding has become commercialized and classified as an extreme sport, questions concerning street skateboarding and professional skateboarding include: Is skating the streets the only authentic mode of practicing the subculture? Is professional skateboarding really competitive like other professional sports, or do skateboarders continually subvert the rules and, if so, why?

Skateboarding originated in the California beach cities. From the late 1950s to the early 1970s, surfers transferred surfing moves in the ocean to the hard surfaces of the streets. From the 1970s, skaters utilized a wide variety of surfaces, from school yards to drainage ditches and concrete pipes. They discovered that the many round, keyhole and kidney-shaped swimming pools in Los Angeles offered something special for skaters when emptied – a curved surface from floor to wall where skaters could ride up the walls and soar beyond in aerial moves. When they committed trespass and began using pools in this manner without the permission of the owners during the drought in Southern California in 1976 to 1977 they were designated "Outlaws" (Carr 2010: 992). Since then, street and "transition" skating – using curved surfaces that transition to steep or vertical walls such as the sides of an empty pool – have become the dominant forms of the subculture (pp. 991, 992).

In the late 1970s, purpose-built commercial skate parks appeared in a number of countries offering a range of skateable surfaces including empty pool-like creations. By the mid-1980s, the popularity of the subculture had declined and it was dismissed as a fad due to overexposure and a lack of transition terrain. During this period almost all the skate parks closed (Carr 2010: 992). As a result, skateboarding returned to its origins on the streets and became a worldwide subculture on city streets. In the United States, it is centered in cities like Los Angeles, San Francisco, Philadelphia, New York and Chicago which offer walls, benches, ledges, railings and other urban artifacts and objects to be skated on and over (Borden 2000: 138). In this period also, the "ollie" was created – a vertical jump accomplished by "popping" the tail of the skateboard on the riding surface. This allows the skater to jump perpendicularly with the skateboard seeming to stick to the feet. Once taken to the streets, the ollie allowed skaters to jump over, on to and up a range of surfaces, and gave new life to skateboarding (Carr 2010: 992).

Skateboarding and cultural values

Skaters' moves or tricks are learned from fellow skaters, through photographs in skating magazines or from videos and the Internet. Each move is named and can be "traded" (Borden 1998). Skaters map their world in terms such as:

"[Y]ou see a post and you think, wow, I can ollie over that and then if I ride this way, I can boardslide or do a noseslide over that bench. You can do it backside or frontside. There are a thousand ways to approach an object."

(Karsten and Pel 2000: 327)

Borden argues that this subculture is totalizing and "rejects work, the family, and normative American values" (2000: 138).

Skaters add art to their equipment by affixing graphics to the bottom of the skateboard deck which remain invisible while the skateboard is on the ground but are revealed in aerial moves, or when the board is being carried. In the 1980s, the thematic graphic was the skull but from the late 1980s the graphics have become more pluralistic to include semi-naked women, cartoons, geometric patterns, aliens, oriental figures and even slogans and political imagery, all typically non-realistic in style (Borden 2000: 139). Most graphics are the work of skaters themselves with the mix of styles suggesting, according to Borden, "an alternative reality, parallel to the everyday world of work, money, leisure time, shopping routines and realist photography" (p. 140).

Rejecting normative American values, skaters in one Arizona town reported to Sefiha (2003: 122) that they had cut off handrails to make them easier to skate, removed anti-skate nubs and poured concrete on certain surfaces to make them more skateable. Skaters who were questioned by adults when skating during afternoon hours about why they were "not in school" or were told to "get a job" seemed to challenge normative conceptions of how youth ought legitimately to occupy their time and in what places (p. 128).

Skaters regard themselves as nonconformists. For example, they do not perceive skating to be a traditional sport and reject the regulative aspects of organized sport such as rules, competition, set plays and referees. Similarly, skating permits many styles of play, something that would not be countenanced in a formally organized sport, and skating lacks standards by which to judge performance. Skating is also seen as a form of freedom of expression – a means of expressing your mood and identity:

"The reason I love to skate is because its [sic] a challenging [sic] sport. It's the way I express myself its something I can do by myself and nobody's there to judge me."

(Beal 1996: 208–209)

Skateboarding and claims to public spaces

Skateboarding is a performative subculture. In the city streets skaters move through urban space and seek encounters with multiple urban objects. In this process skaters relate to a particular ledge or set of handrails, or a set of steps or fire hydrants, as objects, which, for skaters, float free of the structure. In this sense therefore, skateboarding "decenters building-objects in time and space in order to recompose them as a strung-out yet newly synchronous arrangement" (Borden 2000: 145). Thus, "cities can be thought of as a series of micro-spaces" and skaters develop highly local knowledge about places and urban objects and the times when access to them is possible (p. 146). As one skateboarder describes it:

> "Walls aren't just walls, banks aren't just banks, curbs aren't just curbs and so on . . . mapping cities out in your head according to the distribution of blocks and stairs, twisting the meaning of your environment around to fit your own needs and imagination. Its brilliant being a skateboarder isn't it?" (Twisted, 1997).
>
> (Borden 2000: 148)

A skating "session" means creating and practicing techniques, locating places in which to skate and trying out new tricks on objects located in that space (Beal 1996: 208). Skaters leave traces of their paths through the city in the form of "grind marks, traces of wax, and black and silver streaks," the signs of a "sessioned" spot (Carr 2010: 988), and "exploit the ambiguity of the ownership and function of public space" (Woolley and Johns 2001: 215). Street skating is now seen as the authentic "gritty" and "rebellious" aspect of skateboarding (Borden 2001) and as invoking "freedom, non conformity and engagement with risk" (Atencio et al. 2009: 6). A study in Britain found that skaters choose spaces that afford them "accessibility, sociability and compatibility, and the opportunities they offer for tricks" (Woolley and Johns 2001: 211). In Amsterdam, when a trick is accomplished well, "skateboards are drummed on the ground as a kind of alternative applause" (Karsten and Pel 2000: 335).

In a study of skateboarding in New York City that compared skate park skating to skating public streets and plazas, Chiu (2009: 32, 33) found that skaters in the streets select from available spaces, learn the city by traveling through it, and show an appreciation for the architectural details that enable their performance. As one skater expressed it:

> "You see everything different with different eyes. Someone sees something and says, oh yes, it is just up there, you don't even notice that, but as a skater you say yeah, I can skate that, if I hit it like this, I can get all the buzz out" (Kim, 28).
>
> (Chiu 2009: 33)

The parks and plazas of the city become social sites for skaters where they share aspects of their subculture and crystallize social interactions. When skaters skate the city they "just keep cruising" and "It is not just about doing tricks, it is also about who's around, kind of relaxing" (Kim in Chiu 2009: 34). By comparison, skating in the skate parks offers a conformist mode of performing within a designated time and space, and imposes controls including the mandatory wearing of protective gear and monitoring by attendants (Chiu 2009: 38). Typically, a skate park resembles a playground and, by using the objects situated there, skaters can perform as they do in the streets with no fear of retribution. Social interaction is limited because skaters focus on improving their skills. There is a sameness about the facilities that cannot match the diversity of the streets. As explained by one skater:

> "Skateboarding in the park is like walking through the Central Park on the paths. One [street skating] is [that] you are making your own path, the other way is [that] you are making the path that urban planners say, 'this is the path that you should walk on'" (Frank, 24).
>
> (Chiu 2009: 35)

Skate parks function to designate skateboarding as a sport and to give it public legitimacy. Generally, there appears little public toleration of groups of teens, including skaters, gathering in public spaces unless for the purpose of playing a sport such as basketball. One skater summed up the difference between skating in parks and in streets as follows:

> "For real skaters, they want to skate on real things. Because in their minds, there is no validity in skateboarding on something that's made for skateboarding, but if it's something that is natural in the environment then that's considered in their mind something more real" (Roy, 22).
>
> (Chiu 2009: 39)

In the end, being banned from public spaces becomes just another obstacle to be overcome:

> "They can kick us out but we don't care, we'll be back. In the meantime, we'll just go on to the next spot and keep breaking it down."
>
> (Borden 2001: 25)

In Amsterdam, skaters travel in packs like "nomads" and contest with shopkeepers over the use of smooth walkways and entrances to shops. Skaters claim that their presence makes the street livelier and retailers

youth, crime and justice

counter that skaters are a constraint to trade. In Rotterdam, the police erected railings to prevent skating and "the spot became more popular because the railings were perfect for skating" (Karsten and Pel 2000: 337).

Skateboarding and the law

Carr (2010: 990) suggests that it is simplistic to see the relationship between urban youth and the law as one of "punitive exclusion" and that instead youth should be regarded as engaged in a "dialectical relationship with the law by which their use of the city is constantly evolving in response to a variety of legal logics – especially those of private property – which in themselves evolve to respond to these emerging practices" (p. 990). In relation to skateboarders it is suggested that they have responded to the attempts through law to exclude them from public spaces by adapting and managing the urban landscape to their ultimate benefit.

Skateboarders have tended to be included in definitions of those considered "undesirable" in the urban environment such as the homeless, graffiti writers and gang members (Carr 2010: 989). In fact, young people who simply hang out in public spaces – especially working-class male youth – have habitually been regarded as demonstrating lawlessness and disorderly conduct. As much as their mere presence, it is their lack of consumption that seems to indicate their problematic status. In late modern society urban public spaces are intended for consumption, but skate-boarders use and occupy public spaces for "play, expression and sensuality" (p. 993) without consuming or producing marketable goods. As well, skateboarding conveys an impression of unpredictability and mobility that unsettles and seems to conflict with late modern values, especially when skaters mark and damage surfaces and place wax on features (pp. 993–994).

In the U.K., urban policy directives promoting the cultural regeneration of moribund cities to produce public space that is visually appealing are said to remove "the untidy" "so as to beautify the city" and achieve "a safe and sanitized streetscape" (Millie 2008: 387). The mere visibility of youth subcultures and not their conduct is therefore considered problematic (Coleman 2005: 141). In the city of Liverpool skaters can be fined from £250 to £1,000 if they violate a law banning skating passed in 2002. The governing authority of the city claims that skateboarding gives the city a poor image and scares off tourists and consumers as well as creating damage to city property (p. 141). Nevertheless, since 2003, the city has hosted a two-day skateboarding event on specially erected ramps and walls on the city waterfront to promote tourism and the cultural image of the city (p. 139).

In Seattle, skateboarders have taken advantage of changes in the law by asserting claims to unwanted and undeveloped public spaces. They have mobilized skaters into lobby groups, and run media campaigns, and taken possession of unused and unwanted city land, adopting a "build first, ask questions later" approach (Carr 2010: 998). Skaters have raised funds and constructed their own skate parks without government permission and subsequently obtained unofficial city approval (p. 999).

In 1996, New York City legislated to prohibit skateboarding on sidewalks and in public plazas and provided an alternative to the streets in the form of 16 skate parks. In spite of this, skaters continue to skate in non-designated areas (Chiu 2009: 26). The policing of these non-designated areas is not consistent. For example, in Union Square, where old signs announce that skateboarding is prohibited, police usually eject skaters during the early evening and sometimes confiscate boards and issue tickets to pay fines (p. 28). In privately owned but publicly accessible plazas private security agencies provide intensive social control and surveillance, with owners citing the post-9/11 fear of terrorism as the rationale (p. 35). Skateboarders are viewed as antisocial, disorderly and a danger to pedestrians, and property owners fear lawsuits from skaters who injure themselves in these private places. Police issue tickets and summonses on complaints from private guards, and public and private police and security cooperate in policing these spaces.

In Australia, skateboarding first appeared in the 1960s and by the 1990s street skating was the most popular skating mode (Nolan 2003: 312). In 2003, Melbourne hosted the Skateboarding World Cup and in 2002 the Australian Sports Commission was encouraging skating and providing coaching clinics (p. 313). In the city of Newcastle, skateboarding is considered a "transgressive" activity and some public spaces have been closed to skaters (p. 315). In one city mall, uses of its space other than for shopping are considered problematic and shop owners employ a private security guard to patrol it during the day, relying on the power of intimidation and fear. For the retailers it was "common sense" that skating should not be permitted in the mall because the mall is a site for consumption and not for play (pp. 318, 319). As one retailer put it:

> "We can't have skateboarding down that strip. We do try to maintain a good environment so that the space can be shared by everyone . . . they were stealing space from pedestrians because they would use the whole mouth of the Mall. So they were stealing space from other people. You just can't do that. It's there to be shared."
>
> (Nolan 2003: 320)

The rationale for designating skating as transgressive was a concern over damage to public property and to pedestrians (Nolan 2003: 320). Thus, action was taken to construct the urban landscape so as to deter skating, for example, by installing protruding bolts along the edges of public benches, preventing tricks like grinds and slides (p. 320). Police activity is limited because they do not consider skating in no-skate areas to be an activity requiring urgent action, and when they do intervene this is largely in response to actual complaints. Thus, while notionally transgressive, where skating is permitted it is always contested. Skaters tend to ignore prohibitory notices, and in most cases have been asked to move on and are not fined or penalized by having their boards confiscated (p. 322).

Skateboarding in Philadelphia's Love Park, adjacent to City Hall, started in the 1980s, and by the 1990s the Park was renowned as a skate spot with visitors coming from many countries to skate there. In March 2000, a City Council member proposed to ban skateboarding there owing to alleged damage by skaters to concrete ledges and the dangers posed by skaters to other park users. The Council passed but did not strictly enforce a ban on skateboarding in that space (Nemeth 2006: 300).

In April 2002, the Park was closed to skaters and reopened after renovations had been carried out, including the installation of planter boxes to make it unskateable and wooden benches with crossbar dividers to deter skaters and the homeless from using the Park. Skaters and others fought back with demonstrations and Council members were evenly split over the ban on skating (Nemeth 2006: 301). By February 2004 a coalition of activist community groups including the Skateboard Advocacy Network proposed a plan to maximize the use of the Park as a skateboarding site, allowing skating only after 3 p.m. on weekdays to account for other users. Despite commercial support and funding to support it, the plan was turned down by the Council. By late 2004, the Council had relented to the extent of allowing the construction of a street-style skate park in another location. However, this was located over four miles from Love Park.

Protests on the ban in the Park continued however, and the desire to skate the Park proved to be so strong that skaters continued to go there, even posting look-outs to watch for a police presence (Nemeth 2006: 302, 303). The City struck back with a tactic described by one skater:

> "There were just these random dudes, dressed as bums, that would just sit there, and they were undercover cops" (Margera).
>
> (*Love Story* 2004 quoted in Nemeth 2006: 303)

In addition, the City proclaimed the skaters disorderly and unruly, and newspaper articles began to categorize them as "rats" and "vermin." They were compared to "roaches" and described as "dudes in backward baseball caps who dart between cars, plow into pedestrians, and gouge the granite in public plazas . . . [and are] dangerous, destructive, even anti-social" (Nemeth 2006: 304). In this case it was clear that skaters were seen as an impediment to the City's attempts to redevelop and revitalize this part of the city. Only when skaters provided an opportunity to market the city, as when the *X Games* were held there, were they supported (p. 307). Essentially, the City Council's actions in banning skating in Love Park represented "a normative (re)construction of Love Park as a secure space for the consumption of adults, business people and tourists" (p. 307). Youthful skaters were seen as not adults, as transgressive and "out of order" (p. 307).

Commodification of skateboarding

Skateboarding's commercial potential was such that by the late 1980s the business of skateboarding was estimated to be worth between US$300 and US$500 million (Borden 2000). By the 1990s there were about 300 to 400 professional skaters. Some argue that skaters resist commercialization through measures such as establishing cooperatives and co-partnership ventures where skaters can trade with other skaters (p. 141). In reality, what seems superficially to be a fragmented set of marketing organizations is an integrated marketing operation in that, according to estimates, three companies account for about 70 percent of all skateboarding sales (p. 142).

Skateboarders are said to constitute a form of popular culture that resists capitalist social relations constituted by values such as discipline, control, accountability and bureaucratic rationalization (Beal 2001: 48). In Northern Colorado skaters viewed other skaters involved in organized professional skating as "rats." They perceived skating as a style of living and objected to its use as a means to earn income. According to Beal, skaters challenged the commodification of skating through actions such as not buying and displaying advertising stickers on their clothing, by refusing to buy clothing designed specifically for skaters, and by buying commercially produced skateboards but decorating them themselves (p. 49).

In Colorado, in 1991, skaters participating in amateur contests countered and subverted the disciplines of mainstream sports by deliberately wearing their registration numbers upside down, making them difficult to read; by skating with contestants in the warm-up periods even though this was prohibited; by not preparing routines designed to impress the judges within the two minutes of performance allowed but by simply skating with a few tricks; by supporting other skaters in the competition through sharing gear and helping to recover skateboards when a skater lost control; by disregarding time limits; and by ending runs when they felt they had completed the run rather than according to the official time (Beal 2001: 51, 52). Skaters who bragged or competed in contests were considered "uncool." Skaters gained status not through competition but by being recognized as highly skilled and creative and by not belittling others who lacked such skills (p. 53).

By the late 1980s, skateboarding clothing was being mass marketed and purchased by youth who never skated but who enjoyed the style and image of the skateboarder (Borden 2000). Uncomfortable with this appropriation by non-skaters, some skateboarders have given up their own original style of clothing, thus seeking to make an explicit statement that their identity is derived from the act of skateboarding itself and not from clothing styles (p. 144).

Gender in skateboarding

Studies have shown that skateboarding is a highly gendered subculture. It has been suggested that women do not participate because street skateboarding is associated with risk and rebellion, and is represented in skaters' magazines by young males performing high-risk tricks and wearing minimum protective gear (Atencio et al. 2009: 6–7).

In a study of women skateboarders in San Diego and San Francisco, Atencio and others (2009: 9–10) found that male street skaters stressed skating's inherent dangerousness and the potential for serious injury and pain. Women skaters were not regarded as "decent" or "respected" skateboarders because they would not attempt difficult tricks and tended to hang out as if they were groupies. They were referred to as "posers" and "groupies" and were believed to be less capable of dealing with pain. Males thought women lacked the authenticity possessed by real skaters.

All the major skateboarding magazines have promoted skating as masculinist and offered up sexist assumptions. For example, in one publication a professional skater described women as promiscuous "chicks" and "bitches" who wanted only to pick up men (Atencio et al. 2009: 12). Atencio and others (2009: 13) found that women were often harassed or chased away from public spaces by male skaters, as Abby explained:

> "Actually, where I grew [up] I knew about ten girls who have a skateboard but they don't go out anymore. Like they don't like skating in front of the guys cause they will watch them skate board and they get all freaked out. I have been heckled with them before and they will never go out with me again. They get scared of all the guys because they [the guys] are really intimidating."

In contrast, when women-only skateboarding events were held in skate parks, women found these to be positive and empowering experiences (Atencio et al. 2009: 14). In a qualitative study of skateboarding in Ontario,

Canada, Young found that women skateboarders were often labeled as lesbians. This labeling enabled male skaters to restrict women's involvement in the subculture for fear of having their sexuality questioned (Young 2004: 77). According to male skaters in Amsterdam, the risk of injury is claimed to be the principal constraint to girls skating:

"They fall down a lot and I think that girls just don't like falling. Once in a while I go skating with a couple of girls and if they fall, sometimes they start crying. It hurts and that's part of it. I don't think that that attracts them. I don't really know. It's kind of like cars, just a boys thing" (male skateboarder).

(Karsten and Pel 2000: 331)

For male skaters in Amsterdam, the absence of female skaters is never a subject for discussion. Skaters there seemingly reproduce existing gender relations that demarcate some fields of activity as male and others female. Thus, skating is firmly entrenched as a boys' sport and girls just don't belong in it.

A study of the members of the Park Gang girl skaters, aged 14 and 15, in Vancouver found that the Park Gang were harassed by male skaters at the skate park who chose to adopt the role of guardians and gatekeepers of the park. Unless the Park Gang took on the traditionally feminine subject positions of watcher, fan or girlfriend, they were given little space in the park. Gang members were accused of being "posers," namely wearing the correct clothing and carrying a skateboard, but not actually skating. The male skaters assumed the girls would hang out at the park to meet skater boys and flirt with them.

The Park Gang started a boycott of the park and then returned when the boys were absent, intending to show the boys "That we're not there just for the guys and we're not there to watch them and be around them" (Pomerantz et al. 2004: 551–552). This action produced more respect and less harassment, and the Gang was then surveilled to "see how they were doing" (p. 552). The Gang members had effectively constructed a space for girls occupying the subject position of "skater" (p. 552). In contrast to the Park Gang, who wanted to skate and be known and accepted as skaters, the "Bun Girls" were considered watchers in the park who wanted to meet skater boys. The Park Gang created distance between themselves and the Bun Girls by dressing casually and avoiding wearing makeup and sexual displays through style (p. 553).

In a qualitative study of skateboarding in Northern Colorado, Beal found that skaters did not regard skating as a traditional competitive sport. For this reason the hegemonic masculinity commonly associated with the social institution of organized sport did not have the same kind of traction in skateboarding (Beal 1996: 208). Nevertheless, male skaters assumed that women wanted to appear feminine and could not reconcile the risk taking in skateboarding with the likelihood of girls receiving injuries that would mar their physical appearance. This was reflected in comments that skating "is a rough sport where people get scarred and girls don't want to have scars on their shins, it wouldn't look good" and "girls probably don't skate because they don't look good with bruises." One girl skater agreed that "Girls don't want to do anything harsh or bruise their legs" (p. 212). According to male skaters, girls associated with skateboarding were named "Skate Betties" and their aim was to meet male skaters and not to engage fully in the subculture:

> "They do it because they want to meet cute guys, or their boyfriends do it. It's the alternative crowd; it's like the girls that are kind of into alternative music and that stuff and kind of skating goes along with it, not as much punk, but not mainstream, and um they like the clothes; it's a cool look, I think it's a cool look."
>
> (Beal 1996: 214)

Therefore, even while challenging hegemonic masculinity associated with organized sports, these skateboarders still subscribed to the notion that skating was a male activity, and this was reflected in gender relations and the social construction of skateboarding.

Recap

The U.K. cultural studies perspective understood the rise of youth cultures as distinctive within British culture and as a metaphor for social change. Youth subcultures were linked to a general social and cultural historical analysis. In the U.S., youth cultures and subcultures, once generally treated as an aspect of deviance within criminology with a strong focus on youth gangs, have since come to the attention of scholars working in cultural criminology. As a result, studies of the subcultures of skateboarding and graffiti have developed new insights, especially in relation to the thrill-seeking aspects of challenging the law. Critics assert that this scholarly concern with spectacular or highly visible styles, seen through the semiotic lens, fails to capture aspects of gender, class, race and ethnicity that might also be incorporated into youth cultural practices.

Key questions associated with youth cultures and subcultures include: Why are youth involved in a particular subculture? and How does society construct deviance so that some youthful activities are deemed deviant and others not? The broad issue of antisocial behavior, most closely associated with activities in public spaces like writing graffiti and skateboarding, has recently come to be addressed, especially in the U.K., through criminalizing activities that were once regarded as trivial misdemeanors associated with exuberant youthful behaviors. Generally, therefore, a more complete account is needed based on a precise and nuanced explanation of how youth interact with various cultural formations.

The permitted uses of public spaces and the capture of what were once public areas for private purposes are central issues in the ways youth subcultures are said to show resistance to authoritarian policies and to wage the class struggle in the U.K. The notion of youthful resistance is itself problematic because some argue that the evidence shows youth to be more interested in consuming a lifestyle. A broader conception of resistance might explain more precisely just how and what youth subcultures are opposed to. A related issue is the impact of commercialism on subcultures and resistance – does commercialism subvert and corrupt all resistance? Idealists of subcultures argue that commodification actually promotes more resistance but others contend that mainstream culture eventually absorbs subcultures so that they are no longer shocking – perhaps because this is an effective way of helping to sell products. The commercialization of skateboarding and rave parties is a case in point.

Notes

1 Social class has been a constant in British life reflected in areas such as language, education, employment, leisure and home life and lifestyle. The mass media also reflect a class basis and bias with much of the tabloid press adopting a working-class style of presentation while the middle classes and above are catered to by broadsheets.

2 Following World War II Britain experienced a period of economic prosperity, and this affluence was especially felt by the youth market, a substantial part of whose income was spent on leisure consumables including clothing, records, alcohol, movies, etc. Teenage spending power was recognized and their distinct tastes began to be provided for by the market. By 1972, when the punk subculture appeared, Britain was in a state of economic depression and teenagers brought up in the 1960s in affluence and under full employment found it much more difficult to secure employment (Campbell et al. 1982: 78, 86).

3 In a qualitative study of raves in the northeast of Britain, informants said that exhaustion and dehydration were common: "You've got to be careful: keep cool, keep well ventilated, take lots of fluid. Sometimes you get 'deep heat' where you just have to sit down in the corner for twenty minutes, then up and at it again" (Adam) (Merchant and MacDonald 1994: 23).

4 The transit authority responsible for the subway had made rules barring graffiti but writers under 16 years of age could only be given a warning, whereas adult

writers over 16 could be charged with malicious mischief and receive up to one year's imprisonment (Castleman 1982: 135).

5   Austin (1998: 248) states that his informants in New York City were more concerned about being beaten by the police than being prosecuted.

6   In Seattle in 1989 graffiti writers were also predominantly male (Brewer and Miller 1990: 352).

References

Atencio, Matthew, Becky Beal and Charlene Wilson. 2009. "The Distinction of Risk: Urban Skateboarding, Street Habitus and the Construction of Hierarchical Gender Relations." *Qualitative Research in Sport and Exercise* 1(1): 3–20.

Austin, Joe. 1998. "Knowing Their Place: Local Knowledge, Social Prestige and the Writing Formation in New York City." In Joe Austin and Michael Nevin Willard (eds) *Generations of Youth: Youth Cultures and History in Twentieth-Century America.* New York: New York University Press, pp. 240–252.

Beal, Becky. 1996. "Alternative Masculinity and its Effects on Gender Relations in the Subculture of Skateboarding." *Journal of Sport Behavior* 19(3): 204–221.

Beal, Becky. 2001. "Disqualifying the Official: An Exploration of Social Resistance through the Subculture of Skateboarding." In Andrew Yiannakis and Merrill J. Melnick Champaign (eds) *Contemporary Issues in Sociology of Sport.* Champaign, IL: Human Kinetics Publishers, pp. 47–57.

Becker, Howard. 1963. *Outsiders: Studies in the Sociology of Deviance,* New York: Free Press.

Bennett, Andy. 1999. "Subcultures or Neo-Tribes? Rethinking the Relationship between Youth, Style and Musical Taste." *Sociology* 33(3): 599–617.

Bennett, Andy and Keith Kahn-Harris (eds). 2004. *After Subculture: Critical Studies in Contemporary Youth Culture.* Basingstoke: Palgrave Macmillan.

Blackman, Shane and A. France. 2001. "Youth Marginality under 'Postmodernism.'" In Nick Stevenson (ed.) *Culture and Citizenship.* Thousand Oaks, CA: Sage, pp. 180–197.

Borden, Iain. 1998. *The Gift of Freedom? Skateboarding and Socio-Spatial Censorship in the Late Twentieth Century City.* Amsterdam: Archis.

Borden, Iain. 2000. "Speaking the City: Skateboarding Subculture and Recompositions of the Urban Realm." *Research in Urban Sociology* 5: 134–154.

Borden, Iain. 2001. *Skateboarding, Space and the City: Architecture and the Body.* New York: Berg.

Brewer, D.D. and Marc L. Miller. 1990. "Bombing and Burning: The Social Organization and Values of Hip Hop Graffiti Writers and Implications for Policy." *Deviant Behavior* 11(4): 345–369.

Campbell, Anne, Steve Munee and John Gales. 1982. "American Gangs and British Subcultures: A Comparison." *International Journal of Offender Therapy and Comparative Criminology* 26(1): 76–92.

Carr, John. 2010. "Legal Geographies – Skating Around the Edges of the Law: Urban Skateboarding and the Role of Law in Determining Young Peoples' Place in the City." *Urban Geography* 31(7): 988–1003.

Carrabine, Eamonn and Brian Longhurst. 2002. "Consuming the Car: Anticipation, Use and Meaning in Contemporary Youth Culture." *The Sociological Review* 50(2): 181–196.

Castleman, Craig. 1982. *Getting Up.* Cambridge, MA: The MIT Press.

Chiu Chihsin. 2009. "Contestation and Conformity: Street and Park Skateboarding in New York City Public Space." *Space and Culture* 12(1): 25–42.

Clean Denver. 1988. *Denver Graffiti Removal Manual.* Denver, CO: Clean Denver.

Cloward, R.A. and E. Ohlin. 1960. *Delinquency and Opportunity: A Theory of Delinquent Gangs.* Glencoe, IL: Free Press.

Cohen, Albert K. 1955. *Delinquent Boys.* New York: Free Press.

Cohen, Phil. 1972. "Subcultural Conflict and Working Class Community." In *Working Papers in Cultural Studies*, CCCS, University of Birmingham, Spring, pp. 5–51.

Coleman, Roy. 2005. "Surveillance in the City: Primary Definition and Urban Spatial Order." *Crime Media Culture* 1(2): 131–148.

Collin, Matthew. 1998. *Altered State: The Story of Ecstasy Culture and Acid House.* London: Serpents Tail.

Coupland, D. 1991. *Generation X: Tales for an Accelerated Culture.* New York: St Martin's Press.

Cressey, P.G. 1932. *The Taxi-Dance Hall: A Sociological Study in Commercialized Recreation and City Life.* Chicago, IL: The University of Chicago Press.

Critcher, Chas. 2000. "'Still Raving': Social Reaction to Ecstasy." *Leisure Studies* 19: 145–162.

Downes, David and Paul Rock. 1998. *Understanding Deviance: A Guide to the Sociology of Crime and Rule Breaking.* Oxford: Oxford University Press.

Faris, Robert L. 1967. *Chicago Sociology 1920–1932.* San Francisco, CA: Chandler.

Feiner, J.S. and S.M. Klein. 1982. "Graffiti Talks." *Social Policy* 12(3): 47–53.

Ferrell, J. 1993. *Crimes of Style: Urban Graffiti and the Politics of Criminality.* New York: Garland.

Ferrell, Jeff and Neil Websdale. 1999. "Materials for Making Trouble." In Jeff Ferrell and Neil Websdale (eds) *Making Trouble: Cultural Constructions of Crime, Deviance and Control.* Hawthorne, NY: Aldine de Gruyter, pp. 3–24.

Ferrell, Jeff, Keith Hayward and Jock Young. 2008. *Cultural Criminology: An Invitation.* London: Sage.

Fischer, Claude S. 1975. "Towards a Subcultural Theory of Urbanism." *American Journal of Sociology* 80: 1319–1341.

Goffman, Erving. 1968. *Stigma.* Harmondsworth: Penguin.

Goldstein, Richard. 1973. "This Thing has Gotten Completely Out of Hand." *New York Magazine*, March 26, pp. 35–39.

Guardian. 2010a. "Police Injured During Violent Clashes at Illegal Rave in London," October 31. http://www.guardian.co.uk/uk/2010/oct/31/police-hurt-halloween-rave-london (accessed May 25, 2012).

Guardian. 2010b. "Return of Underground Rave Culture is Fuelled by the Recession and Facebook," November 6. http://www.guardian.co.uk/society/2010/nov/06/underground-rave-culture-recession-facebook (accessed May 25, 2012).

Hall, Steve, Simon Winlow and Craig Ancrum. 2008. *Criminal Identities and*

Consumer Culture: Crime, Exclusion and the New Culture of Narcissism. Cullompton, Devon: Willan Publishing.

Hall, Stuart and Tony Jefferson (eds). 1993. *Resistance through Rituals: Youth Subcultures in Post-War Britain.* London: Routledge.

Halsey, Mark and Alison Young. 2002. "The Meanings of Graffiti and Municipal Administration." *The Australian and New Zealand Journal of Criminology* 35(2): 165–186.

Hebdige, Dick. 1979. *Subculture: The Meaning of Style.* London: Methuen.

Hebdige, Dick. 1983. "Posing . . . Threats, Striking . . . Poses: Youth Surveillance and Display." In K. Gelder (2005) (ed.) *The Subcultures Reader.* London: Routledge.

Heidensohn, Frances and Loraine Gelsthorpe. 2007. "Gender and Crime." In Mike Maguire, Rod Morgan and Robert Reiner (eds) *The Oxford Handbook of Criminology.* Oxford: Oxford University Press, pp. 381–420.

Hill, Andrew. 2002. "Acid House and Thatcherism: Noise, the Mob, and the English Countryside." *British Journal of Sociology* 53(1): 89–105.

Howe, Neill and Bill Strauss. 1993. *13th Generation.* New York: Vintage Books.

Karsten, Lia and Eva Pel. 2000. "Skateboarders Exploring Urban Public Space: Ollies, Obstacles and Conflicts." *Journal of Housing and the Built Environment* 15: 327–340.

Katz, Jack. 1988. *Seductions of Crime.* New York: Basic Books.

Lachmann, Richard. 1988. "Graffiti as Career and Ideology." *The American Journal of Sociology* 94(2): 229–250.

Lemert, Edwin M. 1952. *Social Pathology.* New York: McGraw-Hill.

Lemert, Edwin M. 1972. *Human Deviance, Social Problems, and Social Control.* Englewood Cliffs, NJ: Prentice Hall.

Ley, David and Roman Cybriwsky. 1974. "Urban Graffiti as Territorial Markers." *Annals of the Association of American Geographers* 64(4): 491–505.

MacDonald, Nancy. 2001. *The Graffiti Subculture: Youth, Masculinity and Identity in London and New York.* New York: Palgrave.

Malbon, B. 1999. *Clubbing: Dancing, Ecstasy and Vitality.* London: Routledge.

Martin, Peter J. 2004. "Culture, Subculture and Social Organization." In A. Bennett and Keith Kahn-Harris (eds) *After Subculture: Critical Studies in Contemporary Youth Culture.* Basingstoke: Palgrave Macmillan, pp. 21–34.

Matza, David and Gresham M. Sykes. 1961. "Juvenile Delinquency and Subterranean Values." *American Sociological Review* 26: 712–719.

McRobbie, Angela. 1980. "Settling Accounts with Subcultures: A Feminist Critique." *Screen Education* 34: 37–49.

McRobbie, Angela. 1993. "Shut Up and Dance: Youth Culture and Changing Modes of Femininity." *Cultural Studies* 7(3): 406–426.

McRobbie, A. and J. Garber. 1976. "Girls and Subcultures." In Stuart Hall and Tony Jefferson (eds) *Resistance through Rituals: Youth Subcultures in Post-War Britain.* New York: Routledge, pp. 209–222.

McRobbie, Angela and Jenny Garber. 1993. "Girls and Subcultures." In Stuart Hall and Tony Jefferson (eds) *Resistance through Rituals: Youth Subcultures in Post-War Britain.* London: Routledge, pp. 177–189.

Merchant, Jacqueline and Robert MacDonald. 1994. "Youth and the Rave Culture, Ecstasy and Health." *Youth and Policy* 45: 16–48.

Miles, S. 2000. *Youth Lifestyles in a Changing World*. Philadelphia, PA: Open University Press.

Millie, Andrew. 2008. "Anti-Social Behaviour, Behavioural Expectations and an Urban Aesthetic." *British Journal of Criminology* 48: 379–394.

Moore, David. 1995. "Raves and the Bohemian Search for Self and Community: A Contribution to the Anthropology of Public Events." *Anthropological Forum* 7(2): 193–214.

Muggleton, D. 1997. "The Post-Subculturalist." In S. Redhead, J. O'Connor and D. Wynne (eds) *The Clubcultures Reader*. Oxford: Blackwell.

Muggleton, D. 2000. *Inside Subculture: The Postmodern Meaning of Style*. Oxford: Berg.

Nemeth, Jeremy. 2006. "Conflict, Exclusion, Relocation: Skateboarding and Public Space." *Journal of Urban Design* 11(3): 297–318.

Nolan, Nicholas. 2003. "The Ins and Outs of Skateboarding and Transgression in Public Spaces in Newcastle, Australia." *Australian Geographer* 34(3): 311–327.

Owen, Frank. 2003. *Clubland*. New York: Broadway Books.

Parker, Howard, Judith Aldridge and Fiona Measham. 1998. *Illegal Leisure: The Normalization of Adolescent Recreational Drug Use*. London: Routledge.

Pomerantz, Shauna, Dawn H. Currie and Deidre M. Kelly. 2004. "Sk8er Girls: Skateboarders, Girlhood and Feminism in Motion." *Women's Studies International Forum* 27: 547–557.

Presdee, Mike. 2000. *Cultural Criminology and the Carnival of Crime*. London: Routledge.

Rahn, J. 2002. *Painting Without Permission: Hip-Hop Graffiti Subculture*. Westport, CT: Bergin and Garvey.

Redhead, Steve (ed.). 1993. *Rave Off: Politics and Deviance in Contemporary Youth Culture*. Aldershot: Avebury.

Rietveld, Hillegonda C. 1998. *This is Our House: House Music, Cultural Spaces and Technologies*. Aldershot: Ashgate.

Rose, Nikolas. 2000. "Government and Control." *British Journal of Criminology* 40: 321–339.

Rubington, Earl and Martin S. Weinberg. 1999. *Deviance: The Interactionist Perspective*. Needham Heights, MA: Allyn & Bacon.

Saunders, N. and R. Doblin. 1996. *Ecstasy: Dance, Trance and Transformation*. Oakland, CA: Quick American Archives.

Sefiha, Ophir. 2003. "A Social Construction of Skateboarding." Unpublished thesis. MS in Criminal Justice. Northern Arizona University.

Shaw, C. and H. McKay. 1942. *Juvenile Delinquency and the Urban Areas*. Chicago, IL: The University of Chicago Press.

Shildrick, T. and R. MacDonald. 2006. "In Defence of Subculture: Young People, Leisure and Social Divisions." *Journal of Youth Studies* 9(2): 125–140.

Smith, David J. 2010. "Changing Patterns of Youth." In David J. Smith (ed.) *A New Response to Youth Crime*. Cullompton, Devon: Willan Publishing, pp. 17–53.

Stahl, G. 2003 "Tastefully Renovating Subcultural Theory: Making Space for a New

Model." In D. Muggleton and R. Weinzierl (eds) *The Post-Subcultures Reader.* Oxford: Berg, pp. 27–38.

Sumner, Colin. 1994. *The Sociology of Deviance: An Obituary.* New York: Continuum.

The Crime Report. 2010. "Art Crime: Graffiti Wars." Monday, February 22. http://www.thecrimereport.org/archive/art-crime-graffiti-wars/ (accessed June 23, 2012).

Thrasher, F.M. 1927. *The Gang: A Study of 1313 Gangs in Chicago.* Chicago, IL: The University of Chicago Press.

Tomlinson, Lori. 1998. "'This Ain't No Disco'. . . . Or Is It? Youth Culture and the Rave Phenomenon." In Jonathan S. Epstein (ed.) *Youth Culture: Identity in a Postmodern World.* Boston, MA: Blackwell, pp. 195–211.

Twenge, J.M. 2006. *Generation Me: Why Today's Young Americans are More Confident, Assertive, Entitled – and More Miserable Than Ever Before.* New York: Free Press.

Weber, Timothy R. 1999. "Raving in Toronto: Peace, Love, Unity and Respect in Transition." *Journal of Youth Studies* 2(3): 317–336.

Williams, J. Patrick. 2007. "Youth-Subcultural Studies: Sociological Traditions and Core Concepts." *Sociology Compass* 1/2: 572–593.

Woolley, Helen and Ralph Johns. 2001. "Skateboarding: The City as Playground." *Journal of Urban Design* 6(2): 211–230.

Young, Alana. 2004. "Being the 'Alternative' in an Alternative Subculture: Gender Differences in the Experiences of Young Women and Men in Skateboarding and Snowboarding." *Avante* 10(3): 69–82.

chapter 7

Youth and Moral Panic

The focus of this chapter is moral panic theory and specific moral panics associated with youth and youth culture. The moral panics discussed comprise a specific incident or a series of incidents that satisfy the conditions for the presence of a moral panic (Cohen 2002) and comprise school shootings, the James Bulger case, mods and rockers in the U.K., mugging in the U.K., the so-called "juvenile superpredators," girl violence and gang violence. In each of these instances a set of circumstances generated a moral panic, in some cases orchestrated by the media,[1] which led to official action, usually in the form of punitive legislation or a heightened level of social control through government regulation. The actual responses to these moral panics were predicated on the need to confront and control violent youth and prevent further acts of violence. Because of the "threat" they presented, the youth were cast as "folk devils," and therefore, according to officials, justified a punitive response. In explaining the basis for moral panics, Stanley Cohen has noted that in Britain recurrent forms of moral panic have been linked to youth culture and that these cultures have been associated with violence (Cohen 2002: 1). As Thompson explains, "no age group is more associated with risk in the public imagination than that of 'youth'" (1998: 44). It is, first, necessary to explore the theoretical underpinnings of moral panic and to examine how adolescence is conceptualized.

Moral panic theory

The concept of a moral panic has developed significantly since its origin in the 1970s, so that now the study of moral panics has become a subdiscipline in itself (Garland 2008: 9). The notion of moral panic encompasses concepts of deviance, collective behavior, social movements and social problems. In this sense, the notion has explanatory power because it sets moral boundaries within a society (Goode and Ben-Yehuda 1994: 29). Importantly, terming an event a moral panic reveals that irrational and unrealistic social processes may occur within society. Recently, Jock Young (2009: 4) has suggested that moral panics produce "cultural conflict" and are associated with "emotional energy," examples of which include zealous police activity, a media feeding frenzy about a controversy, and fervent public interest in the perceived deviance. Like Katz for crime, Young argues that moral panics also have a seductive quality (2009: 4).

The notion of a moral panic and its theoretical framework were first developed in the 1970s by Stanley Cohen in his book *Folk Devils and Moral Panics* (1972). The now classic explanation of a moral panic given by Cohen (1972: 9) is as follows:

> [S]ocieties appear to be subject, every now and then, to periods of moral panic. A condition, episode, person or group of persons emerges to become defined as a threat to societal values and interests; its nature is presented in a stylized and stereotypical fashion by the mass media; the moral barricades are manned by editors, bishops, politicians and other right-thinking people; socially accredited experts pronounce their diagnosis and solutions; ways of coping are evolved or (more often) resorted to; the condition then disappears, submerges or deteriorates and becomes more visible.

Cohen notes specifically that in postwar Britain moral panics have been associated with modes of youth culture involving forms of violence. Cohen terms such violent groups "folk devils" (1972: 10). In their classic work *Policing the Crisis*, Hall and others (1978: 16) further explain moral panic as follows:

> When the official reaction to a person, groups of persons or series of events is out of all proportion to the actual threat offered, when "experts," in the form of police chiefs, the judiciary, politicians and editors perceive the threat in all but identical terms, and appear to talk "with one voice" of rates, diagnoses, prognoses and solutions, when the media representations universally stress "sudden and dramatic" increases (in numbers involved or events) and "novelty" above and

beyond that which a sober, realistic appraisal could sustain, then we believe it is appropriate to speak of . . . a moral panic.

While Cohen approaches moral panics with a focus on media representation of events, Hall and others (1978) provide a perspective that goes beyond the demands of tabloid journalism and media competition to analyze more deeply why and how moral panics are engineered by elites to divert attention away from challenges to capitalism. It is therefore important to appreciate that Hall and others do not assume that the media acts alone in creating and sustaining moral panics (Schissel 1997: 13).

According to Cohen (1972), the relevant theoretical frameworks for moral panics are social problems and collective behavior. Becker in particular has explained how moral crusades have been forged against particular social conditions, deemed problematic, such as drinking alcohol in the case of Prohibition, and drugs in the case of smoking marijuana (in Cohen 1972: 11). These crusades, focused on perceived social problems, Becker terms "moral enterprises" because, in his view, their activities result in "the creation of a new fragment of the moral constitution of society, its code of right and wrong" (p. 145).

In the field of collective behavior, Cohen highlights cases of "mass hysteria, delusion and panics" and how societies cope with disasters (p. 11). Cohen sees the field of collective behavior as including theories related to social types such as the hero, the villain and the fool. Social typing originates in the interactionist or transactional approach to deviance concerned with labeling deviant groups and typecasting individuals (p. 12). Cohen argues that these theories constitute the major point of reference for studying moral panics.

Becker explains the transactional nature of deviance as follows:

[D]eviance is created by society. I do not mean this in the way that it is ordinarily understood, in which the causes of deviance are located in the social situation of the deviant or in "social factors" which prompt his action. I mean, rather, that social groups create deviance by making the rules whose infraction constitutes deviance and by applying those rules to particular persons and labeling them as outsiders. From this point of view, deviance is not a quality of the act the person commits, but rather a consequence of the application by others of rules and sanctions to an "offender." The deviant is one to whom the label has successfully been applied; deviant behavior that people so label.

(Becker 1963: 8–9)

Becker (1963: 122) points out that enforcing rules is "an enterprising act." He sees an "entrepreneur" as taking it upon him- or herself to punish the rule violators. Furthermore, those who enforce the rule will make known its violation to others so that it cannot be ignored. According to Becker then, enforcement is prompted by some advantage or personal interest which varies according to the complexity of each situation.

Social problem formation, according to Cohen (1972: 111), often involves a known sequence of events commencing with vigorous advocacy by a certain group that a condition is trouble-making, difficult or dangerous, and requires action to be taken. Based on this advocacy, a specific rule is derived and a method of control suggested. Yet, Cohen critiques this notion of a sequence as being too deterministic, and suggests that three elements that he terms "legitimating values, enterprise and power" (p. 112) are conditions found in all social problems. According to this view, values will always be an issue and under challenge; such challenges will lead to rule creation; there will be an enterprise comprising a movement to gain publicity and support to make those rules; and finally there must be someone in a position of power who is able to influence the media and expert authorities. If these conditions are satisfied, a crusade to challenge a social problem is likely to be successful (p. 112).

Becker (1963: 147) suggests that the "crusading reformer" is not satisfied about an existing set of rules and perceives it necessary to correct an evil. As he puts it, "the crusader is fervent and righteous, often self-righteous" (p. 147). In the case of Prohibition in the U.S., Becker notes that the prohibitionists believed they were pursuing a higher moral purpose in trying to provide conditions for a better way of life (p. 148). Yet, the integrity of moral crusaders can be called into question and Becker argues that some industrialists believed that Prohibition would produce a more manageable labor force (p. 149). Moral crusades may be successful, like Prohibition which resulted in the Eighteenth Amendment to the Constitution, or they may fail completely. Also, public attitudes toward a moral issue may change, thus eroding any moral gains (p. 152). Becker suggests that the outcome of a successful moral crusade is likely to be a new set of rules accompanied by the necessary machinery within government to enforce them. At this point the crusade becomes "institutionalized" (p. 155).

According to Goode and Ben-Yehuda (1994: 33–41), a moral panic is characterized by several constituent elements, namely concern, hostility, consensus, disproportionality and volatility. *Concern* relates to feelings of anxiety over the conduct of a particular group and the potential outcome of that conduct for society generally. Concern is revealed through modes of opinion such as public opinion polls, media attention and legislation. *Hostility* is manifested toward the group regarded as rule violators. The group is categorized as the enemy of society, which threatens values and interests and leads to a dichotomy between "them and us" – the respectable citizens and the deviants. Here, Cohen's notion of a folk devil characterizes the deviants (p. 34). In achieving the element of *consensus*, it is necessary that society as a whole see the threat posed by the rule violators as significant and serious. As Goode and Ben-Yehuda note, "moral panics come in different sizes," some exciting only specific segments of society (p. 34).

Disproportionality is a key element, particularly in assessing whether a panic is a moral panic. Of course, disproportionality is a subjective issue and, while some may feel that public concern is warranted, others will not. For this reason, the concept of disproportionality has been critiqued as a meaningless notion (p. 36). For example, Waddington (1986 in Goode and Ben-Yehuda 1994: 42) argues that the concept of a moral panic lacks criteria for assessing disproportionality and, as such is simply a value judgment. In contrast, Jock Young suggests that a disproportionate reaction is a critical element of a moral panic and argues that assessing disproportionality depends on empirical evidence and normative evaluation (Young 2009: 13). He points to moral panics concerning youth and drugs and youth violence as illustrations of this. Similarly, Garland highlights the difficulties associated with measuring and evaluating disproportionality but suggests that they can often be resolved through appropriate data and investigatory methods (Garland 2008: 22). Nevertheless, Garland suggests that for some, the idea of a proportionate response has no validity because empirical facts are subsumed by value judgments based on power and interest (also see Thompson 1998: 10).

Moral panics are *volatile* because they emerge suddenly and then tend to disappear. In some cases, the moral concern becomes institutionalized and is captured by social movements and organizations or government practices and procedures. However, in a typical moral panic the authors suggest that the level of intensity and degree of hostility over the issue are not sustainable (Goode and Ben-Yehuda 1994: 39). Nevertheless, moral panics may resurface over time such as in the case of the enduring concern over satanic rituals. Garland suggests that over time a succession of moral panics can create divisions within society and prompt modes of regulation and control such as a buildup of government regulations and enforcement measures in response to public outcries about alcohol and drugs (Garland 2008: 16). Garland has argued that two further elements should be added to the criteria proposed by Goode and Ben-Yehuda (p. 11). These are the moral dimension of the social reaction to an act of deviance and the notion that the deviance is symptomatic. These two elements, according to Cohen's original thinking, reveal that underneath the moral panic lies an apprehension that a set of values is under threat.

Issues of power and control are also associated with theories that explain moral panics. In particular, social position and motivations are significant elements of any analysis of a moral panic. According to Goode and Ben-Yehuda (1994: 124), societal groups may be positioned as elite, middle level or grass roots. The elite draw their power from position or wealth. A Marxist approach would argue that elites fabricate moral panics for personal interest or power (p. 125). Hall and others (1978) claim in their study of mugging in Britain that not only did the concern about mugging equate to a moral panic, but mugging was seen as a reaction by control agencies and the media to a perceived or symbolic threat to society. In other words, mugging itself was simply a label for the concerns of the powerful. The authors argue that the panic over mugging as a form of street crime served as a means of legitimating a punitive law and order program, helping to divert attention away from Britain's economic recession, which constituted a threat to capitalism (Hall et al. 1978 quoted in Goode and Ben-Yehuda 1994: 136). In the case of mugging, then, it is argued that the capitalist state sought to exercise "total social authority . . . over the subordinate classes" (p. 136). In this situation the news media "reproduced the definitions of the powerful" by promoting the agenda of the powerful (p. 137).

The middle level referred to by Goode and Ben-Yehuda includes professional organizations, the police, political parties and social movements (1994: 124). The remainder of the general public constitutes the grass-roots level. In terms of motivation, questions arise such as "whether the moral crusade develops around a particular issue because of ideology and morality 'genuinely felt' or whether motivation is more concerned with power and personal interest" (p. 124). Middle-level members of society primarily seek material or status advantage, and at the grass-roots level moral panics are generated bottom-up in a spontaneous movement where a large number of people manifest their concern.

McRobbie and Thornton (1995: 560) suggest that moral panics are no longer ad hoc, spontaneous events, but rather have become a means of bringing daily events to the attention of the public. As they put it,

> Used by politicians to orchestrate consent, by business to promote sales in certain niche markets, and by media to make home and social affairs newsworthy, moral panics are constructed on a daily basis.

The notion that moral panics have become institutionalized into persistent fabricated crusades is linked to the development of the culture of control and to the notion of governing through crime (Feeley and Simon 2007: 51). Recently, commentators have tried to link moral panics with the concept of the risk society and with Foucault's notion of discursive formations. As Thompson notes, the risk society, as explained initially by Beck (1992 quoted in Thompson 1998: 22), connects moral panics to notions of anxiety. It is arguable, then, that the socio-cultural term "fear of crime" (Lee 2007) is also linked to notions of anxiety and the risk society. However, as yet, no studies appear to have linked fear of crime to moral panics but clearly they are associated. Foucault's work on the "microphysics" of power relations and discourses in the form of statements that provide a language for talking about a particular topic are clearly relevant to the way in which moral panics become regimes of truth for some and represent power struggles over moral regulation (1977: 26).

Adolescence

Definitions and constructions of the "youth problem" at any given point in time are based on fears that youth are out of control. The following historical context shows that discourses about the conception of adolescence, the association between adolescence and delinquency, and fundamental issues of class and race have always combined to render youth a superlative target for moral panics.

The period of youth known as adolescence is closely associated with delinquency. Notions of childhood and youth are social constructions shaped by social, historical and cultural discourses. Some argue that before the 17th century no conception of childhood existed (Aries 1962: 28), and while this is regarded as problematic (deMause 1976; Pollock 1983), it is generally agreed that in pre-industrial societies childhood did not exist as a separate stage in life because children mixed closely with adults and followed adult ways and practices. During the Middle Ages, the idea emerged that a child ought to have a moral and educational upbringing before entering adulthood, a duty to be exercised by family and school (Muncie 2009: 49).

By the latter part of the 19th century the notion that adolescence was a distinct stage of life had taken hold. Before then, it was quite common for children to be sent away from home for schooling or for an apprenticeship. During this period in the U.S., industrialization reduced the demand for highly skilled workers and young people began to remain at home for longer, maintaining their dependency on their parents for support. Child labor laws prohibited child employment. For much of the 19th century, young persons between the stages of puberty and adulthood were regarded as in need of guidance while they sought independence and maturity (Binder et al. 2001: 42). Their volatility and unpredictability raised concerns about dangerousness and proper character formation, and delinquency was viewed as a natural consequence of adolescence. In Britain, concerns about working-class youth coalesced around fears that working-class parents were not adequately disciplining their children and that working children enjoyed too much freedom from parental control (Muncie 2009: 64).

In 1904 G. Stanley Hall published a study of adolescence which became a highly influential psychological explanation of delinquency. It focused on the idea of gaining maturity through developing control over natural adolescent tendencies (Binder et al. 2001: 44). Hall's work can be seen as part of the growth of psycho-medical discourses during that period rooted in Darwinian notions of evolution (Brown 1998: 15). Hall believed that adolescence was "pre-eminently the criminal age" and that "criminals are like overgrown children" (Hall 1904: 325, 338). Psychological explanations of the problems of adolescence focused on psychological growth and minimized the importance of social and economic factors that caused the working classes to live in conditions of poverty (Muncie 2009: 67). The "child savers"[2] of the 20th century promoted welfare ideologies that called for supervising "sick" and "pathological" working-class delinquents. Contemporary perspectives apply a developmental perspective to adolescence, identifying areas such as cognitive, moral and identity development as indicative of the "dangerousness" of an adolescent, and of his or her susceptibility to treatment. Immature thought processes displayed by adolescents within their cognitive development include: not anticipating (a lack of capacity to plan ahead); reacting to perceived threats (fear affects the ability to make choices); minimizing danger (risk taking, thrill seeking and lack of capacity to manage impulses); having only one choice (adults perceive several options but adolescents often see only one and may consequently feel cornered and act without good judgment). Moral development in adolescents is idealistic and intolerant of unfairness, while identity development is a gradual process open to the influence of peers, family, culture and success. Where a patchwork of conflicting identities forms, adolescents may act unpredictably under stress (Beyer 1999: 16–19).

Having explored the theoretical underpinnings of moral panics and the associations between the concept of adolescence and delinquency, it is now possible to present and analyze a set of incidents and circumstances that satisfy the requirements for a moral panic. This analysis will reveal how moral panics are shaped, how they take effect, and how they finally come to no longer have a presence in the public consciousness.

School shootings

Although the history of public schooling in the U.S. reveals a considerable level of violence, it is only from the 1960s that the discourse of "school violence" has been officially sanctioned and advanced. Today, amassing information on incidents and forms of school violence has become a high priority in schools (McCabe and Martin 2005: 21), and media coverage of such incidents is intense.[3] This is consistent with the association between the media and mass anxiety about youth (Fornas and Bolin 1995).

What historical circumstances have contributed to shaping the conditions of school violence? During the 17th and 18th centuries, education in public schools was viewed as a privilege and children were expected to respect all aspects of education. In disciplining students for rule infractions teachers often resorted to threats, intimidation and beatings to enforce very strict learning regimes, and everyone supported corporal punishment (McCabe and Martin 2005: 14). In the 19th century, punitive punishments were common, including numerous forms of physical punishment. It was considered axiomatic that disobedient children were products of broken families and that they would never accept societal norms without proper controls and direction. With the arrival of immigrants, schools became sites where local cultural norms and values had to be instilled in students from other cultures, causing conflict and deepening forms of social control. States gave teachers the right to sanction children who failed to assimilate dominant norms (p. 16). In the late 1830s, Horace Mann, the first super-intendent of schools in Massachusetts, reported that one school with 250 students had recorded on average over 300 floggings for disciplinary infractions over a five-day week. In addition, almost 400 schools were closed every year due to disciplinary issues (p. 17).

Lawrence Cremin (1961: 8–14) identified three distinct purposes of public schooling at the turn of the century: providing custodial arrangements for children and thereby enforcing social control; acculturating immigrant children into the U.S. culture; and preparing future workers. Each rationale provided its own tensions and became a basis for conflict between students and teachers. In the 20th century, the period up to and including the 1920s was characterized by youth questioning adult authority, while economic prosperity was celebrated through drinking, smoking and dating in cars (McCabe and Martin 2005: 18). During the 1930s, an outcome of the Great Depression was numerous child vagrants, and truancy was the most significant student issue (p. 19). With industrialization came the movement of families and children into the cities and associated issues of tardiness and failure to attend school.

In studies conducted during the 1940s and 1950s, teachers reported a general lack of respect for authority and a range of behaviors that repre-sented challenges to rules (Crews and Montgomery 2001). By the late 1950s, hearings in the Senate revealed that in inner city ghettos, school buildings and property were being routinely vandalized. By the mid-1950s (1954), *Brown v. Board of Education* struck down segregation in schools (McCabe and Martin 2005: 19).

During the 1960s and 1970s, hearings on school violence were con-ducted in both Houses of Congress, costs of vandalism were estimated in hundreds of millions of dollars, and a survey of 750 school districts found significant increases in violence between 1970 and 1973 (for example, increases of 85 percent in student-to-student assaults and 77 percent in student-to-teacher assaults) (Crews and Montgomery 2001: 49). This trend continued into the 1980s and 1990s, with the 1980s seeing severe cuts in education programming, and by 1993, an estimated 9 percent of students were victims of crimes in and around schools (pp. 47–53). According to Noguera (1997), by the latter part of the 1990s, school violence had been identified to a great extent as an issue of race, although some argue that class is in fact the predominant characteristic. Thus, in the same way that crime is seen as a problem caused by black Americans, so too is school violence associated with race (Hirschfield 2008: 92). The correlation between race, class and violence means that educators fail to locate the issue of school violence within the context of race, class and education. Instead, judgments are based on ignorance of the inner cities and poor urban populations, and fear of those communities. Because of the over-riding image of the criminal and prisoner as a black male, schools tend to see black students who consistently flout school rules as "bound for jail" and "unsalvageable" (p. 92).

In the 26 years between 1974 and 2000, there were 37 separate incidents of school shootings in the U.S. that resulted in the injury or death of a student or teacher by another student within the environment of a school (McCabe and Martin 2005: 42).[4] Despite the fact that shootings at schools in the U.S. have been infrequent, mass coverage of these events by the media has tended to ensure that each incident has generated its own moral panic. Some argue that the media construct public opinion responses to these events to such an extent that the media "*is*" public opinion, at least in relation to the version of events presented to the political elite for appropriate responses (Golding and Middleton 1979: 19). It is argued that events like Columbine provide the media with an opportunity to shine a light on the cruel and evil world of teens (Males 1996).

In school shootings, the media have focused on the search for explanations and sought to make sense of incidents that appear to have no rational meaning (Springhall 2008: 50). As Cohen (2002: xiii) points out, "this scurrying around for a causal theory – or, at least a language for making sense, – is found in all moral panic texts." In his analysis of the Columbine and other shootings, Springhall (2008) notes that the media and other commentators have identified causes such as the availability of guns,[5] violent forms of mass entertainment, especially violent movies and cult rock stars, and the institutional culture of the U.S. high school as prime triggers or causes (pp. 51–59). Structural and institutional causes were supplemented by individual psychological explanations that attempted to show how a multitude of structural and individual factors might combine to trigger such events (p. 60).

Often ignored in the search for causes, not only in regard to school shootings but also in other incidents of youth violence, is adolescent masculinities (Messerschmidt 2000: 3). Yet arguably this is a cross-cutting dynamic in all such incidents. Given that all the school shooters were boys, gender – and specifically the association between masculinities and crime – become salient factors in assessing the etiology of these crimes. Structured action theory posits that gender is constructed as a "situated social and interactional accomplishment" that grows out of social practices located in particular settings (p. 6). In the school setting, challenges to adolescent masculinities can stem from threats and insults from other students and teachers, as well as from unrealized expectations associated with masculinities. In his study of nine boys and adolescent masculinity, Messerschmidt (2000) reveals how, as boys progress through schooling, their conception of "being a man" is shaped by their school experience and interactions in that environment. All the violent offenders in his study believed that physical violence was an appropriate response to resolve interpersonal issues. This disposition toward using violence as a remedy originated in parental expectations of how a "real man" would act but was also derived from school culture (p. 88). Thus, explications of school shootings and youth violence that identify bullying, domination, school social cliques and sporting prowess or the lack of it, as well as poor parenting skills as causal factors, should also analyze underlying adolescent mas-culinities for an adequate account of such incidents.

Responses to school shootings and other forms of violence in schools include the adoption of a so-called "zero tolerance" policy by many schools. This involves advising students that there is zero tolerance for weapons in schools; however, the policy has been extended to alcohol, tobacco, drugs and violence generally (Simon 2007: 222). Violation of this rule is commonly sanctioned by expulsion or suspension. While a policy of zero tolerance offers teachers an uncomplicated strategy for dealing with forms of violence, there appears to be little evidence that it actually reduces school violence and it may be responsible for pushing juveniles out of school who subsequently become delinquent (McCabe and Martin 2005: 94–95, 99).

Other measures to prevent and counter school shootings have included placing security officers in schools, installing metal detectors, keeping schools open in the evenings, proposals to fund a huge corps of "youth counselors," a guidebook on risk factors and strategies to counter violence, bullet drills where students practice evasive tactics, having some teachers carry concealed weapons, attempts to include warning labels on violent music, movies and video games, school lock-downs, bag searches and video surveillance cameras (Burns and Crawford 1999: 152; Hirschfield 2008: 82). Other preventive strategies that have been proposed include teaching conflict resolution skills, language skills and music (Girard and Koch 1996; Shafii and Shafii 2001).

Researchers have noted that the discourse of school violence has resulted in the criminalization of school discipline in the U.S. In schools where gangs and violence are very apparent, students who violate rules are more likely to be criminalized and treated as such. Criminalization of gangs is most advanced in schools where the student population comprises disadvantaged urban minorities (Wacquant 2001). Problems that were once resolved through school disciplinary systems are now viewed as issues for crime control agencies and are referred there systematically, even if they are quite minor. Thus, the panoply of security measures now found in schools, such as metal detectors, dogs and armed police, ensures that students are treated as actual or prospective criminals (Hirschfield 2008: 80).

Employing the model devised by Goode and Ben-Yehuda (1994), described earlier in this chapter, Burns and Crawford (1999: 151) analyze school shootings in terms of the elements of concern, hostility, disproportionality, consensus and interests (political and the media) which collectively constitute a moral panic. As would be expected, concern over school shootings has been instantly manifested at all levels of society from the then President Clinton down, while the media provided wall-to-wall coverage and the impetus for the preventive measures noted above.

Hostility was apparent in the punitive measures proposed and implemented which included: no bail for students charged with bringing guns to school; harsher penalties for those who failed to secure firearms against access by children; a variety of gun restrictions intended to prevent children getting access to them; requiring that students found with guns be detained for evaluation for 72 hours; criminalizing as a felony the exposure of children to books, movies and video games portraying actual sex and violence; and a Juvenile Crime Bill that asked for US$1 billion to strengthen juvenile crime control as well as measures to incarcerate juveniles with adults for what would amount to status offenses like running away from home (Burns and Crawford 1999: 153). Other punitive actions included incarcerating parents whose children commit acts of truancy and restricting students' rights in the interests of heightened security. Significantly, several measures focused on inner city youth in urban schools.

Disproportionality in relation to school shootings can be established by reviewing data on school shootings. First, as indicated above, they are relatively infrequent occurrences, especially given the number of schools (80,000) and the number of students (50 million) (Burns and Crawford 1999: 154). Second, the odds of being shot at school are around a million to one (p. 154). Finally, school shootings cannot be considered a trend but are rather distinctive and peculiar events.

In terms of a consensus, while many parents became fearful of their children's safety at school, school shootings provided a platform for the proponents of punitive juvenile justice policy as well as a feast of alarmist images for the media (Burns and Crawford 1999: 156). Research studies indicate that both the media and legislators give the highest level of attention to issues that have a dramatic quality and that are promoted by powerful political and economic interests (Hilgartner and Bosk 1988: 71).

As Burns and Crawford note (1999: 156), the shootings provided interest groups, politicians and the media with ample material for their respective crusades. Among the political elite, attacking children and proposing a hostile legal regime for delinquents is an ever-popular electoral issue especially given that children do not vote. Politicians have been able to leverage the incidents to drive forward their own interests in punitive justice. For the media, the incidents provided a dramatic set of images of criminal children and their victims that appealed to sections of public opinion that appreciate simplistic media depictions of good and evil (p. 158). By categorizing these events as a recent trend and an "all too familiar story," the media perpetuate the fiction that school shootings are a regular occurrence. As is often the case, the media provide little or no context for what happened, preferring instead to present narratives that either construct or contribute to what are arguably classic moral panics.

James Bulger

In February 1993 in the U.K., two boys aged 10 abducted 2-year-old James Bulger from a shopping center, walked with him about two miles to a railway line and there battered him to death with bricks and an iron bar (Brown 1998: 49; Green 2008: 1). The abduction was captured on 16 security video cameras in the shopping center and the blurred image of James Bulger, held by the hand by one of his murderers as he was abducted, burned itself into the public conscience through constant media iterations. In Britain, the murder of children by strangers is a rare event, and the murder of children by other children even more so, given that only 27 such murders had occurred in the previous 250 years (Muncie 2009: 5).

As with school shootings, youth popular culture was seen as being implicated in this crime. According to the trial judge (whose comment was made despite there being no actual evidence whatsoever of video violence at the trial), "it is not for me to pass judgment on their upbringing, but I suspect that exposure to violent video films may in part be an explanation" (Brown 1998: 50). In the last months of 1993, following the trial and conviction of the two assailants,[6] the tabloid media continuously reproduced the face of the character Chucky Doll from the movie Child's Play 3 (p. 50). The day following the verdict in a front-page editorial, the tabloid newspaper The Sun urged readers to burn their video nasties "for the sake of ALL our kids" (Boyle 2005: 2). Tabloid newspapers, in a battle for circulation in a highly competitive tabloid news market, "strongly influenced" all reactions to the murder. In addition, British politicians, taking media pronouncements to represent public opinion, tended to defer to the media and therefore created a feedback loop that aided the media in constructing and framing their narratives of the Bulger case (Green 2008: 11).

In a report published by "child experts" in April 1994, the Bulger murderers are presented as "exemplars of a new cruelty in children" (Boyle 2005: 4–5). The report claimed that children have become more violent due to the availability of videos that depict sadistic behavior and invite identification with the sadists (pp. 4–5). There were few dissenting voices in the report and following a rush to legislate, a law was passed requiring that the potential harm to viewers watching at home, especially under-age viewers, must be considered in the level of classification assigned to a film or video (p. 5). As well, legislative provisions lowered the age at which a child could receive an indeterminate sentence from 14 to 10, doubled the maximum sentence in juvenile institution for 15- to 17-year-olds to two years, and created a new measure called a "Secure Training Order" rendering it easier to incarcerate persistent offenders in the age range of 12 to 14 years. American-style "boot camps" also stirred British interest (Green 2008: 3). As one researcher aptly noted, in moral panics "the mobilization of a control culture becomes perceived as not only legitimate but necessary as perceptions of threat, risk and crisis are mobilized and generalized" (Hay 1995: 205).

It is significant that at the time of the murder, Britain was suffering an economic recession with a rate of unemployment not experienced since the 1930s (Hay 1995: 202). Thus, the Bulger case served as a locus where general anxieties and fears could be unpacked and processed. The media expressed the event as a descent into moral chaos; for example, one quality weekly claimed that there was a "new brutality about Britain" (*Sunday Times*, February 21, 1993) and the tabloid *Daily Mirror* wrote, "there is something rotten at the heart of Britain. A creeping evil of violence and fear" (*Daily Mirror*, February 22, 1993). These apocalyptic statements matched the economic and political malaise of the time. Stanley Cohen sums up the reaction to the murder as follows:

> Long before the trial began in November the Bulger story had become a potent symbol for everything that had gone wrong in Britain; a "breed" of violent children, whether feral or immoral; absent fathers, feckless mothers and dysfunctional underclass families; the exploitation of children by TV violence and video nasties.
>
> (Cohen 2002: ix)

In the Bulger case, the folk devils were two 10-year-old delinquent boys who had been corrupted by popular culture (there was no evidence that the two boys had ever actually seen the movie said to have motivated the murder) (Boyle 2005: 2). The case sparked a public re-examination of the entire concept of childhood with the result that most believed it inconceivable that innocent children could perform such evil acts.[7] It followed therefore that the murderers, through their evil acts, had effectively surrendered their status as innocents and become transformed, as the media variously termed it, into "freaks of nature" with "hearts of evil," "boy brutes," "monsters" and "spawn of Satan" (Muncie 2009: 6).

The contemporary discourse of childhood represents a child as an innocent dependant, thus rendering any connection between a child and a crime of violence extremely problematic (James and Jenks 1996: 320). One resolution to this problem is to exclude children who commit acts of violence from the category "child," as, for example, was exemplified in the trial judges summing up of the case: "The killing of James Bulger was an act of unparalleled evil and barbarity" (p. 322). Labeling children as not-children essentially has the effect of reaffirming the fundamental nature of what constitutes a child (pp. 322, 323).

Mods and Rockers

In Britain, disturbances in 1964 between groups of youths known as Mods and Rockers were studied by Stanley Cohen in the first sociological study of moral panics (Cohen 1972, 2002). The incidents occurred in small coastal towns in the south and southeast on public holidays between the Mods, known for their neat forms of dress and motor scooters, and the Rockers, more unkempt in dress and associated with motorbikes.[8] The ensuing moral panic, and Cohen's analysis of it, reveals how claims makers, moral entrepreneurs and the mass media interacted to produce a discourse that demonized specific groups as immoral (Thompson 1998: 31).

Cohen's account of the first incident between the two groups describes local shopkeepers as irritated because of lack of business on a public holiday. The weather was bad and groups of young people were suffering feelings of frustration due to rumors that cafés and bars would refuse to serve them. Groups of Mods and Rockers began to fight and throw stones at each other on the sidewalks. Those who possessed motorbikes and scooters separated out and rode loudly up and down the street, windows were broken, some beach huts destroyed and someone fired a starting pistol into the air. For two days the general feeling of irritation, the crowded streets, the noise and the activity of an undermanned local police force resulted in an oppressive and even frightening atmosphere (Cohen 2002: 29).

Cohen compared his research on these events with media representations of the same events and was able to reveal substantial discrepancies between the reality and media depictions of that reality. For example, while the media described the Mods and Rockers as gangs terrorizing local people and vacationers, as causing mass havoc and destruction, and engaging in violent assaults, Cohen's research showed that: the conflict was based largely on regional rivalry and did not emanate from one group's identity as Mods and the other as Rockers; that there were no structured gangs as such; and that the violence and damage that did occur was greatly exaggerated (Brown 1998: 40). In fact, of the total number of arrests of 97 in one town, only one-tenth were charged with offenses involving violence (Cohen 2002: 37). In addition, only a minority of those participating actually possessed a scooter or motorbike. Most were not affluent but had traveled to the towns using public transport or by hitching rides.

Generally, the public reacted to the incidents and the deviance through the processed or coded images presented by the media. On the morning following the initial occurrence all national newspapers except one ran a leading report using headlines such as "Day of Terror," "Youngsters Beat up Town," "Wild Ones Invade Seaside" (Cohen 2002: 30). Despite the fact that disturbances of this kind had always been a regular occurrence on public holidays in southern coastal towns during the late 1950s and early 1960s, it was only when the incident was labeled as widespread deviance that it became news (Thompson 1998: 35). Having achieved this label, the incidents came to provide a symbolic framework for other completely unconnected disturbances, causing increased public anxiety and prompting a more robust police response.

For the media, and subsequently for politicians and commentators, the incidents came to symbolize postwar social change in Britain when the mantra of "never having it so good" meant that some were enjoying too much affluence, too quickly. Youth became objects of jealousy and resentment owing to their increased spending power and sexual freedom (Cohen 2002: 162). Anxieties concerning a possible breakdown of class barriers (Mods and Rockers appeared less linked to specific classes) associated with the emergent youth culture and the Mod attitude of seeming indifference to the virtues of promotion through hard work and apparent ingratitude for the bounty society was granting them, cohered, so that the groups were seen as threatening delinquents and as "a marauding army . . . massacring and plundering, living by slaughter and rapacity" (p. 37).

Cohen's discussion of the sociology of moral panics (1972: 191) suggests that the groups of Mods and Rockers symbolized the social change that occurred in Britain in the 1960s. In particular, Cohen points to an emerging youth culture focused on satisfying the needs of the young, high wages, the popularity of pop heroes, the permissive society and the welfare state as perceived causes of this group conflict (p. 191).

Mugging in Britain

In *Policing the Crisis: Mugging, the State, and Law and Order* (1978) Stuart Hall and his colleagues explain how the American expression "mugging" and its underlying themes came to be appropriated and applied in Britain by the media to a set of violent crimes and how this constituted a moral panic. This insightful and richly textured study is a complex analysis of a moral panic constituted by youth, media representation and crime, which the authors regard as "one of the principal forms of ideological consciousness by means of which a 'silent majority' is won over to the support of increasingly coercive measures on the part of the state" (Hall et al. 1978: 221).

According to the social history provided by the authors, this moral panic was precipitated by the death of an elderly man by stabbing in August 1972 and labeled by the media "a mugging gone wrong" (Hall et al. 1978: 3). This was the first time the term had been applied to a particular criminal attack in Britain. On August 17, 1972 the *Daily Mirror* tabloid described it as "a frightening new strain of crime" and explained that it was an American conception involving an assault on a victim's head using an arm lock with the intent to rob, with or without the use of weapons (quoted in Hall et al. 1978: 3). Despite historical evidence of a similar crime occurring almost 100 years previously known as "garrotting," and police information that mugging was essentially the traditional crime of "rolling" a seaman, the media persistently asserted that this was a new crime (Hall et al. 1978: 6).

The ensuing panic about mugging lasted for 13 months from August 1972 and generated crime reports, features, editorials and public statements from judges and the social control agencies as well as politicians (Hall et al. 1978: 3). During this period the courts reacted to the "new" crime by imposing exemplary sentences for acts that were labeled muggings based on the public interest, deterrence or "the need to keep our streets safe," and the police instituted strategies to keep muggers and others out of public parks.

The underlying themes associated with the mugging panic were: claims about massive increases in crimes of violence, especially mugging; claims of lenient sentencing by the courts; and the need to "get tough" to deter such crimes (p. 9). One case in particular demonstrated the judicial response: a 16-year-old mugger was given a sentence of 20 years for mugging and his accomplices 10 years. Arguably, it was no accident that they were black working-class youth. Hall and others (1978) reveal how racial tensions, poor relations between police and black youth, immigration restrictions and populist anti-immigration movements combined to bring a focus on black youth so that mugging came to be defined as a black youth problem.

Hall and others (1978: 9–10) demonstrate that statistical data of the time as well as from previous years did not support the notion of massive increases in violent crime. How then, and why, did mugging enter the crime lexicon in Britain and why did the media fuel a moral panic about a type of crime that was scarcely new? By tracking the roots and subsequent development of the notion of mugging in the U.S., the authors demonstrate that by the 1960s, the term had come not only to refer to a kind of urban crime but also to "a whole complex of social themes in which the 'crisis of American society' was reflected" (Hall et al. 1978: 19), including:

> the involvement of blacks and drug addicts in crime; the expansion of the black ghettos, coupled with the growth of black social and political militancy; the threatened crisis and collapse of the cities; the crime panic and the appeal to "law and order"; the sharpening political tensions and protest movements of the 1960s.
>
> (Hall et al. 1978: 19–20)

Mugging had become a "referential symbol" for a complex set of threatening social and political issues that were avidly followed in the British media (Hall et al. 1978: 21). The media educated the British public about mugging in its broadest conception, asking whether what was happening in the U.S. would be imported into Britain. The media provided the answer: take urgent steps and Britain would avoid the perils of the U.S. Thus, the media provided justification for the extreme reaction and the punitive measures that followed the "discovery" of mugging in Britain. Hall and others (1978) are clear that the reaction to mugging was wholly disproportionate to any actual threat level. Disproportionality was exemplified by the punitive approach of the judiciary and the police. The latter amplified concern by actively formulating and implementing strategies and campaigns rather than simply reacting to the moral panic (p. 52).

The authors identify a media "signification spiral" that amplifies instances of deviant conduct to create a greater sense of risk (Hall et al. 1978: 55). Studies reveal that the media do not simply report news as if it is self-selecting. Instead, news is "the end product of a complex process, which begins with a systematic sorting and selecting of events and topics according to a socially constructed set of categories" (p. 53). "Good news" is judged as such if it possesses the value of being "extraordinary" but subsets of news values relate to: events involving elite persons; events that are dramatic; human interest topics that involve human characteristics such as sadness and humor; occurrences that have negative outcomes; and events that constitute part of an existing newsworthy theme (p. 52). Mugging became a news story simply because of its novelty.

Events deemed to be newsworthy are reported through a frame, which is in part premised on what the authors term a "consensus" – a single perspective on events that we all supposedly share. Hall and others argue that crime marks the boundary of that consensus because crime is an interruption to that consensus. It marks a break in the social order and violent crime "represents a fundamental rupture in the social order" because only the state may legitimately exercise violence (1978: 68). However, the media are not the "primary definers" of news events and do not determine this consensus. Those who have privileged access to the media as "accredited sources" exercise this function and the media "stand in a position of structured subordination to the primary definers" (p. 59). Given that the media are the primary source of knowledge about events for the public, the media connect the primary definers and the public. By mediating in this way, the media are able to mobilize public opinion on issues like law and order within the dominant framework set by the primary definers.

Like Stanley Cohen, Hall and others attribute this moral panic in part to the "social anxiety" arising in the postwar period based on increased affluence and social changes that fundamentally changed working-class culture (1978: 157). A succession of moral panics focused on deviant and antisocial youth and merged into a "general panic" about social order which in turn led to a mobilization to restore stability and law and order. Undisciplined and affluent youth became the scapegoats, and the folk devils comprised a series of working-class youth subcultures that included Cohen's Mods and Rockers (p. 159) as well as the muggers of this study. While Hall and others acknowledge the key role of the media and the linkages between the media and social control agencies, they part company with Cohen's analysis by insisting that an authoritarian state embarked on a campaign to stifle liberalizing influences that threatened the authority of the law itself.

Juvenile superpredators

In the 1990s, the U.S. experienced a moral panic associated with public fear of youth violence. It was thought that a more dangerous variety of youthful offender was emerging whose behavior was vicious and without precedent, and whose numbers would grow to produce a frightening menace in the first decade of the next century (Zimring 1998: xi). These dangerous juveniles, termed "superpredators" by one academic commentator, were supposed to emerge based on demographic projections of a growing juvenile population and a sharp increase in juvenile rates of arrest for violent crimes beginning in the 1980s. The notion soon became accepted as "truth" and attained the status of a moral panic when legislators and policy analysts responded with a crusade of scaremongering and punitive laws (Bilchik 2000).

A principal advocate of this startling proposition was John Dilulio, who, writing with others in 1996, reported,

youth, crime and justice

today's bad boys are far worse than yesteryear's and tomorrow's will be even worse than today's and as a result America is now home to thickening ranks of juvenile "super-predators" – radically impulsive, brutally remorseless youngsters, including ever more pre-teenage boys, who murder, assault, rob, burglarize, deal deadly drugs, join gun-toting gangs, and create serious communal disorders.

(Bennett et al. 1996: 26–27)

Dilulio claimed that "By the year 2010 there will be approximately 270,000 more juvenile super-predators on the streets than there were in 1990" (Bennett et al. 1996: 27). Criminologist James Fox added his voice to the developing moral panic:

So long as we fool ourselves into thinking that we're winning the war against crime, we may be blindsided by this bloodbath of teenage violence that is lurking in the future.

(quoted in Baer and Chambliss 1997: 97)

The cause of this supposed phenomenon of the superpredator was said to be "moral poverty"; that is, "children growing up without love, care, and guidance from responsible adults" (Bennett et al. 1996: 59).

Media contributions to the superpredator moral panic are illustrated by a 1995 story in *Newsweek* stating that "Criminologists are already warning that the United States can expect another wave of violent crime in the coming decade, and some say it will be much worse than the one that is now subsiding" (quoted in Baer and Chambliss 1997: 97). Also, echoing Dilulio's menacing warning was Representative Bill McCollum, the then chair of the House Subcommittee on Crime, who in 1996 said:

It is important to keep in mind that [the current] dramatic increase in youth crime over the past decade occurred while the youth population was declining. Now here is that really bad news: This nation will soon have more teenagers than it has had in decades. In the final years of this decade and throughout the next, America will experience an "echo boom" – a population surge made up of the children of today's aging baby boomers. Today's enormous cohort of five year olds will be tomorrow's teenager. This is ominous news, given that most [sic] violent crime is committed by older juveniles (those fifteen to nineteen years of age) than by any other age group. More of these youths will come from fatherless homes than ever before, at the same time that youth drug use is taking a sharp turn for the worse. Put these demographic facts together and brace yourself for the coming generation of "superpredators."

(quoted in Zimring 1998: 5)

Here, in this apocalyptic narrative, is contained the entire logic of the argument: that the U.S. would soon be overrun by a generation of super-predators, a claim made and given legitimacy by respected criminologists and policy analysts.[9] The emphasis in commentaries on the viciousness of these folk devils separated out and demonized this category of youth, and allowed legislators and policy makers to easily promote a punitive criminal justice response (Zimring 1998: 6–7).

From 1990 to 1997, having denoted a category of youth as folk devils and responding to what was seen as a national emergency, virtually every state amended its laws covering youth violence. Most adopted the strategy of increasing the number of juveniles who could be tried as adults, funda-mentally erasing their identity as juveniles and applying the rationale that "If you're old enough to do the crime, you're old enough to do the time" (Zimring 1998: 9). Other responses to this moral panic included curfews, anti-gang measures, gun controls and allowing much greater public access to juvenile court proceedings or records. Guns and gangs symbolized the new youth violence with gun use by juveniles accounting for over 90 percent of increases in juvenile homicide from 1985 to 1992 (pp. 14–15). The Office of Juvenile Justice and Delinquency Prevention (OJJDP) reported in 2000 that a link between juvenile homicide arrest rates and weapons use was to be found in the FBI's Supplementary Homicide Report data (Bilchik 2000: 5). It showed that the overall trend in homicides committed by juveniles was entirely attributable to homicides committed using firearms (p. 5). The leading explanation for the increase in youth homicide rates was the production and sale of crack cocaine and the conflicts associated with marketing it, resulting in youth turning to guns and gangs for protection (Blumstein 1995; Cork 1997; Reiss and Roth 1993).

The basis for the concern about juvenile superpredators was the projected increase in the adolescent population. The assumption was that the increased population of teenagers of 2010 would be committing serious violent crimes. Predictions made in the mid-1990s about criminal activity by children in 2010 who were as yet either unborn or under 4 years of age imply that the causes of serious juvenile violence are fixed and immutable. How is it possible to argue that rates of violence can be predicted for children of between 2 and 4 years of age?

Fears based on predictions of 270,000 superpredators in 2010 were based on straight-line projections and relied on the existence of a fixed relationship between population and rates of serious violence. However, in truth, the conditions that would influence the rate of homicides among children who were only 4 years old in 1997 had not yet been determined (Zimring 1998: 11). Zimring (1998: 45) points to the absence of any unitary trend in the history of youth arrests for violent crime. Absent this kind of evidence, it is impossible to generalize about the conduct of a cohort of youth from the 1990s into the future.

Levels of predatory crimes committed by juveniles, including rape, robbery and murder, have dropped significantly since 1997. While there was evidence that juvenile violence did increase in the early 1990s, the National Crime Victimization Survey (NCVS) also showed that by 1995, the rate had returned to its traditional level (Bilchik 2000). The NCVS data, therefore, showed no evidence of the advent of superpredators. Rather, in spite of a temporary increase in the rate of serious juvenile offending in the mid-1990s, offending was comparable to that of a generation ago (Bilchik 2000: 1–2). The OJJDP data, for example, showed that in 2000, after years of relative stability, the juvenile violent crime *arrest rate* began to increase in the late 1980s. However, after 1994 the rate began to decline, and by 1997 it had returned to the level near that of 1989 (p. 2). The OJJDP authoritatively concluded that "arrest increases are not always related to an increase in crime. They can reflect positive policy changes. Regardless, it is clear that national crime and arrest statistics provide no evidence for a new breed of juvenile superpredator" (p. 4). More recently, Greenwood and Turner (2011: 89) note that as of 2009 "the number of juveniles arrested for serious crimes and the number of juveniles in custody is at an all-time low."

Girl violence and girl gangs

Beginning in the 1990s and onward, a media discourse about individual girl violence and violent girl gangs set off a moral panic or set of moral panics, incorporating youth as the folk devil, but now in gendered form. In the 1990s, the media focus was on the "gangsta girl" and in the new century on the "bad girl" and on the "bad girls go wild" (Chesney-Lind and Irwin 2008: 31). Concerns about girl violence and girl gangs migrated from the U.S. to Britain and Canada, merging in a supranational media discourse that seems time bound by traditional gender conceptions of appropriate girl conduct.[10]

The media construction of violent and amoral girl gangs in the 1990s included television presentations like *Girls in the Hood* in August 1992, but the media launch of this topic has been traced back to a story in the *Wall Street Journal* of January 25, 1990 entitled "You've Come a Long Way, Moll" (Crittenden 1990: A14). The story argued that over the period between 1978 and 1988 there was a 41.5 percent increase in the number of women arrested for violent crimes as compared to only a 23.1 percent increase for men. The *New York Times* followed this lead in 1991 with a story "For Gold Earrings and Protection, More Girls Take the Road to Violence" (Lee 1991: A1). This was a story about 15-year-old Aleysha who stole gold earrings and designer clothes and who symbolized girls in gangs, girls in the drug trade and "girls carrying guns and knives" (1991: A1). Additional articles and television shows followed, including an NBC broadcast in 1993 linking women's "equality" with girls in gangs:

> Gone are the days when girls were strictly sidekicks for male gang members, around merely to provide sex and money and run guns and drugs. Now girls also do shooting . . . the new members, often as young as twelve, are the most violent. . . . Ironic as it is, just as women are becoming more powerful in business and government, the same thing is happening in gangs.
>
> (quoted in Chesney-Lind 1999: 299)

Conceptualizations of girl gangs in the 1990s followed the "liberation hypothesis" or the "social injury hypothesis" (also see Chapter 2). The former contended that changes in gender roles and responsibilities impacted girl gangs by creating more gangs, provoking a higher level of violence, and causing gangs to take on male activities like the production and sale of drugs.[11] The latter argues that these changes are questionable and asserts that gangs have always represented places of safety for girls from troubled backgrounds who find a sense of belonging and empowerment there (Hagedorn and Devitt 1999: 256; Nurge 2003). The more general liberation argument is linked to advances for women coming from the feminist movement. It postulates a convergence between men's violence and women's violence now that women are claimed to enjoy "equality" with men.

In a thorough and insightful analysis of the liberation hypothesis and contemporary bad girl media representations, Chesney-Lind and Irwin (2008: 2–3) work from a moral panic model and argue that:

> masculinized images of bad girls . . . serve a number of important societal purposes. Notably, they serve to warn all girls and women of the negative consequences of seeking political and social equality with men while also justifying harsh new controls on certain girls – the daughters of the powerless. In a race and class based society, the demonization of certain girls and women as gender outlaws justifies their harsh control and punishment, all the while cautioning the daughters of the powerful about the downside of challenging male dominance.

Moral panics about bad girls and violence have provoked new definitions of appropriate conduct and an increased degree of social control over girls within the family, in schools and by peer groups. Intense monitoring of their activities for violations of appropriate conduct has meant that more girls have entered the juvenile justice system to be dealt with for supposed violence and aggression (Chesney-Lind and Irwin 2008). Conduct previously considered normal within the school and resolved using school procedures has been reclassified as "bullying" and been made the subject of new forms of discipline and control. According to some psychological studies on which anti-bullying programs have been based, girls and boys are now considered equally aggressive, boys directly and girls more indirectly, even though boys use actual physical violence and girls are generally non-violent (p. 7).

Girls are entering the juvenile justice system in increasing numbers principally for cases of "assault." From 1991 to 2003 detentions of girls increased 98 percent as compared to 29 percent for boys, girls' referrals to the juvenile court by 92 percent compared to 29 percent for boys, and girls' commitments 88 percent compared to 23 percent for boys (Chesney-Lind and Irwin 2008: 9). Between 1980 and 2000 girls' arrests for aggravated assault, simple assault and weapons offenses increased by 121 percent, 257 percent and 134 percent respectively, but boys' increases were only 28 percent, 109 percent and 20 percent respectively. The media conclude that girls are becoming more violent and acting more like boys but self-report studies and victim reports fail to corroborate any supposed increases in girls' violence (pp. 25, 26). To add to the confusion, girls' arrests for murder (which would have been expected to show an increase if the gender gap for violence was closing) actually dropped by 36.9 percent between 1995 and 2004.

What therefore accounts for the increased arrest rate for girls? Among the explanations offered by researchers are increased monitoring and surveillance of youth in the home and at school and, due to concerns about school violence, new definitions of violent conduct encompassing activity previously considered non-violent. With the impetus of school shootings and the new conception of "school violence," school bullying has emerged as a social problem and arguably almost a moral panic in itself. Despite the fact that only boys have been responsible for school shootings and that research about the serious effects of bullying has been confined to an examination of the direct violence by boys, the identification of bullying as a risk factor in some school shootings has meant that girls too have been subjected to a new regime of definitions and sanctions associated with the new social problem of bullying.

In an exhaustive analysis of this issue, Chesney-Lind and Irwin (2008) trace the emergence of bullying and its transformation into a form of violence through national anti-bullying campaigns and legislation requiring that school districts adopt bullying prevention and education policies. Expert psychological discourses used in training about bullying have defined bullying to mean exposure "repeatedly and over time, to negative actions on the part of one or more other students" (p. 100) and bullying has been explained as direct physical or verbal attacks or indirect attacks, "making faces or obscene gestures, or intentional exclusion from a group" (p. 100). Conflating the direct and indirect brings actions such as rolling eyes and spreading rumors within the definition of bullying (p. 100). The heightened attention to bullying has promoted increased surveillance and monitoring of student conduct within schools, an atmosphere of intolerance to direct and indirect forms of bullying, and increased flows of information about school violence resulting in increased disciplining and policing.

Aggression is explained by Simmons as "behaviors that are intended to hurt or harm others" (2002: 69). The breadth of this definition means that forms of aggression that are "relational," "covert" or "indirect," like bullying, also qualify as aggression. Researchers have revealed that when indirect forms of aggression are included, girls are as aggressive as boys (p. 69). The existence of relational aggression has been presented as a significant problem and as revelatory, an activity previously hidden from the sight of parents and teachers, and as "the day-to-day aggression that persists among girls, a dark underside of their social universe. . . . We have no language for it" (p. 69). However, the notion that there is parity between relational and direct forms of aggression has been challenged owing to the differing effects of each and because relational aggression may in fact be pro-social and not antisocial for youth (Chesney-Lind and Irwin 2008: 113). Thus, Chesney-Lind and Irwin (2008) argue that when the media represent girls as becoming more aggressive and as achieving "violence parity" with boys based on limited data about arrests, this ignores the wider dimension constituted by new definitions of aggression and new policing practices affecting girls.

"Policing girlhood" in the schools includes modes of disciplining like zero-tolerance policies for school violence and increased reporting of non-serious incidents to the police. Reclassifying less serious incidents into major acts of violence has resulted in only two recognized forms of school violence – "serious violence" and "violence" (Kaufman et al. 2000). Labeling minor events as girls' "violence" augments the social control of girls through the juvenile justice system. Within the family there is evidence that policing domestic violence through policy practices such as mandatory arrest is unfairly penalizing girls who are involved in trivial disputes with their parents[12] (Chesney-Lind and Irwin 2008: 86; Zahn et al. 2008: 7), and that parents are sometimes complicit with police in creating the circumstances for such arrests.

Generally, researchers agree that media reporting of girls' violence and girl gangs draws on statistics that are presented unproblematically as evidence that girls' aggression has converged with boys' aggression. This, despite the fact that crimes committed by girls are principally property crimes of a less serious nature, and the evidence from not only the U.S., but also Canada and Australia, that the supposed increase in girls' violence is accounted for by arrests for the less serious forms of violence, many newly defined as "violence." The media attention to girls' violence appears to be a crusade against inappropriate conduct, now reconstructed as disorder and violence (Alder and Worrall 2004: 3, 7, 11). Sometimes even when there is a degree of violence, authorities can exaggerate the "danger" as seen below. Additionally, a small change in the number of cases is reflected in what seems to be a huge increase in the percentage of cases, thus, highlighting the problem of the "tyranny of numbers" when applied to girls.

GIRLS' GANGS IN WASHINGTON

In March 2006 it was reported that girl gangs were on the increase in Washington, D.C. Princess Galloway, 16, explained that as a younger girl she and her friends had birthday parties, discussed clothes and held sleepovers in their houses. She says, "It was, like, a normal thing females do." But as the girls became older the parties were transformed into trips to go-go clubs, and belts and bags were replaced by blades and bats and so a girl gang was created.

"We started fighting when a different female gang from uptown jumped one of our friends," explained Princess, who left her gang after several detentions in the Oak Hill Youth Facility for assault. Princess' story is now becoming common in the District where officials claim girl gangs are on the rise. Disputes in the school yard are turning into turf battles. Bridget T. Miller, coordinator of the District's Youth Gang Task Force, claims that "In the last three years, female activity . . . has risen. Nobody wanted to acknowledge it because they thought it was just a short trend, but they failed to realize how dangerous a female can be." She says more than 270 girl gangs are found in the District.

In the District the number of Superior Court cases involving female juveniles increased from 445 in 2003 to 571 in 2004 and the number of girls brought to court for violence rose from 225 in 2003 to 322 in 2004, an increase of 43 percent.

Officials are disturbed by the trend. Anita Josey-Herring, the presiding Judge of D.C. Family Court, says, "Women have become more involved in the system for at least a decade. We're trying to get ahead of that before the problem becomes insurmountable."

Source: Adapted from Gary Emerling, Modern Tribalist. http://modern tribalist.blogspot.com/2006/03/girl-gangs-on-rise-in-washington-dc.html

Gang violence

Before the 1980s the gang problem in the U.S. was barely visible in the mass media, although gangs in some form or another, however defined, had been a feature of American society, especially in the urban slums, since the early 19th century (Hagedorn 1998: 366).[13] However, beginning in the 1980s, following police reports of increased gang activity, the media uncovered and revealed publicly the existence of menacing gangs and promoted dramatic images of gangs linked to guns, drugs and violence.[14] In response, legislatures and policy makers poured resources into the policing of gangs, created specialist anti-gang units and tracking systems, and enacted punitive laws or increased existing penalties for gang-type offenses.[15]

Numerous research studies and "gang experts" promoted anti-gang discourses, explaining to school administrators how they could identify gangs and their insignia, and warning the general public that gangs represented a major threat to social order. Some researchers locate the source of this exposure of gangs in law enforcement itself, believing that the police recognized an opportunity to market a gang threat to secure additional resources (McCorkle and Miethe 2002: 5). Thus, applying moral panic theory, middle-level professional interest groups, namely law enforcement, sought to secure an advantage from a crusade against gangs.

Accounts of local panics about gangs and their activities in Arizona, Nevada and California have tended to support the notion that law enforcement has encouraged the media to instigate moral panics about gangs. In California during the 1980s, media reports of gang violence and destruction flourished, creating widespread fear and alarm, and producing a series of anti-gang measures including harsher penalties for drug, gun and drive-by shooting offenses (Geis 2002). The concerns were pitched at a decidedly dramatic level captured in the employment of the term "terrorism" in the *Street Terrorism Enforcement and Prevention Act*.[16]

According to gang researcher Joan Moore, California experienced a moral panic about gang activity following a series of shootings including that of a young woman in a wealthy university community in West Los Angeles. Seizing on this incident, the media declared a crisis, the police declared Los Angeles to be the gang capital of the nation, and law enforcement conducted sweeps aimed at drug gangs. At the height of this "crisis" the California Attorney General announced:

> Criminal street gang members are terrorizing communities throughout California, where the viciousness of the gangs [has] taken away many of the public's individual freedoms. In some parts of the state, gang

members completely control the community where they live and commit their violent crimes.

(quoted in McCorkle and Miethe 2002: 63)

However, few drugs were actually found and few gang members featured among those arrested during these purges (Moore 1991). Arguably, both the rhetoric and the responses were disproportionate to the actual gang problem in the state and relied on formulaic images of gangs deployed by the media and law enforcement:

> The image of gangs that figured prominently in mass media and the discussions at public hearings was of groups who use juveniles, high-power weaponry, and motor vehicles to traffic drugs. These gangs were characterized as instrumental groups or vaguely defined youth street gangs whose overriding purpose was to make large amounts of money through the distribution and sale of crack and other drugs.
>
> (Jackson and Rudman 1990: 258)

In Nevada during the late 1980s, Las Vegas and Reno both experienced a level of hysteria about gangs prompted by several high-profile violent crimes involving minorities with alleged gang associations. Media coverage, based almost entirely on police reports, suggested that drug-dealing gangs were overrunning the cities. The media and local elites neglected to objectively assess law-enforcement claims that gangs represented a clear and present danger to the community. The police pressed for additional resources and lawmakers acquiesced, even though the claims were questionable and even misleading (McCorkle and Miethe 2002: 123).

In their detailed analysis of "gang panics" in Las Vegas and Reno, McCorkle and Miethe (2002) note that gangs have been active in Las Vegas since the 1960s but that the reporting of gang activity increased in 1983 after two gang killings involving rival gangs.[17] These events resulted in the resurrection of a Gang Diversion Unit previously charged with intelligence gathering to conduct that same task again. Gradually, community pressure built for a more robust approach and elected black officials, and law enforcement began to meet with communities promising action. They used the example of gang activity in Los Angeles as a basis for arguing that only a well-resourced anti-gang unit could prevent something similar from happening in Vegas (p. 128). Both private and public "gang experts" arrived in the late 1980s to train teachers in gang recognition and to conduct seminars for youth workers. Law enforcement received increased resources in the form of an additional 16 officers for the Gang Diversion Unit, which now took a more robust approach stressing deterrence and punishment. Customary strategies (such as police sweeps accompanied by the media) targeted gangs, and police claimed that high level gang leaders were now out of circulation. By 1988, more funds and staff were being provided to the Unit following claims "that gangbangers were retreating in the face of superior forces" (p. 134). Yet, gangs continued to be defined as a critical social problem for the city with law enforcement persisting in its claims that street gangs would overrun the city in the absence of greater resources. McCorkle and Miethe (2002) conclude that in the case of Vegas, rhetoric did not match reality. In fact, the events constituted a moral panic, sparked by the claims of law enforcement and amplified by media coverage. In truth, while acts of violence by persons with gang affiliations did take place and there was some increase in gang-related violence, the response of law enforcement and the media was wholly disproportionate to the actual threat.

In Reno, McCorkle and Miethe (2002) found that the media and the community attacked the police for failing to recognize the threat posed by gangs. The local newspaper, the *Reno Gazette Journal*, led the crusade to get tough on gangs with apocalyptic editorials of a city under siege:

> [W]e need to understand – all of us – that this is a war. We are under attack and we must respond forcefully and immediately, with every resource at our command. We must pledge to do whatever it takes to control this scourge. We must promise that our streets will not be overrun by thugs without a conscience, our schools will not be battle-grounds for teen-age hoodlums, our nights not punctuated by gunfire.
> (quoted in McCorkle and Miethe 2002: 150)

Here, as in Vegas, the gang problem was revealed during a period of rapid population increase, racial diversification and economic growth. Fears about members of the Los Angeles gangs, the Crips and the Bloods, migrating to Reno followed an incident in 1988 in which a 16-year-old male was beaten to death by an alleged Crips member. Gang specialists were called in and gave warnings that Reno was a prime target for gang activity but the local police did not share that fear. Only a week after the expert prediction was made, a 13-year-old girl was beaten, robbed and raped by alleged Crips members. By the summer of 1988, a Youth Gang Task Force had been created and while the police participated in this unit, they remained unconvinced that a serious gang threat existed.

The discourse of gang threats gained further traction in 1989 when it was the theme of the annual conference of Juvenile and Family Court Judges and again in 1990 after violence was reported between two rival Hispanic gangs (McCorkle and Miethe 2002). Finally, giving into community pressure, the police department upgraded its gang unit and adopted zero-tolerance anti-gang policies closely monitoring suspected gang members (p. 160). In an atypical response to gang problems, law enforcement adopted a community-based strategy, focusing on prevention and intervention rather than warfare, and took care to ensure that only accurate information about gang activity was released to the community. Data showed that very little criminality in the city could be attributed to gangs or gang activity, and the calm and measured response of law enforcement reflected its belief that while gangs constituted a threat, they did not imperil the community (p. 161).

Police desire to secure an advantage from "discovering" a gang problem is argued to have been the cause of a moral panic over the "Chicano youth gang problem" in Phoenix, Arizona in the late 1970s and early 1980s (Zatz 1987). In 1979, the police reported that the number of youth gangs in the city had doubled in six months. This claim produced additional resources for law enforcement in the form of an information system for storing data on gangs, and an upgraded gang squad. As well, federal grants were secured on the basis of claims that the number of Chicano gangs had increased from five or six to 35 in 18 months, then to 50 or 60 in the following three months, and then to between 100 and 120 (pp. 129, 130). In reality, if police claims were correct, about a quarter of all young Chicano males in the city had been identified as likely gang members, but there was no evidence of a corresponding increase in violent crime. In 1980, 18 percent of the 10- to 14-year-olds and almost 17 percent of the 15- to 19-year-olds in the city were of Spanish origin but in 1981 31.5 percent of youth detained by police were Chicanos, a disproportionality suggesting that law enforcement was profiling Chicanos (pp. 129, 137). In fact, data suggested that Chicano youth were arrested for fighting and property offenses and not for serious violence or for drug offenses (p. 146).

During 1979, the media focus on gangs in the city intensified, with 25 articles published in the two local newspapers detailing gang fights, arrests and gang trials. Once again, like Las Vegas and Reno, Phoenix police asserted claims about the Los Angeles gang problem migrating to Phoenix. The Chief of the Gang Squad stated:

> "The problem could get serious . . . because sometimes what happens in the Chicano communities here seems to be about five years or so behind what is happening in the Los Angeles barrios. And it's bad there. The police spend millions and they cannot even begin to control the gangs and the violence."
>
> (*Phoenix Magazine* 1979: 33)

In 1980, the police continued to present the issue as one of gangs defying societal norms and values through showing contempt for the law, and defiance of parents and civility. As well, gangs were characterized as predators, "vicious" and "cruising the streets spoiling for blood" (Zatz 1987: 132).

Like Vegas and Reno the "Chicano gang problem" in Phoenix occurred at a time of economic expansion and demographic changes that had made Phoenix, a "sun belt city," into one of the ten largest cities in the U.S. Economic growth and population migrations seem to have converged to raise law-enforcement fears of social disorder in the city. There are clear parallels in the situation in Phoenix to the insights of Hall and others (1978) with regard to mugging in Britain. Having designated Chicano gangs as folk devils, as outsiders[18] and as the symbol of potential social disorder, policing these gangs became, at one level of analysis, a means of subordinating and controlling the migratory population in the city in the interests of the city's elite entrepreneurs and developers. At another level, law enforcement's claims about the gang peril facing the city enlarged their powers and resources and reinforced their standing as the only authority on the "Chicano gang problem."

Generally, the preoccupation with gangs that builds into moral panics is almost always aimed at African American and Hispanic gangs (Shelden et al. 2001: 7). These groups are perceived to be the most threatening to society and especially to the elite. The inner city, constructed as a place populated largely by minorities, is seen as the site of mayhem and social disorder, and as potentially menacing the wider community. Alleviating the poverty, unemployment and hopelessness of the inner city environment takes second place to waging a "war" against gangs represented as "terrorists."

Recap

The notion of a "moral panic" provides an important explanatory framework for analyzing social movements that erupt when conditions seem to give rise to a threat to societal interests. Associations between adolescence and deviance, especially in the form of violence, are deeply embedded in the public consciousness, and moral panics therefore often center on youth cultures and practices. When gender is implicated in a moral panic, moral crusaders are often seeking to exercise a heightened social control over women and girls, as, for example, in the panic concerning girl gangs. In fact, to an extent, as David Garland has noted, moral panics can collectively over a period of time create ruptures within society and stimulate modes of government regulation and control which may leave a permanent legacy.

Some scholars have argued that moral panics have become institutionalized into persistent fabricated crusades linked to the development of the culture of control and the notion of governing through crime (Feeley and Simon 2007: 51). In the risk society moral panics seem also to be linked with anxiety about challenges to values. Moral regulation therefore becomes

youth, crime and justice

a site of struggle over how society should be, and is played out in the media and through social movements and collective behavior.

School shootings and heinous crimes committed by children that necessitated a redefinition of childhood in order to comprehend its enormity seem to challenge the fundamental societal order. When the search for causal explanations is exhausted, recourse is made to policy prescriptions that reinforce the culture of control because policy makers have no other adequate response. Perceptions of gang violence, incidents of mugging and adolescent violence that generate apocalyptic rhetoric are almost never contextualized in media accounts, and consequently, the motivations of moral crusaders, and sometimes law enforcement, remain unknown and undiscovered.

Notes

1 As Stanley Cohen (2002: xxiii) has noted, in moral panics the media set the agenda, transmit the images and now, increasingly, make the claims themselves.

2 See Chapter 2.

3 Jonathan Simon (2007: 210, 216–217) argues that crime in schools is now "the subject of almost frantic data collection" largely because schools need data to secure benefits from the federal government under the *Safe Schools Act 1994*. This gives data collection for crime analysis priority over other data flows used for purposes like employment.

4 Details of the various school shootings may be found in numerous publications (see, e.g., McCabe and Martin (2005: 42) and Crews and Montgomery (2001: 55)), but the most notorious, owing to the number of dead and the fact that it occurred in a white middle-class school, was the incident at Columbine on April 20, 1999, when two students, Eric Harris, aged 18, and Dylan Klebold, aged 17, shot 12 students and a teacher at Columbine High School, Littleton, Colorado and then killed themselves.

5 According to Lawrence and Birkland (2004: 1199) the causal frame of guns and gun control was the most prominent in both media coverage and political debate.

6 After nine months awaiting trial and no psychological treatment the boys were charged with murder and kidnapping. They were found guilty of both crimes and received indeterminate life sentences (Green 2008: 2). In June 2001 both boys were released on parole and were granted lifelong anonymity to protect them from vigilante violence (Muncie 2009: 5).

7 The Archbishop of York was quoted in *The Times* (November 25, 1993 in James and Jenks 1996: 322) as saying, "the importance of [the] crime lies in what it says about the potential for evil in children of an age at which innocence was once taken for granted."

8 In terms of dominant associations within the subcultures, Mods were associated with the use of amphetamines, soul music, Italian clothing and scooters, and Rockers with alcohol, rock'n'roll music, leather clothing and motorbikes (Muncie 2009: 219).

9 See, e.g., Bennett et al. 1996; Dole 1996; Fox 1996: Wilson and Petersilia 1995.

10 In Britain, media depictions of girls as "mean, violent, drunk and disorderly" have been common since the mid-1990s and Angela McRobbie has suggested that "young women . . . have replaced youth as a metaphor for social change" (in Burman and Batchelor 2009: 271). An attack on actress Elizabeth Hurley in London in November 1994 by four teenage girls generated significant media interest about girl gangs and a supposed rise in female violence (Thompson 1998: 111). In Canada, the beating and murder of a 14-year-old girl of Asian origin by a group of seven girls and a boy in November 1997 provided "evidence" that girl violence had become a serious problem (Barron and Lacombe 2005: 54). In typical fashion, the Canadian media amplified this case into a trend of girl violence, and media attention and public concern prompted new punitive policies for violent youth (Barron and Lacombe 2005: 59).

11 According to Zahn et al. (2008: 14), "Very little research has examined girl's violence within gangs. The research that has been done shows that boys in gangs are more violent than girls in gangs. Still, girls in gangs are more likely to be delinquent and violent than girls who are not in gangs."

12 Such incidents include "father lunged at her while she was calling the police about a domestic dispute. She (girl) hit him" and a girl arrested "for throwing cookies at her mother," and an arrest for assault for throwing a Barbie doll at her mother (reported in Chesney-Lind and Irwin 2008: 86).

13 A useful chronicle of the history of gangs in the U.S. may be found in McCorkle and Miethe (2002: 32[en]50). The authors conclude that the media "discovery" of gangs in the 1980s disregarded the context of gang development in urban and rural areas since the 19th century.

14 Media coverage of gangs increased by almost 2,500 percent between 1983 and 1999 (McCorkle and Miethe 2002: 84).

15 By 1997 more than half of the largest enforcement agencies had created gang units who waged military-style operations against street gangs employing high-tech weaponry, helicopters and armored vehicles. Recording and tracking systems for gangs include the Gang Reporting Evaluation and Tracking System (GREAT) developed in Los Angels County containing 200,000 records of gang members (McCorkle and Miethe 2002: 71).

16 In similar style, an anti-gang ordinance in California contained the following statement of justification: "California is in a state of crisis which has been caused by violent street gangs whose members threaten, terrorize and commit a multitude of crimes against peaceful citizens in their neighborhood" (in Geis 2002: 260).

17 In 1983 only four stories on gangs appeared in the local media but in 1989 the number was 164 and through 1991 the local media continued to run more than 100 such stories (McCorkle and Miethe 2002: 130).

18 Gilbert Geis notes, "Juvenile gangs, like organized crime syndicates, are part of the world of Others. Their members are ethnically, economically, and socially different from those who wield power and make laws. It is no longer acceptable in American society to demonstrate prejudice overtly. But the same end can be achieved by pinpointing activities that are very largely those of the socially

disenfranchised and inventing special kinds of laws that will bring persons who violate them to grief" (Geis 2002: 259).

References

Alder, C. and A. Worrall (eds). 2004. *Girls' Violence: Myths and Realities.* Albany, NY: State University of New York Press.

Aries, P. 1962. *Centuries of Childhood.* London: Cape.

Baer, J. and W.J. Chambliss. 1997. "The Politics of Crime Reporting." *Crime, Law, and Social Change* 27: 87–107.

Barron, C. and D. Lacombe. 2005. "Moral Panic and the Nasty Girl." *Canadian Review of Sociology and Anthropology* 42: 51–70.

Becker, Howard. 1963. *Outsiders: Studies in the Sociology of Deviance.* New York: Free Press.

Bennett, W.J., J.J. Dilulio and J.P. Walters. 1996. *Body Count: Moral Poverty and How to Win America's War against Crime and Drugs.* New York: Simon and Schuster.

Beyer, Marty. 1999. "Recognizing the Child in the Delinquent." *Kentucky Children's Rights Journal* 7: 16–26.

Bilchik, S. 2000. *Juvenile Justice Bulletin: Challenging the Myths.* Washington D.C.: U.S. Department of Justice, February.

Binder, A., G. Geis and D. Bruce. 2001. *Juvenile Delinquency.* Cincinnati, OH: Anderson Publishing.

Blumstein, A. 1995. "Youth Violence, Guns, and the Illicit-Drug Industry." *Journal of Criminal Law and Criminology* 86: 10–36.

Boyle, K. 2005. *Media and Violence.* London: Sage.

Brown, S. 1998. *Understanding Youth and Crime: Listening to Youth?* Buckingham: Open University Press.

Burman, M. and S. Batchelor. 2009. "Between Two Stools: Responding to Young . . . of American Gangs and British Subcultures." *Deviant Behavior* 10: 271–288.

Burns, R. and C. Crawford. 1999. "School Shootings, the Media, and Public Fear: Ingredients for a Moral Panic." *Crime, Law and Social Change* 32: 147–168.

Chesney-Lind, Meda. 1999. "Girls, Gangs and Violence: Reinventing the Liberated Female Crook in Female Gangs in America." In Meda Chesney-Lind and J.M. Hagedorn (eds) *Female Gangs in America.* Chicago, IL: Lake View Press, pp. 295–310.

Chesney-Lind, Meda and K. Irwin. 2008. *Beyond Bad Girls: Gender, Violence and Hype.* New York: Routledge.

Cohen, Stanley. 1972. *Folk Devils and Moral Panics: The Creation of the Mods and Rockers.* London: MacGibbon & Kee.

Cohen, Stanley. 2002. *Folk Devils and Moral Panics,* 2nd Edition. New York: Routledge.

Cork, D. 1997. "Crack Markets and the Diffusion of Guns among Youth." Pittsburg PA: Carnegie-Mellon University, Heinz School of Urban and Public Affairs.

Cremin, Lawrence A. 1961. *The Transformation of the School: Progressivism in American Education 1876–1957.* New York: Knopf.

Crews, G. and R. Montgomery. 2001. *Chasing Shadows: Confronting Juvenile Violence in America*. Engelwood Cliffs, NJ: Prentice Hall.

Crittenden, D. 1990. "You've Come a Long Way, Moll." *Wall Street Journal*, January 25: A14.

deMause, L. 1976. *The History of Childhood: The Evolution of Parent–Child Relationships as a Factor in History*. London: Souvenir Press.

Dole, Robert. 1996. "Dole Seeks to Get Tough on Young Criminals." *Associated Press* July 7. http://articles.latimes.com/1996-07-07/news/mn-22017_1_bob-dole (accessed May 15, 2012).

Emerling, Gary. 2006. "Girl Gangs on the Rise in Washington D.C." Modern Tribalist, March 30. http://moderntribalist.blogspot.com/2006/03/girl-gangs-on-rise-in-washington-dc.html (accessed June 23, 2012).

Feeley, Malcolm and Jonathan Simon. 2007. "Folk Devils and Moral Panics: An Appreciation from North America." In David Downes, Paul Rock, Christine Chinkin and Conor Gearty (eds) *Crime, Social Control and Human Rights: From Moral Panics to States of Denial, Essays in Honour of Stanley Cohen*. Cullompton, Devon: Willan Publishing, pp. 39–52.

Fornas, J. and G. Bolin (eds). 1995. *Youth Cultures in Late Modernity*. London: Sage.

Foucault, Michel. 1977. *Discipline and Punish: The Birth of Prison*. London: Penguin.

Fox, James. 1996. *Trends in Juvenile Violence: A Report to the United States Attorney General on Current and Future Rates of Juvenile Offending*. Washington D.C.: U.S. Department of Justice.

Garland, David. 2008. "On the Concept of Moral Panic." *Crime Media and Culture* 4(1): 9–30.

Geis, Gilbert. 2002. "Ganging up on *Gangs*: Anti-loitering and Public Nuisance Laws." In C. Huff (ed.) *Gangs in America*. Thousand Oaks, CA: Sage, pp. 257–270.

Girard, K.L. and S.J. Koch. 1996. *National Institute for Dispute Resolution (U.S.) & National Association for Mediation in Education: Conflict Resolution in the Schools: A Manual for Educators*. San Francisco, CA: Jossey-Bass.

Golding, P. and S. Middleton. 1979. "Making Claims: News Media and the Welfare State." *Media, Culture and Society* 1: 5–21.

Goode, Erick and Nachman Ben-Yehuda. 1994. *Moral Panics: The Social Construction of Deviance*. Oxford and Cambridge, MA: Blackwell.

Green, David A. 2008. *When Children Kill Children: Penal Populism and Political Culture*. Oxford: Oxford University Press.

Greenwood, Peter W. and Susan Turner. 2011. "Juvenile Crime and Juvenile Justice." In James Wilson and Joan Petersilia (eds) *Crime and Public Policy*. Oxford and New York: Oxford University Press, pp. 75–108.

Hagedorn, J.M. 1998. "Gang Violence in the Post Industrial Era." In M. Tonry and M. Moore (eds) *Youth Violence*. Chicago, IL: The University of Chicago Press, pp. 365–420.

Hagedorn, J.M. and D.M. Devitt. 1999. "Fighting Female: The Social Construction of Female Gangs." In Meda Chesney-Lind and J.M. Hagedorn (eds) *Female Gangs in America*. Chicago, IL: Lake View Press, pp. 256–276.

Hall, G. Stanley. 1904. *Adolescence : Its Psychology and its Relations to Physiology, Anthropology, Sociology, Sex, Crime, Religion and Education*, 2 Vols. New York: Appleton.

Hall, S., C. Critcher, T. Jefferson, J. Clarke and B. Roberts. 1978. *Policing the Crisis: Mugging, the State, and Law and Order*. New York: Holmes & Meier.

Hay, C. 1995. "Mobilization Through Interpellation: James Bulger, Juvenile Crime and the Construction of a Moral Panic." *Social and Legal Studies* 4: 197–223.

Hilgartner, S. and C.L. Bosk. 1988. "The Rise and Fall of Social Problems: A Public Arenas Model." *American Journal of Sociology* 94(1): 53–78.

Hirschfield, Paul J. 2008. "Preparing for Prison? The Criminalization of School Discipline in the USA." *Theoretical Criminology* 12(1): 79–101.

Jackson, P. and C. Rudman. 1990. "Moral Panic and the Response to Gangs in California." In S. Cummings and D. Monti (eds) *Gangs: The Origin and Impact of Contemporary Youth Gangs in the United States*. Albany, NY: State University of New York Press, pp. 257–276.

James, A. and C. Jenks. 1996. "Public Perceptions of Childhood Criminality." *British Journal of Sociology* 47: 315–331.

Kaufman, P., Gary Phillips and Jan M. Chaiken. 2000. *Indicators of School Crime and Safety*. Washington D.C.: National Center for Education Statistics, Bureau of Justice Statistics.

Lawrence, R.G. and T.A. Birkland. 2004. "Guns, Hollywood, and School Safety: Defining the School-Shooting Problem Across Public Arenas." *Social Science Quarterly* 85(5): 1193–1207.

Lee, F.R. 1991. "For Gold Earrings and Protection, More Girls Take the Road to Violence." *New York Times*, November 25: A1.

Lee, Murray. 2007. *Inventing Fear of Crime: Criminology and the Politics of Anxiety*. Cullumpton, Devon: Willan Publishing.

Males, M. 1996. *The Scapegoat Generation: America's War on Adolescents*. Monroe, ME: Common Courage Press.

McCabe, K. and G. Martin. 2005. *School Violence, The Media and Criminal Justice Responses*. New York: Peter Lang.

McCorkle, R.C. and T.D. Miethe. 2002. *Panic: The Social Construction of the Street Gang Problem*. Engelwood Cliffs, NJ: Prentice Hall.

McRobbie, Angela and Sarah Thornton. 1995. "Rethinking 'Moral Panic' for Multi-mediated Social Worlds." *British Journal of Sociology* 46(4): 559–574.

Messerschmidt, J.W. 2000. *Nine Lives: Adolescent Masculinities, the Body, and Violence*. Boulder, CO: Westview Press.

Moore, J.W. 1991. *Going Down to the Barrio: Homeboys and Homegirls in Change*. Philadelphia, PA: Temple University Press.

Muncie. John. 2009. *Youth & Crime*, 3rd Edition. Los Angeles, CA, London, New Delhi, Singapore and Washington D.C.: Sage.

Noguera, Pedro. 1997. "Preventing Violence in Schools Through the Production of Docile Bodies." *Motion Magazine*, January 12.

Nurge, D. 2003. "Liberating yet Limiting: The Paradox of Female Gang Membership." In D. Brotherton and L. Barrios (eds) *The Almighty Latin King and Queen Nation: Street Politics and the Transformation of a New York City Gang*. New York: Columbia University Press, pp. 161–182.

Phoenix Magazine. 1979. "Chicano Response: The Youth Gang Controversy." August: 152–157.

Pollock, L. 1983. *Forgotten Children: Parent–Child Relations from 1500 to 1900.* Cambridge: Cambridge University Press.

Reiss, A.J. and J.A. Roth (eds). 1993. *Understanding and Preventing Violence.* Washington D.C.: National Academy Press.

Schissel, Bernard. 1997. *Blaming Children: Youth Crime, Moral Panic and the Politics of Hate.* Halifax: Fernwood Publishing.

Shafii, M. and S.L. Shafii. 2001. *School Violence: Assessment, Management, Prevention.* Washington D.C.: American Psychiatric Press.

Shelden, Randall, Sharon Tracy and William Brown. 2001. *Youth Gangs in American Society.* Belmont, CA: Wadsworth.

Simon, J. 2007. *Governing Through Crime: How the War on Crime Transformed American Democracy and Created a Culture of Fear.* New York: Oxford University Press.

Simmons, R. 2002. *Odd Girl Out: The Hidden Culture of Aggression in Girls.* New York: Harcourt.

Springhall, J. 2008. "The Monsters Next Door: What Made Them Do It? Moral Panics over the Causes of High School Multiple Shootings." In C. Krinsky (ed.) *Moral Panics Over Contemporary Children and Youth.* Burlington, VT: Ashgate, pp. 47–69.

Thompson, Kenneth. 1998. *Moral Panics.* London and New York: Routledge.

Wacquant, L. 2001. "Deadly Symbiosis: When Ghetto and Prison meet and Mesh." In D. Garland (ed.) *Mass Imprisonment: Social Causes and Consequences.* London: Sage, pp. 82–120.

Wilson, J.Q. and Petersilia, J. (eds). 1995. *Crime.* San Francisco, CA: Institute for Contemporary Studies Press.

Young, Jock. 2009. "Moral Panic: Its Origins in Resistance, Ressentiment and the Translation of Fantasy into Reality." *British Journal of Criminology* 49: 4–16.

Zahn, M., Susan Brumbaugh, Darrell Steffensmeier, Barry Feld, Merry Morash, Meda Chesney-Lind, Jody Miller, Allison Ann Payne, Denise C. Gottfredson and Candace Kruttschnitt. 2008. *Violence by Teenage Girls: Trends and Context.* Washington D.C.: U.S. Department of Justice.

Zatz, M.S. 1987. "Chicano Youth Gangs and Crime: The Creation of a Moral Panic." *Contemporary Crisis* 11: 129–158.

Zimring, F. 1998. *American Youth Violence.* Oxford: Oxford University Press.

chapter 8

Restorative Justice for Young Offenders

Restorative justice (RJ) is a particular mode of responding to criminality that explicitly invokes an ideology of "doing justice." The proponents of RJ began advocating its virtues and urging its application in the 1970s and while modes of RJ exist in the U.S. and in other countries, RJ has yet to make substantial inroads into formal justice systems. In the U.S., forms of RJ, particularly Victim Offender Mediation (VOM), have been embraced as part of the movement toward victim support and advocacy. RJ has been able to align itself with forms of dispute settlement such as mediation and with the victims' rights movement as part of a wider social exploration of how justice might best be realized (Crawford and Newburn 2003: 20).

It is in the field of juvenile justice that RJ has had its greatest impact worldwide. Proponents of RJ within juvenile justice see RJ becoming a viable alternative justice process through systematic reform and not simply as a "sideshow." This means that all functions within a juvenile justice system would be based on restorative principles, especially that of repairing the harm caused by a wrongful act (Bazemore and Walgrave 1999: 5).

Because RJ encompasses a multitude of practices and policies, a clear-cut definition of RJ is problematic. In practice, RJ tends to define itself by reference to those elements it possesses that are not found in formal or traditional criminal justice systems. Fundamentally, RJ conceives of crime as a violation of one person by another person. It sees the main task in responding to crime as making the offender aware of the harm that has been caused by the wrongful act. The aim is to help the offender understand the wrongfulness of the act and to accept liability to repair the harm caused and therefore ensure that further harms are prevented. RJ is a process by which offenders, victims and the community collectively decide, in a mediatory process, the form and amount of reparation going from the offender to the victim and the measures to be taken to ensure that re-offending does not occur. It is through such a process that the offender is said to be reintegrated into the community.

This chapter aims to provide a clearer understanding of the merits of RJ and to ask a set of questions that include: Why has RJ impacted U.S. juvenile justice systems so modestly?; Are policy makers' and legislators' views about juvenile justice so firmly anchored in penal populism that alternatives such as RJ are ignored?; Is RJ considered a "soft option" for punishment and rejected on that ground?; Does public opinion show any support for RJ and if so in what forms?; To what extent is a change to RJ from a system of punishment applied through the formal justice system feasible and desirable as a normal response to crime?; Is RJ considered unproven and too radical?

In the broad sense, questions about the future of RJ are well expressed by Barbara Hudson:

> [I]s it to be a justice at the margins, or will restorative justice become mainstream justice? Is restorative justice to be established mainly for dealing with juveniles and perhaps some very routine adult offences; is its relationship to established criminal justice to be that of receiving cases and funneling back those where agreement cannot be reached or one or other of the parties decides to withdraw from restorative proceedings? Is it to be at the bottom of an enforcement pyramid . . . to be used for first time, remorseful offenders with repeat or recalcitrant offenders being dealt with by the "big stick" of formal court proceedings carrying the possibility of imprisonment? Or is it to become *the* or *a* major form of justice, dealing with a whole range of offences and offenders?
>
> (Hudson 2002: 617)

The following discussion will respond to these and related questions and issues about RJ.

Explaining restorative justice

Explanations about the nature of RJ often begin by comparing it with retributive justice. For example, Zehr contrasts the main principles of RJ with retributive justice in the following:

[I]t is a violation of the state, defined by law breaking and guilt. Justice determines blame and administers pain in a contest between the offender and the state directed by systematic rules. . . .

Restorative justice sees things differently. . . . Crime is a violation of people and relationships. . . . It creates obligations to make things right. Justice involves the victim, the offender and the community in a search for solutions which promote repair, reconciliation, and reassurance.

(Zehr 1990: 181)

Thus, advocates of RJ present an unproblematic perspective that depicts RJ as an empowering, holistic response to an offense, whereas retribution is seen as oppressive and divisive as well as being deeply embedded in our institutions, a natural and inevitable response to crime, and therefore not open to question. This oppositional ideology offered by RJ proponents has been critiqued as dichotomous and simplistic because the implication is that RJ is good and retributive justice is evil (Daly 2002: 61), and because the implementation of RJ commonly includes multiple justice aims, as well as some elements of retributive justice in the form of censure for past offenses.

RJ advocates reject the existing punishment paradigm within most criminal justice systems, perhaps for similar reasons as Garland, who argues that "Punishing today is a deeply problematic and barely understood aspect of social life, the rationale for which is by no means clear" (1990: 3). In place of the conventional punishment paradigm, RJ argues for a new RJ-centered paradigm that focuses not on the infliction of pain but on a socially constructive obligation to repair the harm caused by the crime (Walgrave 2001: 28). Nevertheless, some RJ outcomes almost certainly result in forms of pain, loss or deprivation, even when the agreements and sanctions offered by RJ processes have the consent of the offender. Examples include the payment of reparations, carrying out work for a victim or the community, and writing a letter of apology. In some cases both the offender and the victim may see these reparative acts as punishment. An example is seen in Gray's (2005) qualitative study concerning young offenders' experience of RJ in England. As one youth explained, his view of community reparation is that "'It punishes young people so that they don't offend again' (YP148: Community Reparation)" (Gray 2005: 946).

Duff (1992) contends that RJ reparations do not constitute "alternatives to punishment" but instead represent "alternative punishments," while Wright (1991) and McCold (2000) insist that punitive sanctions never inhabit the framework of RJ. More recently, desert theorists like Von Hirsch and Ashworth have conceded that there is a model that could satisfy the aims of both retribution and RJ, and Howard Zehr has recognized that common ground exists between these two conceptions (Roche 2007: 85).

RJ has its origins in indigenous and customary responses to crime, past and present, and in victim offender mediation programs developed in Canada in the 1970s (Van Ness et al. 2001: 4). There are numerous definitions of RJ but the one most often cited focuses on the process of RJ:

> Restorative justice is a process whereby all the parties with a stake in a particular offence come together to resolve collectively how to deal with the aftermath of the offence and its implications for the future.
>
> (Marshall 1996: 37)

Bazemore and Walgrave (1999: 48) critique Marshall's definition for failing to refer to repairing harm and for limiting RJ to a process. They offer the following definition which adds specificity by referring to the aims and outcome of RJ:

> [E]very action that is primarily oriented toward doing justice by repairing the harm that has been caused by a crime.
>
> (Bazemore and Walgrave 1999: 48)

Yet, as Daly (2002: 196) and others have noted, it is difficult to define RJ satisfactorily because it covers a wide range of practices that occur at different stages in the criminal justice process.

The focus on the *harm* caused by the wrongful act is said to be the distinguishing feature of RJ (Bazemore and Walgrave 1999). Unlike retributive systems where the harm caused is regarded as creating an imbalance that must be corrected by imposing a proportionate harm on the offender, RJ responds to the wrongful act, not with punishment as such, but with the objective of repairing or compensating for the harm caused (p. 49). In terms of victimization, while it is clear that the individual victim(s) must be the focus of restorative action, proponents of RJ argue that the victimized community must also be included.

Of course, defining a "community" for this purpose is no easy task and in some cases it will be difficult to specify the actual harm that the community has suffered. An example is the case of driving under the influence of alcohol (Bazemore and Walgrave 1999: 49). The community as a set of "dense networks of individual interdependencies with strong cultural commitments to mutuality of obligations" (Braithwaite 1989: 85) can be difficult to locate in contemporary society. Even where it is possible to identify a discrete community for a particular context, it is still necessary to determine who will represent the community and how they will be appointed (Walgrave 1999: 135). RJ advocates downplay the idea that community is a geographical place, arguing instead that each person possesses a community that is centered on themselves like a concentric circle of relatives

youth, crime and justice

and/or significant others (Marshall 1998: 30–31). Crawford and Newburn (2003: 55) stress the social control aspects of the community:

> Reference to communities in restorative justice generally alludes to some form of regulatory authority or moral value system with powers to induce conformity beyond the family and below the state (the political community).

In RJ conferences community involvement is often limited to kinship networks or supporters of the offender or victim, but in sentencing circles a more extended notion of community may be employed. It still not clear exactly why the community is involved and how representation from a community is to be secured, nor its degree of legitimacy in any particular RJ process (Crawford and Newburn 2003: 56). Generally, there is a tendency to see communities as places and not to acknowledge the diversity within a community. Moreover, communities do not occupy some moral high ground but are differentiated according to power relations and exist in the real world. Thus, different communities enjoy varying levels of access to resources and may not be able to offer or mobilize the same modes of reparation, for example, in relation to community work as a form of compensation.

Questions about *restoration* center on the process to be followed and the outcome desired. Restitution, compensation, service to the victims and apology are all considered accepted forms of reparation and may be directed at the victims alone or at an entire community. The process to be followed need not always involve face-to-face encounters because victims may decide not to participate. Nevertheless, advocates of RJ contend that when participants express themselves, moral accountability emerges as an explanation for the motivation for their criminal acts. The emotional environment created when an offender explains their behavior encourages remorse, shame and social reintegration (Cook 2006: 110). Diverse modes of restoration can be accepted as legitimate if they are aligned to meet the needs of different victims, varying circumstances and diverse communities (Bazemore and Walgrave 1999: 51–52).

Proportionality is a central RJ issue for desert theorists who contend that punishment should always be proportionate to the degree of seriousness of the harm caused. According to Ashworth (2002), it is difficult for RJ to accommodate this principle because the views of victims in determining punishment may vary and proportionality cannot be guaranteed. Crawford and Newburn have suggested that one way of addressing proportionality in RJ is to set upper and lower limits to restorative outcomes so as to avoid RJ itself becoming a forum where victims may pursue punitive outcomes (2003: 49). However, Tonry (1999) points out that sentencing systems in the

U.S. have not cohered because even states which maintain sentencing guidelines have disrupted them with initiatives such as mandatory minimum sentences and three-strikes laws. Those opposing RJ because of lack of proportionality in sentencing point to the use of untrained and nonqualified volunteers in the process, who, they argue, are bound to make arbitrary and capricious decisions on sanctions (Kurki 2000: 287).

Restorative justice and community justice

The notion of "community justice" has been used interchangeably with RJ but some commentators see distinct differences between these concepts. For example, McCold (2004: 13) critiques the Balanced and Restorative Justice Project (BARJ) of the Office of Juvenile Justice and Delinquency Prevention (OJJDP) for merging the practice of community justice with RJ and thereby distorting the RJ paradigm "almost beyond recognition" (McCold 2004: 14). He explains community justice as a local intervention, based on neighborhoods and using a variety of programming with the aims of including the community in criminal justice processes, improving the quality of community life, and enhancing the capacity of communities to prevent and respond to crime. In this process, community justice seeks to empower local stakeholders such as volunteer groups and to encourage collaboration between those groups and citizens and justice agencies. Crime is seen as a social problem and therefore justice agencies should be concerned to widen their mission to incorporate crime prevention and solving conflicts in neighborhoods (Kurki 2000: 236). According to Clear and Karp (1998: 14), community justice comprises four core elements: coordination of activities at the neighborhood level; long- and short-term problem solving; decentralization of authority; and accountability and citizen participation.

Community justice commonly includes programs like community policing, Neighborhood Watch, drug courts and so on which are aimed at increased surveillance and the detection of offenders (McCold 2004: 16). Community policing has been a significant component of the community justice approach but research suggests it has not been very successful in achieving its aim of involving the community in the policing task. Ordinarily, roles adopted by the community in such projects have been as the "eyes and ears of the police" in providing information about crime, as cheerleader for police, to provide support for community policing, to provide monetary assistance for policing and to provide public signage for rallies and so on (Buerger 1994). It seems clear that community justice encompasses a wide range of programs intended to repair the effects of criminality in a community, only some of which may include RJ processes. Similarly, Kurki (2000: 237) argues that while most RJ initiatives are community based, only a few community justice programs incorporate RJ values and principles. Unlike RJ, conceptions of community justice do not delineate roles for victims and offenders.

The differentiation proposed by McCold between community justice and RJ relates to the community. He contends that in RJ "because the stake-holders own the conflict, they have moral authority and legitimacy to be part of the outcome," but in community justice "stakeholders' legitimacy is based on the fact that they live and work in the neighborhood affected by crime" (2004: 20). Thus, in his view, community justice relies on the formal criminal justice system where RJ empowers victims, offenders and com-munities of care (McCold 2004: 21).

The project, noted above, is an initiative of the Department of Justice, OJJDP, launched in 1993. The focus of the BARJ project requires that juvenile justice professionals devote balanced attention to the goals of offender accountability, offender competency development and community protection (McCold 2004: 23). When linked together, these three concepts are said to establish balance with no one objective taking precedence (p. 23). Balanced approach proponents argue that these three elements provide a coherent philosophy for organizing resources, supervising and assisting juveniles. Several states have incorporated the balanced approach into their juvenile justice legislation (Hemmens et al. 1999: 359).

BARJ objectives include that the harm caused to the community is repaired through sanctions that have meaningful consequences (McCold 2004). In practice, this has meant that the most frequent BARJ programs are court-ordered community service projects, which while producing worth-while outcomes, do not amount to RJ because the victim and offender do not participate in the decision making. Thus, it is argued, the planned convergence between community justice and RJ treats RJ merely as a subset of the larger concept of community justice, and RJ cannot be described as community justice (p. 28).

Authentic restorative justice?

McCold (2000) has proposed a classification of various modes of RJ according to the extent to which various stakeholders are involved in the process. His typology identifies three stakeholders as being the victim, the offender and the community (see Figure 8.1). The degree to which each is involved in the process determines the level of restorativeness. According to this view, when all three stakeholders are involved, the maximum level of restorativeness is achieved and the process is judged "fully restorative." When only two stakeholders are involved, the process is "mostly restorative" such as South Africa's Truth and Reconciliation Committee, victim restitution and victim–offender mediation (p. 404) and,

Types and degrees of restorative justice practice

Victim reparation

Communities of care reconciliation

Victim support circles

Victim services

Offender family services

RESTORATIVE JUSTICE

Crime compensation

Family-centered social work

Peace circles   Family group conferencing

Victim restitution

Victimless conferences

Community conferencing

Positive discipline

Victim–offender mediation

Therapeutic communities

Related community service

Reparative boards

Youth aid panels

Victim sensitivity training

Offender responsibility

Fully restorative

Mostly restorative

Partly restorative

Figure 8.1 Restorative practices typology
Source: McCold and Watchel (2003: 3).

when only one, this is judged "partly restorative" such as Mothers Against Drunk Driving (MADD), Students Against Destructive Decisions (SADD) and Parents of Murder Victims Against the Death Penalty (p. 403). To take the example of VOM, it is judged "mostly restorative" because of the absence of the community. Reparative boards qualify only as "partly restorative."

In discussing whether or not RJ is a fully fledged alternative for juvenile offenders, Walgrave (1995: 239) suggests that within the judicial framework the concept of a collection of sanctioning practices called "alternative sanctions," all with differing objectives and practices, constitutes a "threat" to the status of RJ. Walgrave (1995: 239) argues that aggregating these measures under this terminology denies individual RJ measures their innovatory aspects. The potential consequence of this aggregation is that the distinctiveness of RJ will be ignored and blurred into a category of so-called "alternative sanctions" (such as mediation and community service) and risk being directly incorporated into traditional penal sanctions (p. 239). For example, in the U.S., the term "restorative justice" has been employed to describe sex offender notification laws and the right of relatives of murder victims to attend executions (Rock 2004: 288). In New Zealand, the Justice Minister described legislation that required offenders to recompense their victims as restorative, despite the fact that the compensation provided for far exceeded RJ norms (Pratt 2007: 141).

youth, crime and justice

Restorative justice: theoretical foundations

RJ professes to offer a model of justice but, as Crawford and Newburn argue, "in large part Restorative Justice constitutes a practice in search of a theory" (2003: 19). Similarly, Marshall (1999: 30) notes:

> As it currently stands Restorative Justice still lacks a definitive theoretical statement. . . . Whether or not it is capable of becoming more than just a model of practice and becoming a complete theory of justice remains to be seen.

As Marshall (1999) has noted, many theories have been incorporated into or become associated with RJ. Accounts of the theoretical foundations of RJ therefore tend to present RJ as loosely underpinned or influenced by numerous justice conceptions, including, in broad terms, shame theory, restorative theory as contrasted with retributive theory, and notions of reintegration and forgiveness. As Crawford and Newburn (2003: 21) note, and Kurki (2000: 240) agrees, religions and moral theories have provided a great deal of the fundamentals of RJ. For example, the Mennonite community in the U.S. and the Quakers in the U.K. have provided some of the basic building blocks, along with theories about republicanism and communitarianism (Crawford and Newburn 2003: 21).

In an influential article in the field of RJ, "Conflicts as Property," Christie (1977) posits that crime is not simply a wrongful act against society but is also a private wrong committed by an offender against a specific victim. He argues that the conflict brought about in this way should be seen as something of value to be cultivated, and as an opportunity for clarifying norms. The process for engaging with this conflict, in his view, should not be handed over to professionals, or, as he puts it, the state should not be allowed to "steal" conflicts.

Karp (2001) identifies a variety of "overarching" theoretical concepts with which RJ is associated. These are: the "balanced approach"; reintegrative shaming; dominion and republican justice; peacemaking; and the community justice ideal. Similarly, Marshall (1999: 31) suggests that peacemaking, conflict resolution theory and feminist criminology are "strands of thought" that have impacted RJ. Peacemaking is associated with the work of Pepinsky and Quinney (1991) in particular, and advances an ideology of social harmony and unity that some see as more of a belief system than an intellectual statement (Thomas et al. 2003: 101). Defining peacemaking or its principles and precepts presents a challenge because, as Thomas et al. (2003) argue, it constitutes a perspective and not a theory, and it possesses "no integrating set of systematic theories or method or immediately obvious policy-oriented guidelines" (p. 103).

According to Kurki (2000: 264), RJ is associated with social movements as well as theories including informal justice, restitution, the victim movement, conferencing, and reconciliation movements and social justice. She also links RJ with broader social movements such as civil rights, indigenous justice, the women's movement and penal abolition. Perhaps the broadest conception of RJ is suggested by John Braithwaite (1999: 2):

> If we take restorative justice seriously, it involves a very different way of thinking about traditional notions such as deterrence, rehabilitation, incapacitation, and crime prevention. It also means transformed foundations of criminal jurisprudence and of our notions of freedom, democracy, and community.

According to Van Ness and Strong (2010: 24), the "explorers of restorative justice theory" include Howard Zehr, termed "the grandfather" of RJ and author of a seminal RJ text *Changing Lenses,* and Martin Wright for his 1991 text, *Justice for Victims and Offenders.* The lens Zehr wants to change is the formal criminal justice system which views crime as lawbreaking and justice as dispensing blame and punishment. Zehr sees the formal system as oppositional to RJ and therefore suggests that as a theoretical construct RJ offers what formal justice does not. For Llewellyn this oppositional stance renders RJ a theory about "the meaning of justice" (2007: 355). As she explains it (p. 356),

> Understood in its full sense, restorative justice as a theory of justice focused on the harms resulting from wrongdoing issues a challenge to the private/public dichotomy existing in traditional Western legal systems.

She sees RJ as offering a lens to "see the world relationally" (p. 356).

Martin Wright (1991: 117) argues that the basic rationale of criminal justice should not be retributive but restorative. Punishment is justified as retribution and denunciation, regardless of its ability to reduce crime, but if more constructive methods can be identified they should be employed. Under a new justice paradigm, he sees the courts as having the function of restoring the community and the individual victim, rather than the punishment of the offender (p. 117).

Reintegrative shaming makes up part of the theoretical discourse concerning RJ and has been called "the most influential theoretical model underlying restorative justice in juvenile proceedings" (Hudson 2002: 619). In his book *Crime, Shame and Reintegration,* Braithwaite (1989) proposed that societies that employ the notion of reintegrative shaming enjoy lower levels of crime and violence. The process itself involves encouraging offenders to experience a level of shame for their wrongful acts while still

youth, crime and justice

permitting them to retain their human dignity. Thus, the shaming is said to be "reintegrative" and not simply a negative blaming exercise. An analogy is to the good parent who makes a child aware of wrong actions, but does not diminish the care he or she has for the child in the process. Braithwaite argued that most Western societies had rejected reintegrative shaming. Braithwaite stresses the "crucial" distinction between shaming that is disintegrative or stigmatizing, and reintegrative shaming:

> Reintegrative shaming means the expressions of community disapproval . . . are followed by gestures of reacceptance into the community of law abiding citizens. . . . Disintegrative shaming (stigmatization), in contrast, divides the community by creating a class of outcasts.
>
> (Braithwaite 1989: 55)

According to Braithwaite, the community itself must exercise social control through reintegrative shaming and not rely solely on the state to do so. This is achieved by ensuring that the community is a community of care, and that the shaming is followed by an effort to reconcile the offender with the community. Braithwaite's theory essentially seeks to revive what is claimed to be an ancient and widely employed method of social control long abandoned in the West.

Restorative justice programs

Three programs exemplify the principles of RJ processes: victim offender mediation, conferencing and circles (Van Ness et al. 2001: 6).

Victim offender mediation (VOM)

This was the first of the modern RJ processes. It began in Kitchener, Ontario, Canada in 1974 when two teenagers met with their victims after acts of vandalism and agreed to pay restitution. In the U.S., the Community Justice Initiatives Association began the first VOM in 1975 with support from the Mennonite Central Committee and the local probation authority. VOM programs are derived from the experience of Mennonite communities and are therefore faith based (McCold 2001: 43). The victims' rights movement that has developed over the past two decades has also influenced VOM. By 2000 more than 300 VOM programs were operating within the U.S., with about two-thirds being private community or faith based and about a quarter operating under probation or correctional authority (Umbreit et al. 2001: 122–123). VOM brings together victims and offenders with a mediator whose job it is to coordinate and facilitate the process. The mediator does not take sides, builds trust and creates a space for the parties within which to conduct a dialogue (McCold 2001: 44). Commonly, victims explain how they experienced the crime and offenders why they committed the crime and what they did, while responding to the questions of the mediator. After both victim and offender have spoken, the mediator focuses on how to make things "right" between the parties through an act of restitution that takes effect in a signed restitution agreement. VOM need not involve a direct confrontation between the parties. For example, European practice has adopted a model that has the mediator shuttling between victim and offender until a restitution agreement is achieved. In the U.S. and Canada, VOM may well involve other participants who support the principals. In some programs, cases are diverted to VOM from prosecution provided that the agreement is successfully completed while in others the referral is made following an admission of guilt, with VOM being a condition of probation (Umbreit et al. 2001: 124).

Surveys have revealed that victims who participate in VOM experience a significant degree of satisfaction with the process itself and the agreed outcomes. Five studies of juvenile programs and four studies of mixed programs reported 90 to 97 percent satisfaction by victims with the mediation itself and, in the case of outcomes, seven studies of juvenile programs reported satisfaction levels of 80 to 97 percent (Umbreit et al. 2001: 130, 133; Van Ness et al. 2001: 7). Encounters between victims and offenders now take place in prisons in the U.S., Canada, the U.K., Belgium, the Netherlands and elsewhere, and include sexual assault victims and offenders (Van Ness et al. 2001: 9).

Accounts by burglary victims during Victim Offender Reconciliation Program (VORP) sessions convey the emotional nature of these encounters. Victims made the following statements in Umbreit's (1990: 49–51) study:

> "It's like we were raped. The stuff they took was all given to us for wedding presents . . . they went through our clothes. . . . It's kind of like somebody raping me or seeing me naked. . . . I just felt hurt that somebody invaded my privacy. . . . I couldn't sleep for a few nights . . . somebody may come in again. . . . My goals were to have the offender see face to face that it was a person he had violated, not just an object, an empty house, that he had to deal with the person he hurt, and to be able to have him understand that it was a loss and a hurt."

However, sometimes juveniles consciously manipulate VOM sessions, as one juvenile explained:

> "It depends on what the victim was like. If you have an old lady you would try to win her over not so much by the reasons you have done it,

but by talking to her and making her feel at home with you. If it was a younger person you would take to them and make them see the reasons why you have done it hoping they would understand plus bring a lot of bluff with it."

(Launay and Murray 1989: 126)

Victims in VOM often gain a sense of empowerment from being able to interact with the offender. For example, Gray (2005: 946) reports that victims in a study of VOM in England described the process as follows:

"It's an important part of you being able to get on with your own life. . . . I felt relieved that I saw them personally, spoke to them personally, told them how I felt . . . it gave me peace of mind. It's a part of the healing process" (V66/69: Victim Offender Mediation).

However, dissatisfied victims in England, believing that young offenders were not sufficiently punished in VOM, noted:

"I didn't think they were really sorry, but that's not to say they don't deserve a second chance. Everybody makes mistakes but I felt they weren't sorry if that makes sense. It's like they were sorry because they got caught and they were in a load of trouble but they weren't sorry about the consequences for me" (V138: Shuttle Mediation).

(Gray 2005: 947)

Conferencing

Originally developed in New Zealand and to a certain extent reflective of some aspects of the "traditional" dispute settlement processes of the indigenous Maori, conferencing has passed through several iterations and been applied in a number of countries. Claims that conferencing is based on indigenous justice practices are erroneous and, as Daly (2001: 65) puts it,

conferencing is better understood as a fragmented justice form: it splices white, bureaucratic forms of justice with elements of informal justice that may include non-white (or non-Western) values or methods of judgment.

Unlike VOM, conferencing involves not only the victim and offender but also persons connected to the victim such as family and friends and also supporters of the offender. It is essentially a bigger tent within which all those affected in some way by the crime can come together and join in making a final agreement. Conferences are managed by facilitators, and some facilitators also guide the discussions following a script prepared for that form of conferencing (Van Ness et al. 2001: 7). Sometimes the police or other representatives of the justice system will be present. Conferencing procedure commonly involves offenders starting out by explaining the crime and how others were affected by it. Following this, the victims discuss the harm that was caused, their family members and others discuss how it affected them, and the offender's supporters then round off the discussion. The aim is to decide as a group what the offender should do to repair the harm he or she has caused, and the kind of assistance the offender might require to execute an agreement that is entered into at the conference and registered with justice officials.

The New Zealand experience

In New Zealand conferencing has been given legislative status in the *Children, Young Persons and their Families Act 1989*. The original impetus for conferencing was political pressure to incorporate indigenous Maori concerns and practices into the youth justice system and especially to allow families to play a role in deciding the appropriate response to youth offending. Thus, a more culturally specific approach to justice for Maori youth became institutionalized into a new form of youth justice (Crawford and Newburn 2003: 27).

Youth justice family group conferences are facilitated by public servants, offenders are provided with legal representation and the Court exercises overall jurisdiction over conference agreements which commonly provide for reparative sanctions such as apologies, restitution and community service (McCold 2001: 45). Research studies in New Zealand have revealed that conferencing holds offenders accountable and is responsive to victims. Interviews conducted between 1990 and 1991 showed that 84 percent and 85 percent respectively of young offenders and their parents were satisfied with the outcome of family conferencing but only half of the victims reported satisfaction (Maxwell and Morris 1993: 115). Conferences have tended to be too much under the control of the professionals and to focus overly on the offender with victims receiving minimal concern. In practice, victims attended only about half of the conferences, and of those who participated, about a quarter felt re-victimized by the process (p. 121).

In the past decade in New Zealand, 70 percent to 80 percent of juvenile justice cases were disposed of through police diversion out of the juvenile justice system and the remaining 20 percent to 30 percent were referred to conferences (Daly 2001: 70). Family group conferences are employed for dealing with the more serious and persistent juvenile offenders. They should not be regarded as limited to trivial offenses or as an alternative to police cautions or diversion out of the system (Crawford and Newburn 2003: 28).

The Wagga Wagga model

In Australia, a different approach to conferencing was developed in Wagga Wagga, New South Wales, in 1991 by a police officer drawing heavily on the theoretical work of John Braithwaite (1989) on reintegrative shaming. These conferences are facilitated by police officers (itself a source of critique of this process), who encourage participants to reach an agreement with arrangements for restitution and reparation (McCold 2001: 47).

The Wagga Wagga scheme has not been adopted by most Australian states, which have followed instead the New Zealand conferencing model that does not include police-run conferencing (Daly 2001: 64) and in fact the model is no longer operating in Wagga Wagga. In Canberra, the Reintegrative Shaming Experiment (RISE) study tested the Wagga Wagga model against formal court processing, applying Braithwaite's reintegrative shaming theory. The hypothesis was that formal courts stigmatize and label offenders and therefore adversely impact offenders' lives in the community. In contrast, the shame engendered by a family conference should allow an offender to repair the harm and confront his or her wrongful action. The argument is that by inducing a sense of shame in an offender but permitting him or her to retain human dignity while reintegrating into the community is the best method to control crime (Crawford and Newburn 2003: 30).

In England, the police-controlled Wagga Wagga mode of restorative cautioning was actively employed by one police force with the police being trained to follow a script to facilitate a conference about how to repair the harm caused (Crawford and Newburn 2003: 31). This scheme focused on less serious offenders and is thus open to arguments about "net widening." Typically, the outcome of the conference was a written or verbal apology.

The "Wagga Wagga model" was introduced into North America in 1995 by the Real Justice organization, and more than 2,000 police, probation officers, educators and others in the United States and Canada were subsequently trained as conference facilitators. In October 1995, 20 full-time police officers in Bethlehem, Pennsylvania volunteered to be trained and to conduct conferences. Over an 18-month period, first-time juvenile offenders arrested for selected misdemeanor and summary offenses were randomly assigned either to formal adjudication or to a diversionary restorative policing conference.

A study of this project, the Bethlehem, Pennsylvania, Police Family Group Conferencing Project, revealed that over 90 percent of victims, offenders and parents of offenders would recommend conferencing, would chose conferencing again, found the process helpful, believed they were treated fairly and found the experience friendly (McCold and Wachtel 1998). Of the victims, 94 percent believed their views were adequately considered and 92 percent found conferencing a more humane response to crime. However, the study also found that conferencing had little effect on re-offending and that while it was possible to train police to conduct conferences, overall police attitudes did not change as a result of using RJ practices.

Circles

Circles are derived from the practice of Canadian First Nations people. The participants, including the victim, the offender and their respective supporters, sit in a circle. Usually between 15 and 50 persons will attend (Lilles 2001: 163). A typical circle will commence with the offender's explanation of the crime and then each person sitting in the circle is permitted to talk until all who wish to have spoken. Circles have a "keeper" whose task it is to ensure that the process is respected. Usually circles employ a talking piece in the form of a feather or an object that carries a meaning to circle members. It is passed from speaker to speaker and only the holder of the piece may speak (Van Ness et al. 2001: 9). Circles are being utilized with serious sexual offenders in Canada who are released into communities at the end of their sentences. The circles comprise communities of faith who agree to provide the offender with support through a reintegration plan that establishes a basis for the community to involve itself with the offender's needs and to ensure his or her accountability (Van Ness et al. 2001: 9, 10). Circles may be used for healing purposes or for sentencing, with the latter remaining under the control of the Court and limited to making recommendations for actual case disposition by the Court (McCold 2001: 49). Circles are used in sentencing serious cases because the process is lengthy and requires a sustained commitment from all parties (Lilles 2001: 163). The outcome of a circle sentencing hearing is usually a community-related disposition involving supervision and a program. The terms are quite detailed, requiring attendance at treatment and counseling, and may include culturally appropriate conditions. Few offenders fail to complete the disposition. Most reported cases involve Canadian First Nations people living on reserves or in small communities in rural and remote areas where the offender's community is well delineated (pp. 166, 169). In the U.S., sentencing circles are used in Minnesota in Native American and inner city black communities where they deal only with minor crimes (Kurki 2000: 282).

Vermont Reparative Boards

The Vermont Reparative Probation Program has been available since 1996 for adults and juveniles whose cases are referred to boards following conviction for an offense and as a condition of probation. Vermont is the only state to have mandated such a program and implemented it statewide. Its stated aims include: "implement the restorative justice program of seeking to obtain probationer accountability, repair harm and compensate a victim or victims and the community" (quoted in Karp 2001: 731).

The task of the Board is to meet with the offender in the presence of victims and other affected parties to devise a solution to address the harm caused by the offender in that community. Citizen volunteers receive training, staff the boards and in that role seek to conclude a reparative agreement with an offender. When an agreement cannot be reached the offender is referred back to the Court. The Board's tasks include: enabling the offender to better understand the harmful consequences of his or her act; devising ways in which the offender can repair that harm; engaging the offender in making amends within the community; and in collaboration with the offender, determining how re-offending can best be prevented (Crawford and Newburn 2003: 36). In 1998 only about 15 percent of victims attended board meetings but 52 percent of offenders completed their reparative agreements. Research has shown considerable variation in the process and outcomes as between different boards, and there are concerns that the volunteer board members are disproportionately older, middle class and well educated, in contrast to the less educated working-class and more youthful offenders (Crawford and Newburn 2003: 37).

In his study of Vermont Reparative Boards, Karp (2001) analyzed the RJ discourse and the interactions between boards and participants. He found that the majority of cases he studied (52 video tapes of board meetings with offenders) were restorative and that the single most common restorative activity was community service, which was an element in 73 percent of all reparative contracts entered into (2001: 740). However, the community service was rarely linked to the actual offense. In one case where there was such a link, the offender, a high school student, was arrested for drag racing at 130mph down a busy street. The Board and the offender decided that an apology to the arresting officer (because of the dangerous driving and the threat to his safety) and an explanation by the offender to his classmates of what occurred (as a service task) were the most appropriate forms of reparation. In their view, these tasks symbolically linked the risk of such reckless driving to the general community (p. 743).

In another case, a store owner who sold alcohol to a minor agreed to write a letter to the local retail association newsletter giving her account of the offense and explaining steps she had taken to reduce the risk of another offense. In this way, the Board linked the issue of easy access to alcohol to problem drinking in the community (Karp 2001: 744).

RJ programs are well represented in Europe, especially in Austria, Germany and Finland. VOM has been part of the Austrian juvenile justice system since the 1980s (Beale 2003). In Germany, mediation was made available in 1994 as an option for adult offenders where the penalty would otherwise be imprisonment for up to one year or a fine. In both Germany and Austria VOM is used for serious offenses and in Germany in 1995, about 70 percent of the cases mediated were violent crimes. In Austria, almost three-quarters of the adult cases dealt with under VOM involved forms of violence such as fighting and road rage. In Finland, VOM programs handle up to 20 percent of the Court caseload (Beale 2003: 420).

International norm formation

RJ has established itself as a mode of justice practice endorsed by the international community in the form of the *Basic Principles on the Use of Restorative Justice Programmes in Criminal Matters* (*Basic Principles* 2000). In relation to children's rights and protections, the *United Nations Standard Minimum Rules for the Administration of Juvenile Justice* (*Beijing Rules* 1985) enhance the broad norms of the 1989 Convention on the Rights of the Child (CRC) in relation to non-institutional dispositions by referring specifically to diversion. Rule 11 of the *Beijing Rules* (1985), for example, mandates generally that:

> Consideration shall be given, wherever appropriate, to dealing with juvenile offenders without resorting to formal trial by the competent authority.

Rule 11 concerns specifically applying diversion to policing and prosecution as follows:

> The police, the prosecution or other agencies dealing with juvenile cases shall be empowered to dispose of such cases, at their discretion, without recourse to formal hearings, in accordance with the criteria laid down for that purpose in the respective legal system and also in accordance with the principles contained in these Rules.

The *Beijing Rules* (1985) make it clear that any form of diversion must have the consent of the juvenile or his or her parents or guardian. They also suggest that appropriate forms of diversion include "community programmes, such as temporary supervision and guidance, restitution, and compensation of victims" and the Commentary to the Rules specifies:

> Programmes that involve settlement by victim restitution and those that seek to avoid future conflict with the law through temporary supervision and guidance are especially commended.
>
> (*Beijing Rules* 1985, Commentary to the Rules)

Similar to the *Beijing Rules*, the Fundamental Principles enumerated in the *United Nations Guidelines for the Prevention of Juvenile Delinquency* (*Riyadh Guidelines* 1990) include:

> Community-based services and programmes should be developed for the prevention of juvenile delinquency, particularly where no agencies have yet been established. Formal agencies of social control should only be utilized as a means of last resort.
>
> (*Riyadh Guidelines* 1990, Fundamental Principle 6)

There are now at least two further international instruments where the term "restorative justice" is explicitly employed in connection with criminal justice proceedings. The first is the *Guidelines for Action on Children in the Criminal Justice System* (1997) which are intended to assist states in implementing the CRC. Under the heading of specific implementation plans for implementing the CRC, these *Guidelines* set specific targets, including:

> A review of existing procedures should be undertaken and, where possible, diversion or other alternative initiatives to the classical criminal justice systems should be developed to avoid recourse to the criminal justice systems for young persons accused of an offence. Appropriate steps should be taken to make available throughout the State a broad range of alternative and educative measures at the pre-arrest, pre-trial, trial and post-trial stages, in order to prevent recidivism and promote the social rehabilitation of child offenders. Whenever appropriate, mechanisms for the informal resolution of disputes in cases involving a child offender should be utilized, including mediation and restorative justice practices, particularly processes involving victims.
>
> (*Guidelines for Action on Children in the Criminal Justice System* 1997)

The second instrument, the *Basic Principles on the Use of Restorative Justice Programmes in Criminal Matters* (2000), is devoted entirely to the employment of RJ programs in criminal matters. It is beyond the scope of this chapter to discuss these principles in detail but significantly the preamble recognizes that "restorative justice initiatives" "often draw upon traditional and indigenous forms of justice which view crime as fundamentally harmful to people." The principles incorporate many of the general principles and practices that comprise RJ as it is widely defined and practiced in a number of jurisdictions. The *Basic Principles* (2000) adopt the concept of "restorative process" defined as:

> any process in which the victim and the offender, and, where appropriate, any other individuals or community members affected by a crime,

participate together actively in the resolution of matters arising from the crime, generally with the help of a facilitator. Restorative processes may include mediation, conciliation, conferencing and sentencing circles.

(*Basic Principles* 2000, Preamble, Section 1.2)

Elaborating on the restorative process, the *Basic Principles* (2000) identify the following as elements of the concept:

■ RJ respects the dignity and equality of each person, builds under-standing, and promotes social harmony through the healing of victims, offenders and communities.
■ RJ enables those affected by crime to share openly their feelings and experiences, and aims at addressing their needs.
■ RJ provides an opportunity for victims to obtain reparation, feel safer and seek closure.
■ RJ allows offenders to gain insight into the causes and effects of their behavior and to take responsibility in a meaningful way.
■ RJ enables communities to understand the underlying causes of crime, to promote community well-being and to prevent crime.

A comparison of this set of standards or elements with the various theo-retical formulations and practical schemes and applications of RJ worldwide indicates that this normative international statement echoes national standards. For example, Van Ness (1989 quoted in McErea 1996: 72) sets out three fundamental principles of RJ that resonate with the international norms:

1 Crime results in injuries to victims, communities and offenders; there-fore the criminal justice process must repair those injuries.
2 Not only the state, but also victims, offenders and communities should be actively involved in the criminal justice system at the earliest point and to the greatest possible extent.
3 The state is responsible for preserving order, and the community is responsible for establishing peace.

Finally, it is worth noting that the *Basic Principles* (2000) call upon states to:

consider the formulation of national strategies and policies aimed at the development of restorative justice and at the promotion of a culture favorable to the use of restorative justice among law enforcement, judicial and social authorities, as well as local communities.

(*Basic Principles* 2000, Point 6)

The *Basic Principles* (2000) clearly recognize that implementing RJ measures would require some fundamental changes in the punishment culture of certain states.

Critiques of restorative justice

Critical positions on RJ include, as noted above, objections to the stance taken by many proponents of RJ that opposes RJ to retributive justice, favoring the former and tending to see RJ as "good" and retributive justice as "evil." Kurki (2000: 287) points out that if crime is seen as an act against persons (in the RJ sense) and against the state (in the formal justice system sense) a double system of punishments may evolve, with offenders being processed through the formal system and then through a RJ process for a reparative sanction. This suggests more social control and double punishment, or perhaps "net widening" attracting minor criminality that was previously ignored. In relation to "net widening," Maxwell and Morris (1996) did not find evidence of this following the changes in New Zealand juvenile justice law in 1989 to incorporate RJ. For example, the number of places in residences for young offenders was reduced from 200 to 76, and custody sentences declined from an average of 374 a year to 112 in 1990 (p. 94).

The account that is usually offered of RJ presents ancient forms of dispute settlement, still practiced in indigenous communities, and modernized as RJ in its various forms, as a model of what justice ought to be. Romanticizing the past in this way allows RJ advocates to claim that RJ is somehow a truer or more legitimate form of justice than the modern systems based on retribution and punishment. In its present modes of operation, RJ can be seen as peripheral to the formal or traditional criminal justice system because many modes of doing RJ require that cases be referred from the formal justice system to a forum where RJ is applied and implemented. Without those referrals, RJ has no constituency and in this sense the criminal justice system can be seen as a barrier to the growth and implementation of RJ (Crawford and Newburn 2003: 40, 41). Kurki questions whether the aims and values of RJ will ever be adopted by the bureaucratic criminal justice agencies who are accustomed to and who value routinized, specialized and technical modes of operation (Kurki 2000: 265). The uniformity, regularity and predictability encouraged and supported by the criminal justice bureaucracy is unlikely to give way to the flexibility and creativeness associated with RJ practices.

The notion that RJ is derived from forms of indigenous justice, and is therefore in some way timeless, has been called into question in relation to Australian RJ practice. In Australia, the statutory schemes for RJ in various states that claim linkage with indigenous justice forms have been criticized for ignoring the structural problems faced by the indigenous peoples and for failing to map out "a new decolonized terrain, where genuine reconciliation with indigenous peoples can take place" (Blagg 2001: 227). In states with indigenous populations, Aboriginal youth are greatly overrepresented in the juvenile justice system. For example, as compared to whites with an arrest rate in 1997 of 16 per 1,000, the Aboriginal arrest rate was 137 per 1,000 (p. 228). The RJ movement is said to have appropriated elements of traditional practice while ignoring associated aspects of obligation, reciprocity and meaning, and repackaged them into a form that meets the needs of the dominant culture. Moreover, it is argued that a series of culturally specific traditional practices have been merged into a singular form of traditional practice and assigned the label "restorative," ignoring the heterogeneity of specific cultural groups and their practices. Ironically, despite the appropriation of modes of Aboriginal dispute settlement, Aboriginal youth themselves in Western Australia continue to be underrepresented in conferencing (p. 230). Blagg calls for RJ to be responsive to Aboriginal needs, especially in regard to the recognition of Aboriginal customary law, and for conferencing to generate modes of operation that are specific to local indigenous groups (pp. 238–239).

Conferences are seen by RJ advocates as both empowering and as deliberative democracy but may also be negatively seen as naïve, idealistic, and as disregarding structural inequalities and the social context affecting victims and offenders. Arguably, offenders will suffer a diminution of rights in restorative processes that they would not experience in the criminal justice system and empowering victims may produce an imbalance to the detriment of an offender. Some forms of conferencing give power to the police, allowing them to dominate the process (Braithwaite and Parker 1999: 108). All in all, RJ "purports to restore a social peace that never existed" (Abel 1982: 8). Some question whether it is actually possible to reintegrate offenders within a community that has been abused on the basis of one RJ intervention such as a family group conference. This is especially so where any structural, social or even economic issues are not addressed through the RJ process (Crawford and Newburn 2003: 52).

Class may also have a detrimental effect in RJ proceedings. For example, mediators in VOM programs tend to be white, male and well educated (Levrant et al. 1999). It is possible that more affluent offenders will be perceived to do better in conferencing because they present themselves more appropriately and are more skilled verbally. In terms of affluence, it is likely that disadvantaged offenders will find it difficult to meet the needs of victim restitution. More affluent offenders will have an advantage in meeting conditions like drug treatment and parental monitoring (p. 16).

Whatever may be the merits of inculcating shame about an offense and participating in a conference to discuss the wrongness and harmfulness of the offender's conduct, it is important to note that "formal criminal justice is still the recognized way of demonstrating that society takes something seriously . . . there remains the demand for authoritative condemnation of the class of behaviours of which the incident is part" (Hudson 2002: 629). Hudson argues for an integration of the aims and principles of retributive justice and RJ with regard for due process and standards like proportionality (p. 631). Currently, RJ interventions operate "on the margins of criminal justice, offsetting the central tendencies without much changing the overall balance of the system" (Garland 2000: 104). The proponents of RJ therefore need to convince the public and criminal justice professionals that the essential tasks performed reasonably well by the formal criminal justice system will continue to be performed at least as well (Johnstone 2002: 7). However, there remains the fundamental problem that some serious crimes, especially those considered morally blameworthy because they are carried out deliberately and not simply carelessly or recklessly, cannot be repaired through compensation or reparation. They are seen as warranting a more serious response that causes the wrongdoers to suffer because they are perceived as more threatening to the community. Johnstone argues that the issue is therefore whether RJ, in offering merely compensation or reparation, is trivializing crime (2002: 27).

Critics of RJ draw attention to the absence of procedural safeguards in practices like conferencing. While offenders may be legally represented in some programs, commonly, the only right available to an offender is to withdraw from the program and be processed through the formal criminal justice system (Kurki 2000: 286). Lawyers are generally discouraged from attending mediation hearings and the informality of RJ practice results in more lenient rules concerning the presentation of evidence. Information used in conferences may be used in a trial in the formal system if the offender and victim fail to agree on reparations (Levrant et al. 1999: 7–8). In response to this kind of criticism, Morris (2002: 601) points out that the RJ process usually requires that guidelines or standards be followed and sometimes there are legal regulations that must be complied with. She notes that in RJ conferencing in the U.S., lawyers hold a watching brief and can interrupt if they believe that a juvenile's rights are likely to be violated. In New Zealand, facilitators at a family conference are able to request that a lawyer be provided at the expense of the state. The difference in RJ practice is that lawyers are not the main protagonists. In any event, in practice, juveniles often go unrepresented in the formal juvenile justice system because they tend to waive the right to counsel (p. 602).

Face-to-face meetings in the nature of mediation typically give rise to concerns about power imbalances, especially when young offenders and indigenous peoples are participating. For example, in the RISE project in Canberra, Australia, about one-third of juvenile offenders believed they lacked control over the outcome or felt too intimidated to speak (Sherman et al. 1998). As Braithwaite has argued, "any attempt by a participant at a conference to silence or dominate another participant must be countered" (2002: 565). In her study of 12 conferences in Australia in 2001, Cook found that class, gender and ethnicity come under scrutiny in RJ conferences and that socially constructed differences are "used as subtle devices of domination" (Cook 2006: 120). Moreover, participants must adhere to the master discourse of RJ and so the truth that is offered must be appropriate to that discourse. Thus, when explanations do not conform to the expected discourse, the speaker's empowerment is displaced, raising the issue of just how empowering RJ practices may actually be (p. 120). Kurki (2000: 240) observes that face-to-face meetings between victim and offender can be highly emotional affairs in contrast to the formality of a courtroom trial, but it is not yet clear that the emotional catharsis engendered by this interaction actually produces results in the form of reduced recidivism.

Restorative justice and the public

While RJ has emerged as a global movement over the past decade, retributive justice still dominates thinking on justice punishment policy. The public reaction to RJ will, to some extent, determine whether legislators and policy makers are willing to afford RJ a greater role within criminal justice systems. Thus, it is significant that research conducted in 2004 into the public reaction to RJ (Roberts and Stalans 2004: 315) revealed that there is significant public support for RJ. Generally, public reaction to restorative sentencing options like restitution and community service is favorable compared to more punitive sentences. In this study 79 percent favored restitution and only 54 percent favored a military-style discipline program, with 56 percent supporting house arrest (p. 319).

In relation to proportionality in sentencing, the public generally supports proportional sentencing, with the severity of the punishment increasing according to the seriousness of the crime. In research conducted in Germany, it was found that public support for a RJ response to a crime declined the more serious was the crime committed (Roberts and Stalans 2004: 320). Consequently, the public sees crime seriousness as a central issue in views about sentencing (p. 320).

Reparative boards were supported as a concept by 92 percent of respondents in one survey but the level of support fell to less than 5 percent for serious crimes like rape and armed robbery (Roberts and Stalans 2004). Less serious offenses attracted more support for reparative boards including shoplifting, auto theft and theft where two-thirds of a sample preferred reparative boards to imprisonment (p. 320). Similarly, VOM programs are regarded as inappropriate for more serious offences (p. 323). In terms of specific reparative actions, there is significant support for restitution and compensation among the public, as compared to imprisonment, for a range of property offenses (p. 325). Community service has attracted support in Canada where a sample showed that 72 percent favored such service for a minor assault over imprisonment (p. 326).

Despite public support for RJ sanctions the public appears to regard RJ as a more appropriate punishment for juveniles, especially juvenile offenders without previous adjudications. So, for example, in one study, when asked to sentence a 15-year-old first offender for shoplifting, 43 percent supported a RJ caution, 15 percent an order for reparation and 28 percent some other form of community sanction. Only 3 percent supported a custody order (Roberts and Stalans 2004: 327).

Similarly, the public regards RJ sanctions to be more appropriate for first offenders than for repeat offenders but where the current offense is nonviolent restorative sanctions are still considered appropriate. A study in Vermont (Roberts and Stalans 2004) showed that for a recidivist shoplifter, 76 percent favored the use of a community board, for a repeat bad check writer, 73 percent, and even for a repeat unarmed burglar, 66 percent. However, only 4 percent regarded a community board as appropriate for a first-time armed robber (p. 328).

Given the support that exists for RJ sanctions, why have they made so little impact as compared to retributive sentencing? Roberts and Stalans suggest that public support for RJ measures has not caught the attention of policy makers or politicians (2004: 331). Even if it did, the U.S. is renowned for "penal populism"[1] to the extent that judgments about crime tend to be founded on a "visceral sense of danger" promoted avidly by media sensationalism that becomes translated into calls for more punitive penalties for all offenders (Beale 2003: 432).

It seems that RJ advocates envisage the inclusion of RJ within existing formal justice systems along the following lines: the police divert suitable cases out of the system and into an alternative RJ track such as a family group conference; cases which are not diverted at this early stage may be transferred subsequently, for example, a person convicted may be transferred to a sentencing circle; and where a person is convicted and serving a sentence of imprisonment he or she may participate in a VOM program. As a result, RJ will gradually become the norm and prosecution, trial and punishment will be the exception, used only where RJ has failed (Johnstone 2002: 17). Nevertheless, Braithwaite, while insisting that RJ processes should be tried over and over, also accepts that punishment should be applied where RJ repeatedly fails. He blurs the punishment and RJ distinction by alluding to formal punishment as something lurking in the background of RJ practice that may "sharpen our perceptions of how bad the punitive consequences would be if we were caught again" (Braithwaite 1999: 63).

Proponents of RJ argue that it has now become an international movement, is ever expanding, and has established its place as part of contemporary criminal justice (Van Ness and Strong 2010: 172). It is true that internationally RJ has gained recognition, and RJ norms and standards have been agreed to by the international community. The CRC and its associated instruments are especially important for the development of RJ in juvenile justice systems owing to their emphasis on diversion and because all states except two (the U.S. and Somalia) are parties to the CRC and bound to implement its provisions in their domestic laws.

At the same time, there is general recognition that rigorous empirical research and enhanced theory building is necessary to better understand the nature and the processes of RJ within the general field of justice (Johnstone 2002: 170). In the present climate of penal populism, RJ does little to address key issues such as fear of crime, although it does contribute to the overwhelming belief that satisfying victims of criminality is as important as punishing offenders. The greatest resistance to moving RJ from the margins of the criminal justice system to its center comes from prosecutors and judges who adhere to a firm belief in the merits of punishment as provided by the formal criminal justice system.

Recap

The new paradigm offered by RJ focuses not on the infliction of pain but on a socially constructive obligation to repair the harm caused by the crime. RJ seeks to do justice by repairing the harm that has been caused by a crime. By including the victim in the process, RJ clearly appeals to the public sense that a victim's needs are important. However, while it is clear that individual victims must be the focus of restorative action, proponents of RJ argue that the victimized community must also be included. This approach presents theoretical and practical difficulties in terms of deciding just what constitutes a community. Complex questions also arise in relation to proportionality of "punishment." Thus, at the same time as RJ seeks to do justice, it raises numerous procedural and substantive issues, noted above, that remain unresolved. Forms of community justice that incorporate RJ tenets, but are nevertheless judged not fully authentic by RJ proponents, complicate the issue still further, blurring the boundaries for policy makers and unsettling notions of RJ purity.

Will RJ remain forever justice at the margins or can it become mainstream justice? This is the key issue in RJ. Despite advances in its development, its international recognition and practice and increased research into

youth, crime and justice

its efficacy, RJ has not been able to secure even a moderate degree of acceptance within formal justice systems. Only in the field of juvenile justice, and only then in a few countries, has RJ been recognized as an effective policy choice in terms of "punishment." There remains a consistent tension between the social justice and reparative underpinnings of RJ and the penal populism that prevails in contemporary justice policy.

Note

1   "Penal populism" is explained by John Pratt as comprising a number of elements including "the way in which criminals and prisoners are thought to have been favored at the expense of crime victims in particular and the law-abiding public in general" (2007: 12). According to Pratt, penal populism reflects a highly critical view of the criminal justice establishment, disparages technical expertise on crime control, and seeks to substitute a "commonsense" view based on feelings and intuitions for technical expertise in policy making (p. 13).

References

Abel, R. 1982. "Introduction." In *The Politics of Informal Justice: Volume One: The American Experience*. New York: Academic Press, pp. 1–13.

Ashworth, A. 2002. "Responsibilities, Rights and Restorative Justice." *British Journal of Criminology* 42: 578–595.

Basic Principles. 2000. *Basic Principles on the Use of Restorative Justice Programmes in Criminal Matters*. Economic and Social Council Resolution 2000/14, U.N. Doc. E/2000/INF/2/Add.2 at 35.

Bazemore, Gordon and Lode Walgrave. 1999. "Restorative Juvenile Justice: In Search of Fundamentals and on Outline for Systemic Reform." In Gordon Bazemore and Lode Walgrave (eds) *Restorative Juvenile Justice: Repairing the Harm of Youth Crime*. Monsey, NY: Criminal Justice Press, pp. 45–74.

Beale, Sara Sun. 2003. "Still Tough on Crime? Prospects for Restorative Justice in the United States." *Utah Law Review*: 413–437.

Beijing Rules. 1985. *United Nations Standard Minimum Rules for the Administration of Juvenile Justice (The Beijing Rules)*. Adopted by General Assembly Resolution 40/33 of November 29.

Blagg, Harry. 2001. "Aboriginal Youth and Restorative Justice: Critical Notes from the Australian Frontier." In Daniel Van Ness, Allison Morris and Gabrielle Maxwell (eds) *Restorative Justice for Juveniles*. Portland, OR: Hart Publishing, pp. 227–242.

Braithwaite, John. 1989. *Crime, Shame and Reintegration*. Cambridge: Cambridge University Press.

Braithwaite, John. 1999. "Restorative Justice: Assessing Optimistic and Pessimistic Accounts." *Crime and Justice: A Review of Research* 25: 1–127.

Braithwaite, John. 2002. "Setting Standards for Restorative Justice." *British Journal of Criminology* 42(3): 563–577.

Braithwaite, John and Christine Parker. 1999. "Restorative Justice is Republican Justice." In Gordon Bazemore and Lode Walgrave (eds) *Restorative Juvenile Justice: Repairing the Harm of Youth Crime*. Monsey, NY: Criminal Justice Press, pp. 103–126.

Buerger, Michael. 1994. "A Tale of Two Targets: Limitations of Community Anticrime Actions." *Crime and Delinquency* 40: 411–436.

Christie, Nils. 1977. "Conflicts as Property." *British Journal of Criminology* 17(1): 1–15.

Clear, Todd and David R. Karp. 1998. "The Community Justice Movement." In David R. Karp (ed.) *Community Justice: An Emerging Field*. Lanham, MD: Rowman and Littlefield, pp. 3–30.

Convention on the Rights of the Child. 1989. U.N. General Assembly. Document A/RES/44/25 (December 12) with Annex.

Cook, Kimberly J. 2006. "Doing Difference and Accountability in Restorative Justice Conferences." *Theoretical Criminology* 10(1): 107–124.

Crawford, Adam and Tim Newburn. 2003. *Youth Offending and Restorative Justice: Implementing Reform in Youth Justice*. Cullompton, Devon: Willan Publishing.

Daly, Kathleen. 2001. "Conferencing in Australia and New Zealand: Variations, Research Findings and Prospects." In Daniel Van Ness, Allison Morris and Gabrielle Maxwell (eds) *Restorative Justice for Juveniles*. Portland, OR: Hart Publishing, pp. 59–83.

Daly, Kathleen. 2002. "Restorative Justice: The Real Story." *Punishment and Society* 4(1): 55–79.

Duff, R.A. 1992. "Alternatives to Punishment or Alternative Punishments." In W. Cragg (ed.) *Retributivism and its Critics*. Stuttgart: Franz Steiner, pp. 44–68.

Garland, David. 1990. *Punishment and Modern Society*. Oxford: Clarendon Press.

Garland, David. 2000. *The Culture of Control: Crime and Social Order in Contemporary Society*. Oxford: Oxford University Press.

Gray, Patricia. 2005. "The Politics of Risk and Young Offenders' Experience of Social Exclusion and Restorative Justice." *British Journal of Criminology* 45: 938–957.

Guidelines for Action on Children in the Criminal Justice System. 1997. Recommended by Economic and Social Council Resolution 1997/30 of July 21.

Hemmens, Craig, Eric J. Fritsch and Tory J. Caeti. 1999. "The Rhetoric of Juvenile Justice Reform." *Quinnipiac Law Review* 18: 351–372.

Hudson, Barbara. 2002. "Restorative Justice and Gendered Violence: Diversion or Effective Justice?" *British Journal of Criminology* 42: 616–634.

Johnstone, G. 2002. *Restorative Justice: Ideas, Values, Debates*. Portland, OR: Willan Publishing.

Karp, David R. 2001. "Harm and Repair: Observing Restorative Justice in Vermont." *Justice Quarterly* 18(4): 727–757.

Kurki, Leena. 2000. "Restorative and Community Justice in the United States." In Michael Tonry (ed.) *Crime and Justice: A Review of Research, Volume 27*. Chicago, IL: The University of Chicago Press, pp. 235–303.

Launay, Gilles and Peter Murray. 1989. "Victim/Offender Groups." In Martin Wright and Burt Galaway (eds) *Mediation and Criminal Justice*. London: Sage, pp. 113–131.

Levrant, Sharon, Francis T. Cullen, Betsy Fulton and John F. Wozniak. 1999. "Reconsidering Restorative Justice: The Corruption of Benevolence Revisited?" *Crime and Delinquency* 45(1): 3–27.

Lilles, Heino. 2001. "Circle Sentencing: Part of the Restorative Justice Continuum." In Daniel Van Ness, Allison Morris and Gabrielle Maxwell (eds) *Restorative Justice for Juveniles*. Portland, OR: Hart Publishing, pp. 161–179.

Llewellyn, Jennifer. 2007. "Truth Commissions and Restorative Justice." In Gerry Johnstone and Daniel W. Van Ness (eds) *Handbook of Restorative Justice*. Cullompton, Devon: Willan Publishing, pp. 351–371.

Marshall, Tony. 1996. "Criminal Mediation in Great Britain 1980-1996." *European Journal on Criminal Policy and Research* 4(4): 21–43.

Marshall, Tony. 1998. "Restorative Justice: An Overview." http://ssw.che.umn.edu/rjp/Resources/Resource.htm (accessed May 25, 2012).

Marshall, Tony. 1999. *Restorative Justice: An Overview*. Home Office, Research Development and Statistics Directorate. London: Home Office.

Maxwell, Gabrielle and Allison Morris. 1993. *Family, Victims and Culture: Youth Justice New Zealand*. Wellington, NZ: Victoria University, Social Policy Agency and Institute of Criminology.

Maxwell, Gabrielle and Allison Morris. 1996. "Research on Family Group Conferences with Young Offenders in New Zealand." In Joe Hudson, Allison Morris, Gabrielle Maxwell and Burt Galaway (eds) *Family Group Conferences: Perspectives on Policy and Practice*. Sydney: Federation Press and Criminal Justice Press, pp. 88–110.

McCold, Paul. 2000. "Towards a Mid-range Theory of Restorative Criminal Justice: A Reply to the Maximalist Model." *Contemporary Justice Review* 3(4): 357–414.

McCold, Paul. 2001. "Primary Restorative Justice Practices." In Daniel Van Ness, Allison Morris and Gabrielle Maxwell (eds) *Restorative Justice for Juveniles*. Portland, OR: Hart Publishing, pp. 41–58.

McCold, Paul. 2004. "Paradigm Muddle: The Threat to Restorative Justice Posed by its Merger with Community Justice." *Contemporary Justice Review* 7(1): 13–35.

McCold, Paul and Benjamin Wachtel. 1998. *Restorative Policing Experiment: The Bethlehem Pennsylvania Police Family Group Conferencing Project*. Pipersville, PA: Community Service Foundation.

McCold, Paul and Ted Wachtel. 2003. "In Pursuit of Paradigm: A Theory of Restorative Justice." Restorative Practices EForum, August 12. www.restorativepractices.org. http://www.realjustice.org/articles.html?articleId=424 (accessed May 25, 2012).

McErea, F.W.M. 1996. "The New Zealand Youth Court: A Model for Use with Adults." In B. Galaway and J. Hudson (eds) *Restorative Justice: International Perspectives*. Monsey, NY: Criminal Justice Press, pp. 69–83.

Morris, Allison. 2002. "Critiquing the Critics: A Brief Response to Critics of Restorative Justice." *British Journal of Criminology* 42: 596–615.

Pepinsky, Howard E. and Richard Quinney. 1991. *Criminology as Peacemaking*. Bloomington: Indiana University Press.

Pratt, John. 2007. *Penal Populism*. London: Routledge.

Riyadh Guidelines. 1990. *United Nations Guidelines for the Prevention of Juvenile Delinquency (The Riyadh Guidelines)*. Adopted and proclaimed by General Assembly Resolution 45/112 of December 14.

Roberts, Julian V. and Loretta J. Stalans. 2004. "Restorative Justice: Exploring the Views of the Public." *Social Justice Research* 17(3): 315–334.

Roche, D. 2007. "Retribution and Restorative Justice." In G. Johnstone and D.W. Van Ness (eds) *Handbook of Restorative Justice*. Cullompton, Devon: Willan Publishing.

Rock, Paul. 2004. *Constructing Victims Rights: The Home Office, New Labour, and Victims*. New York: Oxford University Press.

Sherman, Lawrence W., Heather Strang, Geoffrey C. Barnes, John Braithwaite, Nova Ipken and Min-Mee. 1998. *Experiments in Restorative Policing: A Progress Report to the National Police Research Unit on the Canberra Reintegrative Shaming Experiments (RISE)*. Canberra: Australian Federal Police and Australian National University.

Thomas, Jim, Julie Capps, James Carr, Tammie Evans, Wendy Lewin-Gladney, Deborah Jackson, Chris Maier, Scott Moran and Sean Thompson. 2003. "Critiquing the Critics of Peacemaking Criminology: Some Rather Ambivalent Reflections on the Theory of 'Being Nice.'" In Kieran McEvoy and Tim Newburn (eds) *Criminology, Conflict Resolution and Restorative Justice*. Basingstoke: Palgrave Macmillan, pp. 101–134.

Tonry, Michael. 1999. *The Fragmentation of Sentencing and Corrections in America*. Washington D.C.: U.S. Department of Justice, National Institute of Justice.

Umbreit, Mark. 1990. "The Meaning of Fairness to Burglary Victims." In Burt Galaway and Joe Hudson (eds) *Criminal Justice, Restitution and Reconciliation*. Monsey, NY: Criminal Justice Press, pp. 47–57.

Umbreit, Mark S., Robert B. Coates and Betty Vos. 2001. "Victim Impact of Meeting with Young Offenders: Two Decades of Victim Offender Mediation Practice and Research." In Daniel Van Ness, Allison Morris and Gabrielle Maxwell (eds) *Restorative Justice for Juveniles*. Portland, OR: Hart Publishing, pp. 122–143.

Van Ness, Daniel W. and Karen Heetderks Strong. 2010. *Restoring Justice: An Introduction to Restorative Justice*. New Providence, NJ: Matthew Bender.

Van Ness, Daniel, Allison Morris and Gabrielle Maxwell. 2001. "Introducing Restorative Justice." In Daniel Van Ness, Allison Morris and Gabrielle Maxwell (eds) *Restorative Justice for Juveniles*. Portland, OR: Hart Publishing, pp. 3–16.

Walgrave, Lode. 1995. "Restorative Justice for Juveniles: Just a Technique or a Fully Fledged Alternative?" *The Howard Journal* 34(3): 228–249.

Walgrave, Lode. 1999. "Community Service as a Cornerstone of a Systemic Restorative Response to (Juvenile) Crime." In Gordon Bazemore and Lode Walgrave (eds) *Restorative Juvenile Justice: Repairing the Harm of Youth Crime*. Monsey, NY: Criminal Justice Press, pp. 129–154.

Walgrave, Lode. 2001. "On Restoration and Punishment: Favourable Similarities and Fortunate Differences." In Daniel Van Ness, Allison Morris and Gabrielle Maxwell (eds) *Restorative Justice for Juveniles*. Portland, OR: Hart Publishing, pp. 17–37.

Wright, Martin. 1991. *Justice for Victims and Offenders*. Milton Keynes: Open University Press.

Zehr, Howard. 1990. *Changing Lenses: A New Focus for Crime and Justice*. Scottdale, PA: Herald Press.

chapter 9

What Works?

This chapter will explore questions of what works in delinquency prevention and what works in treatment and rehabilitation. A number of related issues relevant to treatment will be discussed, such as the need for specificity in treatment for different cultures and modes of treatment that have been shown to be ineffective. Treatment issues and programming for girls are discussed in Chapter 4.

There are now a host of prevention and treatment programs for juveniles and at-risk youth. What constitutes a good treatment or prevention program? What are the risk factors that such programs target? What principles may be applied to treatment and prevention, and what mechanisms exist for evaluating programs? Juvenile drug courts are a favored treatment option for youth with drug or alcohol issues but how do they operate and how effective are they? Proponents of restorative justice (see Chapter 8) argue that it represents the best hope in juvenile rehabilitation. Has its time arrived or is it merely a marginal option?

Delinquency prevention: what works?

The field of *early prevention* focuses on measures implemented in the early years of life through to early adolescence. Early prevention in this sense does not relate to crime prevention in the form of law-enforcement measures such as improved lighting or environmental safety, nor in taking a public health approach that links prevention to alcohol abuse or gun use. Rather, early delinquency prevention is concerned with reducing individual long-term tendencies toward criminality and is usually targeted at youth or families who have an increased risk of involvement in delinquent behavior

(Greenwood 2006: 6). The purpose is to intervene in the lives of children and youth *before* they engage in delinquent behaviors because certain risk factors are deemed to be present. Most adult criminals begin their criminal careers as juveniles, and in general, the greater the number of risk factors, the more likely it is that a child will show continued antisocial behavior, such as assault, aggression, theft, cruelty to animals and serious rule violations into adulthood.

Current theories of delinquency prevention argue that there is an interaction between risk and protective factors in the developmental course of a person (Greenwood 2006). Prevention programs attempt to reduce risk factors and enhance protective factors. For example, risk factors for an individual may include: pregnancy and delivery complications for the mother; violent behavior; risk taking; and involvement in forms of antisocial behavior (p. 25). In the case of a family, risk factors can include: living with a criminal parent; excessive disciplining; physical abuse; child neglect; and low levels of parental involvement with children. Additional risk factors include academic failure, truancy, early drop-out from school, delinquent peers or siblings, and community risks such as drug availability, and community disorganization. The theory asserts that lower levels of delinquency will result from interventions that are able to reduce these risk factors. Designing and testing possible interventions and gaining a deeper understanding of how these risk factors interact are the principal tasks of delinquency prevention research (p. 25).

Early prevention measures are of a developmental or social nature – preventing the development of an individual's criminal potential or improving social conditions such as families or those who have some influence on offending. Developmental prevention is regarded as a major strategy in preventing delinquency and later adult criminality (Welsh and Farrington 2011). It is based on the notion that the early years of life are the most influential in shaping later experiences and that as a person ages, interventions become more costly, complex and problematic (p. 101). Early prevention strategies have benefited from decades of research using prospective longitudinal studies that have identified risk factors for delinquency. In addition, evaluations of a large number of early prevention programs intended to target these risk factors have shown that effective programs exist and that others show promise for the future. There is also widespread public support for these programs. Cost-benefit analysis shows they offer value for money and are a worthwhile investment compared to criminal justice responses such as incarceration (p. 102). The best programs are risk focused and evidence based.

In their review of early prevention programs Welsh and Farrington (2011: 104–110) categorize programs as: *individual, family* and *school and community. Individual programs* target risk factors in the person such as "low intelligence and attainment, personality and temperament, low empathy, and impulsiveness" (p. 104). According to Welsh and Farrington, two main types of programs in this category have been found to be effective – preschool intellectual enrichment (aimed at low intelligence and attainment) and child social skills training (targeted at impulsivity, low empathy and self-centeredness).

In the category of *family prevention programs*, Welsh and Farrington (2011) identify programs that target risk factors associated with the family, including poor child rearing, poor parental supervision, and inconsistent or overly harsh discipline. These programs aim to change the family environment so that children are rewarded for pro-social behaviors and punished for antisocial behaviors. Programs in this category include home visiting for at-risk mothers to improve prenatal health and reduce complications at birth and deliver general parent education, and parent education and parent management training programs. The latter is concerned to correct parents' failure to tell their children how to behave, failure to monitor behavior, and failure to enforce rules and impose appropriate sanctions.

The category of *school and community prevention programs* includes school-based programs that focus on discipline management, classroom management and self-control based on cognitive approaches (Welsh and Farrington 2011). These programs are also effective in preventing drug and alcohol abuse. Community-based programs utilize community associations and clubs as well as churches to address delinquency problems. After-school and mentoring programs also fall within this category, involving organizations like Big Brothers and Big Sisters (a Blueprints Model Program: see p. 263 below).

Rehabilitation and treatment: what works?

Underlying the question of what works in treating delinquency is the ideal of rehabilitation. While some early attempts were made to correct criminality in the 19th century, it was not until the 20th century that therapeutic disciplines began to be developed to rehabilitate criminal offenders. As Cullen and Gendreau (2000: 114) illustrate, from the 1800s when they were first established, penitentiaries were a site not for warehousing prisoners but for transforming them into useful, law-abiding citizens. Corrections therefore were exactly that – places for reform.

According to Blomberg and Lucken (2000: 100–101), four principles formed the foundation of the ideal of rehabilitation:

1   Human behavior was the outcome of past causes such as upbringing and environment, and these events caused and shaped a person.

2   These causes could be discovered and individual case histories developed.
3   Gaining enough knowledge about a person's individual history would enable behavior issues to be treated through various technical therapies.
4   Treating an offender in order to eradicate criminality was not only in the best interest of the offender but also a public good, because recidivism would be reduced and the offender reintegrated into society.

It is here that the association between rehabilitation and religion is strongest, especially in relation to the Christian ideal of helping those who fall by the wayside (Cullen and Gendreau 2000: 114).

Individualized treatment became the principal means of rehabilitating criminality. This meant designing a range of treatment programs that could be applied to the needs of a specific offender. The objective was to isolate the causes of an individual's criminality, determine treatment needs and then apply the treatment (Blomberg and Lucken 2000: 107). Chapter 3 discusses the emergence of the House of Refuge and Child Savers and points out how, by the 1950s and 1960s, psychologically directed treatment programs had begun to populate juvenile institutions. During that period, the ideal of rehabilitation was generally endorsed and supported by policy makers, legislators and the general public.

In assessing what works in the treatment of juvenile offenders, researchers increasingly rely on evaluations, reports, reviews and meta-analyses (Guerra et al. 2008). Some treatment programs have been evaluated, found to be effective and have been replicated. Other programs are graded as "promising" (p. 79). In spite of this bias toward scientific evidence there is still an almost instinctive urge to select populist programs that rely heavily on military discipline and "tough love." Examples are boot camps and similar, get-tough programs (p. 79).

"Nothing works"

In the early 1970s, the ideal of rehabilitation came under serious challenge through a landmark event that proclaimed rehabilitation to be a lost cause because "nothing works." In 1974, Robert Martinson at the City University of New York published a celebrated study of reviews of treatment studies entitled "What Works? Questions and Answers about Prison Reform" which concluded that "with few and isolated exceptions, the rehabilitative efforts that have been reported so far have had no appreciable impact on recidivism" (Martinson 1974: 25). The notion that "nothing works" became a rallying cry for penal conservatism, leading to an increase in media and political attention to crime control and punishment. Martinson's announce-ment coincided with a general discontent within society and with the criminal justice system. Liberals accused rehabilitation of coercing offenders and conservatives claimed that too much leniency was being shown toward them (Cullen and Gendreau 2000: 109, 119).

Martinson's conclusions shocked the discipline, but according to Cullen and Gendreau (2000: 122), by the time Martinson's study appeared many criminologists had already decided that rehabilitation had failed. In their study, Cullen and Gendreau (2000: 127) draw attention to the deficiencies of 1970s analytical techniques that did not, for example, include contem-porary meta-analytic techniques, now commonly employed to compile a quantitative synthesis of research studies. A meta-analysis is a statistical analysis of a collection of studies involving a literature review, data collection and data analysis. Meta-analyses are regarded as a superior method of research synthesis compared to the traditional narrative reviews (Rosenthal 1991: 17). During a meta-analysis, a database is constructed by coders who are guided by questionnaires concerning data elements and program characteristics. Criticisms of this evaluation method generally focus on the fact that it cannot overcome poor research design problems and that summarizing studies with varying methodological features means that studies do not cohere well (Howell 2009: 172). It is of note that Martinson did not review any cognitive-behavioral programs, which today have been evaluated as among the most effective in reducing recidivism (Cullen and Gendreau 2000: 127). In 1979 Martinson retracted his "nothing works" conclusion.

Re-evaluating

In 1979 and 1987 Gendreau and Ross conducted two narrative views of research post-1974 and arrived at three major conclusions (Cullen and Gendreau 2000: 132–133).

1   Correctional programs failed because they lacked therapeutic integrity; that is to say, they contained elements that were inadequate in some respect, for example, poorly trained teachers.
2   There were many examples of treatment programs which had success-fully reduced recidivism, so that, in fact, some things did work.
3   Individual responses to treatment can affect the viability of treatment programs. Examples of this include the fact that high-risk offenders benefit most from treatment and that structured learning most benefits offenders with low intellectual capacity.

Researchers such as Gendreau, Lipsey, Andrews and Cullen have identified the characteristics most associated with effective programs (quoted in Levrant et al. 1999: 18). These "principles of effective intervention" are:

- Risk principle – treatment should be provided primarily to higher risk offenders – studies have shown that intensive services are required to achieve a reduction in recidivism among high-risk offenders, but when applied to low-risk offenders the effect is minimal.
- Need principle – target the known criminogenic predictors of crime and recidivism such as antisocial attitudes, poor family communication, antisocial peer associations. Reducing these factors decreases the likelihood of recidivism.
- Treatment principle – use behavioral or cognitive-behavioral models.
- Fidelity principle – maintain the integrity of a program during the period of delivery of services.

Meta-analyses find that programs which satisfy these principles achieve, on average, a reduction in recidivism of 50 percent and treatment that fails to follow these principles does not succeed (Levrant et al. 1999: 19). For example, deterrence and control-oriented programs like boot camps and scared straight produce slight increases in recidivism.

According to Guerra and others (2008: 87), evaluations of programs reveal that there are four critical components in juvenile programming. These are:

1 Highly structured programs produce better results than unstructured interventions.
2 Cognitive programs with skill development are more effective.
3 Programs that engage with families and reduce delinquency risks from that source are more effective.
4 Comprehensive interventions that address multiple risk factors work better then single component programs.

There is now a consensus on what works to reduce recidivism and what does not. As will be explored in more detail below, deterrence-based interventions such as boot camps, scared straight programs and intensive supervision on probation or parole are ineffective, as are "less structured approaches such as casework or individual and group counseling" (Cullen and Gendreau 2000: 139). Successful interventions are evidence-based cognitive-behavioral and multi-modal programs based on social learning that use more than one mode of treatment to target an offender's multiple problems. To be effective, the treatment should last from three to nine months (p. 145). Treatment effectiveness is increased by a range of factors that include: conducting interventions in a community rather than in an institution; using well-trained, sensitive staff whose performance is properly monitored; and monitoring offenders after release and providing forms of aftercare to prevent relapses. It is equally important to match styles of treatment to offenders' learning styles (p. 147).

According to Guerra and others, "there are very few proven treatment programs for delinquent youth and no proven program models in custodial settings" (2008: 80–83). Only three programs meet the standard of careful evaluation in multiple settings, longer term outcomes, review by an advisory group and wide use. These are multisystemic therapy (MST), functional family therapy (FFT) and multidimensional treatment foster care (MTFC). A further possible addition is aggression replacement training (ART). Except for ART, which can be administered to youth in institutions, or who no longer live with their families, the other programs are designed for youth who live with their families or foster families. Removing offenders from their families by institutionalizing them should be a last resort because programs are more effective when sited within a community (Guerra et al. 2008: 93).

These "gold standard" programs noted above are considered *Blueprints Model Programs* and are endorsed by the Center for the Study and Prevention of Violence at the University of Colorado. In the early 1990s, this university center took the lead in identifying proven programs aimed at reducing violence. A program is only considered proven by Blueprints if it has demonstrated its impact with a rigorous design, its impact is shown to be persistent and it has been successfully replicated in another site (Elliot 1997).

Despite the evidence and expert consensus that evidence-based programs are the most beneficial, these high-quality proven programs are the exception and not the rule in most states – less than 10 percent of youth participate in such programs. According to Greenwood and Edwards (2011: 380), the reasons for this include: a lack of accountability within the juvenile justice system for performance and outcome measurement; funding – because evidence-based programs are seen as expensive to implement; competitors in the marketplace for programs who claim to offer similar programs at lower cost; the absence of an overall rating system for programs – many entities claim to be able to judge program effectiveness but their methods may be less rigorous than are applied in Blueprints Programs; staff resistance – they may have to follow new processes and adopt new behaviors when they are accustomed to autonomy and relying on their intuition; and agencies may lack the competency to administer a Blueprint Program.

Often, programs that are not evidence based receive political support or are simply programs in vogue at a particular time. A good example is the scared straight type of program which, despite many times having been shown to be totally ineffective, continues to collect adherents both in the U.S. and in other countries. Some non-evidence-based programs simply resonate with the public because they possess an instinctive appeal that is often related to the notion of imposing order and discipline. For example, boot camps have an enduring popularity among the public and exemplify the concept of "tough love" where treatment is blended with punishment.

Greenwood (2006: 90–97), in a comprehensive discussion of the Drug Abuse Resistance Training (DARE) program, notes that this program "provides one of the most dramatic examples of how a program can be put into practice nationwide with little in the way of supportive evidence, and then continue to flourish and prosper despite mounting evidence that it is ineffective in reducing drug use." DARE was organized and administered by former LAPD police officers in the belief that classroom education by trained police will make students less vulnerable to pressures to use alcohol and drugs, give them a clearer sense of values and engender more responsible decision making (Greenwood 2006: 92). It built a network of support and was heavily marketed. Despite rigorous evaluations of DARE showing that it is ineffective, the program gained public support, was lauded in the media and by lawmakers, and has been able to resist all criticisms over many years.

As well as addressing the issue of what works, it is essential to address the question of *why some interventions work better than others*, and what makes that difference when applying interventions in practice. Dowden and Andrews (2004: 204) make the point:

> Despite these impressive findings regarding what program characteristics are most effective for offenders, very little research has focused on the characteristics of effective staff practice to use in the delivery of these interventions.

Dowden and Andrews (2004: 205) characterize the qualities and techniques required of practitioners for successful programs as "core correctional practices." These include: the capacity to employ authority in an appropriate manner; to teach cognitive skills; and to act as advocate and broker. They suggest that the most critical component is "relationship factors" and call for "conditions characterized by open, warm, enthusiastic communication" (p. 205). Similarly, McNeill (2006) cautions against rigidly implementing structured interventions so as to overlook the importance of individual needs and particular social contexts relevant to youths' lives. Hence, the process of administering a program must be shaped by relational and contextual factors. McNeill describes the "core conditions of effectiveness" as including "empathy and genuineness; the establishment of a working alliance; and the adoption of person-centered, collaborative, and client-driven approaches" (p. 130). More research on engagement with youth that matches the substantial body of work now completed on the effectiveness of different types of programs would complement each other and help shape a comprehensive treatment strategy.

Rehabilitating offenders, as opposed to warehousing them in correctional institutions, is still the most favored punishment option by the general public. While U.S. public opinion does support a punitive approach, surveys show that the public does not support a corrections system whose *only* aim is incarceration. Rather, both punishment and rehabilitation are the favored approach (Cullen and Gendreau 2000: 161). In relation to juveniles, one survey measuring willingness to pay for rehabilitation and childhood prevention programs found the public at least as willing to pay for rehabilitation as they were for punishment for juvenile offenders and also found substantial support for early childhood prevention (Nagin et al. 2006: 301). In another survey in 1998, respondents saw rehabilitation as an integral goal of the juvenile correctional system. They also endorsed a range of community-based treatment interventions and favored early intervention programs over imprisonment. The researchers concluded that the public's belief in "child saving" remains firm, and that citizens do not support an exclusively punitive response to juvenile offenders (Moon et al. 2000: 38). As indicated above, however, it seems likely that the public favors rehabilitation that is blended with punishment, especially where the element of punishment is expressive, as in the case of boot camps, where juveniles are seen to be under significant physical stress.

Effective interventions: examples

Cognitive-behavioral interventions

This approach is psychological in nature and attempts to restructure an offender's cognition – the mental process of knowing, thinking, judging and problem solving – and to assist in learning new cognitive skills. The thinking behind these approaches is that an offender has thoughts and values that support antisocial activity and devalue pro-social activities like work, education and relationships. Thus, effective cognitive-behavioral programs attempt to help offenders: they define the problems that led to the offense; select future goals; adopt new pro-social ways of thinking; and implement these solutions (Guerra et al. 2008).

Most cognitive-behavioral programs contain components of: cognitive self-control; anger management; social problem solving; social perspective taking; empathy; moral reasoning; and changing attitudes and beliefs

(Guerra et al. 2008). Techniques used include role playing, modeling and group discussions, and these programs work best when they are multi-component, for example, not focusing only on anger management (p. 84). The approach followed within a cognitive-behavioral program involves telling an offender that his or her beliefs are unacceptable and that alternative pro-social ways need to be acquired through a process of therapeutic modeling in one-on-one sessions or in groups. Over time, it is hoped that the offender's thinking will be reinforced toward appropriate pro-social thinking until his or her behavior reaches a level that is acceptable (Cullen and Gendreau 2000: 146–147). Comprehensive cognitive-behavioral programs have been found to produce significant improvements in cognitions and skills (Guerra et al. 2008: 85).

Multisystemic therapy (MST)

This treatment form has been implemented in the U.S. and Canada and is shown to produce marked reductions in recidivism and problem behaviors among youth with serious antisocial issues. Its focus is mainly high-risk youth and it employs multiple techniques including family therapies, cognitive-behavioral, and behavioral parent training. A family systems approach supplements the individual personality focus because the process perceives offenders to be embedded in multiple systems such as family, school, peer groups and the community. Therefore interventions must be multisystemic, targeting the individual and his or her life context. This requires engaging with family and parents in particular, ensuring that youth peers are pro-social and working with schools to improve skill levels. In terms of the family, risk factors for delinquency include low levels of parental monitoring of activities and poor discipline. A broad set of goals is defined as well as intermediate goals that will collectively support the broader overall goals. Interventions last from three to five months. The treatment provides intensive services within the community and the home with the aim of avoiding institutionalization. The program is costly because it provides 24/7 support for families. Typically, trained teams of MST therapists have caseloads of four to six families and the overall cost is US$5,000 per family (Cullen and Gendreau 2000: 152, 153; Guerra et al. 2008: 81, 82).

Functional family therapy (FFT)

This intervention combines family systems concepts with social learning and behavior management and recently, with cognitive processes. It was designed several decades ago, is short term, and is administered by therapists in the home. It is less intensive and less expensive than MST with a cost of about US$2,000 for a family (Guerra et al. 2008: 82). It targets youth of 11 to 18 years of age who have issues with delinquency, substance abuse or violence. It seeks to improve the functioning of the family unit through enhancing problem-solving skills and emotional connections within the family as well as strengthening family structure (Greenwood and Edwards 2011: 376).

Multidimensional treatment foster care (MTFC)

This program differs from MST and FFT in that the youth being treated do not live at home but in a therapeutic living environment with foster parents. Families from a community are trained to provide structure and behavior management to youth with serious delinquency issues. After completing pre-service training MTFC parents attend a weekly group meeting run by a case manager where ongoing supervision is provided. As well, family therapy is provided to the youths' families. The cost for each youth is about US$2,000 (Guerra et al. 2008: 83).

Aggression replacement training (ART)

This program is targeted at aggressive offenders and stresses acquisition of skills designed to teach a broad curriculum of pro-social behavior, impulse and anger control training intended to empower youth to modify their own anger responsiveness, and moral reasoning training, to help motivate youth to employ the skills learned in the other components. The program runs for 30 hours and is administered with groups of offenders three times a week for 10 weeks. The cost is about US$750 for each youth. It can be administered to youth in custody and has been evaluated as showing some positive effects (Goldstein and Glick 1994: 9; Guerra et al. 2008: 83).

Ineffective interventions: control-oriented programs

Programs that attempt to impose greater controls on offenders are a product of the "get tough on crime" movement along with the massively increased use of incarceration. These kinds of programs cannot claim to be founded on social-scientific principles based on empirical knowledge. Rather, they are based on "commonsense" understandings of what is thought to be effective, primarily the belief that intensifying the pain of punishment and deepening surveillance will turn offenders away from crime (Cullen and Gendreau 2000: 154).

Scared straight

Scared straight programs began in the 1970s and involve bringing youth considered at risk for delinquency to prisons to meet with prisoners so as to be exposed to graphic stories of crime and prison life. Later programs were less confrontational and functioned more as an experience of prison in an educational sense. The program rationale is that experience of prison will shock participants and deter them from delinquent acts. These programs remain popular worldwide. Shock programs of this nature have no effect on offending and results show that some participants actually do worse in such programs compared to youth on probation who did not participate in them (Guerra and Leaf 2008: 117). After reviewing a number of scared straight programs, Finckenauer (1982: 169) suggested that they could actually be harmful to participants because:

> the project actually sets in motion a "delinquency fulfilling prophecy" in which it increases rather than decreases the chances of juvenile delinquency. . . . The project may romanticize the Lifers – and by extension other prison inmates – in young, impressionable minds.

Boot camps

Boot camps draw heavily on a military model and privilege notions of discipline, routine and the ethos of the military. In many ways, boot camps can be regarded as extensions of forms of discipline once found in the home but now considered out of line with modern parenting practice. Consequently, they reflect what are perceived to be traditional disciplinary practices that are no longer condoned in society. As Welch (1999: 113) notes, such camps are also "normalizing institutions" in the sense that they are intended to bring persons in line with a set of standards considered to be "normal." Welch suggests that they are directed at satisfying middle-class attitudes of appropriate punishment, the middle class having lost faith in the efficacy of incarceration (p. 118). The thinking behind such programs is that offenders are antisocial because they lack character, and that breaking them down and then building them up through boot camp techniques will remedy their defects. This folk understanding of criminal conduct has proven to be totally misconceived (Cullen and Gendreau 2000: 154). Several evaluations have shown that boot camps, especially the mainstream military-style programs, do not affect rates of recidivism. More recent programs that have added treatment components still have no effect on recidivism (Guerra and Leaf 2008: 117; MacKenzie et al. 2001: 578).

WHY WE SHOULD GIVE BOOT CAMPS THE BOOT

On December 8, 1999 the *Chicago Tribune* reported that the FBI had started an investigation into a girls' boot camp operated out of the South Dakota State Training School. The investigation resulted from the death of Gina Score, aged 14, who died during a forced long-distance run only two days after entering the boot camp. She had been adjudicated delinquent for shoplifting. The leader of the Democratic minority in the South Dakota House commented on boot camps: "In general the concept lends itself to abuse. Basically the boot camp concept attempts to turn troubled children around by pushing them around. It doesn't make sense to me." However, the South Dakota secretary of corrections said of boot camps: "It's not intended to be a pleasant experience."

At the Arizona Boys' Ranch, also a boot camp for juveniles, a 16-year-old boy from Sacramento died in 1998 as a result of punishment. His delinquent act was stealing a car and then absconding while in custody.

In a one-day boot camp in Brazoria County, Texas, physical exercise was removed from the punishment regime after a 15-year-old boy was hospitalized for six days following a collapse from heat stroke.

Source: Adapted from Page, Clarence. 1999. "Why Should We Give Boot Camps the Boot?" *Chicago Tribune*, December 8. http://articles.chicago tribune.com/1999-12-08/news/9912080053_1_boot-camps-arizona-boys-ranch-juvenile-facilities.

Wilderness programs

In these programs youth take part in physically challenging activities, such as backpacking or rock climbing, usually in an outdoor environment. Programs vary widely in terms of settings, types of physical activities and therapeutic goals, but their treatment concepts are grounded in the field of experiential education – learning by doing. According to Guerra and others (2008: 88), these programs lack support in evaluations and are now considered to fall within the "doesn't work" category. However, there is evidence that they can be effective if they include a well-structured therapy component. Wilson and Lipsey (2000: 1) conducted a meta-analysis of 28 such programs involving some 300 youth aged between 13 and 15. Most programs exceeded two weeks in length and most contained no therapeutic elements. They concluded that such programs did, to some extent, prove effective in reducing delinquent behaviors, especially where programs contained a therapeutic element. Wilson and Lipsey caution, however, that more evidence needs to be collected before any conclusive statements can be made about the effects of these programs.

Intensive supervision, probation or parole (ISP)

The rationale for this type of intensive supervision program on probation or on parole was that offenders could be subjected to rigorous punishment in the community as a means of reducing prison overcrowding (Cullen and Gendreau 2000). These programs involve strict and close supervision of probationers and parolees, thereby increasing the chances that any violations would be detected. This, it is thought, will discourage re-offending (p. 156). Random drug testing, electronic monitoring and house arrest are also features of these programs. While there is some evidence that ISP which included actual treatment did result in some reductions in recidivism, overall, studies indicate that they did not achieve any success (p. 156).

Understanding culture: culturally specific programming

According to Guerra and others (2008: 94), there is an absence of research examining the effectiveness of interventions for youth with different ethnicities. Nevertheless, there is a broad consensus among practitioners that treatment programs should be culturally appropriate. Notwithstanding, most studies of treatment of delinquent youth treat them as homogeneous groups and ignore their cultural diversity and distinct cultural worldviews. Evidence from family therapy research shows that programs sensitive to cultural difference will be more effective and that youth treatment programs need to incorporate culturally specific approaches to assist in increasing treatment engagement (McGoldrick et al. 1996; Santisteban and Szapocznik 1994). As well, a number of studies have revealed the operation of cultural difference in psychological testing. For example, Beauvais (2000: 128) notes that "the conditions, definitions and descriptions of what constitute a 'normal' mental status are highly saturated with cultural meaning." Duran and Duran (1995) explain that most attempts to integrate culture into treatment programs make use of traditional ceremonies and healers to build pride and self-esteem.

In an extensive exploration of the place of culture in treating Alaskan Native juveniles in a juvenile institution in Fairbanks, Alaska, Banks (2009: 41–61) explains how Alaskan Native cultures define themselves by reference to the subsistence lifestyle that many continue to experience in small communities in Alaska, and "to social practices that reinforce cultural identity through an emphasis on unity, equality, cooperation and sharing goods, especially those obtained through hunting and trapping" (pp. 41–42). Cultural characteristics associated with Alaskan Natives include less focus on verbal communication in interpersonal relations. For example, unlike Western cultures, Alaskan Native parents do not engage in lengthy dialogues with their children and they express intimacy in modulated forms such as through a simple smile or nod of the head, or through a father showing his son how to build a sledge. There are few parental pressures for success, and the notion that it is the responsibility of the parents when children turn out bad has no place in this culture. Rather, children are allowed to develop according to their natures. Appropriate social behaviors learned through modeling include conflict avoidance, emotional inhibition and a reliance on joking and humor to diffuse tense situations. Culturally specific child-rearing practices include encouraging a child to channel anger into amusement and fear into laughter. For example, adults will laugh when a child becomes angry or frightened to help that child learn how to channel such emotions.

Banks (2009) notes that these behaviors become salient in the environment of a cognitive-behavioral treatment program based on Western psychological models and applied to Alaskan Native youth in the Fairbanks Youth Facility, Alaska. Specifically, Banks points to the reactions of the Alaskan Native juveniles to correction and to group therapy as instances of conflicting cultures. For example, the reliance on intensive verbalization of issues in cognitive treatment is at odds with the Alaskan Native propensity to communicate nonverbally. Juveniles experience severe homesickness, and, being accustomed to an expansive outdoor environment, react adversely to the closed environment of incarceration (p. 94). Staff tend to regard Alaskan Native silence and passivity in group therapy as a form of resistance to their power and authority. Structure and rules are alien to many Alaskan Native juveniles because at home they enjoy a high level of autonomy, but staff continue to read cultural specificity as resistance. The institutional psychologist pointed out that tests applied to all residents at the facility tend to "artificially lower the IQ of Native Alaskan youth" (p. 220) and explained that Alaskan Native youth find the complexity of the treatment process challenging:

Like most Native youth he will get lost in the wording of many of the workbooks and not necessarily bring it to the counselor's attention. The helper should not make assumptions about his abilities which would prevent "A" from being successful by using his most effective skills.

(Banks 2009: 220–221)

One psychological report in a youth's file usefully illuminates the issue of cultural difference:

Recommends – substance abuse – anger management – all staff approach him with an understanding of his ethnicity – this is essential and to not provide him with culturally sensitive help will only serve to deepen his problem. He does not relate to the typical norms established for Caucasian youth.

(Banks 2009: 223)

Staff at the institution had little or no training in cultural sensitivity, and were often indifferent and sometimes wholly resistant to cultural difference. Banks argues that cultural differences prevail within the institution and must be addressed because simply administering Western models of psychological treatment that assume a common set of cultural experiences and values among the detainees will be ineffective in addressing the needs of incarcerated Alaskan Native youth.

Cultural difference is also a critical factor in developing prevention programs (Valentine et al. 1998: 53) but little is known about what works for minority youth (Greene and Penn 2006: 230). For example, Afrocentric programs are administered by schools and community organizations including the so-called "rites of passage" programs intended to help African American youth identify with their cultural heritage. Such programs have proven effective in addressing drug and alcohol abuse. One such program is targeted at attitudes and beliefs of incarcerated African American males concerning masculinity and may be appropriate for black youth because it seeks to build resilience and therefore coping strategies in difficult environments (Greene and Penn 2006: 232).

Juvenile drug courts

Juvenile drug courts (JDCs) are an adaptation of the specialist adult drug court model widely regarded as effective. They aim to provide the comprehensive services needed to treat substance-involved juvenile offenders. Studies show that risk and protective factors relevant to substance abuse in adults mirror those relevant to delinquency. This suggests that targeting

youth, crime and justice

substance abusers for JDC treatment is an appropriate strategy (Belenko and Logan 2003: 197).

In 2008 the police arrested 180,100 juveniles for drug abuse violations and 162,400 for alcohol violations (DUI, liquor laws and drunkenness) (Puzzanchera 2009: 3). The extent of substance abuse among juvenile offenders measured by the 1997 Arrestee Drug Abuse Monitoring Program indicated that 35 percent of all arrested and detained youth reported "alcohol involvement," 70 percent reported "drug involvement" and 75 percent reported either drug or alcohol involvement (Belenko and Logan 2003: 190). In light of the high rates of substance abuse among juvenile offenders, effective treatment programs are essential. Standard adjudication processes in juvenile courts fail to provide these services and have prompted the integration of drug treatment into the criminal courts, as had first occurred with adult drug abuse cases in the mid-1980s.

The first JDC began operations in Key West in October 1993 (Belenko and Logan 2003: 191). As of June 30, 2010 there were 483 JDCs (Drugs Court 2010). Generally, when compared to traditional juvenile court adjudication processes, JDCs provide benefits in the form of:

- a focus on the individual offender;
- the capacity to address issues in treatment programs;
- a high level of supervision and monitoring;
- provision of appropriate services in the community;
- better informed judges.

JDCs provide judicial monitoring of treatment programs,[1] drug testing and services for drug-involved offenders within structured programs that contain sanctions for non-compliance and rewards[2] for compliance. The drug court model typically comprises: identification of potential participants as soon as possible following arrest; specific program requirements administered by the Judge of the JDC; mandatory periodic drug testing; a series of graduated sanctions and rewards based on performance; regular status hearings to monitor progress and compliance with program requirements; a non-adversarial approach; a team approach within the justice system; and, following successful completion of the program, dismissal of the case against the juvenile (Belenko and Logan 2003: 190–191). Most JDCs are brought into play post-adjudication after a juvenile has been adjudicated delinquent. This model is preferred over a diversion model because, according to the U.S. Department of Justice (2001: 5), "the court has more authority after guilt has been established and more options are available in the event the youth fails to complete the program."

A typical drug treatment program associated with a JDC is the Marin County Juvenile Drug Court Program, Marin County, California.

THE MARIN COUNTY JUVENILE DRUG COURT PROGRAM

This is an intensive, court-supervised treatment program for youth aged between 14 and 18 who are facing non-violent criminal charges and have a history of drug or alcohol use. The Program is administered by the Drug Court Team comprising the Judge, Deputy Probation Officer, Deputy District Attorney, Deputy Public Defender and treatment providers. Regular meetings are held with a probation officer and regular court appearances are required. A participating youth is required to undergo Urinary Analysis (UA) tests and treatment, and if the treatment program is completed successfully, all charges are dismissed.

Treatment is for a minimum period of nine months. If a participant behaves inappropriately, graduated sanctions may be imposed and if behavior is appropriate or extraordinary, rewards can be earned.

Parents must be willing to participate in the program. Participants are required to express a willingness to change. They must acknowledge that their drug and alcohol use is causing problems, and commit to leading a clean and honest life. Participants are asked to stop blaming others for their problems and to take responsibility for their choices.

The program is designed in three phases as follows:

Phase I (approximately three to four months)
The focus of Phase I is to begin treatment and to recognize responsibility to others. You will participate in a treatment plan. You will be tested frequently for use.

Focus: Treatment, accountability to others, recovery

Components:
- School attendance – no unexcused absences or tardies
- Multiple weekly drug tests
- Two weekly 12-step meetings (Alcoholics Anonymous (AA), Narcotics Anonymous (NA), Meth Anonymous (MA))
- Exercise three times weekly for 30 minutes
- Create drug court journal
- Weekly court appearances and homework
- Regular contact with Probation Officer
- Write an autobiography (1,000 words).

Promotion to Phase II will be determined by your participation and task accomplishments during Phase I and must be preceded by a minimum of two weeks without any sanctions for violation of your Drug Court Orders.

Phase II (approximately three to four months)

The focus of Phase II is to maintain treatment and recognize responsibility to others. You will be required to find a sponsor, complete 25 hours of community service, appear in court as directed, give regular UAs, attend counseling meetings and attend school or maintain employment as directed.

Focus: Maintenance of treatment, community service work

Components:

   School attendance – no unexcused absences or tardies
   Regular exercise, maintain journal, complete drug court homework
   Exercise increased responsibility
■ Drug counseling – no unexcused absences
   Drug testing – as directed
   Two weekly 12-step meetings (AA, NA, MA)
   Court appearances – generally weekly or as directed
   Contact with Probation Officer as directed
   Community service – complete 25 hours of community service work prior to promotion to Phase III.

Promotion to Phase III will be determined by your participation and task accomplishment during Phase I, and must be preceded by a minimum of two weeks without any sanctions for violation of your Drug Court Orders.

Phase III (approximately three to four months)

The focus of Phase III is continued recovery and responsibility to self and others. You are expected to recognize responsibility to yourself, to your family and to the community. Remember that during any phase of the juvenile drug court, you can request specific goals to be included in your contract. This may be an appropriate time to consider educational and vocational goals.

Focus: Maintenance of recovery, complete treatment, aftercare plan, accountability, job development and career counseling, leadership

Components:
- School attendance – no unexcused absences or tardies
- Regular exercise, maintain journal, complete drug court homework
- Exercise increased responsibility
- Drug counseling – no unexcused absences
- Drug testing – as directed
- Two weekly 12-step meetings (AA, NA, MA)
- Court appearances – generally every other week or as directed
- Contact with Probation Officer as directed
- Act as a mentor to Phase I participants as directed
- Education plan/job training.

Source: Adapted from http:www.marincourt.org/PDF/JuvDrCtHandbook.
pdf

Many JDCs simply follow the adult court model and therefore fail to take into account the special needs of juveniles such as the impact that peers and the family environment have on substance abuse, or of developmental differences concerning the motivation for abuse, different patterns of use and different treatment needs (Belenko and Logan 2003: 191, 195). JDCs still lack gender and culturally specific treatment programs. As well, few JDC programs include any aftercare component so that upon completion of treatment, there is an abrupt cessation of support. This may mean a relapse because a youth is unable to be completely responsible or may live in an environment where substance abuse and/or criminality are accepted behaviors (p. 202).

Evaluating drug courts

In terms of evaluating JDC treatment programs, JDCs are still relatively new and studies are continuing. In general, drug courts have tended to produce good treatment retention rates and reduced rates of recidivism in the year following treatment. Drug courts, both adult and juvenile, continue to be established regardless of the lack of robust empirical studies showing positive outcomes from treatment (Belenko and Logan 2003: 202). After reviewing assessments of drug court treatment programs, Wilson and others (2006: 462) suggest that despite the popularity of drug courts and belief in their effectiveness, "the evidence justifying these beliefs requires careful scrutiny." One excellent study of adult drug courts by Gottfredson and colleagues (2003) reported a very large difference in any re-arrest between the drug court and comparison conditions 24 months after admission into the program. Wilson and others (2006: 475) argue that the large variations in effects across evaluation studies of drug courts suggest that some courts are effective and others not. Their findings, based on a meta-analysis, were that "drug offenders participating in a drug court are less likely to re-offend than similar offenders sentenced to traditional correctional options, such as probation" (p. 475). They found a reduction in overall offending of about 26 percent across all studies and 14 percent for two high-quality randomized studies.

A three-year study of a JDC in Arizona which compared juveniles assigned to a drug program to another group assigned to probation found that drug court participants were less likely to recidivate than youth in the comparison group (Rodriguez and Webb 2004: 292). The authors suggest that future research should address how youth in treatment programs regard these programs because this would help generate data on the issue of whether drug courts keep offenders drug free as well as reducing recidivism. It would also generate information of a more qualitative and subjective nature about the challenges faced in the experience of actually undergoing a drug court program (p. 310).

Reports of JDCs tend to show that outcomes for participants vary between different programs, with programs that fail to offer evidence-based treatment faring poorly similar to programs that fail to include family members in the treatment, or make no real effort to customize programs according to the developmental level of the offender (Marlowe 2010).

Juvenile drug courts: operations and performance

Butts and Roman (2004: 11) point out that between 1990 and 1997 the arrest rate for juvenile drug violations more than doubled (a 145 percent increase) and that in 1985 juvenile courts dealt with about 74,000 drug cases, but this had risen to 198,500 by 2000. Following this period of growth during the 1990s, the juvenile arrest rate for drug abuse violations declined after 1997 (by 28 percent between 1997 and 2008) (Puzzanchera 2009: 10). Adult drug courts originated as a strategy for coping with huge increases in drug arrests of adults and were spurred on by the availability of federal funding. They became a social movement boosted by private organizations which included treatment providers and specialist drug practitioners (Butts and Roman 2004: 52). Similar workload concerns and rationales drove the development of JDCs, with the first being created in 1995.

JDCs are individualized courts but tend to conform to a fairly standard model. A youth must qualify to actually enter a JDC program. This raises questions about "What are the criteria required to be satisfied to be accepted into a JDC?" and "Is the program intended for youthful drug addicts or, if not, what level of abuse is required to qualify for treatment?" In practice, qualifying criteria tend to be vague, such as those seen in the Marin County JDC example above requiring only a history of drug or alcohol abuse (Butts and Roman 2004: 17).

In their survey of JDCs, Butts and Roman (2004: 16) routinely asked JDC officials about youth drug use and received a consensus view that 80 to 90 percent of youth participating in JDC programs were non-dependent users of alcohol and marijuana. The lowest estimate they received of the non-dependent category of participants was 75 percent. As they point out, a JDC system intended to intervene with all youth at the first sign of drug abuse is simply unaffordable and unworkable given the fact that the average JDC handles only 40 to 50 cases each year and that 15 percent of youth between the ages of 14 and 17 would be expected to have used an illegal drug at least once in the past 30 days (Butts and Roman 2004: 17).

Eligibility is therefore a key question for a JDC and it is important to understand that JDCs, unlike adult drug courts, are very rarely involved with juveniles addicted to drugs or alcohol because there are very few such youth (Butts and Roman 2004: 142). The breadth of the JDC mission applies very broad intervention criteria and therefore raises concerns about the net-widening and labeling effects of JDCs. Local considerations seem to determine the breadth of the JDC mandate – is it to focus on youth with serious or severe substance abuse problems or on youth who are just starting to use alcohol or drugs?

JDC judges have very broad discretionary powers within the parameters of the JDC program. The U.S. Department of Justice (2001: 5) describes the role of the judge in the following terms:

> The judge is the key leader for the juvenile drug court program. The judge oversees not only the juvenile's performance and that of his or her family, but also the coordination and delivery of treatment and other core services.

As explained by Wilson and others (2006: 461), the power of the judge is utilized to compel treatment compliance. Sanford and Arrigo (2005: 249) note that reports indicate that judges are regarded as "pivotal figures" and that, according to one study of drug courts in Hawaii, "the judicial discretion of the drug court judge is unprecedented within contemporary criminal justice policy settings." In a study of a California JDC, Paik (2011: 21) suggests that the judges become "quasi social workers" but must rely on the drug treatment counselor for technical expertise. Nolan's study of adult drug courts reveals how drug court judges were themselves instrumental in launching drug courts as a social movement. While they lack proper theoretical underpinnings, Nolan argues that drug courts give expression to judicial yearnings to do "therapeutic jurisprudence" (2001: 185).

In a detailed and insightful study of performance, process and decision making in a California JDC, Paik (2011) reveals how collective JDC decisions blend therapy with punishment and reject law in favor of expediency by ignoring legal standards of evidence. Above all, Paik argues that the JDC functions as an instrument of intense social control for those who enter the drug program. In this Californian JDC, process and performance are far from flawless. Members of the treatment team seem to invert and subvert the supposed certainties of the law with bureaucratic maneuvers, acts of gender and racial bias, and constant reversals of the process. Thus, for example, a positive urine test does not always invoke a sanction but a negative test may do so;[3] a youth does not have an overall treatment plan but the treatment team makes its decisions based on constantly evolving knowledge of a youth's activity, always with the aim of assessing his or her "workability"; that is, "how they can most effectively persuade youth to comply with the court's expectations" (p. 177). Youth can spend many months in custody while undertaking treatment even though the program is founded on a sentence of probation. Notably, the treatment discourse of personal accountability means that youth are sanctioned for events over which they have no control and the treatment team focuses more on updates on a participant's compliance rather than on actual treatment.

The complexities of the treatment team's decision-making processes reveal how this model of specialist court reinvents the original model of the juvenile court and how youth lose legal protection as they did under the pre-Gault model. Many decisions are arrived at informally and are never reduced to writing while the backstage discussions become the therapeutic master discourse of the JDC. This poses problems for defense lawyers who are told to discard their normal role of protecting their client's rights in favor of a therapeutic approach to problem solving. Describing an adult drug court, Nolan observes (2001: 71):

> When during one drug court session a defense attorney objected to the judge's therapeutically styled questioning of a client, the judge leaned back, shook his head and smiled with knowing irritation, as though accustomed to dealing with defense attorneys untrained in the peculiarities of the drug court format.

The rigors of JDC social control of youth may adversely affect the lives of parents and families as, for example, when youth are sanctioned with home supervision for lack of accountability (they cannot even step outside the house) for which their parents are charged a daily fee.[4] Parents complain that the JDC feels like a punishment imposed on them (Paik 2011: 124). The youth express their frustration as follows:

> "They make you do so much, and if you don't do it, then you get in trouble really fast. . . . You would think that you only get in trouble if you test dirty, but they get you in trouble if you don't do all these other things, even if you're staying clean. . . . Like if you miss school sometimes. . . . But it's like, if I'm staying clean, then what's the big deal?" (Michaela, a white seventeen year old in the east court).
>
> (Paik 2011: 41)

As Whiteacre notes (2008: 59), the JDC is often a more onerous alternative than traditional probation; a point that underscores why they are not "soft on crime." Paik argues that the intensity of the surveillance and control exercised by the drug court overwhelms the treatment objective so much so that the JDC in effect administers surveillance disguised as treatment, and that a JDC is constituted as a total institution (Goffman 1961), a "panopticon without walls" (Paik 2011: 7).

Graduating from this California program is a challenge because a youth must have accumulated 365 consecutive sober days in addition to completing all other program requirements such as school attendance. When a youth tests positive for drugs, the sober day count is reset to zero even if he or she has accumulated 364 days. According to one participant, Rita, a white 15-year-old, being continually punished for non-compliance was counter-productive:

> "It's too hard, you get locked up for everything, and that's stupid. Let's get locked up for this long and come out and do the same shit, and then get locked up again. . . . For me, getting locked up makes me want to use. So, the more they lock me up, the more I'm going to probably use, because that makes me want to use. It's not helping us, it's just making shit worse. . . . Locking you in a cell doesn't do nothing. . . . It makes it very unhealthy in there, it causes depression, doesn't help nothing."
>
> (Paik 2011: 71)

Many youth saw the JDC as simply monitoring their behaviors. As one 17-year-old Latino put it, "they emphasize a lot on the bad things. . . . They're trying to catch you," and another observed, "They're basically trying to whip us into shape" (Paik 2011: 70). In his study of a JDC, Whiteacre (2008: 41) observes that youth who deny they have a problem with drug use are deemed by treatment staff to be "in denial" even when their use is only occasional. For treatment staff, the only salient fact is that cannabis is a prohibited substance and they equate any use of it as abuse and as a gateway to addiction (p. 41). As an example, one youth explained to his counselor that he drank alcohol every couple of months and, when asked if he experienced any problems from drinking, responded that he had suffered a hangover. His counselor told him he was an alcoholic:

> "Because I had a problem from the time I drank and I continued to drink later on, whether it's too much, then by definition I was an alcoholic. . . . When I said no, I wasn't an alcoholic she'd say that I was in denial."
> (Whiteacre 2008: 41)

Drug testing is a key element of the treatment, but Paik (2011: 90, 91) has observed:

- Tests are subject to interpretation according to the youth's broader pattern of drug use.
- Tests are subject to information the team receives, for example, from a parent to whom a youth who tested negative admitted taking drugs.
- Tests are subject to whether the team believes the youth deliberately diluted a test to deceive the court (test results cannot be verified if they are diluted by large fluid intakes).

Thus, in practice all drug test results are highly contingent. The dominance of drug tests is confirmed by a staff member's comments to Whiteacre (2008: 83):

> "The drug tests to me are phenomenally important. . . . [They are] the foundation. . . . If I had nothing else but a drug test each week I would be happy."

Thus, the drug test has become almost a form of treatment and constitutes an end in itself.

The treatment team frequently sanction youth for activities that would not be criminal outside the JDC, such as being late for school. As Paik notes (2011: 4), the reality of the treatment process is that the treatment outcome is an aggregation of team decisions that classify trivial actions (such as being late for school, or stepping outside the home while on home supervision or disrespecting parents) as compliant or non-compliant. However, incidents of non-compliance are not merely bad behavior – they constitute breaches of probation. Moreover, the focus of the JDC on accountability and on changing bad behaviors ignores any structural factors that continually impact choices about engaging in bad behaviors. This is especially the case in relation to parents. While the team expect active support from parents, this contradicts the personal accountability message given to youth in the program (p. 103). Some parents see the program as a form of social control beyond the terms of the treatment program. As an example, Hector's mother, a 38-year-old Latina, clearly sees the program as disciplinary leverage over her son:

> MOTHER: Right now . . . I was mad at Hector because he did not want to help me fix the bed. He said that he needed to take a shower. I told him that he just took a shower. . . . I told him, "I need your help, Junior, Please help me." . . . He knows that if he raises his voice, I'll call like this. I immediately call his probation and let him know that Hector is misbehaving. I cannot tolerate that he yell at me . . .
>
> LESLIE: And do you feel that through the program you can control him?
>
> MOTHER: I have Hector here [signals to the palm of her hand].
>
> (Paik 2011: 107)

Accountability is key in JDC programs and, as Whiteacre observes (2008: 69), the traditional juvenile court was criticized for "neglecting to impose accountability" for crimes. When the Department of Justice created a Block Grants Program in 1998, it explained "accountability" in the following terms:

> Accountability means that each offender is assured of facing individualized consequences through which he or she is made aware of and held responsible for the loss, damage or injury perpetrated on the victim. . . . Accountability involves a new set of expectations and demands for the juvenile justice system.
>
> (Flores and Thompson 2007: 1)

In the JDC, accountability is achieved by punishing youth for non-compliance when they fail to take advantage of the resources allocated to them, and above all, for failing to value and validate the program and its treatment staff (Whiteacre 2008: 74).

In terms of gender, the parents of female participants police them more zealously and are more likely to tell treatment staff when their daughter violates curfew or has inappropriate boyfriends (Paik 2011). Treatment staff take a gendered approach when a girl becomes pregnant by immediately transferring her out of the JDC to a probation program for expectant mothers in the belief that a pregnant youth would not be able to fulfill the treatment program (p. 5). Expectant fathers, on the other hand, were considered to have an additional motivation to stay off drugs.

The treatment team applies two categories associated with race and class – "mentally ill" and "gang involved" (Paik 2011). When a youth is judged mentally ill he or she is not held responsible for bad behaviors; however, only the white middle-class parents had the resources to secure a speedy diagnosis of mental illness. Other youth had to be referred to the local mental health authority for an assessment – a process that could take many months. This meant that white youth escaped sanctions for non-compliance due to mental illness while others did not. Race was also a factor in relation to gangs. Latino youth gangs were regarded as a more serious threat while a white youth's gang membership would be ignored or judged irrelevant (p. 51).

Serious limitations affect the JDC model described by Paik. For example, the treatment team is constrained by the availability of other programs where it can place youth to sanction them and by the rule that time spent in custody during treatment may not exceed the maximum sentence the youth could have received as a disposition for the original offense (Paik 2011: 135). Consequently, each instance of custody draws on the bank of custodial time, and when that time runs out the team can no longer impose any further custodial sanctions.

Nolan (2001: 179) argues that the adult drug courts have discarded common law notions of justice and have instead adopted the "therapeutic ideal," where the self takes precedence over social purposes or the interests of others, and emotivism dominates the court room discourse. Expressing one's emotions is equated to truth while keeping silent is therefore seen as a form of dishonesty. In the adult drug court, judges impose punishment for violation of treatment agreements but relabel sanctions as "providing help" while at the same time asserting that "treatment regimes are not punishment, but the restructuring of the defendant's lifestyle" (p. 195). In this way, judges deny that they are imposing punishment because punishment is reframed as treatment, and the dominance of the therapeutic ideal renders debate over traditional forms of punishment irrelevant. Intermingling punishment and treatment characterizes both adult and juvenile drug courts. Given this blurring of the boundaries between treatment and punishment, drug courts appeal to both conservative and liberal ideologies (Whiteacre 2008: 50).

This exploration of adult drug courts and JDCs has revealed the complexities associated with the management and performance of these institutions as well as the problematic status of actual treatment programs when assessing "what works." Nevertheless, drug courts have taken hold of the public imagination; they enjoy widespread political support and flourish under the technologies of the therapeutic ideal. Specialist problem-solving courts may lack adequate theoretical foundations but populist notions of accountability and the supposed capacity of these courts to change behaviors (and even to transform offenders), together with the now vast array of specialist services, will continue to ensure their existence.

Restorative justice (RJ)

While proponents of RJ claim it is an effective form of punishment (see Chapter 8) Levrant and others (1999: 18) caution that RJ does not share the features of programs that have been shown to achieve a reduction in recidivism; the so-called *principles of effective intervention*. They argue that the primary criterion for matching sanctions to offenders is the harm caused by the crime and not the seriousness of the offense. This approach, then, violates the principle of risk because the needs of high-risk offenders may not be properly addressed in RJ programs and typically programs treat low-risk non-violent offenders. Given that studies show the need for intensive services for high-risk offenders, it remains unclear how limited RJ sessions can provide the required range and depth of treatment that is required. Levrant and others (1999: 20) suggest that in terms of criminogenic needs, RJ addresses only empathy and is largely concerned with victim restoration. Consequently, in their view, RJ fails to meet the principles of effective intervention because it lacks any behavioral framework (p. 20).

Compared to behaviorally oriented programs, RJ has not been shown to have a significant effect on recidivism. More recently, Bergseth and Bouffard (2007: 433) note that while numerous evaluations of RJ programs have shown high levels of victim and offender satisfaction and compliance with restorative agreements, "evidence regarding the impact on recidivism is less consistent" (p. 434). Some meta-analyses demonstrate positive effects of RJ programming but others do not. To an extent, this reflects weak methodology in evaluations. However, Bergseth and Bouffard's study found that juveniles referred for RJ fared better than those undergoing traditional juvenile court processing on a number of outcome measures – prevalence, number of later police contacts, seriousness of later behavior, time to first re-offense and so on (p. 448).

In another evaluation Rodriguez (2007: 355) found that juveniles who participated in a RJ diversion program had slightly lower rates of recidivism after 24 months than juveniles who formed a comparison group. As well, girls and offenders with minor criminal histories showed the greatest benefits from such programming. The author stresses that these results relate to a particular RJ program and are not generalizable to all RJ programs, and that more research is needed to establish how effective RJ can be in reducing crime for girls (p. 372).

Similar cautionary language is used by Latimer and others (2005: 138). They conducted a meta-analysis of RJ programs and found that RJ was a more effective method of decreasing offender recidivism when compared to traditional juvenile justice responses. The authors point out, however, that the results are mitigated by a self-selection bias because RJ is by its very nature a voluntary process. Consequently, the members of the offender treatment group choose to participate and therefore may be more motivated than a control group. Self-selection continues therefore to be an inherent problem in RJ studies. As well, Latimer and others (2005) argue that the RJ outcomes in terms of recidivism do not satisfy the principles of effective intervention (Levrant et al. 1999), even though RJ programs may "yield reductions in recidivism compared to more traditional criminal justice responses to crime, they did not have nearly as strong an impact on reoffending as psychologically informed treatment" (Latimer et al. 2005: 140). Latimer and others therefore suggest that employing both restorative and rehabilitative components would be a valuable exercise.

Recap

Early delinquency prevention targets risk factors identified in youth and adolescence and applies mainly psychological solutions that aim to transform antisocial tendencies into pro-social drives. This positivist approach, based on the science of longitudinal studies, aims to discipline impulses in youth that are judged non-normative and therefore potentially dangerous to society. A few treatment and rehabilitation programs claim success in eradicating delinquency and recidivism. The principles of effective intervention for treatment programs are predisposed toward psychological approaches and claim that evidence-based cognitive-behavioral and multimodal programs based on social learning that use more than one mode of treatment to target an offender's multiple problems are the most successful interventions.

Despite the efforts of researchers and practitioners to apply science and empirical evidence to prevention and treatment, the general public, policy makers and legislators continue to demonstrate an almost visceral urge to support populist programs that rely heavily on military-style discipline and "tough love." The public consciousness is that imposing order and discipline should be effected through expressive modes of treatment that satisfy instinctive concerns about "building character," even though cognitive programs also seek to discipline those same delinquent impulses.

Cultural differences and gender issues remain problematic and under-researched in the cognitive-behavioral environment as do judicial yearnings to do "therapeutic jurisprudence" in the JDC. The extensive exploration of the operations of the JDC in this chapter reveals how compliance with the institutional regime often matters more than the actual treatment, and how the JDC negatively impacts the lives of participants' families and disregards legal protections by merging treatment and punishment.

RJ fails the tests set by the principles of effective intervention but may nevertheless be a viable alternative if combined with cognitive programs. To the extent that RJ is an expressive mode of treatment through practices such as conferencing, it may, if combined with psychological forms of treatment, satisfy the treatment and punishment nexus favored by practitioners and researchers as well as by the general public.

Notes

1   The U.S. Department of Justice (2001: 9) suggests that some JDCs have been adopting the MST approach to treatment.
2   The U.S. Department of Justice (2001: 6) suggests that JDCs generally offer the following types of rewards: "(1) promotion to a subsequent program phase; (2) award of a gift voucher or a ticket to a local sports or other event contributed by local merchants, and/or (3) presentation of a certificate or other token acknowledging the participant's accomplishments. The praise of the judge is, as always, of immeasurable motivational value."
3   According to Paik (2011: 78–79), time sensitivity is the main problem with drug testing. Metamphetamine and alcohol traces disappear from urine between 24 and 48 hours after use but marijuana can remain in the system for up to ten days. A patch overcomes the sensitivity issue because it is a continuous measure of drug use but after being on a youth's skin for at least a week, a further two weeks is required for it to be analyzed. This means treatment staff cannot respond immediately to possible drug use.
4   Paik (2011: 115) reports that each time a youth appears in court the parents are charged a fee. Most sanctions also involve a fee, for example, home supervision at US$35 a day, juvenile hall US$37 a day, and each offense carries a restitution fine of a minimum of US$50. Amounts owed to the court by parents ranged from US$200 to almost US$30,000.

References

Banks, Cyndi. 2009. *Alaska Native Juveniles in Detention: A Qualitative Study of Treatment and Resistance.* Lewiston, NY: The Edwin Mellen Press.

Beauvais, F. 2000. "Indian Adolescence: Opportunity and Challenge." In R. Montemayor, G. Adams and T. Gullota (eds) *Adolescent Diversity in Ethnic, Economic, and Cultural Contexts.* Thousand Oaks, CA: Sage, pp. 110–140.

Belenko, Steven and T.K. Logan. 2003. "Delivering More Effective Treatment to Adolescents: Improving the Juvenile Drug Court Model." *Journal of Substance Abuse Treatment* 25: 189–211.

Bergseth, Kathleen J. and Jeffrey Bouffard. 2007. "The Long-term Impact of

Restorative Justice Programming for Juvenile Offenders." *Journal of Criminal Justice* 35: 433–451.

Blomberg, T.G. and K. Lucken. 2000. *American Penology: A History of Control*. New York: Aldine de Gruyter.

Butts, Jeffrey A. and John Roman. 2004. *Juvenile Drug Courts and Teen Substance Abuse*. Washington D.C.: The Urban Institute Press.

Cullen, Francis T. and Paul Gendreau. 2000. "Assessing Correctional Rehabilitation: Policy, Practice, and Prospects." *Criminal Justice* 3: 109–175.

Dowden, Craig and D.A. Andrews. 2004. "The Importance of Staff Practice in Delivering Effective Correctional Treatment: A Meta-analytic Review of Core Correctional Practice." *International Journal of Offender Therapy and Comparative Criminology* 48: 203–214.

Drug Courts. 2010. Washington D.C.: U.S. Department of Justice, Office of Justice Programs, National Institute of Justice.

Duran, E. and B. Duran. 1995. *Native American Postcolonial Psychology*. Albany, NY: State University of New York.

Elliot, D.S. 1997. *Blueprints for Violence Prevention*. Boulder, CO: Center for the Study and Prevention of Violence, University of Colorado.

Finckenauer, J.O. 1982. *Scared Straight and the Panacea Phenomenon*. Engelwood Cliffs, NJ: Prentice Hall.

Flores, J.R. and G. Thompson. 2007. *Juvenile Accountability Block Grants Program Guidance Manual 2007*. Washington D.C.: U.S. Department of Justice, Office of Justice Programs, Office of Juvenile Justice and Delinquency Prevention.

Goffman, E. 1961. *Asylums: Essays on the Social Situation of Mental Patients and Other Inmates*. Garden City, NY: Anchor Books.

Goldstein, Arnold P. and Barry Glick. 1994. "Aggression Replacement Training: Curriculum and Evaluation." *Simulation and Gaming* 25(1): 9–26.

Gottfredson, D.C., S.S. Najaka and B. Kearley. 2003. "Effectiveness of Drug Treatment Courts: Evidence from a Randomized Trial." *Criminology and Public Policy* 2: 171–196.

Greene, Helen Taylor and Everette B. Penn. 2006. "Reducing Juvenile Delinquency: Lessons Learned." In Everette B. Penn, Helen Taylor Greene and Shaun L. Gabbidon (eds) *Race and Juvenile Justice*. Durham, NC: Carolina Academic Press, pp. 223–241.

Greenwood, Peter W. 2006. *Changing Lives: Delinquency Prevention as Crime-control Policy*. Chicago, IL: The University of Chicago Press.

Greenwood, Peter W. and Daniel L. Edwards. 2011. "Evidence-based Programs for At-risk Youth and Juvenile Offenders: A Review of Proven Prevention and Intervention Models." In David W. Springer and Albert R. Roberts (eds) *Juvenile Justice and Delinquency*. Sudbury, MA: Jones and Bartlett, pp. 369–390.

Guerra Nancy G., Tia E. Kim and Paul Boxer. 2008. "What Works: Best Practices with Juvenile Offenders." In Robert D. Hoge, Nancy G. Guerra and Paul Boxer (eds) *Treating the Juvenile Offender*. New York: The Guilford Press, pp. 79–102.

Guerra, Nancy G. and Caren Leaf. 2008. "Implementing Treatment Programs in Community and Institutional Settings." In Robert D. Hoge, Nancy G. Guerra and Paul Boxer (eds) *Treating the Juvenile Offender*. New York: The Guilford Press, pp. 103–126.

Howell, James C. 2009. *Preventing and Reducing Juvenile Delinquency: A Comprehensive Framework*. Thousand Oaks, CA: Sage.

Latimer, Jeff, Craig Dowden and Danielle Muise. 2005. "The Effectiveness of Restorative Justice Practices: A Meta-Analysis." *The Prison Journal* 85: 127–144.

Levrant, Sharon, Francis T. Cullen, Betsy Fulton and John F. Wozniak. 1999. "Reconsidering Restorative Justice: The Corruption of Benevolence Revisited?" *Crime and Delinquency* 45(1): 3–27.

MacKenzie, Doris Layton, David B. Wilson and Suzanne B. Kidder. 2001. "Effects of Correctional Boot Camps on Offending." *Annals, AAPSS* 578: 126–143.

Marlowe, Douglas B. 2010. "Research Update on Juvenile Drug Treatment Courts." *Need To Know*. National Association of Drug Court Professionals. http://www.udetc.org/documents/judicial/201205eNews/nadcp.pdf (accessed January 2, 2013).

Martinson, Robert. 1974. "What Works? Questions and Answers about Prison Reform." *The Public Interest* 35(Spring): 22–54.

McGoldrick, M., J. Giordano and J. Pearce (eds). 1996. *Ethnicity and Family Therapy*. New York: The Guilford Press.

McNeill, Fergus. 2006. "Community Supervision: Context and Relationships Matter." In Barry Goldson and John Muncie (eds) *Youth, Crime and Justice*. London: Sage, pp. 125–136.

Moon, Melissa M., Jody L. Sundt, Francis T. Cullen and John Paul Wright. 2000. "Is Child Saving Dead? Public Support for Juvenile Rehabilitation." *Crime and Delinquency* 46(1): 38–60.

Nagin, Daniel S., Alex R. Piquero, Elizabeth S. Scott and Laurence Steinberg. 2006. "Public Preferences for Rehabilitation Versus Incarceration of Juvenile Offenders: Evidence from a Contingent Valuation Survey." *Criminology and Public Policy* 5(4): 301–326.

Nolan, James L. Jr. 2001. *Reinventing Justice: The American Drug Court Movement*. Princeton, NJ: Princeton University Press.

Page, Clarence. 1999. "Why Should We Give Boot Camps the Boot?" *Chicago Tribune*, December 8. http://articles.chicagotribune.com/1999-12-08/news/99 12080053_1_boot-camps-arizona-boys-ranch-juvenile-facilities (accessed June 23, 2012).

Paik, Leslie. 2011. *Discretionary Justice: Looking Inside a Juvenile Drug Court*. New Brunswick, NJ: Rutgers University Press.

Puzzanchera, Charles. 2009. *Juvenile Arrests 2008*. Washington D.C.: U.S. Department of Justice, Office of Justice Programs, Office of Juvenile Justice and Delinquency Prevention.

Rodriguez, Nancy. 2007. "Restorative Justice at Work: Examining the Impact of Restorative Justice Resolutions on Juvenile Recidivism." *Crime and Delinquency* 53: 355–379.

Rodriquez, Nancy and Vincent J. Webb. 2004. "Multiple Measures of Juvenile Drug Court Effectiveness: Results of a Quasi-experimental Design." *Crime and Delinquency* 50: 292–314.

Rosenthal, R. 1991. *Meta-analytic Procedures for Social Research*. Newbury Park, CA: Sage.

Sanford, J. Scott and Bruce Arrigo. 2005. "Lifting the Cover on Drug Courts: Evaluation Findings and Policy Concerns." *International Journal of Offender Therapy and Comparative Criminology* 49: 239–259.

Santisteban, D.A. and J. Szapocznik. 1994. "Bridging Theory, Research and Practice to More Successfully Engage Substance Abusing Youth and Their Families in Therapy." *Journal of Child and Adolescent Substance Abuse* 3: 9–24.

U.S. Department of Justice. 2001. *Juvenile Accountability Incentive Block Grants Program. Juvenile Drug Court Programs.* Washington D.C.: Office of Justice Programs, Office of Juvenile Justice and Delinquency Prevention.

Valentine, J., J.A. De Jong and N. Kennedy (eds). 1998. *Substance Abuse Prevention in Multicultural Communities.* New York: The Haworth Press.

Welch, Michael. 1999. *Punishment in America: Social Control and the Ironies of Imprisonment.* Thousand Oaks, CA: Sage.

Welsh, Brandon C. and David P. Farrington. 2011. "Effectiveness of Early Crime Prevention in Juvenile Justice and Delinquency." In David W. Springer and Albert R. Roberts (eds) *Juvenile Justice and Delinquency.* Sudbury, MA: Jones and Bartlett, pp. 101–116.

Whiteacre, Kevin. 2008. *Drug Court Justice: Experiences in a Juvenile Drug Court.* New York: Peter Lang.

Wilson, David B., Ojmarrh Mitchell and Doris L. McKenzie. 2006. "A Systematic Review of Drug Court Effects on Recidivism." *Journal of Experimental Criminology* 2: 459–487.

Wilson, Sandra Jo and Mark W. Lipsey. 2000. "Wilderness Challenge Programs for Delinquent Youth: A Meta-analysis of Outcome Evaluations." *Evaluation and Program Planning* 23: 1–12.

chapter 10

Transnational Youth Justice

This chapter engages with aspects of transnational youth justice (in international usage "youth justice" is the preferred terminology and not "juvenile justice") within a thematic framework. It focuses on topics rather than individual countries and is not intended to be a comparative discussion of transnational youth justice. Rather, it seeks to explore themes that connect youth justice with policy initiatives, youth legislation, international norms concerning child rights and child protection, and the articulation between youth and culture.

Comparative criminologists have observed that the constraints associated with studying comparative youth justice exceed those for comparative adult justice because so little is known about youth justice, especially in developing countries (Hartjen 2008: xvii). In any event, the notion of comparing how justice works in different nations has itself been questioned. Wide ranging discussions of the issue of "comparing" in comparative criminal justice generally can be found in Beirne and Nelken (1997: 3). As well, Nelken, in *Comparative Criminal Justice* (2010), explores many of the troubling questions about comparative analysis in criminal justice. As he notes, core issues in this field may call for an interpretive approach. For example, how exactly does a particular culture conceive of "disorder," how is its legal culture constituted, and how does that impact perceptions of crime and criminality? (Nelken 2010: 5). At the root of comparative inquiry lies the issue of what Sztompka (1990: 48) calls "the incommensurability of concepts" even though, in his view, historical tendencies work toward a conceptual convergence (p. 50). Understanding the cultural specificity of a particular culture is arguably a prerequisite to comprehending how that culture perceives criminality, both adult and juvenile. Banks (2000a) contends that the idea of cultural specificity in relation to a culture must include an understanding of the pre-colonial history, colonial and post-colonial changes within a specific culture,[1] an analysis of the commonalties and differences (where there are diverse societies within a culture) and an explicit statement of local definitions and conceptions. The aim is to emphasize the importance of the whole and the interdependence of its parts so that specific acts and events of interest to criminology can be viewed within the particular cultural context.[2]

Building cultural specificity means discarding Western definitions of acts that constitute "crime" and "offense" and identifying local definitions. For example, in her research in Papua New Guinea, in seeking to overcome the definitional problems associated with terminologies such as "offenses" and "crimes," Banks elected to study acts representing responses to injury (or grievances) rather than examining only acts constitutive of "criminal offenses." In this way, the cultural context of any act can be revealed along with its meaning. In pursuing this research trajectory Banks sought to establish the cultural specificity of the concept of "violence" in Papua New Guinea (Banks 2000b).[3] Questions such as how violence is defined locally, how violence is addressed in indigenous processes and what perceptions prevail about the nature of violence itself, such as appropriate modes of redress, can be addressed by taking a broad perspective that seeks to define the cultural specificity of violence as a response to a perceived injury.

Ultimately, research of this kind, especially concerning local meanings of "justice," assists in formulating appropriate justice policies and addressing questions such as the legitimacy of law and the local configuration of the concept known in the West as "the rule of law." It can even contribute to the building of a "rule of law culture" (Stromseth et al. 2006).

Specificity of delinquency in Bangladesh

As discussed above, developing a cultural criminology for a post-colonial state includes addressing local expectations and beliefs that are culturally embedded. Explanations relevant to a particular project in criminology should be teased out of the cultural matrix and located together with other elements that collectively comprise the cultural specificity of that culture. Gaining knowledge of local beliefs, values and expectations will often be an interdisciplinary exercise and in many criminological projects the discipline of anthropology will have special salience. Nelken (2010: 43) suggests that an interpretive inquiry is the preferred approach, "where the aim is to show congruence between meanings and values in criminal justice and the larger culture."

One aspect of youth justice, namely that of age, represents a critical issue for police and the courts in managing delinquency. As noted above, it should not be assumed that concepts of childhood are identical in all cultures. Instead, an analysis that assists in understanding the cultural specificity of age and childhood in a country should be undertaken. An example of that approach is provided in the following section concerned with childhood and its meaning in Bangladesh.

In Bangladesh, age and childhood are topics infused with local definitions and cultural meanings that may not figure at all in legislation regulating youth justice. In terms of legality, like other post-colonial states, Bangladesh opted to follow colonial or post-colonial legislative models that derive from Western cultural conceptions regardless of divergences in cultural categories and practices.

Local practices and formulations render "childhood" a contested term in Bangladesh. In its report to the Committee on the Rights of the Child of September 2003 the Government of Bangladesh (GOB) stated, "until recently, adolescence was not widely recognized in Bangladesh as a distinct phase of life. This is especially true in relation to girls" (Committee on the Rights of the Child 2003b: 5).

In the Bangladesh juvenile justice system children cease to be protected at the age of 16, and not 18 as required by the Convention on the Rights of the Child (CRC). More generally, in its Written Replies to the Committee on the Rights of the Child (Committee on the Rights of the Child 2003a: 11) the GOB notes that most of its laws define children for various purposes in an age range of 12 to 18. Siddiqui (2001: 5–7) describes 18 distinct laws affecting children which fix the age of a "child" for discrete purposes ranging from the legal age of criminal responsibility, to laws regulating child labor, to minimum wages for children, to the age fixed for a vagrant (over 14 years). Many of these laws pre-date the creation of both Pakistan and Bangladesh, and the GOB is faced with a major task of legal reform in bringing its definitions of childhood into line with the requirements of the CRC. The age of criminal responsibility was until very recently fixed by the Penal Code at 7 years but was raised to 9 years in late 2004. Below that age a child is deemed to be incapable of committing a crime. A child over 9 and below 12 years of age may be considered capable of committing a crime depending on his or her state of mind and a child over 12 years of age is considered fully capable of criminal intent and is treated legally as an adult.

In the area of juvenile justice, it is often difficult in practice in Bangladesh to determine a child's actual age owing to ineffective systems of birth registration. An Alternative Report to the Committee on the Rights of the Child submitted by the NGO Bangladesh Shishu Adhikar Forum (BSAF) comments that "in [the] majority [of] case[s] there is no sound system for recording and presentation of documentary proof of the exact age of a child"

(BSAF 2007). According to Therese Blanchet (1996: 43), there is no perceived social need for birth registration and it is not a government priority, especially when registration would have significant implications in relation to both laws and institutional practices.

Age is determined for youth justice purposes by the *Children Act 1974*. In criminal court proceedings, the Act requires that whenever a person coming before a court appears to the court to be a child, the court has a duty to conduct an inquiry concerning the age of that person and after taking evidence must record a finding stating the person's age. The Act does not require that there be medical evidence of age and the courts may act on any appropriate evidence such as school records, other official records and statements by relatives as to age.

After interviewing court officials and examining records, Odhikar (2002), a leading Bangladesh NGO, reported that magistrates did not often conduct enquiries as to age. Records of cases are forwarded to them by the police who either do not mention the age of the arrested person or increase the actual age. Lawyers were reluctant to raise the issue of age and, in the absence of any argument, the magistrate usually did not enquire into the age of the arrested person. Rohfritsch and Sattar (1995: 33), in their research, discovered that magistrates believe it is the responsibility of the police to fix the age of an offender and that once a person is referred to them categorized as an 'adult' the issue is effectively decided.

Odhikar (2002) argues that in most cases, the police do not record the age of an arrested person, even though the Criminal Procedure Code requires an accused to be examined before trial and to provide particulars, including age. According to Odhikar (2002), the police arrest records commonly describe children under age 16 who have been arrested as aged above 16 in order to avoid them gaining the protection of the *Children Act*. Where children are arrested with adults, police treat the children as though they are also adults, asserting that if they are old enough to commit serious crimes with adults they must themselves be adults. Rohfritsch and Sattar (1995) found that the police and magistrates had scant knowledge of the *Children Act* and that when dealing with juvenile crime, the age of the offender was rarely considered. Instead, the nature and seriousness of the offense was the foremost consideration.

Blanchet (1996: 41) provides an insightful discussion of the cultural and social context of age in Bengali culture, revealing that while life stages are recognized, a person's actual age may be elusive. Thus, for example, illiterate people are not aware of their age, and children, when asked their age, are likely to reply, "How do I know, ask my mother." Illiterate fathers are uninterested in the ages of their children and sometimes even literate fathers do not know precise ages. Mothers pressed to give the age of their child will commonly provide an age range, such as "8 to 9 years."

This mutability of age is demonstrated in transactions with government authorities and institutions. For example, parents registering their children in schools often give an age which they know to be incorrect. Urban children entering competitions are often recorded as being younger than their real age. Similarly, parents will reduce a child's age, especially that of a girl, when contemplating arranging a marriage, to enhance marriage prospects, and, as noted above, there is no consistency in the age assigned to children accused of criminal offenses. Often, the police, the parents, the accusers and the defendants assign different ages depending on the case they are arguing.

As between children, seniority is acknowledged and considered important in both childhood and adulthood, and the Bangla language contains formal terms of address and respect based on seniority. Professional persons fixing seniority often refer to their year of matriculation or graduation as a benchmark. While birthdays are sometimes celebrated in the urban middle and upper classes, this custom is widely perceived as foreign.

Blanchet (1996) observes that young sex workers, no older than 11 or 12, sometimes hold affidavit documents stamped by a magistrate stating their age as 18. She concludes that although there is general acceptance that age information has to be captured and made explicit for official documentary purposes, it need not be credible. Sometimes the margin between the age on paper and the likely biological age can be considerable, and Blanchet cites the example of a Muslim marriage registrar who married a 5-year-old girl to a 12-year-old boy in 1988, recording the age of the bride as 18 and the groom as 21. The registrar explained that he had recorded these ages because both guardians had agreed to the marriage and he wanted to comply with the law in relation to the age of marriage. Overall, age-stating norms and practices are well established and legal requirements are frequently subverted.

Naming a person as "child" or "not child" is contingent on concrete situations involving the person (Blanchet 1996: 48). For example, a child may be said to be "too small" or "old enough" to undertake certain work or "old enough" to "understand" or to "not understand." The context of the discussion is always crucial. Another key concept is possessing "understanding" because it signifies being "grown up" in one form or another. When small children "do not understand," parents show great tolerance and leniency. Gaining understanding does not depend upon physical growth or age but relates to life circumstances and to one's *jati*; that is, what one should understand and know, and practice according to one's path and duty in life. For example, an orphan child, a poor child hired out as a domestic servant, or a young girl given in marriage, are all expected to rapidly develop their understanding, and there is no toleration for lengthy periods of irresponsibility associated with childhood. In contrast, while middle-class children are expected to show early maturity in their school work they must

youth, crime and justice

remain innocent about sexuality. Parents and their children continually negotiate stages of "understanding" and this has important ramifications, especially in terms of guilt and punishment.

Thus, child development in the cultural context of Bangladesh is best viewed as an organic process unrelated to age (Blanchet 1996: 62). For example, a mother living in the *bustee* (urban slum) told Blanchet that she sent her 7-year-old son to school but discovered that he was unable to understand the proceedings, did not like the experience and dropped out within a few weeks. His illiterate mother concluded that her son's brain was not ready for school and perhaps he might try again in a year or two. In contrast, a middle-class mother gives milk and eggs to her 4-year-old child in the belief that this particular nourishment will develop his or her intelligence and enable the child to excel in school. Middle-class parents believe that with better food, good care, extensive coaching and the impetus of parental ambition, their child can be made clever. While middle-class and village and *bustee* mothers negotiate the division between ignorance and understanding differently, none relate child development to the child's actual age.

Blanchet (1996: 63) argues that the circumstances of birth, including class, largely determine when an adult with authority will acknowledge the state of understanding of a particular child. For example, middle-class women believe that the young girls they employ as maidservants "understand" and develop a maturity about domestic work much earlier than their own daughters. Therefore, they expect a 9- or 10-year-old maidservant, who they regard as "grown up," to obey orders, perform duties and take their punishment for mistakes. Similarly, the daughters of sex workers who reach 11 or 12 years old "naturally" take up their mother's occupation because they are regarded as lacking innocence and as having achieved "understanding" much earlier than village girls. However, all classes acknowledge that girls "understand" earlier than boys.

"Understanding" connotes loss of innocence and therefore the possibility of guilt and punishment. Thus, children who have lost their innocence are assimilated with adults, and adolescents who have committed crimes are said to "understand" and bear the same guilt and responsibility as adults. This may help reveal police motivations in their habit of writing higher ages for children on the first information reports (FIRs) they complete when recording a child's offense.

In all cultures, age is always socially constructed. Assumptions about age being a cultural universal have been challenged by criminologists who have become aware of culturally specificity. For example, Maureen Cain (2000: 243) points out that in the Caribbean "age is lived differently" and that the crime of drug trafficking is dependent on the participation of mature persons. Thus, in that region, the age profile of offenders differs to that found in the West.

In Bangladesh age is never a fixity and, in relation to youth justice, is often contested according to the context in which it becomes an issue. Thus, while positivist law fixes the age for delinquency, culturally specific Bangladesh practices challenge legal definitions with local definitions and values. In formulating a cultural criminology of delinquency in Bangladesh the divergences and complexities associated with age determination must be accounted for. Bangladesh's cultural practices and beliefs do not match Western conceptions of age, determined by Western cultural values, and contained in the CRC. In seeking a convergence between local beliefs and conceptions and CRC norms, age will continue to be contested. However, cultural practices are fluid and, as David Nelken (1998: 323) reminds us:

> the contrast between rights and traditions can be overdrawn. Traditions can be "invented" or reinvented, and the evolution of the liberal notion of individual rights is itself part of tradition. Traditions are not and cannot be static.

This discussion has shown the complexities associated with age determination in Bangladesh. Local definitions and conceptions about age pay little regard to legal definitions. The incommensurability of cultural conceptions of childhood in Bangladesh and the requirements of the CRC is apparent and will continue to be contested. This exploration of an element of great importance to juvenile justice policy-making reveals how building a cultural criminology ought to include an adequate account of the cultural specificity of childhood in Bangladesh. A criminological project focused on childhood and age can therefore initiate a debate on the congruence between meanings and values in criminal justice and the larger culture.

Policy convergences and policy transfer of youth justice policies

There are numerous definitions and explanations of globalization, but the broad conception of the term offered by Tomlinson (1999: 2) is a useful starting point: "globalization refers to the rapidly developing and ever-densening network of interconnections and interdependences that characterize modern social life." In particular, it is now possible for information to be exchanged (at least between developed states and to a lesser extent between developed and less developed states) so that social relations are no longer bounded by territoriality. Some argue that globalization is associated with homogenization in the form of global conformity and ubiquity (Tomlinson 1999: 6), with the result that local happenings are penetrated and shaped by events occurring in the distance (Giddens 1990: 64).

While some see globalization as an overarching hegemonic process ordering outcomes at the level of nations, economies and cultures, it is generally accepted that in terms of power relations between the global and the local, there is a "push and pull" between globalizing forces and countervailing forces (Tomlinson 1999: 61). This is largely because the local interprets, translates, adapts and indigenizes global imports. Accordingly, in complex ways, local forms of knowledge are constantly being reordered and worked in a process of interaction with changing external forces.

In the field of criminal justice policy making, globalization has been associated with what is described as the new punitiveness or populist punitiveness. The latter term, according to Bottoms (1995: 40), "is intended to convey the notion of politicians tapping into, and using for their purposes, what they believe to be the public's generally punitive stance." It is contended, therefore, that trends in penal policy, essentially punitive in nature, have emerged in a number of Western societies, consistent with processes of globalization (Baker and Roberts 2005: 121–122). These trends, represented in easily understood, compressed forms by slogans such as "three strikes and you're out" and "zero tolerance," as well as a shift in focus away from the offender to the plight of the victim, signify a set of policies that are "tough on crime" and have been diffused among Western states, including Australia and New Zealand. However, Jones and Newburn (2007: 162, 163), in comparing U.S. and U.K. policy measures, argue that while labels and nomenclature were easily exported from the U.S., there may still be considerable variation in policies that are actually implemented in the receiving states.

According to Wacquant (1999: 327), the network responsible for disseminating these policies originates them in Washington D.C. and New York, and transmits them to London before moving to Europe and beyond. As a result, there has emerged a "global consciousness" within which policy makers and others are said to locate their thinking as they take advantage of a rich and diverse set of knowledges available to them on criminological issues and debates (Baker and Roberts 2005: 124). At the same time, neo-liberalism may have shifted power away from nations and narrowed their choice of justice policy options, causing justice pathways to converge across a so-called "global North" of Western societies (Drake et al. 2010: 29–30).

While of course criminal justice systems between states are far from identical, within Western nations, commonalities have been identified in the form of populist responses to crime that are skeptical of expert advice, that insist that crime is increasing even when official data indicate otherwise, and that remain convinced that the courts are "soft" on criminals. Nevertheless, it is also acknowledged that globalization in the form of the new punitiveness is unable to account for all developments in criminal justice. Restorative justice (see Chapter 8), for example, is seen as one approach to criminal justice that has grown and become accepted as one policy option in many countries, and that resists the punitive trend (Baker and Roberts 2005: 124).

Youth justice, in the forms of laws and practices concerned with youth coming into contact with the law, is a discrete topic within Western criminal justice policy making. Western states generally have well-developed systems of youth justice and extensive bureaucratic and civil society networks that engineer and promote policy changes. It is expected that the same forces of globalization that affect criminal justice policies would generally similarly impact youth justice policies and that there would be a convergence of youth justice policies toward Western models, such as those existing in the U.S. (Muncie 2005: 38). Primarily this means a shift away from a welfare-based model[4] to a justice-based managerialist model (p. 38).

In most states in the U.S., the original welfare-based model of juvenile justice has come under pressure and been challenged by forces that have promoted a set of policies as punitive in their nature and effect as those applying to adult offenders. Measures such as trying youth as adults, broadening the scope of criminality to criminalize antisocial youth conduct, imposing youth curfews, and adopting zero-tolerance policies for violence in schools constitute a new punitiveness in penal and crime control discourses and policies toward youth (see Chapter 7, where policy responses to moral panics about youth are discussed).

In global terms, youth justice has also been impacted by the CRC to which all states other than the U.S. and Somalia are party. The CRC impact arises from its mandating a set of norms on youth rights and justice that promote a welfare rather than a punishment approach to youth justice, arguably setting up a countervailing tendency to populist punitiveness.[5] For example, it encourages diversion from custody, stipulates that custody should be a last resort and requires that for those under 18 years of age "the best interests of the child shall be a primary consideration" (CRC, Article 3.1; Muncie 2005: 45). This leads to questions such as: To what extent has the universalist child rights discourse of the CRC been privileged in state policy making on youth justice, and, despite the CRC, are local forces and modes of practice still prevalent?

In a comprehensive analysis of the effects of globalization on youth justice, Muncie (2005) traces the shifts to punitiveness in Western policies on youth justice and reveals how policy makers have abandoned policies of social inclusion and discarded the welfare model. While some argue that this shift may bring about a global youth justice based on that representation, Muncie counters that there are contrary developments and modes of thinking in youth justice in many countries, including movements for RJ and mediation which favor policy heterogeneity rather than policy homogenization (p. 44). He concludes that youth justice policy transfer is "rarely

youth, crime and justice

direct and complete but is partial and mediated through national and local cultures" (p. 44).

Muncie (2005) argues that globalization has not produced and will not deliver a universalistic juvenile justice system such as that advocated by the CRC. Instead, he asserts that local contingencies, and especially assertions about cultural specificity, will figure in debates about implementing these universalistic discourses, and "the argument that youth justice has become a global product can only be sustained at the very highest level of generality" (p. 56). He characterizes state implementation of the CRC as "half-hearted and piecemeal" and claims that violations attract no formal sanctions (p. 46). He calls for an analysis at the level of the nation state which recognizes that global policy norms will be "reworked, challenged and contested" (Muncie 2005: 56) by particular cultures and practices through the local politics of law reform.

Sites of tension

In responding to this challenge, Banks (2007: 391) examines youth justice in Bangladesh by presenting a case study of the articulation between some of the international norms concerning the rights and status of children under the CRC and local practices and customs about punishing children in Bangladesh. Banks argues that in adopting and endorsing international norms concerning children's rights contained in the CRC, the GOB has contradicted local contingencies and practices that resist and offer a counter-discourse to the CRC. For example, where the CRC mandates deinstitutionalization and urges diversion out of the juvenile justice system, counter-discourses promoted by GOB officials and some parents favor institutionalization of so-called "uncontrollable" children.

Bangladesh signed the CRC in January 1990, one of the first states to do so following the promulgation of the Convention on November 20, 1990 (Harris-Short 2003: 134). International human rights treaties like the CRC propagate a kind of transnational juvenile justice policy which signatories are required to put into action in their laws and administrative practices.[6] In discovering how the rights-based normative discourse of the CRC is materialized in the context of Bangladesh, and in revealing the tensions between global and local formulations of child rights in that state, Banks focuses on areas where CRC discourse and local oppositional discourses collide (2007: 393).

One area of contention between the CRC and local practices is the field of local culture as it impacts children. In her examination of reservations and statements by various states to the Committee on the Rights of the Child established by the CRC to examine the progress made by states in meeting their CRC obligations, Sonia Harris-Short (2003) explains how cultural relativism is deployed before the Committee to explain and justify a lack of effective action to implement the CRC. As Muncie (2005: 47) notes, non-Western states comprise the majority of countries where the Committee on the Rights of the Child has identified tradition and culture as constraints to implementation. Harris-Short concludes that these states do not cynically deploy cultural relativist arguments but offer genuine explanations rooted in local cultures. These states lack local-level human rights cultures that support international norms and are deficient in grass-roots support for obligations accepted by their governments, especially "when the rights in question impinge upon traditions and practices relating to children and the family" (Harris-Short 2003: 134).

How has the GOB responded to the discourse of the CRC represented by the Committee? The GOB has offered an explanation for its admitted lack of activity in juvenile law reform. In its Written Replies to the Committee the GOB (Committee on the Rights of the Child 2003a: 3) stated:

[L]ike most developing countries, poverty and resource constraints remain serious obstacles for Bangladesh in fulfilling the goals of child rights. However, the government remains fully committed, and with the active support from NGOs, the civil society and international organizations, it is determined to move forward with its agenda to provide children with better conditions and opportunities to grow in a safe and secure environment.

UNICEF has noted the difficulty in obtaining any reliable data on the extent and nature of crime committed by children in Bangladesh. However, data provided to the Committee by the GOB indicate that most recorded delinquency was categorized as "miscellaneous." UNICEF suggests that these offenses may represent behaviors considered antisocial such as truancy, wandering in the streets, staying out at night, smoking cigarettes, watching an excessive number of movies and running away from home.

In its statement to the Committee on the Rights of the Child of September 2003 the GOB (Committee on the Rights of the Child 2003b: 4) noted that:

[A] baseline survey in 2001 revealed major gaps in the knowledge and practices of early childhood care and development . . . [with] about one third of parents and guardians interviewed, reported using physical punishment as a means to discipline their child.

The cultural context of parental discipline in Bangladesh is complex. According to Blanchet (1996), all classes of society hold the belief that children will be "spoiled" if parental control and authority is weak. This sometimes leads to parents imposing severe physical punishments to correct them. Accordingly, when parents volunteer information about the punishments they inflict on their children they are sending the message to family and the community that they have not neglected their parental responsibilities. For example, in one study of boys adjudicated to the country's two juvenile institutions, Sarker (2001: 240) found that parents had used both physical and psychological punishment in responding to perceived delinquency. In most cases boys had been physically punished by parental assaults involving hands or sticks. Other sanctions included refusing to provide food or delaying meals, restrictions on movement, chaining the youth's legs and locking the child away in a room for a period. Eighty-two percent of the guardians and parents interviewed admitted having beaten boys using their hands, and over 64 percent had used wooden, iron or bamboo sticks. As an alternative to physical punishment, some parents and guardians had sent their children to hostels, placed children under the care of relatives, or changed the child's schooling from academic to religious education.

About 50 percent per cent of the boys interviewed in Sarker's (2001: 170) study indicated that physical punishment and other sanctions applied by their parents had made them feel hostile toward them. As a consequence, many of the youth would stay away from their homes for most of the day and this often led their parents or guardians to conclude that they had become habitual offenders. Once measures of control and punishment had failed, parents often applied formally to the juvenile court for their children to be detained in institutions under the *Children Act 1974* as so-called "uncontrollable" children. Cultural pressures mandate parental control. As Sarker (2001: 171) affirms: "in a traditional society like ours the loss of control over children is considered as an 'utter defeat' on the part of the parents/guardians."

Blanchet (1996: 64) explains how Bangladeshi children come to be regarded as "spoiled" and therefore delinquent, or potentially so, in the eyes of their parents. Both boys and girls may be "spoiled" as the outcome of early, untimely maturity. Spoiling can come about from non-attendance at school, hanging around with friends, being addicted to sports, showing an interest in girls or simply refusing to obey one's parents. Even in the slums, parents avoid any possible action that might result in neighbors calling their children "spoiled." However, once a child is regarded as "spoiled," his or her parents may be ostracized if they do not sever relationships with the affected child. This kind of community sanction may explain the willingness of parents to have their children confined in a juvenile institution as "uncontrollable" under the *Children Act*.

Institutionalizing children for up to three years reflects certain cultural norms held by Bangladeshi parents which require that they "protect" their reputations and instill discipline when their children become "uncontrollable." For that reason, in Bangladesh parental physical punishments are sanctioned by culture and values, and are legitimized by the law. However, they are condemned by the discourse of the CRC which prohibits physical or mental violence and cruel and degrading treatment.[7]

As noted earlier, the GOB response to the Committee on the issue of punishment is not to justify local practices on cultural relativist grounds, but rather to attribute their existence to lack of awareness of early childhood development. Embedding a set of Western liberal values within the complex social structure of Bangladesh is a challenging task. Arguably, even the relatively weak enforcement mechanisms of the CRC encourage action and transparency by requiring states to explicitly reveal their progress toward the incorporation of international norms of protection. However, a Committee that merely monitors progress may suggest that child protection is less a matter of urgency and more a lengthy process of negotiation. Accordingly, devising explanations for non-implementation becomes a preoccupation of some states.

Child soldiers

Relatively recently criminology has begun to engage with the subject of state crime, explained by Green and Ward (2004: 2) as "state organizational deviance involving the violation of human rights" or more broadly by Kauzlarich and others (2001: 175) as "illegal, socially injurious, or unjust acts which are committed for the benefit of a state or its agencies, and not for the personal gain of some individual agent of the state." In their review of research into state crime and victims of state crime, Kauzlarich and others (2001: 173) argue that the study of state crime has yet to become accepted as a major sub-field of criminology, and that "beyond brief descriptions, there has been no attempt to establish the nature, extent and distribution of the victimology of state crime" (p. 175). The same point might be made about the study of human rights in criminology despite the salience of the rights discourse over the past 60 years or so. The authors offer a working definition of victims of state crime as follows:

> Individuals or groups of individuals who have experienced economic, cultural, or physical harm, pain, exclusion, or exploitation because of tacit or explicit state actions or policies which violate law or generally defined human rights.
>
> (Kauzlarich et al. 2001: 7)

Many of the events analyzed below fall within the parameters of state crimes and the victimology of state crime but they remain generally

youth, crime and justice

unexplored and untouched by criminology. A framework of international law, although created in piecemeal fashion, now governs and regulates the employment of children in armed conflicts, sets normative standards and provides for war crime prosecutions for those who violate those norms. There remains, however, a substantial gap between the normative ideal of human rights and its promotion and application by states and their instrumentalities. In the case of child soldiers, questions of structure and agency, issues of the gap between the need for protection and its achievement in practice, and empirical investigation into the experiences of child soldiers are salient subjects for criminological enquiry. The following discussion seeks to establish a foundation of knowledge and to draw attention to the need for further research by a criminology that investigates human rights and engages more with issues of state power.

The term "child soldier" is not used under international law but the concept that children should not be participants in armed conflict is expressed most recently in the *Optional Protocol to the Convention on the Rights of the Child on the Involvement of Children in Armed Conflict* of May 2000 and in the *Statute of the International Criminal Court* of 1988.[8] In the case of the Protocol, there are prohibitions against using persons under the age of 18 in armed conflicts. In the case of the International Criminal Court, its Statute provides that it is a war crime to conscript or enlist children under the age of 15 or to use them to participate actively in hostilities in national or international armed conflicts.

The *Cape Town Principles and Best Practices* adopted at a UNICEF symposium on child soldiers in Africa in 1997 provides a broad informal definition of "child soldier" as follows (UNICEF 1997: 8):

> "Child soldier" in this document is any person under 18 years of age who is part of any kind of regular or irregular armed force or armed group in any capacity, including but not limited to cooks, porters, messengers and anyone accompanying such groups, other than family members. The definition includes girls recruited for sexual purposes and for forced marriage. It does not, therefore, only refer to a child who is carrying or has carried arms.

This definition therefore acknowledges the diversity of roles that children, both boys and girls, may play in armed groups and explicitly includes children not engaged in actual combat but who nevertheless participate in an armed force or group. The terminology calls attention to a multiplicity of experiences and practices represented by the signifier "child soldier."

As noted in the definition, child soldiers are not an exclusive feature of irregular, non-government forces – governments also recruit children as soldiers. Both the U.S. and the United Kingdom have recruited children for many years and, until recently, the U.K. permitted children aged 17 to enter combat. The U.K. still recruits children of 16 and 17 years with their parent's consent. The U.S. also recruits young men and women at age 17 and trains them so that they can be deployed to combat units by the age of 18 (Wessells 2006: 17). Accordingly, the child soldier is constituted in both developed and developing worlds.

Over the past 15 years, conflicts in Africa and elsewhere have established the child soldier as a new cause for concern worldwide. The discovery of the scale of employment of children in armed conflicts has led to a set of questions. How has it come about that children as young as 6 have been trained and armed to fight in local and international conflicts? What social, cultural, political and economic contexts and circumstances require or permit children to fight as soldiers in contemporary Africa? How can we understand the conditions that replace childhood innocence with the capacity to willingly torture and kill? Researchers have explored these and other associated issues, and governments and civil society have cooperated to establish an international legal regime to constrain those who would recruit children as soldiers and to punish the criminality of warlords.

Modern forms of warfare bear little resemblance to conventional wars between the armed forces of two or more states to gain territory or conquer the opposing force for some other purpose. Contemporary wars often occur within the borders of one state (although they may spill over to other states) and comprise attacks by warring factions involving armed civilians as well as regular forces attacking and killing unarmed civilians, adults and children, often to gain natural resources or political power. In this mode of violent conflict, torture, killing, rape and the slaughter of ethnic groups have been frequent outcomes. Children have not only suffered as the victims of this violence but have themselves perpetrated it. Significant numbers of children now participate in local wars as armed combatants, some as young as 6 years old (Singer 2006: 6). In Liberia and Sierra Leone, militias created "small-boy units" where the boys typically were under 12 years old and were renowned for their fearlessness. Worldwide, most child soldiers are aged between 13 and 18 (Wessells 2006: 7).

Historically, at least in Europe, children were generally excluded from armed conflict although there have been some rare exceptions such as the Hitler Jugend in World War II. One reason they were excluded is that they lacked the physical strength to wield the weapons of the times. However, children did participate in wars in non-combat roles such as squires who assisted knights, and as drummer boys and "powder monkeys" (boys who supplied ammunition to canons) in support roles (Singer 2006: 11–14). In the modern day, however, the extent of the employment of child soldiers in armed conflicts has radically distorted established past practices.

Child soldiers have participated in conflicts in Columbia (11,000 child soldiers), Ecuador, El Salvador, Guatemala, Mexico, Nicaragua, Paraguay and Peru; in Northern Ireland and Bosnia; in Turkey (in the Kurdish Workers' Party (PKK)); in Sierra Leone (where they were used from the onset of the civil war in 1991 and comprised as much as 80 percent of the Revolutionary United Front (RUF)); Liberia (where the United Nations estimates that some 20,000 served in combat); Angola (where as many as one million children were exposed to the conflict as civilians and combatants (Honwana 2006: 14)); Mozambique (where between 8 and 10,000 children participated in the conflict (Honwana 2006: 11)); Uganda (where the Lord's Resistance Army (LRA) is notorious for its abduction of more than 14,000 children with the youngest being only 5 years of age); the Democratic Republic of the Congo (DRC) (where one protagonist had an army of some 10,000 child solders between the ages of 7 and 16); in Palestine; in the war between Iran and Iraq (some 100,000 child soldiers from Iran are thought to have died in child-led human wave attacks); in Sudan (estimates are 100,000 on both sides of the civil war); Ethiopia; Afghanistan (with the Taliban and the Northern Alliance); and in many conflicts in Asia, especially in Myanmar and Sri Lanka (Singer 2006: 15–28).

According to Singer (2006: 29), in 68 percent of ongoing or recently ended conflicts, children under the age of 18 served in combat roles and in 80 percent of these conflicts child soldiers under the age of 15 participated.

Girl soldiers

Gender has not been a constraint to the employment of child soldiers. Notably, the Liberation Tigers of Tamil Eelam (LTTE) in Sri Lanka established brigades of fighters of 16 years of age and under with about half of them girls. Similarly, in Nepal, the Maoist Lal Sena group recruited girls to fight, and in Uganda the LRA specifically abducts attractive girls who are "married" to its leaders in a form of sexual slavery (Singer 2006: 33). The LRA is known for using extreme brutality on young girls assigned to work as servants of commanders, as one account confirms:

> "The commander would call to us to come and lie down. He would say, 'Do you know why I am beating you?' We didn't know, so the soldiers caned us, fifty strokes. This happened every day. They beat us on the buttocks, but if you cry, they will beat every part of your body and not count the strokes."
>
> (Wessells 2006: 93)

In a comprehensive discussion of girls abducted and held captive by the militias in Angola and Mozambique, Honwana (2006: 75) notes that in

Mozambique girls and young women served as guards, ammunition and supplies carriers, messengers, spies, so-called wives and sometimes as fighters. They were abducted and taken to military camps where they were raped and held as sexual slaves. One account expresses the horror:

> "The nights were dreadful because we were there to be used by the soldiers. A soldier per night . . . the lucky ones were those who were chosen by an officer who had a hut for them to live in and who protected them as his wives."
>
> (Honwana 2006: 84)

In Liberia, it was important to be taken under the protection of a soldier and then develop the necessary coping skills to sustain that relationship. Accordingly, some girls were able to shape their role within a group through sex and relationships, and to actively manage their survival. In Colombia, a similar system operated with girls competing for access to important fighters for protection:

> "When girls join the FARC, the commanders choose among them. There's pressure. The women have the final say, but they want to be with a commander to be protected. The commanders buy them. They give a girl money and presents. When you're with a commander, you don't have to do the hard work. So most of the prettiest girls are with the commanders."
>
> (Honwana 2006: 85, 86)

In Columbia and Sierra Leone, girls were recruited and trained for combat (Honwana 2006: 93). In Angola, girls were used for domestic tasks in the camps, and for sexual purposes. Reportedly, if a girl refused to have sex with a soldier she would be taken away and killed (Honwana 2006: 86). The sexual violence directed against girls forms part of the wide-ranging pattern of violence used against girls and women in zones of war, but it is important to note the diversity of experiences suffered by girls, and that some groups expressly prohibited sexual violence (Wessells 2006: 86–87). Stereotypes of the passive victim are inappropriate in view of the survival strategies girls employed to actively manage their predicament. As well, some girls joined groups willingly for ideological reasons.

Honwana (2006: 79) notes the secrecy that still surrounds the participation of girls in internal conflicts, largely because few girls are willing to share their experiences due to the social implications within the family and community. Explicit discussion of sexual matters is ordinarily proscribed, and rape and forms of sexual slavery even more so.

Questioning childhood

At the center of the condition of being a child soldier is its disturbing and unsettling nature. Involving children in war as combatants defies and subverts the category of childhood, which, under conditions of modernity, denotes a time of innocence, weakness and a dependency on adults for guidance and instruction. As Honwana (2006) notes, children participating in combat are located between the categories of child and adult, still children but without innocence, and removed from childhood by possessing and using the means to kill others, as if an adult. As she puts it:

> Child soldiers live between a world of make-believe – a child's world of games and fantasy, of playing with guns – and reality – where the playful becomes shockingly lethal and the game turns deadly. Here the ludic is transformed into the grotesque and the macabre.
>
> (Honwana 2006: 3)

The contradictory position occupied by child soldiers, culturally and socially, challenges our most fundamental assumptions about childhood. Should child soldiers always be regarded as victimized children or do we recognize their agency and exclude them from the category "child" because of their actions? Honwana (2006: 4) contends that children affected by conflict "do not constitute a homogeneous group of helpless victims but exercise an agency of their own, which is shaped by their particular experiences and circumstances." When child soldiers disrupt so many cultural and social categories and dualities, such as protector and protected, victim and perpetrator, and civilian and soldier, they lack a fixed identity and "occupy a world of their own" (p. 4).

However, the condition of childhood must be understood as a social construction that varies across cultures and that will change over time. It is crucial not to universalize the position of youth in developed Western societies to their status in less developed regions. In Africa and Asia, it has long been common for children to be involved in economic activity, and the boundary between childhood and adulthood is not sharply defined. For example, Honwana (2006: 41) explains in relation to children in Angola and Mozambique that:

> children are often portrayed as strong and resilient, as survivors who grow in difficult conditions. Being a child in this particular setting may have little to do with age . . . and is centrally linked to social roles, expectations and responsibilities.

She notes that the majority of children in these states were forcibly recruited, at a very young age, and before they were able to transition into adulthood through ritual initiation ceremonies that designate them as responsible and morally competent persons (Honwana 2006: 43). Commonly, in such societies, warfare and soldiering are regarded as activities only for the initiated and therefore these children lacked the preparation culturally necessary to assume the role of a soldier (Honwana 2006: 52, 53).

According to Wessells (2006: 5), initiation rites in Africa typically occur around the age of 14, and therefore a 15-year-old child soldier, armed and part of a militia, may well be regarded as a young adult by rural African villagers. Nevertheless, local elders speak of 15-year-old soldiers as "under-age soldiers" or "minor soldiers" because they regard a person of that age as too young to join an armed group.

Why use child soldiers?

Despite the prohibitions under international law, children continue to be used as fighters in violent conflicts. Singer (2006: 38) identifies three contributing factors: (1) abortive development and structural failure has led to conflict and generational dislocation; (2) weaponizing children is now possible because small arms are light and portable so that children can easily deploy and use them; and (3) mobilizing children to fight is a cost-effective way to participate in the violent internal conflicts that represent contemporary warfare.

HIV/AIDS has impacted African states dramatically and children now constitute an overall majority of persons with 51 percent of the continent's population of 340 million under the age of majority. Singer (2006) argues that the death of so many mature adults due to HIV/AIDS has destabilized the large youth population and that the young males, lacking parental controls and family structure, and feeling "angry" and "listless," find themselves drawn into violence. More specifically, a large pool of orphans has been created who are susceptible to the attractions of child soldiering (pp. 41–42). At the same time, an acceleration in the number and extent of violent internal conflicts has created a demand for fighters. The lack of basic needs such as food and shelter in a war zone means that the poor and least educated children are vulnerable to recruitment in order to survive. In some states, children have experienced only violence and conflict. As one child in northern Uganda noted:

> "If you are under 20 and living here, you have known virtually nothing else your whole life but what's it like to live in a community enduring armed conflict – conflict in which you are a prime target."
>
> (Singer 2006: 44)

Honwana (2006: 46, 47) contends that economic and structural issues in post-colonial Africa have impacted households and communities, and weakened their capacity to maintain established norms and value systems that once protected and nurtured children. Children have therefore become commodified because their labor has become vital for the survival of the family group. In such conditions child soldiering can function and flourish as a survival strategy because failed states are unable to provide any protection to their citizens. Children are drawn into internal conflicts as they move to towns searching for employment following the collapse of social and economic structures in the rural areas.

Incorporating plastics into small arms, especially automatic weapons, has made them light and portable and suitable for child fighters, and such weapons proliferate throughout Africa, making them a part of everyday life. A plentiful supply of cheap weapons enables local warlords to join conflicts, and guarantees violence and death (Singer 2006: 49). At the same time, especially in Africa, wars are often struggles to gain control of valuable natural resources like the diamond fields of Sierra Leone and the coltan mines of the Democratic Republic of Congo. In Asia and South America, the huge profits of the drug trade constitute a powerful incentive to make war. New wars have been likened to organized crime or massive violations of human rights and involve civilians to an extent never seen before both as targets and as assets in making war (Honwana 2006: 32). Like organized crime, violent conflicts are led and managed by leaders, often referred to as "warlords" (local leaders who are able to mobilize forces using terror tactics and tribal loyalty) eager for the plunder and spoils of war (Honwana 2006: 34).

Socio-economic factors, cheap and plentiful weapons and changes in warfare have contributed to the growth of the child soldier, but the strategy of using children is so appealing because it provides a ready source of "manpower" at very little cost to almost any protagonist because children are rarely paid (Singer 2006: 52). Wessells (2006: 34) draws attention to a more sinister basis for recruiting children – their tactical value as shock troops. Adult soldiers opposing children are asked to confront the prospect of killing them, sowing confusion and doubt in their minds, and adversely affecting their cohesion as a unit and force.

Recruitment and training

A common means of recruiting children is through abduction, sometimes directly, for example, from a school, or a marketplace, or simply by sweeps in the streets, or by imposing conscription targets in an area (Singer 2006: 58, 59). Camps for refugees as well as for internally displaced persons are also favored by recruiters because they are not well policed and contain large numbers of children (Wessells 2006: 38).

Sometimes children choose to join a group through their own initiative and in fact their agency accounts for about two out of every three children who are recruited (Singer 2006: 61). Joining a group may be prompted most often by the need for food and shelter, but the desire to exact revenge for the loss of a family member may also be a precipitating factor, as may be a simple desire to experience the excitement of having weapons and fighting. Recent research has shown that some children join groups to escape negative family pressures and situations such as parental abuse, perhaps seeing the group as a better "family" than the one they have escaped from (Wessells 2006: 48). Some join simply to better themselves by acquiring skills and training, as explained by one 16-year-old girl who had been a commander with the RUF in Sierra Leone:

> "I'm proud of what I learned – how to speak to groups, organize people, command, use weapons. I never got this from [the] government. How else am I supposed to have a future? If I had to do it again, I'd join again,"
>
> (Wessells 2006: 50)

Children may also respond to ideological messages and propaganda, and acquire a genuine desire to serve a particular cause (Wessells 2006: 53).

It is important then to recognize that children become soldiers for a diversity of reasons and there is no single narrative, such as forced recruitment, that adequately encapsulates their experience. It is important that the actual context of the recruitment be examined, embedded within wider structures of violence and oppression (Wessells 2006: 32, 55).

Agents or passive victims?

Children should not be regarded as victims devoid of agency, even though there are of course questions about their capacity to make such rational decisions. According to Honwana (2006: 51), in Mozambique and Angola, child soldiers were not without agency but displayed what she terms "tactical agency," a limited mode of agency, "an agency of the weak," necessary as a coping mechanism in the environment in which they had to survive. In this sense, the children lacked power to exercise a full "strategic" agency where they would have been aware of the purposes of their actions and any long-term gains or benefits. Even so, they were conscious of the immediate outcomes of their actions. Former boy soldiers report that "insecurity, vulnerability, and lack of food" were among the causes that led them to volunteer, but in some cases the main inducement was "wearing military gear and carrying an AK-47" (p. 58). Honwana warns against applying Western conceptions of responsibility to the actions of child soldiers. Asking if they should be regarded as victims or perpetrators, she concludes, "Although these boy soldiers cannot be considered fully responsible for their actions, they cannot be seen as entirely deprived of agency either" (p. 69).

The issue of agency also arises in relation to girls. One perspective is that girls are devoid of agency in the context of a war in which they have no capacity to resist, and the other argues that girls retain agency and devise strategies to exercise it. Applying the distinction between "tactical" and "strategic" agency, Honwana argues (2006: 95) that while girls have adapted to the living circumstances with tactical agency they have not created the "little worlds of their own" (p. 95) as do boy soldiers. She points to the need for more research into the subjective experiences of these girls given the silence that surrounds so much of what they have experienced.

Wessells (2006: 3–4) suggests that children have often been represented as "passive innocents whom adults have forced and intimidated into soldiering." Nevertheless, he argues, although forced recruitment does occur, children who live in war zones may not see any future for themselves, are oppressed, lack education and are powerless. In such circumstances they may see violence as offering a form of social justice. They may be attracted by the rhetoric of an insurgent group, or may secure a sense of family by belonging to one, or gain other benefits such as protection, food and shelter. Consequently, joining a group confers a sense of identity they cannot find in their routine life. Children may specifically construct an identity in the form of a "combat name" derived from their combat experience, for example, "Rambo" and "Cock and Fire" (p. 83). A disturbing account of combat naming is given by a 12-year-old Liberian boy who fought with a "small boys" unit:

> "As a commander, I was in charge of nine others, four girls and five boys. We were used mostly for guarding checkpoints but also fighting. I shot my gun many times. I was wounded during World War 1 . . . shot in the leg. I was not afraid, when I killed LURD soldiers, I would laugh at them, this is how I got my nickname, 'Laughing and Killing.'"
>
> (Wessells 2006: 83)

Studies show that once recruited, children are indoctrinated, often through the use of physical and psychological force, to motivate them and instill obedience. As Singer explains, "the overall intent of the process is to create a sort of 'moral disengagement' from the violence they will encounter as child fighters" (Singer 2006: 72). Horrific accounts of torture, ritualized killing of family members or other children, and even acts of cannibalism reveal the mechanisms used to destroy their resistance to killing others and ensure absolute compliance with leaders' orders (p. 74). In Angola and Mozambique, militia commanders appropriated features of peacetime initiation rituals or used local healers to give boys traditional forms of protection for forthcoming combat (Honwana 2006: 62). Actual training for combat was given by having them complete programs that copied those designed for adults, including the application of rigorous discipline.

Child soldiers in combat

A rebel commander in the Democratic Republic of the Congo (DRC) is quoted as saying, "Children make good fighters because they are young. . . . They think it's a game, so they're fearless" (Singer 2006: 80). Drugs or alcohol are sometimes supplied to augment this lack of fear, making them willing to undertake the most dangerous missions without question. A report chillingly summarizes the value of the child soldier to a commander in the field:

> "Children make very effective combatants. They don't ask a lot of questions. They follow instructions, and they often don't understand and aren't able to evaluate the risks of going to war. Victims and witnesses often said they feared the children more than the adults because the child combatants had not developed an understanding of the value of life. They would do anything. They knew no fear. Especially when they were pumped up on drugs. They saw it as fun to go into battle."
>
> (Singer 2006: 83)

While child fighters may be deployed according to the needs of a commander, for example, in concert with adult forces, or to attack soft targets such as villages, it is common for them to be used in human wave attacks, in a mass charge, firing automatic weapons, screaming and yelling (Singer 2006: 85). Newly recruited child fighters experience the same fears of combat as adults but rapidly adapt partly because commanders punish those who show fear (Wessells 2006: 75). Over time children can become extremely proficient soldiers, like the child fighters of the LTTE Leopard Brigade whose members grew up in LTTE orphanages and who took on elite Sri Lanka commando forces, surrounding and killing nearly 200, or the Sierra Leone West Side Boys who fought the highly trained British special forces, the SAS, for six hours and killed one and wounded 25 others (Singer 2006: 87, 88).

Some children attempt escape, but many do not wish to leave, especially after one year or longer in a group, even if they were originally abductees

(Singer 2006). Indoctrination, bonds of loyalty to comrades and psychological factors such as bonding together in conditions of hardship all militate against escaping. As well, if they do succeed in escaping they cannot expect necessarily to be welcomed back into their former community, if it even continues to exist (p. 89). However, escape is always problematic and children fear what will happen to them if they are caught trying to escape. As one account describes:

> "One boy tried to escape, but he was caught. His hands were tied, and then they made us, the other new captives, kill him with a stick. . . . I refused to kill him and they told me they would shoot me. . . . After we killed him, they made us smear his blood on our arms" (S., 15).
>
> (Singer 2006: 91)

As well as making efforts to escape, child soldiers will sometimes resist or reject commands and may develop a knowledge of which orders can be disobeyed without running the risk of being put to death. A 16-year-old male from Sierra Leone, abducted by the RUF, provides this example:

> "The leader told us to beat women and saw it [watched us] with his eyes. Also the leader told us to have sex with women older than your mother. I told him 'no' and was flogged and made to do hard work."
>
> (Wessells 2006: 73)

Sometimes girls resist commands. In one case a girl abducted by the RUF at 14 years of age told her captors that she was too young for sex. She tried to shame her captors by telling them they should be ashamed of themselves for wanting sex with her at her age. The RUF cut off her left arm above the elbow (Wessells 2006: 95).

The stereotype of all child soldiers as bloodthirsty killers should be challenged because only a small minority participate willingly and become hardened to extremes of violence and killing (Wessells 2006: 74). According to Wessells (2006: 79), the operation of five psychological processes enables an ordinary child to kill initially and then to do so time after time. These are:

- The will to survive.
- Obedience – enabling the guilt to be transferred to the person giving the orders.
- The normalization of violence – continual exposure to violence breaks down sensitivities and killing once enables more killing.
- Satisfaction that is derived from killing – for example, where a child takes revenge for harm caused to his or her family, or where rewards are earned by killing or peer approval is gained.

■ Ideology – where the child believes that fighting is regarded as a legitimate means of achieving some form of social justice.

Restoring the child soldier

In light of the experiences described above, how best can a child soldier be restored to his or her community and regain his or her childhood? After disarming and demobilizing them, child soldiers become ex-combatants, many of them now adults but still in need of support services. Many suffer from post-traumatic stress which may continue for months or even years. Reintegrating former child fighters into their communities has proved to be a difficult process (Singer 2006: 193). For example, one survey in Africa found that 82 percent of parents considered that former child soldiers represent a potential danger to the population (p. 200).

Wessells (2006: 23) argues for a perspective of former child soldiers which recognizes that although they may have suffered greatly they are "neither uniquely vulnerable nor definable in terms of vulnerability," and that most display "remarkable resilience." He contends that the suffering of child soldiers should be seen in the context of the overall suffering of all children living in war zones. Modern internal conflicts are an assault on the well-being of all children and there are "intimate connections between child soldiering and the wider suffering of war-affected children" (p. 23).

Honwana (2006: 4) argues that, based on her research on child soldiers in Angola and Mozambique where internal wars lasted for more than 20 years and 15 years respectively, "the healing and reintegration of children affected by armed conflict need to be embedded in local world views and meaning systems in order to be effective and sustainable." She explains that in Angola, societies have long established rituals for healing those who participate in wars because "When he returns he has to be treated to become his own self again" (p. 105). A process of ritual purification is required to reincorporate a child into the community, and the community itself is understood as disturbed and in need of rituals to cleanse and reconcile (p. 106). Similar rituals are employed in Mozambique in a holistic approach to health and healing. In Sierra Leone, addressing a group of similarly abducted girls, one girl explained the need for purification:

> "We are not like other girls, because we were taken in the bush. Our minds are not steady, and we cannot eat off the same plates as our families. People call us bad names and do not accept us. They call us bad names. How can they do that? We worry about where we will get money to live and feed our babies. Our hearts are heavy even after the war."
>
> (Wessells 2006: 195)

These culturally and societal specific forms of treatment are preferred to the Westernized therapeutic models that look back into events and involve individual verbal externalization of the traumatic experience of being a child soldier. Thus, local understandings, deeply embedded in the life-worlds of the people involved, are vital tools for the reintegration of these populations (Honwana 2006: 134).

Wessells (2006: 137) agrees that Western models and measures such as those employed in diagnosing post-traumatic stress might not generalize to other cultures which have their own understandings about trauma. He reports that former child soldiers often express their desire to see a traditional healer who can cleanse them (Wessells 2006: 194). As he points out, the trauma approach is ethnocentric, and imposing outsider categories runs the risk of marginalizing or even entirely displacing local knowledge. He urges a focus on children's assets, those qualities that enabled them to survive and to develop coping strategies for the times when they needed protection. In practical terms, Wessells (2006: 141) suggests, "the reintegration of former child soldiers is less a matter of helping individual children than of strengthening family and community supports, enabling children to adapt and function well despite difficult past experiences and current living situations."

The task of mobilizing governments against those who recruit and employ child soldiers was undertaken by a group of international non-government organizations which ensured that the subject was placed on the global agenda, despite the resistance of some nation states. Justice for child soldiers became an issue that, by its very nature, had to transcend territorial limits. In this case, therefore, an international mobilization into a domain of relevance to criminology offered protection and empowerment to those in need and created new definitions of criminality. Global justice and global interconnections should encourage an examination of the narrow boundaries of criminological research so that, in the future, war crimes and state crime become regular objects of inquiry and study within the discipline.

Recap

Focusing only on developing countries, this chapter has investigated the articulation between childhood and culture in Bangladesh, and in a number of African countries where child soldiers have fought in internal wars. An analysis of this nature can aid in identifying the cultural specificity of childhood in those countries so that criminological projects concerned with justice policy are informed by local meanings and definitions, and do not simply assume that Western conceptions of childhood are taken for granted in all cultures.

In Bangladesh, values and practices about parental discipline are culturally constructed, complex and deeply embedded in society. Thus, international norms about punishing children are likely to be contested. Despite assertions that globalization has forced justice policy convergences in all countries, it appears that global forces have not created a homogenization of criminal justice problems and policies. Rather, youth justice policy transfer is only partial and will be mediated through national and local cultures. Similarly, the concept of childhood itself in Bangladesh is associated with cultural meanings about conceptions of "being old enough" and possessing "understanding."

The analysis of the creation and development of the child soldier shows how the conditions for child soldiering permit a measure of agency so that regarding these children as without agency or as bloodthirsty killers is to adopt simplistic stereotypes. Addressing African conceptions of childhood reveals again how the complexities of culture impact the life-worlds of African societies. Exploring the role of child soldiers draws attention to the need for further research by a criminology that investigates human rights and engages with issues of state power.

Notes

1   Beirne (1983: 388) advocates a methodological approach that allows a focus on identifying the historical roots of behavior defined as criminal so as to enable greater understanding of how and why criminal behavior is defined in the way it is within a particular cultural context.

2   Loomba (1993) and Mohanty (1993), writing from a post-colonial perspective, make similar arguments that it is context which provides the fundamental "construction of meaning."

3   Authors who have produced ethnographies of violence include Bourgois (1996), Feldman (1991) and Scheper-Hughes (1992).

4   Doob and Tonry (2004: 2) remind us that the notion of a "pure" welfare model or a "pure" punishment model is a simplistic dualism.

5   The CRC (1989) states four general principles: *non-discrimination* (Article 2); *best interests* of the child (Article 3); *survival, protection and development* of the child (Article 6); and *respect for the views* of the child (Article 12). The CRC is a rights-creating text prescribing 54 rights that can be grouped into four broad categories: *survival rights*, covering the child's right to life and the needs that are most basic to his or her existence, such as an adequate standard of living, shelter, nutrition and access to medical services; *development rights*, including what children require in order to achieve their fullest potential, for example, the right to education, play and leisure, cultural activities, access to information and freedom of thought, conscience and religion; *protection rights*, requiring that children be safeguarded against all forms of abuse, neglect and exploitation, and covering issues such as special care for refugee children, torture, abuses in the criminal

justice system, involvement in armed conflicts, child labor, drug use and sexual exploitation; and *participation rights*, allowing children to take an active role in their communities and nations, including the freedom to express opinions, to have a say in all matters affecting their own lives, to join associations and to assemble peacefully.

6   Article 4 of the CRC (1989) requires that "State Parties shall undertake all appropriate legislative, administrative, and other measures for the implementation of the rights recognized in the . . . Convention." General Comment No. 5 issued by the Committee on the Rights of the Child (2003) advises that when a state ratifies the CRC it takes on obligations under international law to implement it. Therefore, says the Committee, state parties should undertake a comprehensive review of all domestic legislation and related administrative guidance to ensure full compliance with the CRC (p. 5).

7   Article 19 of the CRC (1989) states, "States Parties shall take all appropriate legislative, administrative, social and educational measures to protect the child from all forms of physical or mental violence, injury or abuse, neglect or negligent treatment, maltreatment or exploitation, including sexual abuse, while in the care of parent(s), legal guardian(s) or any other person who has the care of the child." Article 37 states, "No child shall be subjected to torture or other cruel, inhuman or degrading treatment or punishment."

8   Additional Protocol 1 to the Geneva Conventions 1977 states that parties involved in armed conflicts "shall take all feasible measures in order that children who have not attained the age of fifteen years do not take a direct part in hostilities and, in particular, they shall refrain from recruiting them into their armed forces" (Article 77). In addition, the International Labor Organization Convention on the Worst Forms of Child Labor of 1999 lists "forced or compulsory recruitment of children for use in armed conflict" as among the worst forms of child labor.

References

Baker, Estelle and Julian V. Roberts. 2005. "Globalization and the New Punitiveness." In John Pratt, David Brown, Mark Brown, Simon Hallsworth and Wayne Morrison (eds) *The New Punitiveness: Trends, Theories, Perspectives*. Portland, OR: Willan Publishing, pp. 121–138.

Bangladesh Shishu Adhikar Forum (BSAF). 2007. "BSAF's Alternative Report on the Implementation of UNCRC in Bangladesh 1996–2000." http://www.crin. org/docs/resources/treaties/crc.34/BangladeshBSAFngoreport.doc (accessed January 23, 2012).

Banks, Cyndi. 2000a. "Developing Cultural Specificity for a Cultural Criminology." In C. Banks (ed.) *Developing Cultural Criminology: Theory and Practice in Papua New Guinea*. Sydney: Institute of Criminology, pp. 15–50.

Banks, Cyndi. 2000b. "Deconstructing Violence in Papua New Guinea." In C. Banks (ed.) *Developing Cultural Criminology: Theory and Practice in Papua New Guinea*. Sydney: Institute of Criminology, pp. 79–128.

Banks, Cyndi. 2007. "The Discourse of Children's Rights in Bangladesh: International Norms and Local Definitions." *The International Journal of Children's Rights* 15(3–4): 391–414.

Beirne, P. 1983. "Cultural Relativism and Comparative Criminology." In P. Beirne and D. Nelken (eds) *Issues in Comparative Criminology*. Aldershot: Dartmouth, pp. 3–24.

Beirne, Piers and David Nelken (eds). 1997. *Issues in Comparative Criminology*. Aldershot, UK: Ashgate Dartmouth.

Blanchet, Therese. 1996. *Lost Innocence, Stolen Childhoods*. Dhaka, Bangladesh: The University Press.

Bottoms, Anthony. 1995. "The Philosophy and Politics of Punishment and Sentencing." In C.M.V. Clarkson and Rod Morgan (eds) *The Politics of Sentencing Reform*. Oxford: Oxford University Press, pp. 17–50.

Bourgois, P. 1996. *In Search of Respect: Selling Crack in El Barrio*. New York: Cambridge University Press.

Cain, Maureen. 2000. "Orientalism, Occidentalism and the Sociology of Crime." *British Journal of Criminology* 40: 239–260.

Committee on the Rights of the Child. 2003a. Written Replies by the Government of Bangladesh Concerning the List of Issues received by the Committee on the Rights of the Child Relating to the Consideration of the Second Periodic Report of Bangladesh received August 27, 2003, document CRC/C/RESP/41.

Committee on the Rights of the Child. 2003b. Session on Bangladesh, Second Periodic Report, September 30, Geneva, Switzerland. Statement by Government of Bangladesh, unpublished.

Committee on the Rights of the Child. 2003. General Comment No. 5, General Measures of Implementation of the Convention on the Rights of the Child, November 27, CRC/GC/2003/5. http://www.unhcr.org./refworld/docid/45388 34f11.html (accessed January 13, 2013).

Convention on the Rights of the Child (CRC). 1989. U.N. General Assembly. Document A/RES/44/25 (December 12), with Annex.

Doob, Anthony N. and Michael Tonry. 2004. "Varieties of Youth Justice." In Michael Tonry and Anthony N. Doob (eds) *Youth Crime and Youth Justice: Comparative and Cross-national Perspectives*. Chicago, IL: The University of Chicago Press, pp. 1–20.

Drake, Deborah, John Muncie and Louise Westmarland. 2010. *Criminal Justice: Local and Global*. Cullompton, Devon: Willan Publishing and The Open University.

Feldman, A. 1991. *Formations of Violence: The Narrative of the Body and Political Terror in Northern Ireland*. Chicago, IL: The University of Chicago Press.

Giddens, Anthony. 1990. *The Consequences of Modernity*. Cambridge: Polity Press.

Green, Penny and Tony Ward. 2004. *State Crime: Governments, Violence and Corruption*. London: Pluto Press.

Harris-Short, Sonia. 2003. "International Human Rights Law: Imperialist, Inept and Ineffective? Cultural Relativism and the UN Convention on the Rights of the Child." *Human Rights Quarterly* 25(1): 130–181.

Hartjen, C.A. 2008. *Youth, Crime and Justice: A Global Inquiry*. New Brunswick, NJ: Rutgers University Press.

Honwana, Alcinda. 2006. *Child Soldiers in Africa*. Philadelphia, PA: University of Pennsylvania Press.

Jones, Trevor and Tim Newburn. 2007. *Policy Transfer and Criminal Justice: Exploring U.S. Influence over British Crime Control Policy*. Maidenhead: Open University Press.

Kauzlarich, David, Rick A. Matthews and William J. Miller. 2001. "Toward a Victimology of State Crime." *Critical Criminology* 10: 173–194.

Loomba, A. 1993. "Overworlding the 'Third World.'" In P. Williams and L. Chrisman (eds) *Colonial Discourse and Post-Colonial Theory*. Hertfordshire: Harvester Wheatsheaf, pp. 305–323.

Mohanty, C. 1993. "Under Western Eyes: Feminist Scholarship and Colonial Discourses." In P. Williams and L. Chrisman (eds) *Colonial Discourse and Post-Colonial Theory*. Hertfordshire: Harvester Wheatsheaf, pp. 196–220.

Muncie, John. 2005. "The Globalization of Crime Control: The Case of Youth and Juvenile Justice: Neo-liberalism, Policy Convergence and International Conventions." *Theoretical Criminology* 9(1): 35–64.

Nelken, David. 1998. "Afterword: Choosing Rights for Children." In Gillian Douglas and Leslie Sebba (eds) *Children's Rights and Traditional Values*. Aldershot, Hants: Ashgate, pp. 315–335.

Nelken, David. 2010. *Comparative Criminal Justice*. Thousand Oaks, CA: Sage.

Odhikar. 2002. *Summary of Selected Topics for Discussion*. Dhaka, Bangladesh: Unpublished notes. July.

Rohfritsch, Agnes and Naeela Sattar. 1995. *A Critical Review of the Judicial Institutions in Relation to the Rights of the Child*. Dhaka, Bangladesh: A Radda Barnen Study.

Sarker, Abdul Hakim. 2001. *Juvenile Delinquency, Dhaka City Experience*. Dhaka, Bangladesh: Human Nursery for Development.

Scheper-Hughes, N. 1992. *Death Without Weeping: The Violence of Everyday Life in Brazil*. Berkeley: University of California Press.

Siddiqui, Kamal. 2001. *Better Days, Better Lives: Towards a Strategy for Implementing the Convention on the Rights of the Child in Bangladesh*. Dhaka, Bangladesh: The University Press.

Singer, P.W. 2006. *Children at War*. Berkeley: University of California Press.

Stromseth, J., D. Wippman and R. Brooks. 2006. *Can Might Make Right? Building the Rule of Law After Military Interventions*. Cambridge: Cambridge University Press.

Sztompka, Piotr. 1990. "Conceptual Frameworks in Comparative Inquiry: Divergent or Convergent?" In Martin Albrow and Elizabeth King (eds) *Globalization, Knowledge and Society*. London: Sage, pp. 207–218.

Tomlinson, John. 1999. *Globalization and Culture*. Chicago, IL: The University of Chicago Press.

UNICEF. 1997. *Cape Town Principles and Best Pratices*.

Wacquant, Loic. 1999. "How Penal Common Sense Comes to Europeans: Notes on the Transatlantic Diffusion of the Neoliberal Doxa." *European Societies* 1(3): 319–352.

Wessells, Michael. 2006. *Child Soldiers: From Violence to Protection*. Cambridge, MA: Harvard University Press.

Index

Note: Page numbers followed by 'n' refer to notes.

accountability 282–3
acid house parties *see* rave subculture
adjudication process and race 105, 120
Adler, F. 36, 93
adolescence 196–7, 199–200, 210–11
adult courts 51–2, 81, 210; transfer of juvenile cases to 105, 116, 119–20
adult drug courts 272, 273, 276–7, 278–9, 283
adult prisons 52–3, 54–5, 81, 201; early history of 3, 43–4, 259
African Americans 103, 106–14, 125, 272
age 292–6
aggression replacement training (ART) 263, 267
Agnew, R. 13, 15, 17, 18, 20, 21, 23, 25, 26, 27, 28, 29, 30, 31, 32
Akers, R. 20, 21, 38
Alaskan Natives 103, 126, 127, 132, 271–2
alcohol 127, 128, 128–9, 259, 272, 273
American Indians 103–4, 104–5, 125, 126–9
anger management 58, 265, 266
Angola 305, 306, 307–8, 310, 312, 314
anti-gang measures 125, 210, 216, 217, 218

apprenticeships 6–7, 45
arraignments 116
arrests: increases reflecting policy changes 80–1, 83, 84, 211; increasing numbers of 93, 213; racial disparities in 116–18
assault: arrests 82, 84–5, 98n, 213, 222n; girls held in custody for 55, 81–2, 213; policing of domestic violence and increase in arrests for 82, 83, 97, 214, 222n; reclassification of offenses as 81, 83; review of cases of 85; in schools 198
Asylums 58
Australia: Aborigines 129, 248; girls' violence 214–15; graffiti writing 164; racial disparities in justice system 129; rave scene 152–3; RISE project 249–50; RJ 241–2, 247–8, 250; skateboarding 178–9
Austria 243, 244
autonomy, seeking 16

Baizerman, M. 54, 55, 59
Balanced and Restorative Justice Project (BARJ) 232, 233
Bangladesh 291–6, 300–2
Banks, C. 56, 59, 60, 61, 65, 66, 67, 68, 69, 71n, 271, 272, 291, 299

Basic Principles on the Use of Restorative Justice Programmes in Criminal Matters 244, 245–7
Becker, H. 8, 29, 30, 140–1, 192, 193
Beijing Rules 244
Belgium 131, 238
Ben-Yehuda, N. 191, 193, 194, 195, 201
Bernard, T. 2, 3, 5, 48–9
Bethlehem, Pennsylvania Police Family Group Conferencing Project 241–2
Bishop, D. 84, 114, 115, 117, 118, 119, 120, 121, 123, 124
blacks: disparities in juvenile justice for 104–5, 114–25; economic trends and employment 108, 109–10, 111, 112; gang membership 112, 125; ghettos 106–14, 117–18, 132; girls 86–7, 88–9, 91; incarceration rates for youths 55, 111, 129; isolation 107, 108, 113; masculinities 88; middle-class 89, 109; poverty 107–8, 110, 111, 113–14; race category 103; urban underclass 106–14
Blueprints Model Programs 263
"blurred boundaries" theory 86, 88
boot camps 262, 268–9
Bortner, M.A. 54, 57, 58, 64, 65, 66, 68
Bourgois, P. 106, 107, 111, 112, 133n
Braithwaite, J. 31, 230, 236, 236–7, 241, 248, 250, 251, 252
Bulger, J. 202–4
bullying 81, 85, 87, 213–14
Burgess, R. 20
Burman, M. 89, 222
Butts, J. 115, 116, 277, 278

California Youth Authority 47
Canada: girls' violence 214–15, 222n; racial disparities in justice system 129; RJ 237–9, 241, 242, 251; youth subcultures 150–1, 157, 181–2
Cape Town Principles and Best Practices 303
Capital Offenders Group 62–3
capital punishment 3, 42, 49, 51, 77
Castleman, C. 158, 159, 160, 161, 162, 163, 185n
Causes of Delinquency 24, 25
Center for Contemporary Cultural Studies, Birmingham 139, 141–3, 144–5

Center for the Study and Prevention of Violence 263
Chambliss, W. 29–30, 209
Changing Lenses 236
Chesney-Lind, M. 33, 35, 36–7, 38, 76, 77, 82, 83, 85, 86, 87, 96, 97, 98n, 125, 211, 212, 213, 214, 222n
Chicago School 138, 139, 143–4
child labor 6, 47, 196, 292, 317n
child neglect 2, 4, 5, 6, 37, 45, 209; blurring of boundaries with delinquency 44, 46; risk factor for delinquency 86, 258
child poverty 124, 126
child savers 3–5, 46, 78, 197
child soldiers 302–15
childhood, concepts of: African 307–8; in Bangladesh 292, 293, 294, 295; child soldiers challenging 307–8; and problem of violent children 204
Children Act 1974 (Bangladesh) 293, 301
Children's Aid Society 3
Chiu, C. 175, 176, 178
Christie, N. 235
circles 242
class: impact on drug treatment programs 283; race and school violence 199; and RJ proceedings 248, 250; and strain theory 16, 19; struggle 143, 184; study of gangs and 29–30 *see also* middle-class; working-class
Cloward, R.A. 15, 16, 17, 139
cocaine 147, 150
cognitive-behavioral programs 56, 95, 261, 262, 265–6, 271, 301
Cohen, A. 15, 16, 17, 139
Cohen, P. 142
Cohen, S. 190, 191, 192, 193, 199, 203, 204, 205, 208, 221n
collective behavior 192
Committee on the Rights of the Child 292, 299–300, 302, 317n
community justice 232–3
community prevention programs 259
community service 233, 234, 243, 251
comparative: racial disparities 129–31; youth justice 290–1
Comparative Criminal Justice 290
conferencing 239–42, 248, 249, 250

"Conflicts as Property" 235
constructing juvenile delinquency 2–3
consumerism and consumption 15, 145, 146, 147, 177, 178
containment approach 23–4
The Contemporary Woman and Crime 36
control-oriented intervention programs 263–4, 267–70
control theories 14, 23–7
Convention on the Rights of the Child (CRC) 244, 252, 292, 298, 316–17n; and tensions over local cultures 299–302
Cook, K. 231, 250
corporal punishment 3, 198
crack cocaine 112, 117, 210
Crime and the Community 28
Crime, Shame and Reintegration 236
The Criminality of Women 35–6
criminology 209, 261; explanations of youth subcultures 138, 139, 140–1, 143–4, 146, 148; feminist 13–14, 33–4, 37–8, 39; and gender 13–14, 33–8
Cullen, F.T. 20, 23, 25, 26, 27, 28, 29, 30, 31, 32, 259, 260, 261, 262, 265, 266, 268, 270
cultural criminology 139, 146–7, 291, 296
cultural studies perspective on youth culture 139, 141–3, 144–5
cultural values 173–4, 198, 296
culturally specificity 144–5, 290–1, 299; of childhood 307–8; in programs 270–2, 276; in treatment of trauma 315
culture, tensions with local 299–302
cycle of juvenile justice 48–52

Daly, K. 33, 36, 37, 86, 229, 230, 239, 240, 241
Darwinism 126, 128, 197
death penalty 3, 42, 49, 51, 77
decriminalization 5, 33
defiance theory 30, 31
Delinquency and Opportunity 139
delinquency prevention 257–9, 272
Delinquent Boys 139
The Delinquent Child and the Home 80

dependency 5, 44, 46, 70, 78
developmental perspective 86, 197
developmental prevention 258
deviance: criminology perspective on youth culture 138, 139, 140–1, 143–4, 148; of girls 76, 97; interacting with youth culture 146; labeling of 29, 30, 38; primary and secondary 28–9; transactional nature of 192–3
differential association theory 14, 20, 23
"differential offending"/"differential treatment" 114
discipline 44, 45; and control 56, 63–9, 260, 268; parental 77–8, 300–2, 316; in schools 7–8, 200–1, 213
discrimination 115
disparity 114–15
dispositions, juvenile court 121–4
disproportionality 194, 201
disproportionate minority confinement (DMC) 122
disproportionate minority representation 122–4, 132
diversion, juvenile justice 28, 84, 115–16, 118, 238, 251
domestic violence 81, 82, 83, 97, 214, 222n
Drug Abuse Resistance Training (DARE) program 264
drug courts: adult 272, 273, 276–7, 278–9, 283; juvenile 272–84
drugs: arrests for 115, 273, 277; culturally specific treatment programs 272; and firearms 117, 120; and gangs 212, 216, 217; given to child soldiers 312; juvenile detention for offenses 53; moral panics over 192, 194; prevention programs 259; racial disparities in cases of 104, 115, 119; of rave subculture 147, 149–50, 152, 153, 154; strain and use of 18; testing 281; treatment programs 273–7; war on 53, 115

early prevention 257–9
economic trends and employment 108, 109–10, 111, 112
ecstasy 147, 150, 153, 154

education, introduction of compulsory 7–8
Eisikovits, Z. 54, 55, 59
empathy 62–3
employment: child 196, 303, 304; illicit 15, 124–5; trends for blacks 108, 109–10, 111, 112; of women 78–9
England 129, 130–1, 229, 238, 239, 241 see also Great Britain
English law 5, 42
ex parte Crouse 5–6, 45, 77–8

families: as central mode for juvenile control 42, 46, 77; effect of JDC on 279–80, 281–2; girls challenging authority of 80; group conferences in RJ programs 240; influence on juvenile behavior 21, 24, 25; risk factors for delinquency 258; support and supervision by 118, 119, 121, 122, 123
family prevention programs 259
Female Detention Project 96
The Female Offender 35
feminism, categories of 33–4
feminist criminology 13–14, 33–4, 37–8, 39
Ferrell, J. 146, 147, 155, 156, 157, 158, 159, 160, 162, 164, 165, 166, 167, 168, 169
Finland 244
firearms 50, 117, 199, 201, 210, 213, 304, 309
first hearings 116
folk devils 10, 148, 190, 191, 203, 208, 210, 220
Folk Devils and Moral Panics 191
Foucault, M. 44, 56, 59, 63, 68, 195, 196
four-pointing 54
France 129, 131
Frazier, C. 84, 123, 124
functional family therapy (FFT) 263, 266–7

"Game of Law" 56–7, 63–4
gangs: attitude of drug treatment programs to 283; in California 216–17; class and 29–30; criminalization of school 201; Crips and the Bloods 218; ghetto membership of 112; girl gangs and violence 211–15; in Las Vegas 217–18; minorities and 124–5; moral panic over violence of 216–20; in Phoenix, Arizona 219–20; in Reno 218–19; subcultural theories and 16–17, 139
Garbarino, J. 92
gender: construction of 200; and control theory 27; and criminology 13–14, 33–8; gap in crime 36, 37, 81, 84; and graffiti 161, 170–2; in skateboarding 181–3; stratification 76, 90 see also girls
gender-specific treatment programs 95, 276
"gendered pathways" approach 37
Gendreau, I. 259, 260, 261, 262, 265, 266, 268, 270
general strain theory (GST) 17–18
A General Theory of Crime 25
generalizability issue 37–8, 39
Germany 148, 243–4, 250
ghettos 106–14, 117–18, 132
girls: black 86–7, 88–9, 91; bullying by 81, 85, 213–14; child soldiers 305–6, 311, 314; comparing boys with 96–7; controlling 37, 76, 77–87, 212, 214, 220; deviance of 76, 97; in drug treatment programs 276, 282; gangs and violence 211–15; "immorality" of 77, 78, 79; offending 81–5; pathways to delinquency 86–7; policing of domestic violence 82, 83, 97, 214, 222n; pregnant 97, 282; programming inadequacies in treatment of 93–7; residential placements 55; violence of 81, 82–3, 84–5, 87–93, 211–15, 222n
globalization 296–7, 298–9, 316
Goffman, E. 58, 62, 141, 280
Goode, E. 191, 193, 194, 195, 201
Gottfredson, D.C. 14, 25, 26, 276
graffiti writing 155–72; as art 156–7, 167, 169; challenging 162–4, 165; conflict between old and new school thinking on 167–8, 169; Denver's war against 164–7, 168; gender and 161, 170–2; hip-hop and 167; and law 162–4, 165–6; motivations for 168; in New York subway 161–2, 162–3, 169, 170; and politics of

public space 167, 168–9; terminology 157–61; thrill of 168–70
Gramsci, A. 143
Gray, P. 229, 239
Great Britain: army recruitment 304; concerns over parenting of working-class youth 196; James Bulger case 202–4; mods and rockers 204–5; muggings 206–8; rave subculture in 148–50, 151, 152, 153; skateboarding in 175, 177; working-class youth culture 142–3, 144, 153, 154, 184 see also England
group discussions 56, 58, 59, 69, 70, 266, 271
Guerra, N. 56, 260, 262, 263, 265, 266, 267, 268, 269, 270
Guidelines for Action on Children in the Criminal Justice System 245

Hagan, J. 27
Hall, Stanley 196, 197
Hall, Stuart 139, 143, 144, 145, 146, 178, 191, 192, 195, 206–7, 208, 220
handcuffs 53–4
Hawaii 81, 104, 125, 278
hip-hop 157, 167
Hirschi, T. 14, 19, 23, 24, 25, 26
Hispanics 104, 111, 112, 124, 133n, 218, 220
HIV/AIDS 308
homicide: age of adulthood for 51; arrests 116, 117, 124, 213; drop in juvenile 211; drugs, weapons and increase in 114, 210; Supreme Court ruling on sentences for 49–50
Honolulu robbery study 87–8
Honwana, A. 305, 306, 307, 308, 309, 310, 311, 312, 314, 315
Houses of Refuge 6, 44–5, 46–7, 53, 69
housing 108, 109, 110
Hubbard, D. 95, 96
Hubner, J. 62–3
Hudson, B. 228, 236, 249

"immorality" of girls 77, 78, 79
incarceration: economic rationale for 44; experiences of 54, 113; failing as a deterrent 47–8, 69, 268; increasing use of 48, 267; of parents of delinquents 201; racial disparities

in rates of 55, 111, 129; Secure Training Orders 203
indigenous justice 240, 245, 247–8
individual prevention programs 258–9
intake decisions 52, 115–16, 118, 123, 127
interventions: effective 261, 262–3, 265–7; ineffective 263–4, 267–70
Irwin, K. 76, 82, 211, 212, 213, 214, 222n
isolation: black ghetto 107, 108, 113; practice 53

Jefferson, T. 142, 143, 144, 145
Jones, N. 76, 85, 88, 89, 91
judicial waiver 105, 119–20
Justice for Victims and Offenders 236
juvenile courts: criticism of 282, 284; differential treatment of girls 79, 84; dispositions 121–4; establishment 7, 8, 47, 79; foundations 5–6; parental requests in Bangladesh to 301; procedures 115–16, 118; public access 210; and referrals to 82, 105, 115–16, 122, 127, 213; secure detention decisions 116, 119; waivers to adult courts 119–20
Juvenile Crime Bill 201
juvenile drug courts 272–84
juvenile institutions: in American Indian areas 127–8; in Bangladesh 301–2; contemporary 48–55; discipline and control 63–9; experiencing treatment in 55–63, 267; girls in 93, 95, 96, 213; history and development of 42–8; pre-trial detention 116, 118, 119, 121; racial disparities in 119, 121, 122, 132
Juvenile Justice and Delinquency Prevention Act (1974) 48, 52–3, 71n, 84, 122
Juvenile Justice and Delinquency Prevention Act (1992) 94
juvenile superpredators 208–11

Kerner Report 107
Krisberg, B. 3, 42, 44, 46–7, 48, 52, 53, 70n, 77

labeling theory 14–15, 27–33, 140–1
Laub, J. 26, 27, 86
lawyers 116, 120, 249, 279

Lemert, E. 28, 29, 141
"liberation hypothesis" 36, 76, 91–3, 212
Liberia 304, 305, 306, 311
life course theory 26, 37, 86
Lombroso, C. 35

MacDonald, N. 155, 156, 157, 160, 161, 170, 171, 172
Marin County Juvenile Drug Court Program 274–6
Martinson, R. 260, 261
Marxism 29, 44, 143, 195
masculinities 16, 34–5, 56–7, 171, 172; adolescent 199–200; black 88; hegemonic 56, 88, 172, 182, 183
Massachusetts 48
Matthews, B. 95, 96
Matza, D. 22, 168
May, T. 130, 131
media: contributing to moral panics 143, 192, 197, 199, 202, 204–5, 206, 207, 209, 211–12, 214–15, 217, 218, 251; interest in graffiti 162, 163, 167; James Bulger case coverage 202–3; mediators between public opinion and primary definers of news 207–8; treatment of girls in 77, 222n; underclass representations in 114; on youth subcultures 144, 148, 179
men, overprepresentation in criminal behavior 36, 37, 81
mental illness 283
Merton, R. 15, 16, 17
Messerschmidt, J. 34, 35, 56, 75, 199, 200
meta-analyses 261, 262
middle-class: blacks 89, 109; delinquency 15, 19, 29, 124, 283; values 2, 4, 8, 16, 79, 122
Miller v. Alabama 50
modelling 266, 271
mods and rockers 204–5
moral crusaders 192, 193, 195, 220
moral panics 143, 190–226; adolescence and delinquency 196–7; characteristics 193–4; gang violence 216–20; girls' violence 76–7, 211–15; graffiti 156, 163, 165; James Bulger case 202–4; juvenile superpredators 208–11; mods and rockers 204–5;

muggings 195, 206–8, 220; rave subculture 148; school shootings 197–202; theory 191–6
Mozambique 305, 306, 307–8, 310, 312, 314
muggings 195, 206–8, 220
multidimensional treatment foster care (MTFC) 263, 267
multisystemic therapy (MST) 263, 266
Muncie, J. 2, 3, 6, 32, 33, 34, 35, 129, 130, 196, 197, 202, 204, 221n, 298, 299, 300

National Commission on the Causes and Prevention of Violence (1969) 47
National Crime Victimization Survey (NCVS) 211
Nelken, D. 290, 291, 296
Netherlands: racial disparities in justice system 129–30, 131; restorative justice 238; skateboarding in 175, 176–7, 182
New York: graffiti writing in subway 161–2, 162–3, 169, 170; skateboarding in 175–6, 178; Spanish Harlem study 111, 112, 133n
New York Times 51, 162, 163, 211
New Zealand 234, 239, 240, 247, 249
Newsweek 209
Nolan, J. 278, 279, 283

O'Connell, D. 7
offense exclusion 119
Office of Juvenile Justice and Delinquency Prevention (OJJDP) 94, 104, 105, 122, 210, 211, 232, 233
Ohlin, E. 15, 16, 17, 139
Outsiders 140–1

Paik, L. 278.279, 280, 281, 282, 286n
Papua New Guinea 291
parens patriae 5–7, 45, 47
parents: of Alaskan Native youth 271; of boys 36; control and effectiveness of 25; discipline 77–8, 300–2, 316; incarceration of juveniles' 201; support and supervision by 118, 119, 121, 123
"pathways to crime" 37, 86–7
patriarchy 34, 36, 38, 75, 91

peacemaking 235
peer groups, influence of 21, 22, 23, 26, 76, 86, 276
penal populism 228, 252, 253
physical abuse 62, 75, 86, 96, 258
physical aggression 68, 85
Platt, A. 3, 4–5, 8, 46, 78
police: approach to gangs in Reno 218–19; community policing 232; control of RJ process 241–2, 248; gang units 216, 217, 218, 222n; proactive and reactive policing 80–1, 130–1; racial bias in arrests and decision making 116–18, 122; referrals 115; surveillance 117–18, 154
Policing the Crisis 191–2, 206
policy: changes and impacts 80–1, 83, 84, 211; convergence and transfer of 296–9
Pollak, O. 35, 36
populist punitiveness 297, 298
post-subcultural theory 145
poverty 107–8, 110, 111, 113–14, 132–3n; child 124, 126
power-control theory 27
power relationships 58, 63–9, 194–5
practitioners of interventions 264–5
pre-trial detention 116, 118, 119, 121
predisposition reports 121–2
President's Commission on Law Enforcement and the Administration of Justice (1967) 47–8
prevention programs, delinquency 257–9, 272
private facilities 53, 55, 123–4
probation 32, 84, 105, 116, 123, 130, 270; comparing drug programs and 280, 281; and RJ 237, 238, 242–3
probation officers 94, 96, 118, 121–2, 274
property crime 17, 36, 114, 115, 116, 127, 170, 214, 251
prosecutorial discretion 119
prostitution 82, 87, 94
Prothrow-Stith, D. 76, 92
psychology 20, 47, 59, 70, 79, 95, 197, 213, 260, 272, 285
Public Entertainments (Drug Misuse) Act 1997 149

public opinion 199, 202–3, 208, 250–2, 265, 285
public space 147, 177, 184; graffiti and politics of 167, 168–9; skateboarding in 172–3, 175–8
punishment 43–4; cycle of juvenile justice 48–52; in drug courts 283; in juvenile institutions 53–4, 65; and RJ 229, 247, 251–2

qualitative research 55–6, 95, 106

race: African American urban underclass 106–14; American Indians and Alaskan Natives 126–9; bias and operation of juvenile justice system 55, 104–6, 114–25, 132, 283; categories 103–4; class and school violence 199; comparative disparities 129–31; and study of girls' offending 86–7
racial profiling 32
Rahn, J. 157, 158, 159, 160, 167–8, 169, 170
rape 54, 211, 250, 304
rave subculture 147–55
re Gault (1967) 7, 120
recidivism 31, 95; drug treatment programs and 276, 277; effective interventions for 261, 262–3, 265–7; ineffective interventions for 263–4, 268–9, 270; restorative justice and reducing of 284–5
Reckless, W. 23–4
referrals 82, 105, 115–16, 122, 127, 213
reform schools 6, 7, 8, 46–7, 78
rehabilitation 4, 43, 57, 64; under challenge 260–1; founding principles of 259–60; re-evaluation of 261–5
Reich, A. 56, 57, 64, 71n
reinforcement 20, 21–3
reintegrative shaming 30, 31, 236–7, 241
relational aggression 81, 85, 90, 214
religion 235, 260
reparative boards 234, 242–3, 250
residential homes 47, 51, 53, 55, 105, 116, 122, 123
"residential space availability" 123–4

restorative justice (RJ) 227–56; circles 242; and community justice 232–3; conferencing 239–42, 248, 249, 250; critiques of 247–50; definitions 227–8, 230; effectiveness 284–5, 286; explaining 228–32; international norms on 244–7; programs 237–44; and public opinion 250–2; theoretical foundations 235–7; typology 233–4; Vermont Reparative Probation Program 242–4; Victim Offender Mediation (VOM) 227, 234, 237–9, 250–1

restraints 53–4

RISE project 249–50

risk assessment instruments (RAIs) 52

risk factors for delinquency 258

risk-taking 16, 27, 50, 83, 197

Riyadh Guidelines 245

robbery 50, 87–8, 90, 211, 250

Roman, J. 277, 278

Roper v. *Simmons* 51

Rothman, D. 24, 42, 43–4, 45

runaways 37, 75, 82, 87, 201

Sampson, R. 26, 27, 111

scared straight 262, 263–4, 268

Schall v. *Martin* 119

school prevention programs 259

schools: data collection in 221n; discipline in 7–8, 200–1, 213; girls' bullying in 81, 85, 213–14; girls' violence in 81; physical punishment in 198; segregation in 198; sexual harassment in 91; shootings 197–202; violence in 214

Secure Training Orders 203

"seductions of crime" 35, 170

See Jane Hit 92

self-control theory 25–6

self-mutilation 67, 68, 71n

sexual abuse 37, 52, 86, 87, 96, 97

sexual double standard 75, 76, 91, 97, 98

sexual harassment 91

sexuality and female delinquency 35–6, 75, 76, 97

Sherman, L. 30, 31, 250

shoplifting 16, 170, 250, 251

Sierra Leone 304, 305, 306, 310, 312, 313, 314

Simon, R. 36

Singer, P.W. 304, 305, 308, 309, 310, 312, 313, 314

single-parent families 118, 123

Sisters in Crime 36, 93

skateboarding 172–83; commodification of 180–1; cultural values and 173–4; gender in 181–3; graffiti in parks 164; and law 177–80; in public space 172–3, 175–8

Smart, C. 34, 36

social anxiety 205, 208

social bond theory 24–5, 26

social control 14, 24, 26; aspects of community 231, 237; contested power relations and emergence of 146, 148, 178; family as central mode of juvenile 42, 46, 77; of girls 37, 76, 77–87, 212, 214, 220; in industrial era 3, 4, 46; JDCs as instrument of 278, 279–80, 282; labelling theory confronting progression of 141; media and links with agencies of 208; and moral panics 190, 206, 208, 212, 214, 220; in schools 198

"social injury hypothesis" 212

social learning 14, 20–3

social order 44, 69, 139, 148–9, 208, 220

socialization 75–6, 86, 87, 125

sociological theories of crime and delinquency 138–9

South Africa 233

Spivak, H.R. 76, 92

state crime 302–3

state intervention, and labelling 32–3

status and respect 15–16

status offenses 37, 80, 81, 84; custody for 82, 84, 201; decriminalization of 5, 33; reclassification of 83, 84

Steffensmeier, D. 36, 81, 84

stereotypes 27, 78, 85, 96, 115, 118, 122

stigmatization 28–9, 31, 32

strain theory 14, 15, 16, 17–20, 19

subcultural theories 16–18, 138–45

Sugar and Spice and No Longer Nice 92

suicide rates 126–7

superpredators, juvenile 208–11
Sutherland, E. 14, 20
Sweden 129
Sykes, M. 22, 168

Tannenbaum, F. 28, 29
techniques of neutralization 22–3
theories of juvenile delinquency 13–41
Thomas, W.I. 35
thrill seeking 16, 168–70
Tonry, M. 129, 231, 316n
'tough love' approach 9, 62, 260, 264, 285
training schools 48, 52, 55
transnational youth justice 290–319; child soldiers 302–15; convergence and transfer of policies 296–9; delinquency in Bangladesh 291–6; local culture and tensions in 299–302
trauma 96, 315
treatment programs: approaches in 1950s and 60s 47–8; culturally specific 270–2, 276; drug court programs 274–6, 283; effective interventions 261, 262–3, 265–7; effectiveness of RJ 284–5, 286; gender-specific 95, 276; inadequacies in girls' 93–7; ineffective interventions 263–4, 267–70; in juvenile corrections 55–63, 267; language of 58, 59, 60–2, 70; and "learning to play the game" 57–8, 65; political and public support for non-evidence-based 263–4, 267–8, 285; practitioner skills and qualities 264–5; private 123–4; re-evaluation of 261–5

Uganda 305, 308
The Unadjusted Girl 35
unemployment 15, 106, 107, 112, 114, 115, 121
UNICEF 300, 303
United Nations Guidelines for the Prevention of Juvenile Delinquency (Riyadh Guidelines) 245
United Nations Standard Minimum Rules for the Administration of Juvenile Justice (Beijing Rules) 244
urban underclass 106–14
U.S. Supreme Court 7, 49–50, 119

Vermont Reparative Probation Program 242–4
victim awareness courses 61–2
victim blaming 91
Victim Offender Mediation (VOM) 227, 234, 237–9, 250–1
victimization 80, 83, 86, 87, 88, 91
victims: RJ experience 238, 239, 240, 241–2, 243, 252; of state crime 302–3
violence: arrests 82, 84–5, 116–17, 127, 211; in black ghettos 111–12, 114; black girls' experience of 88–9, 91; 'charging up' policy 80–1; culturally specific meanings of 291; gang 211–15, 216–20; girls' 81, 82–3, 84–5, 87–93, 211–15, 222n; growing up in an environment of 90–1; James Bulger case and debate on child 202–4; moral panic over fear of youth 191, 208–11; mugging moral panic in Britain 206–8; school shootings 197–202; in schools 214; video 202, 203, 292; by whites to sustain black ghettos 109

Wagga Wagga scheme 241–2
welfare model 298
Wessells, M. 206, 304, 305, 308, 309, 310, 311, 312, 313, 314, 315
wilderness programs 269–70
Williams, L.M. 57, 58, 64
working-class: parenting of youth 196; youth culture in Britain 142–3, 144, 153, 154, 184
Wright, M. 229, 236

Young, A. 111, 112, 113
youth culture: cultural criminology and 139, 146–7; defining 138; and deviance 140–1, 146; graffiti writing 155–72; rave subculture 147–55; skateboarding 172–83; subcultural theories of 16–18, 138–45; working-class British 142–3, 144, 153, 154, 184
Youth Risk Behavior Survey 83

Zehr, H. 228, 229, 236
zero-tolerance tactics 80, 82, 85, 200, 214, 298